Lecture Notes in Artificial Intelligence 1434

Subseries of Lecture Notes in Computer Science
Edited by J. G. Carbonell and J. Siekmann

Lecture Notes in Computer Science
Edited by G. Goos, J. Hartmanis and J. van Leeuwen

Springer
*Berlin
Heidelberg
New York
Barcelona
Budapest
Hong Kong
London
Milan
Paris
Singapore
Tokyo*

Jean-Claude Heudin (Ed.)

Virtual Worlds

First International Conference, VW'98
Paris, France, July 1-3, 1998
Proceedings

Springer

Series Editors
Jaime G. Carbonell, Carnegie Mellon University, Pittsburgh, PA, USA
Jörg Siekmann, University of Saarland, Saarbrücken, Germany

Volume Editor

Jean-Claude Heudin
International Institute of Multimedia
Pôle Universitaire Léonard de Vinci
F-92916 Paris La Defense Cedex, France
E-mail: Jean-Claude.Heudin@devinci.fr

Cataloging-in-Publication Data applied for

Die Deutsche Bibliothek - CIP-Einheitsaufnahme

Virtual worlds : first international conference ; proceedings / VW '98, Paris, France, July 1 - 3, 1998. Jean-Claude Heudin (ed.). - Berlin ; Heidelberg ; New York ; Barcelona ; Budapest ; Hong Kong ; London ; Milan ; Paris ; Santa Clara ; Singapore ; Tokyo : Springer, 1998
  (Lecture notes in computer science ; Vol. 1434 : Lecture notes in artificial intelligence)
ISBN 3-540-64780-5

CR Subject Classification (1991): I.3.7, I.2.10, I.2, I.3, H.5, J.5

ISBN 3-540-64780-5 Springer-Verlag Berlin Heidelberg New York

This work is subject to copyright. All rights are reserved, whether the whole or part of the material is concerned, specifically the rights of translation, reprinting, re-use of illustrations, recitation, broadcasting, reproduction on microfilms or in any other way, and storage in data banks. Duplication of this publication or parts thereof is permitted only under the provisions of the German Copyright Law of September 9, 1965, in its current version, and permission for use must always be obtained from Springer-Verlag. Violations are liable for prosecution under the German Copyright Law.

© Springer-Verlag Berlin Heidelberg 1998
Printed in Germany

Typesetting: Camera ready by author
SPIN 10637689   06/3142 – 5 4 3 2 1 0   Printed on acid-free paper

Preface

1 Introduction

Imagine a virtual world with digital creatures that looks like real life, sounds like real life, and even feels like real life. Imagine a virtual world not only with nice three-dimensional graphics and animations, but also with realistic physical laws and forces. This virtual world could be familiar, reproducing some parts of our reality, or unfamiliar, with strange "physical" laws and artificial life forms.

As a researcher interested in the sciences of complexity, the idea of a conference about virtual worlds emerged from frustration. In the last few years, there has been an increasing interest in the design of artificial environments using image synthesis and virtual reality. The emergence of industry standards such as VRML [1] is an illustration of this growing interest. At the same time, the field of Artificial Life has addressed and modeled complex phenomena such as self-organization, reproduction, development, and evolution of artificial life-like systems [2]. One of the most popular works in this field has been Tierra designed by Tom Ray: an environment producing synthetic organisms based on a computer metaphor of organic life in which CPU time is the "energy" resource and memory is the "material" resource [3]. Memory is organized into informational patterns that exploit CPU time for self-replication. Mutation generates new forms, and evolution proceeds by natural selection as different creatures compete for CPU time and memory space.

However, very few works have used an Artificial Life approach together with Virtual Reality, or at least with advanced three-dimensional graphics. Karl Sims was probably one of the first researchers working in this direction. He designed a flexible genetic system to specify solutions to the problem of being a "creature" built of collections of blocks, linked by flexible joints powered by "muscles" controlled by circuits based on an evolvable network of functions [4]. Sims embedded these "block creatures" in simulations of real physics, such as in water or on a surface. These experiments produced a bewildering and fascinating array of creatures, like the swimming "snake" or the walking "crab". Demetri Terzopoulos and his colleagues have also created a virtual marine world inhabited by realistic artificial fishes [5]. They have emulated not only the appearance, movement, and behavior of individual animals, but also the complex group behaviors evident in many aquatic ecosystems. Each animal was modeled holistically as an autonomous agent situated in a simulated physical world.

Considering recent advances in both Artificial Life and Virtual Reality, catalyzed by the development of Internet , a unified approach seemed to be one of the most promising trend for the synthesis of realistic and imaginary virtual worlds. Thus, the primary goal of this conference was to set up an opportunity for researchers from both fields to meet and exchange ideas.

In July 1998, the first international conference on virtual worlds was held at the International Institute of Multimedia. It brought together scientists involved in Virtual Reality, Artificial Life, Multi-agent Systems, and other fields of computer science and electronic art, all of whom share a common interest in the synthesis of digital worlds on computers. The diversity and quality of the work reported herein reflects the impact that this new trend of research has had on the scientific community.

2 The Proceedings

The production of these proceedings was a major task, involving all the authors and reviewers. As the editor, I have managed the proceedings in a classical way. Every contribution that was accepted for presentation at the conference is in the proceedings. The program committee felt that these papers represented mature work of a level suitable for being recorded, most of them without modification, some of them requiring modifications to be definitively accepted. Besides the classical goal of a proceedings volume, the idea was to recapture in print the stimulating mix of ideas and works that were presented. Therefore, the papers are organized to reflect their presentation at the conference. There were three invited plenary speakers: Nadia Thalmann, Jeffrey Ventrella, and Yaneer Bar-Yam. Two of them choose to provide a printed version of their lecture. There were nine sessions, most of them in parallel, for a total of 36 papers in all, recorded here roughly in the order in which they were presented.

The material covered in these proceedings is diverse and falls naturally into a number of categories: Virtual Reality, Artificial Life, Multi-agent Systems, Complexity, Applications of Virtual Worlds, and last but not least, Virtual Worlds and Art. This collection of papers constitutes a good sample of works that appear necessary if we want to design large and realistic virtual worlds on the Internet in the near future.

3 Acknowledgments

Many people and groups contributed to the success of the conference. My sincere thanks go out to all of them. I would like to thank first all the distinguished authors who contributed to this volume for their willingness to share the excitement of a new enterprise. The committee which selected the papers included the editor along with :

Michael *Best* (MIT Media Lab., USA),
Yaneer *Bar-Yam* (NECSI, USA),
Bruce *Blumberg* (MIT Media Lab., USA),
Eric *Bonabeau* (Santa Fe Institute, USA),
Terry *Bossomaier* (Charles Sturt University, Australia),
Philippe *Coiffet* (Versailles & St Quentin en Yvelines University, France),
Bruce *Damer* (Contact Consortium, USA),
Guillaume *Deffuant* (CEMAGREF, France),
Karine *Douplitzky* (Galimard NRF, France),
Steve *Grand* (Cyberlife, UK),
Bob *Jacobson* (SRI, USA),
Takeo *Kanade* (Carnegie Mellon University, USA),
Hiroaki *Kitano* (Sony Computer Science Lab., Japan),

Jean *Louchet* (ENSTA, France),
Nadia *Magnenat-Thalmann* (University of Geneva, Switzerland),
Daniel *Mange* (EPFL, Switzerland),
Jean-Arcady *Meyer* (ENS, France),
Thomas S. *Ray* (ATR Human Information Research Lab., Japan),
Tim *Regan* (Bristish Telecom, UK),
Bob *Rockwell* (Blaxxun Interactive, Germany),
Scot Thrane *Refsland* (Gifu University, Japan),
Demetri *Terzopoulos* (University of Toronto, Canada),
Jeffrey *Ventrella* (Rocket Science Games, USA),
Marie-Luce *Viaud* (INA, France),
Claude *Vogel* (Semio, USA),
Chris *Winter* (British Telecom, UK).

I am also grateful to Silicon Graphics (official partner of the conference), Canal+ Virtuel, and Softimage for their financial support. Special thanks are due to the New England Complex System Institute, the EvoNet Network of Excellence in Evolutionary Computation, the Contact Consortium, and the International Society on Virtual Systems and Multimedia for their support.

I had a significant help for organizing and running this conference. Most of the staff of the International Institute of Multimedia fall under this category. First and foremost, I have to thank Claude Vogel who was encouraging and supporting me at every step of the project. Monika Siejka performed an enormous amount of work. She was effectively my co-organizer. It was a pleasure to work with Monika. Olga Kisseleva was another co-organizer. Olga was in charge of the artistic part of the conference. Thanks are also due to Sophie Dussault and Sylvie Perret for their help. Finally, all the staff of the Pôle Universitaire Léonard de Vinci were once again a pleasure to work with.

4 Conclusion

The terms "virtual worlds" generally refer to Virtual Reality applications or experiences. In this volume, I have extended the use of these terms to describe experiments that deal with the idea of synthesizing digital worlds on computers. Thus, Virtual Worlds (VW) could be defined as the study of computer programs that implement digital worlds with their own "physical" and "biological" laws. Constructing such complex artificial worlds seems to be extremely difficult to do in any sort of complete and realistic manner. Such a new discipline must benefit from a large amount of work in various fields: Virtual Reality, Artificial life, Cellular Automata, Evolutionary Computation, Simulation of Physical Systems, and more. Whereas Virtual Reality has largely concerned itself with the design of three-dimensional graphical spaces and Artificial Life with the simulation of living organisms, VW is concerned with the simulation of worlds and the synthesis of digital universes.

This approach is something broader and more fundamental. Throughout the natural world, at any scale, from particles to galaxies, one can observe phenomena of great complexity. Research done in traditional sciences such as biology and physics has shown that the basic components of complex systems are quite simple. It is now a crucial problem to elucidate the universal principles by which large numbers of simple components, acting together, can self-organize and produce the complexity observed in our universe [6]. Therefore, VW is also concerned with the formal basis of synthetic universes. In this framework, the synthesis of virtual worlds offers a new approach for studying complexity.

I hope that the reader will find in this volume many motivating and enlightening ideas. My wish is that this book will contribute to the development and further awareness of the new and fascinating field of Virtual Worlds. As of now, the future looks bright.

References

1. Hartman, J., Wernecke, J.: The VRML 2.0 Handbook – Building Moving Worlds on the Web. Reading, Addison Wesley Developers Press (1996)
2. Langton, C.G.: Artificial Life. SFI Studies in the Sciences of Complexity, Vol. VI. Addison-Wesley (1988)
3. Ray, T.: An Approach to the Synthesis of Life. In Artificial Life II, SFI Studies in the Sciences of Complexity, Vol. X. Edited by C.G. Langton, C. Taylor, J.D. Farmer and S. Rasmussen. Addison-Wesley (1991)
4. Sims, K.: Evolving 3D Morphology and Behavior by Competition. Artificial Life, Vol. 1. MIT Press 4 (1995) 353–372
5. Terzopoulos, D., Xiaoyuan, T., Radek, G.: Artificial Fishes: Autonomous Locomotion, Perception, Behavior, and Learning in a Simulated Physical World. Artificial Life, Vol. 1. MIT Press 4 (1995) 327–351
6. Heudin, J.C.: L'évolution au bord du chaos. Editions Hermès, Paris (1998)

May 1998   Jean-Claude Heudin

Table of Contents

Invited Paper

Real Face Communication in a Virtual World   1
W.-S. Lee, E. Lee, and N. Magnenat Thalmann

Virtual Reality (1)

Animated Impostors for Real-Time Display of Numerous Virtual Humans   14
A. Aubel, R. Boulic, and D. Thalmann

Can We Define Virtual Reality ? The MRIC Model   29
D. Verna and A. Grumbach

Distortion in Distributed Virtual Environments   42
M.D. Ryan and P.M. Sharkey

VRML Based Behaviour Database Editor   49
J.F. Richardson

Virtual Reality (2)

The Scan&Track Virtual Environment   63
S.K. Semwal and J. Ohya

CyberGlass: Vision-Based VRML2 Navigator   81
C. Numaoka

Work Task Analysis and Selection of Interaction Devices
in Virtual Environments
T. Flaig   88

Effect of Stereoscopic Viewing on Human Tracking Performance
in Dynamic Virtual Environments   97
P. Richard, P. Hareux, P. Coiffet, and G. Burdea

Virtual Reality (3)

Interactive Movie: A Virtual World with Narratives 107
R. Nakatsu, N. Tosa, and T. Ochi

Real-Image-Based Virtual Studio 117
J.I. Park and S. Inoue

Pop-Out Videos 123
G.U. Carraro, J.T. Edmark, and J.R. Ensor

Color Segmentation and Color Correction Using Lighting
and White Balance Shifts 129
P. Gerard, C.B. Philips, and R. Jain

Invited Paper

Designing Emergence in Animated Artificial Life Worlds 143
J. Ventrella

Artificial Life

ALife Meets the Web: Lessons Learned 156
L. Pagliarini, A. Dolan, F. Menczer, and H.H. Lund

Information Flocking: Data Visualisation in Virtual Worlds
Using Emergent Behaviours 168
G. Proctor and C. Winter

Nerve Garden: A Public Terrarium in Cyberspace 177
B. Damer, K. Marcelo, and F. Revi

A Two-Dimensional Virtual World to Explain
the Genetic Code Structure ? 186
J.L. Tyran

Multi-Agent

Grounding Agents in EMud Artificial Worlds 193
A. Robert, F. Chantemargue, and M. Courant

Towards Virtual Experiment Laboratories: How Multi-Agent Simulations
Can Cope with Multiple Scales of Analysis and Viewpoints 205
D. Servat, E. Perrier, J.P. Treuil, and A. Drogoul

A Model for the Evolution of Environments 218
C. Lattaud and C. Cuenca

AReVi: A Virtual Reality Multi-Agent Platform 229
P. Reigner, F. Harrouet, S. Morvan, J. Tisseau, and T. Duval

Complexity

Investigating the Complex with Virtual Soccer 241
I. Noda and I. Frank

Webots: Symbiosis Between Virtual and Real Mobile Robots 254
O. Michel

Vision Sensors on the Webots Simulator 264
Y.L. de Meneses and O. Michel

Grounding Virtual Worlds in Reality 274
G. Hutzler, B. Gortais, and A. Drogoul

Applications (1)

Growing Virtual Communities in 3D Meeting Spaces 286
F. Kaplan, A. McIntyre, C. Numaoka, and S. Tajan

A Mixed 2D/3D Interface for Music Spatialization 298
F. Pachet and O. Delerue

Organizing Information in 3D 308
D. Doegl and C. Cavallar

Human Centered Virtual Interactive Image World for Image Retrieval 315
H. Kimoto

Applications (2)

Virtual Great Barrier Reef: A Theoretical Approach Towards an Evolving,
Interactive VR Environment Using a Distributed DOME and CAVE System ... 323
S.T. Refsland, T. Ojika, T. Defanti, A. Johnson, J. Leigh,
C. Loeffler, and X. Tu

The Developement of an Intelligent Haulage Truck Simulator
for Improving the Safety of Operation in Surface Mines ... 337
M. Williams, D. Schofield, and B. Denby

Navigation in Large VR Urban Models ... 345
V. Bourdakis

Virtual Worlds and Art

Art and Virtual Worlds ... 357
O. Kisseleva

Las Meninas in VR: Storytelling and the Illusion in Art ... 360
H. Bizri, A. Johnson, and C. Vasilakis

Mitologies: Traveling in the Labyrinths of a Virtual World ... 373
M. Roussos and H. Bizri

Aggregate Worlds: Virtual Architecture Aftermath ... 384
V. Muzhesky

Zeuxis vs. Reality Engine: Digital Realism and Virtual Worlds ... 394
L. Manovich

Avatars: New Fields of Implication ... 406
R. Hayem, T. Fourmaintraux, K. Petit, N. Rauber, and O. Kisseleva

Author Index ... 411

Real Face Communication in a Virtual World

Won-Sook Lee, Elwin Lee, Nadia Magnenat Thalmann

MIRALab, CUI, University of Geneva
24, rue General-Dufour, CH-1211, Geneva, Switzerland
Tel: +41-22-705-7763 Fax: +41-22-705-7780
E-mail: {wslee, lee, thalmann}@cui.unige.ch

Abstract. This paper describes an efficient method to make an individual face for animation from several possible inputs and how to use this result for a realistic talking head communication in a virtual world. We present a method to reconstruct 3D facial model from two orthogonal pictures taken from front and side views. The method is based on extracting features from a face in a semiautomatic way and deforming a generic model. Texture mapping based on cylindrical projection is employed using a composed image from the two images. A reconstructed head is animated immediately and is able to talk with given text, which is transformed to corresponding phonemes and visemes. We also propose a system for individualized face-to-face communication through network using MPEG4.

Keywords: Cloning, orthogonal pictures, DFFD, texture mapping, talking head, visemes, animation

1. Introduction

Individualized facial communication is becoming more important in modern computer-user interfaces. To visualize ones own face in a virtual world and let people talk with given input, such as text or video, is now a very attractive research area. With the fast pace in computing, graphics and networking technologies, real-time face-to-face communication in a virtual world is now realizable. It is necessary to reconstruct an individual head in an efficient way to decrease data transmission size, and send few parameters for real-time performance.

Cloning a real person's face has practical limitations in the sense of time, simple equipment and realistic shape. We present our approach to clone a real face from two orthogonal views, emphasizing accessibility for anybody with low price equipment. Our method to give animation structure on a range data from a laser scanner or stereoscopic camera is also described, but not in detail. This is because of the high price of this equipments. Therefore, it may not be a very practical idea to make use of them. The main idea is to detect feature points and modify a generic model with animation structure. After creating virtual clones, we can use them to animate and talk in a virtual world.

The organization of this paper is as follows. We give a review in Section 2 with classification for existing methods to get a realistic face reconstruction and talking head. In Section 3, we describe the idea of a system for individualized face-to-face communication through a network and our system for creating/animating talking head with given text. Section 4 is dedicated to the reconstruction process from feature detection to texture mapping and then the detailed process for talking head is explained in Section 5. Finally conclusion is given.

2. Related Work

2.1. Face Cloning for Animation

There have been many approaches to reconstruct a realistic face in a virtual world. There are many possible ways such as using a plaster model [12][1], or interactive deformation and texture mapping [2][15], which are time-consuming jobs. More efficient methods are classified into four categories.

Laser Scanning In range image vision system some sensors, such as laser scanners, yield range images. For each pixel of the image, the range to the visible surface of the objects in the scene is known. Therefore, spatial location is determined for a large number of points on this surface. An example of commercial 3D digitizer based on laser-light scanning is Cyberware Color Digitizer^{TM} [14].

Stripe Generator As an example of structured light camera range digitizer, a light striper with a camera and stripe pattern generator can be used for face reconstruction with relatively cheap equipment compared to laser scanners. With information of positions of projector and camera and stripe pattern, a 3D shape can be calculated. Proesmans et al. [13] shows a good dynamic 3D shape using a slide projector, by a frame-by-frame reconstruction of a video. However, it is a passive animation and new expressions cannot be generated.

Stereoscopy A distance measurement method such as stereoscopy can establish the correspondence at certain characteristic points. The method uses the geometric relation over stereo images to recover the surface depth. C3D 2020 capture system [3] by the Turing Institute produces many VRML models using stereoscopy method.

Most of the above methods concentrate on recovering a good shape, but the biggest drawback is that they provide only the shape without structured information. To get a structured shape for animation, the most typical way is to modify an available generic model with structural information such that eyes, lips, nose, hair and so on. Starting with a structured facial mesh, Lee et al. [13] developed algorithms that automatically construct functional models of the heads of human subjects from laser-scanned range and reflection data [14]. However, the approach based on 3D digitization to get range data often requires special purpose high-cost hardware. Therefore, a common way of creating 3D objects is the reconstruction from 2D photo information, which is accessible at a low price.

Modification with Feature Points on Pictures There are faster approaches to reconstruct a face shape from only a few pictures of a face. In this method, a generic model with an animation structure in 3D is provided in advance and a limited number of feature points. These feature points are the most characteristic points to recognize people, detected either automatically or interactively on two or more orthogonal pictures, and the other points on the generic model are modified by a special function. Then 3D points are calculated by just combining several 2D coordinates. Kurihara and Arai [9], Akimoto et al. [4], Ip and Yin [7], and Lee et al. [16] use an interactive, semiautomatic or automatic methods to detect feature points and modify a generic model. Some have drawbacks such as too few points to guarantee appropriate shape from a very different generic head or accurate texture fitting, or automatic methods, which are not robust enough for satisfactory result, like simple filtering and texture image generation using simple linear interpolation blending.

2.2. Talking Head

There are two approaches for the synthesis of talking heads. Pearce et al. [17] have used an approach to create an animation sequence with the input being a string of phonemes corresponding to the speech. In this case, the face is represented by a 3D model and animated by altering the position of various points in the 3D model. A the more recent work of Cohen and Massaro [18], english text is used as the input to generate the animation. The alternative is the image-based morphing approach. Ezzat and Poggio [19] have proposed a method of concatenating a collection of images, using a set of optical flow vectors to define the morphing transition paths, to create an animated talking head. In another recent work of Cosatto and Graf [20], they have proposed an automatic method of extracting samples from a video sequence of a talking person using image recognition techniques. In this case, the face image is being partitioned into several facial parts and later combined to generate a talking head. They focused to reduce the number of samples that are needed and photo-realistic movements of lips.

2.3. Shared Virtual World

There have been numerous works being done on the topic of shared virtual environments. In most of these works [23][24][25], each user is represented by a fairly simple embodiment, ranging from cube-like appearances, non-articulated human-like or cartoon-like avatars to articulated body representations using rigid body segments. In the work of Pandzic et al. [26], a fully articulated body with skin deformations and facial animation is used. However, none of these works discussed about the process of creating individual face model in an efficient manner. In other words, each individual face model usually takes hours of effort to complete. The MPEG-4 framework [30] under standardization can be used to achieve a low bandwidth face-to-face communication between two or more users, using individualized faces.

3. System Overview

In networked collaborative virtual environments, each user can be represented by a virtual human with the ability to feel like "being together" by watching each other's face. Our idea for face-to-face communication through a network is to clone a face with texture as starting process and send the parameters for the reconstruction of the head model to other users in the virtual environment. After this, only animation and audio parameters are sent to others in real time to communicate. The actual facial animation can be done on a local host and all the users can see every virtual human's animation. This provides a low bandwidth solution for having a teleconference between distanced users, compared to traditional video conferencing, which sends video stream in real time through network. At the same time, it is able to retain a high level of realism with individualized textured 3D head.

The general idea of a system for individualized face-to-face communication through network is shown in Fig. 1. There are two hosts, host1 and host2. Each host has a generic model and a program to clone a person from a given input such as two orthogonal pictures or range data. A person in host1 is reconstructed with pictures or range data obtained in any range data equipment. The parameters for reconstruction will be sent to host2 through network. They are texture image data, texture coordinates and either modification parameters or geometric position data for points on a 3D head surface. The same procedure happens in host2. Finally, both host1 and host2 have two 3D heads which are textured. Although we send a texture image, which takes large bandwidth, it is only one time process for reconstruction. After this process, only animation parameters and audio data are sent to another host through network. With animation parameters given, each host will animate two heads in their own platforms.

The part of this system showing the proceedure of producing an individualized talking head is shown in Fig. 2. We reconstruct a real face from a given input. For reconstruction, only some points (so called feature points) are extracted from front and side views or only from front view if range data is available and then a generic model is modified. After reconstructing a head, it is ready to animate with given animation parameters. We use this model and apply it to talking head, which has animation abilities given text input. The input speech text is transformed to corresponding phonemes and animation parameters, so called visemes. In addition, expression parameters are added to produce final face with audio output.

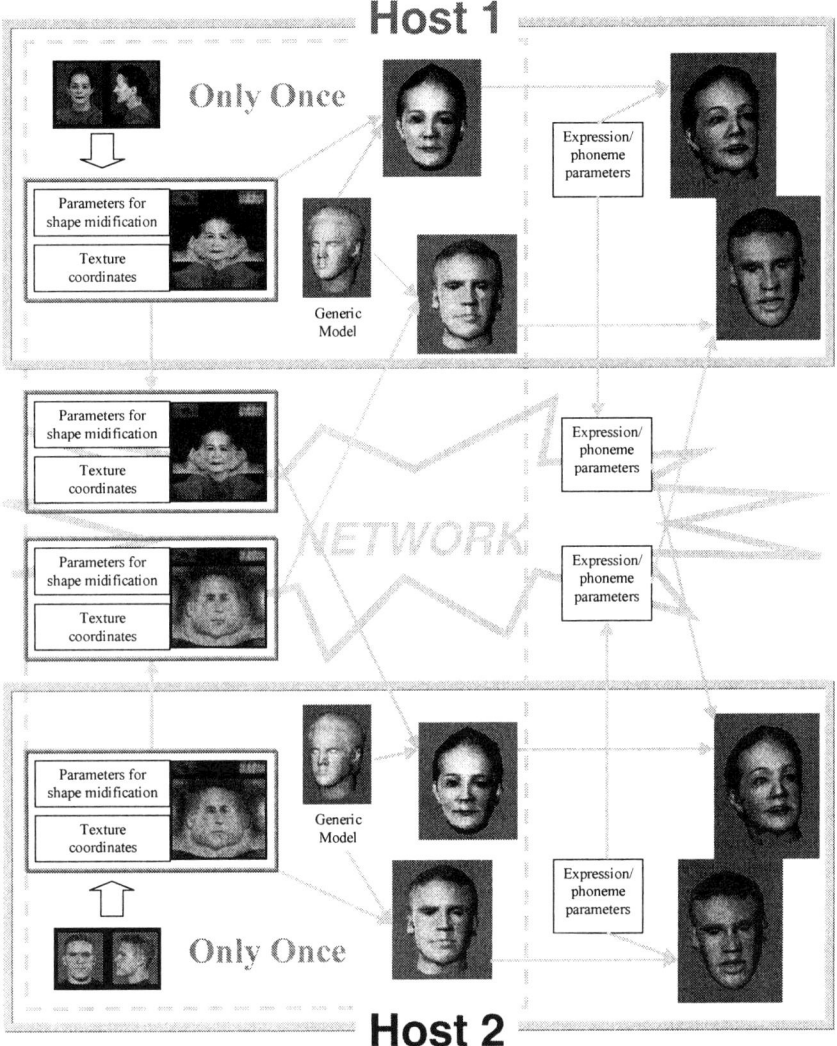

Fig. 1. A system overview for individualized face-to-face communication through network.

4. Face Cloning

We reconstruct a face from two kinds of input, such as an orthogonal picture or range data in VRML format. The main idea is to modify a generic animation model with detected feature points and apply automatic texture mapping. In this paper, we focus on orthogonal picture input rather than range data input since the approach based on 3D digitization to get a range data often requires special purpose (and high-cost) hardware and the process is quite similar to orthogonal picture case.

We consider hair outline, face outline and some interior points such as eyes, nose, lips, eyebrows and ears as feature points.

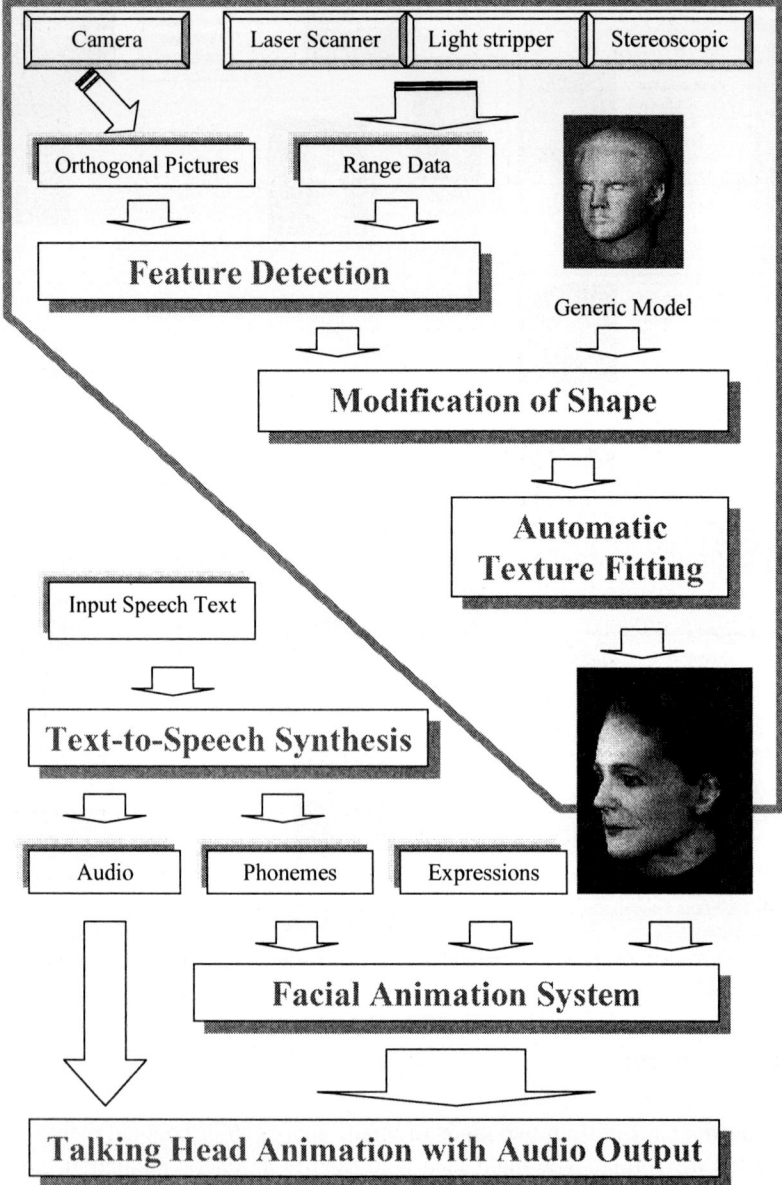

Fig. 2. Overall structure for individualized talking head.

4.1. Preparation and Normalization

First, we prepare two 2D wire frames composed of feature points with predefined relations for front and side views. The frames are designed to be used as an initial position for the snake method later. Then we take pictures from front and side views of the head. The picture is taken with maximum resolution and the face is in the neutral expression and pose.

To make the head heights of side and front views the same, we measure them, and choose one point from each view to matching them with corresponding points in prepared frame. Then we use transformation (scaling and translation) to bring the pictures to the wire frame coordinate, overlaying frames on pictures.

4.2. Feature Detection

We provide an automatic feature point extraction method with an interface for interactive correction when needed. There are methods to detect them just using special background information and predefined threshold [4][7] and then use an edge detection method and apply threshold again. In addition, image segmentation by clustering method is used [4]. However, it is not very reliable since the boundary between hair and face and chin lines are not easy to detect in many cases. Moreover color thresholding is too sensitive and depends on each individual's facial image and therefore requires many trials and experiments. We therefore use a structured snake, which has functionality to keep the structure of contours. It does not depend much on the background color and is more robust than simple thresholding method.

Structured Snake First developed by Kass et al. [8] the active contour method, also called snakes, is widely used to fit a contour on a given image. Above the conventional snake, we add three more functions. First, we interactively move a few points to the corresponding position, and anchor them to keep the structure of points when snakes are involved, which is also useful to get more reliable result when the edge we would like to detect is not very strong. We then use color blending for a special area, so that it can be attracted by a special color [5]. When the color is not very helpful and Sobel operator is not enough to get good edge detection, we use a multiresolution technique [6] to obtain strong edges. It has two main operators, REDUCE with Gaussian operator and EXPAND. The subtraction produces an image resembling the result after Laplacian operators commonly used in the image processing. More times the REDUCE operator is applied stronger are the edges.

4.3. Modifying a Generic Model

3D Points from Two 2D Points We produce 3D points from two 2D points on frames with predefined relation between points from the front view and from the side view. Some points have x, y_f, y_s, z, so we take y_s, y_f or average of y_s and y_f for y coordinate (subscripts s and f mean side and front view). Some others have only x, y_f

and others x, y_s. Using predefined relation from a typical face, we get 3D position (x, y, z).

Dirichlet Free-Form Deformations (DFFD) Distance-related functions have been employed by many researchers [4][7][9] to calculate the displacement of non-feature points related to feature points detected. We propose to use DFFD [11] since it has capacity for non-linear deformations as opposed to generally applied linear interpolation, which gives smooth result for the surface. We apply the DFFD on the points of the generic head. The displacement of non-feature points depends on the distance between control points. Since DFFD applies Voronoi and Delaunay triangulation, some points outside triangles of control points are not modified, the out-box of 27 points can be adjusted locally. Then the orginal shape of eyes and teeth are recovered since modifications may create unexpected deformation for them. Our system also provides a feedback modification of a head between feature detection and a resulted head.

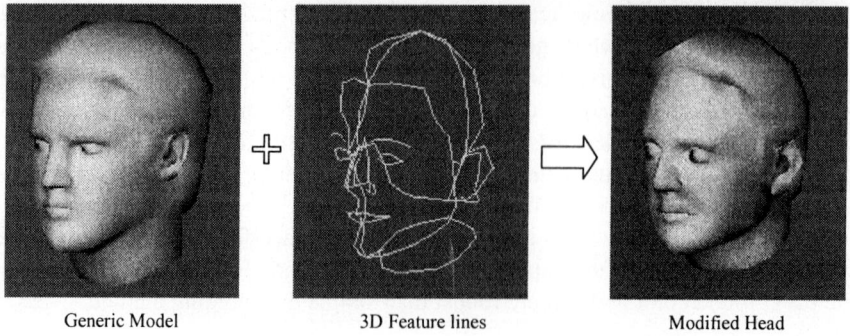

Generic Model   3D Feature lines   Modified Head

Fig. 3. A result of DFFD modification comparing with the original head.

4.4. Automatic Texture Mapping

To increase realism, we utilize texture mapping. Texture mapping needs a 2D texture image and coordinate for each point on a 3D head. Since our input is two pictures, texture image generation to combine them to one picture is needed.

Texture Image Generation For smooth texture mapping, we assemble two images from the front and side views to be one. Boundaries of two pictures are detected using boundary color information or using detected feature points for face and hair boundaries. Since the hair shape is simple in a generic model, the boundary of a side view is modified automatically using information of back head profile feature points detected to have nice texture for back part of a neck. Then cylindrical projection of each image is processed. Two projected images are cropped at a certain position (we use eye extremes because eyes are important to keep at a high resolution), so that the range of combined image to make the final assembled image is 360^0. Finally, a multiresolution spline assembling method is used to produce one image for texture mapping preventing visible boundary for image mosaic.

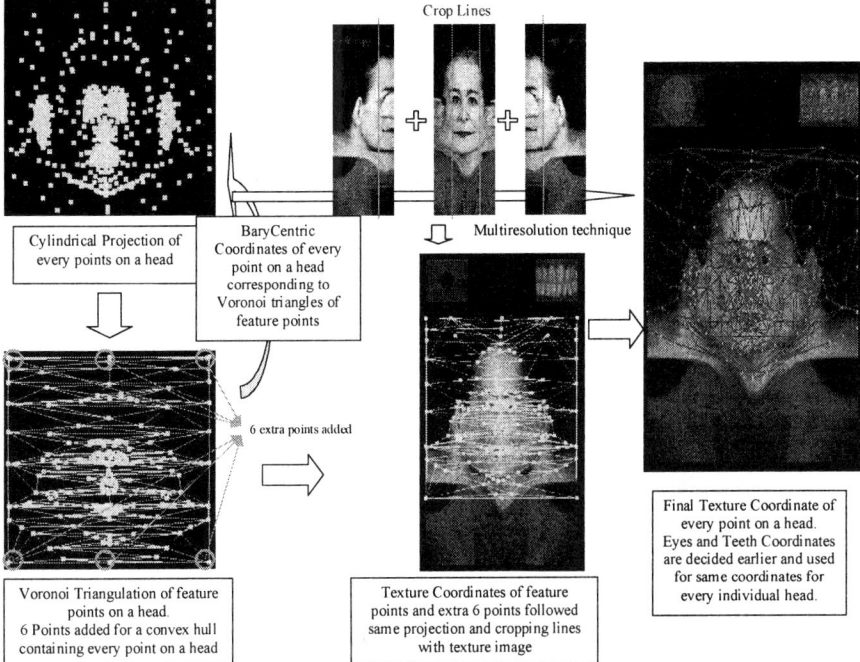

Fig. 4. Texture mapping process.

Texture Fitting The main idea for the texture fitting is to map a 2D image on a 3D shape. Texture coordinates of feature points are calculated using detected position data and function applied for texture image generation. The problem for texture fitting is how to decide texture coordinates of all points on a surface of a head. We first apply a cylindrical projection of every point on a 3D head surface. Extra points are added to make a convex hull containing all points, so that a coordinate of every point is located on an image. Then the Voronoi triangulation on control (feature) points and extra points are processed and the local Barycentric coordinates of every point with a surrounding Voronoi triangle are calculated. Finally the texture coordinates of each point on a 2D-texture image are obtained using texture coordinates of control points and extra points and correspond Barycentric coordinate.

4.5. Result

A final textured head is shown in Fig. 5 with input images, whose process from normalization to texture mapping takes a few minutes.

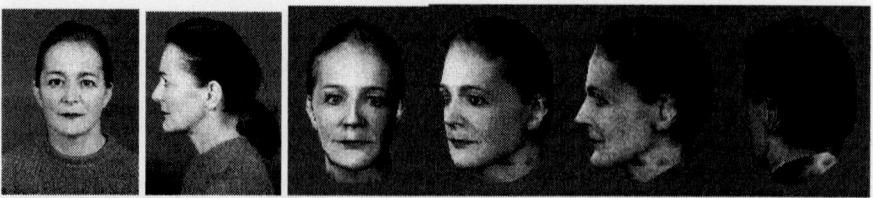

Fig. 5. A final reconstructed head with two input images in left side. The back of head has proper texture too.

5. Talking Head and Animation

In this section, we will describe the steps for animating a 3D face model according to an input speech text, that has been reconstructed as described in the previous section.

Firstly, the input text is being provided to a text-to-speech synthesis system. In this case, we are using the Festival Speech Synthesis System [21] that is being developed at the University of Edinburgh. It produces the audio stream that is subsequently played back in synchronization with the facial animation. The other output that is needed from this system is the temporized phoneme information, which is used for generating the facial animation.

In the facial animation system [22] that is used in our work, the basic motion parameter for animating the face is called Minimum Perceptible Action (MPA). Each MPA describes a corresponding set of visible features such as movement of eyebrows, jaw, or mouth occurring as a result of muscle contractions and pulls.

In order to produce facial animation based on the input speech text, we have defined a visual correlation to each phoneme, which are commonly known as visemes. In other words, each viseme is simply corresponding to a set of MPAs. In Fig. 6, it shows a cloned head model with a few visemes corresponding to the pronunciation of the words indicated.

With the temporized phoneme information, facial animation is then generated by concatenating the visemes. We have limited the set of phonemes to those used in the Oxford English Dictionary. However, it is easy to extend the set of phonemes in order to generate facial animation for languages other than English, as this can be easily done by adding the corresponding visemes.

The facial animation described so far is mainly concerned with the lip movement corresponding to the input speech text. However, this animation will appear artificial without the eyes blinking, and movement of the eyes and head. Therefore, we have also included random eyes blinking and movement of the eyes and head to add more realism into the generated animation. An analysis of the input speech text can also be done to infer the emotional state of the sentence. Then, the corresponding emotional facial expression can also be applied to the animation. For example, the eyebrows can be raised when the emotional state is surprise.

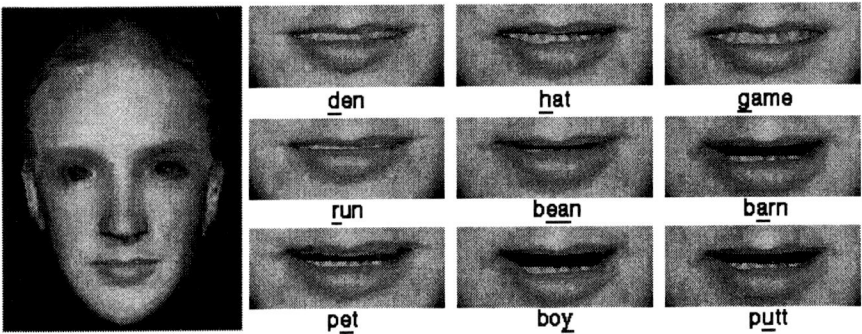

Fig. 6. A cloned head model with some examples of visemes for the indicated words. Our talking head system utilizes 44 visemes and some facial expression parameters.

An example of cloned persons interacting in a shared virtual environment is shown in Fig. 7. Two kinds of generic bodies, female and male, are provided in advance. The generic bodies can be adjusted according to several ratios using Bodylib [28]. We connect individualized heads onto bodies by specifying a transformation matrix. Basically we need four types of data, namely the geometrical shape, animation structure, texture image and texture coordinates. In our case, every individualized head shares the same animation structure. Final rendering is then produced in real time. Our whole process from individualization to final talking head with body in a virtual world takes only few minutes.

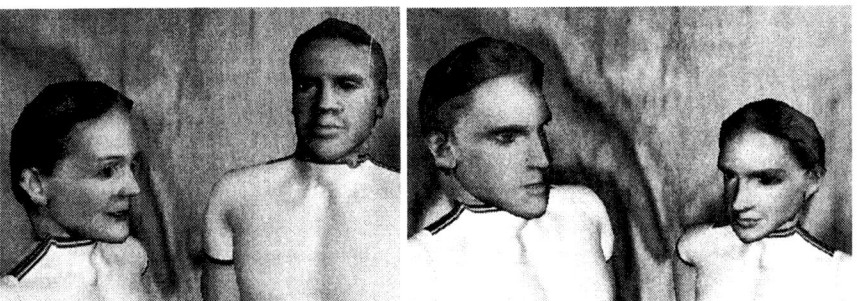

Fig. 7. Cloned persons interacting in shared virtual environments.

6. Conclusion and Future Research

In this paper, we proposed an efficient way of creating the individual face model, in terms of time needed for the creation and transmitting the information to other users, and sending parameters for facial animation. The input of two orthogonal pictures can be easily obtained from any kind of conventional camera. The process of individualization consists of several steps including feature detection on 2D pictures,

Animated Impostors for Real-Time Display of Numerous Virtual Humans

Amaury Aubel, Ronan Boulic and Daniel Thalmann

Computer Graphics Lab, Swiss Federal Institute of Technology
CH-1015 Lausanne, Switzerland
{aubel, boulic, thalmann}@lig.di.epfl.ch

Abstract. Rendering and animating in real-time a multitude of articulated characters presents a real challenge and few hardware systems are up to the task. Up to now little research has been conducted to tackle the issue of real-time rendering of numerous virtual humans. However, due to the growing interest in collaborative virtual environments the demand for numerous realistic avatars is becoming stronger. This paper presents a hardware-independent technique that improves the display rate of animated characters by acting on the sole geometric and rendering information. We first review the acceleration techniques traditionally in use in computer graphics and highlight their suitability to articulated characters. Then we show how impostors can be used to render virtual humans. Finally we introduce a concrete case study that demonstrates the effectiveness of our approach.

1 Introduction

Even though our visual system is not deceived yet when confronted with virtual humans, our acceptance of virtual characters has greatly improved over the past few years. Today's virtual humans faithfully embody real participants in collaborative virtual environments for example and are even capable of conveying emotions through facial animation [1]. Therefore, the demand for realistic real-time virtual humans is becoming stronger. Yet, despite the ever-increasing power of graphics workstations, rendering and animating virtual humans remain a very expensive task. Even a very high-end graphics system can have trouble sustaining a sufficient frame rate when it has to render numerous moving human figures commonly made up of thousands of polygons. While there is little doubt that hardware systems will eventually be fast enough, a few simple yet powerful software techniques can be used to speed up rendering of virtual humans by an order of magnitude.

Because 3D chips were not affordable or did not even exist in the 80s, video game characters, human-like or not, were then represented with 2D sprites. A sprite can be thought of as a block of pixels and a mask. The pixels give the color information of the final 2++D image while the mask corresponds to a binary transparency channel. Using sprites, a human figure could easily be integrated into the decor. As more computing power was available in the 90s, the video game industry shifted towards 3D. However, the notion of sprites can also be used in the context of 3D rendering. This has been successfully demonstrated with billboards, which are basically 3D sprites, used for rendering very complex objects like trees or plants. In our opinion image-based rendering can also be used in the case of virtual humans by relying on the intrinsic temporal coherence of the animation.

Current graphics systems rarely take advantage of temporal coherence during animation. Yet, changes from frame to frame in a static scene are typically very small, which can obviously be exploited [9]. This still holds true for moving objects such as virtual humans providing that the motion remains slow in comparison with the graphics frame rate. We present in this paper a software approach to accelerated rendering of moving, articulated characters, which could easily be extended to any moving and/or self-deforming object. Our method is based on impostors, a combination of traditional level-of-detail techniques and image-based rendering and relies on the principle of temporal coherence. It does not require special hardware (except texture mapping and Z-buffering capabilities, which are commonplace on high-end workstations nowadays) though fast texture paging and frame buffer texturing is desirable for optimal performance.

The next section gives an overview of the existing schemes that are used to yield significant rendering speedups. Section 3 briefly describes our virtual human model and discusses the limitations of geometry level-of-detail techniques. The notion of dynamically generated impostors is introduced in section 4 with the presentation of an algorithm that generates virtual humans from previous rasterized images. In section 5 the duration of the validity of the image cache is discussed. The following section then shows how this method can be embedded in a large-scale simulation of a human flow. Finally section 7 concludes the paper with a summary of the results we obtained and leads on to some possible future work.

2 Background

There exist various techniques to speed up the rendering of a geometrical scene. They roughly fall into three categories: culling, geometric level-of-detail and image-based rendering which encompasses the concept of image caching. They all have in common the idea of reducing the complexity of the scene while retaining its visual characteristics. Besides, they can often be combined to produce better results, as shown in sections 3 and 4.

Culling algorithms basically discard objects or parts of objects that are not visible in the final rendered image: an object is not sent to the graphics pipeline if it lies outside the viewing frustum (visibility culling) or if it is occluded by other parts of the scene (occlusion culling). Luebke and Georges described an occlusion culling system well suited for highly occluded architectural models that determines potentially visible sets at render-time [3]. One major drawback of occlusion culling algorithms is that they usually require a specific organization of the whole geometry database: the scene is typically divided into smaller units or cells to accelerate the culling process. There-link. The intersection is a sample point on the cross-section contour. Once all the sampling is done it is quite straightforward to construct a mesh from the sample points. Thus, we can generate more or less detailed polygonal meshes by simply varying the sample density i.e. the number of sampled contours as well as the number of sampled points per contour. And yet, since the implicit surface remains the same no matter the sampling frequency, the generated meshes look very similar (Fig. 2).

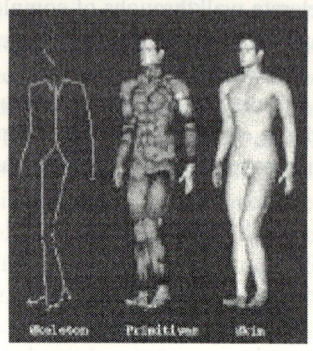

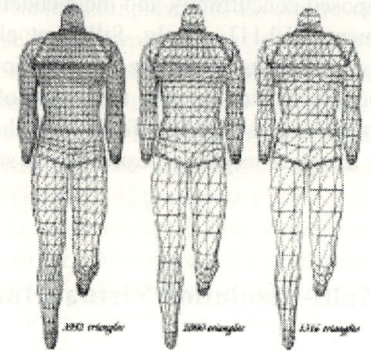

Fig. 1. Multi-layered model [13]

Fig. 2. Body meshes of decreasing complexity

As for the head, hands and feet, we still have to rely on a traditional decimation technique to simplify the original mesh. Manual intervention is still needed at the end of this process to smooth the transition between LODs. The body extremities can cleverly be replaced with simple textured geometry for the lowest resolution (Fig. 3), which dramatically cuts down the number of triangles.

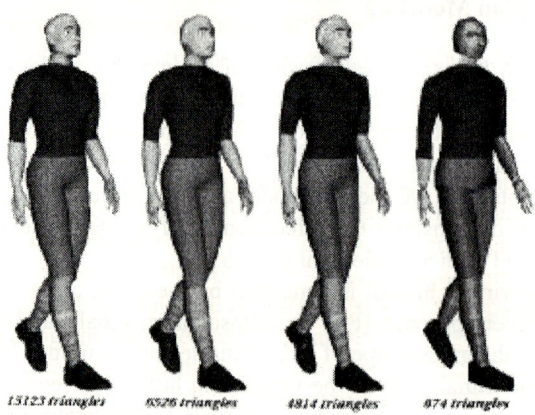

Fig. 3. Levels of detail

3.2 Animation

The skeleton of our virtual human comprises a total of 74 DOFs corresponding to the real human joints plus a few global mobility nodes, which are used to orient and position the virtual human in the world. In the broad lines, animating a virtual human consists in updating this skeleton hierarchy including the global mobility joints at a fixed frame rate. There exist several techniques to feed the joints with new angle/position values. Motion capture for instance is used to record the body joint values for a given lapse of time. The motion can later be played back on demand for any virtual human. Key frame animation is another popular technique in which the animator explicitly specifies the kinematics by supplying key-frame values and lets the computer interpolate the values for the in-between frames.

During animation the appropriate resolution is selected for each individual according to the euclidian distance to the viewpoint. Therefore far objects and those on the periphery contribute less to the final image. Note that we could also take the general motion of the virtual human into account. Finally at a higher level, typically the application layer, virtual humans could be assigned different rendering priorities too. For example, in the context of a human crowd simulation where individuals move and act in clusters the application could decide to privilege some groups.

3.3 Limitations of Geometric LODs

LOD is a very popular technique probably because of its simplicity. It is no wonder that LOD has widely been used in computer graphics, whether in virtual reality applications or in video games. There are some limitations to LOD though. First, shading artifacts may arise when the geometry is extremely simplified. This is conspicuous when Gouraud shading is used because the shading function is evaluated for fewer points, as the geometry is decimated. Popping is another recurrent problem: however look-alike two successive LODs may be, the switch can sometimes be obvious to the viewer. The most widespread solution to this problem relies on a transition zone to smooth the switch. In this special zone both LODs images are blended using a transparency channel. However, this method presents the disadvantage of displaying twice the geometry for a given lapse of time. Lastly, geometric LOD has physical limits in the sense that it is not possible to represent properly a human being with fewer than a few hundred polygons. For example, if we consider textured bounding boxes as the lowest resolution, the number of triangles for our model still amounts to about two hundred in all. Such a representation allows a scene that is made up of dozens of virtual actors to be refreshed at a high frame rate - typically 20 Hz - but to the detriment of the visual quality that drops to a level that is barely acceptable. For all that, LOD remains a very efficient technique that can be used without difficulty in conjunction with impostors.

4 Animated Impostors for Articulated Characters

As first defined by Maciel et al. [8] an impostor is in essence some very simple geometry that manages to fool the viewer. As traditionally the case in the existing literature, what we mean by impostor is a set of transparent polygons onto which we map a meaningful, opaque image. More specifically our impostor corresponding to a virtual human is a simple textured plane that rotates to face continuously the viewer. The image or texture that is mapped onto this plane is merely a "snapshot" of the virtual human. Under these conditions if we take for granted that the picture of the virtual human can be re-used over several frames then we have virtually decreased the polygon complexity of a human character to a single plane (Fig. 4).

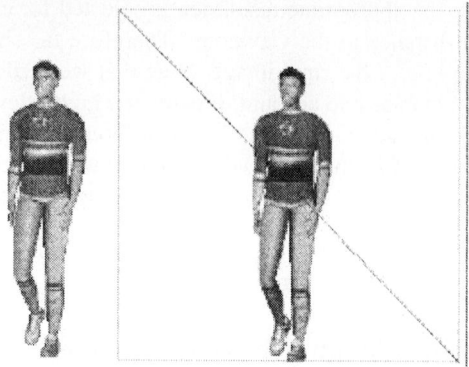

Fig. 4. A Brazilian football player and its impostor

4.1 Impostor Refreshment Approach

The texture that is mapped onto the transparent plane still needs to be refreshed from time to time because of the virtual human's mobility or camera motion. Whenever the texture needs to be updated a snapshot of the virtual human is taken. This process is done in three steps:

1. Set up an off-screen buffer that will receive the snapshot
2. Place the virtual human in front of the camera in the right posture
3. Render the actor and copy the result into texture memory

The first stage typically comes down to clearing the buffer. The buffer should be a part of the frame buffer so as to benefit from hardware acceleration. The purpose of the second step is to set up the proper view to take a picture: first, we let the actor strike the right pose depending on joint values. Second, it is moved in front of the camera or alternately, the camera itself is moved. Note that the latter is preferable because the skeleton hierarchy remains unchanged in this case, which may save some time. In the last stage the virtual human is rendered and the resulting image is copied into texture memory. Once the texture has been generated there only remains to render the textured billboard to have a virtual human on screen. The whole process is hardly any slower than rendering the actual 3D geometry of the virtual human for the following reasons: setting the off-screen buffer up can be done once for all in a preprocessing step. It chiefly consists in adjusting the viewing frustum to the virtual human. Furthermore, this buffer can be re-used to generate several textures of different actors providing that they have approximately the same size. Clearing the buffer is definitely not a costly operation. Letting the virtual human assume the right posture and rendering it would also have to be carried out if the real geometry was used instead. Finally, if the hardware features frame buffer texturing, the frame buffer to texture memory copy is performed within no time. If not, clearing the off-screen buffer and transferring its content still remain all the less costly that the buffer size is small, typically 128 by 128 pixels or less. As a consequence even in the worst cases (very high texture refreshment rates), impostors prove not to be slower than rendering the actual 3D geometry.

4.2 Impostor Viewing and Projection

For the sake of clarity, when speaking respectively in the following of texture windows and scene window, we will mean the off-screen buffers where textures of virtual humans are generated and the window where the final, global scene with impostors is rendered.

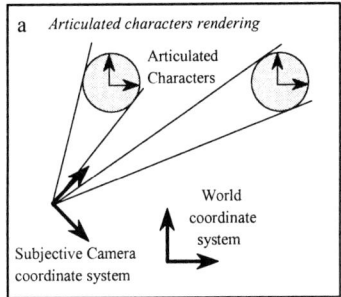

Drawing a. represents a top view of a scene containing two articulated characters. Each character has its own coordinates system. The subjective camera coordinate system defines the user's viewpoint and corresponds to the camera in the scene window. All coordinates systems are expressed with respect to the world.

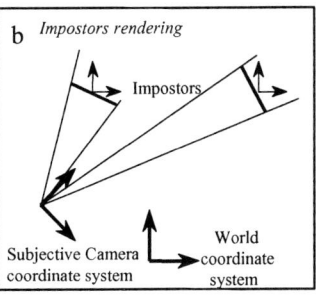

Drawing b. shows a top view of the same scene rendered with impostors. Each character's geometry is replaced with a single textured plane. Each plane is oriented so that its normal vector points back to the eye i.e. the origin of the subjective camera coordinate system.

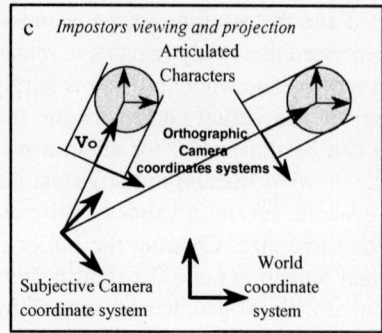

c *Impostors viewing and projection*

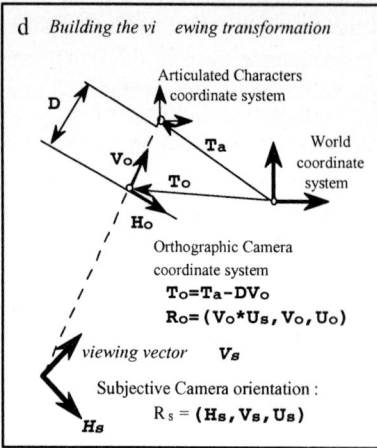

d *Building the viewing transformation*

Drawing c. explains how the textures mapped onto the planes in *drawing b.* are generated i.e. how snapshots of virtual humans are taken. In the drawing there are two orthographic camera coordinates systems corresponding to the cameras in the texture windows associated with each articulated character. The viewing direction **Vo** of the orthographic camera is determined by the eye's position and a fixed point (later referred to as **Ta**) of the articulated character, as will be explained.

Drawing d. is a more detailed version of the previous drawing. It mainly shows how the orthographic camera coordinate system is constructed. **Vo** is the unit vector derived from **Ta** and the position of the subjective camera. The two other unit vectors that give the orthographic camera's orientation **Ro** are determined as follows: the first vector **Ho** is the cross product of **Vo** and **Us** where **Us** is the normalized up vector of the subjective camera's frame. The cross product of **Ho** and **Vo** then yields **Uo**. Note that this method ensures we obtain a correct frame (**Ho**□0) as long as the field of view is smaller than a half sphere.

Finally, the camera of the texture window (termed orthographic camera so far) must be positioned so that the virtual human is always entirely visible and of a constant global size when we take a snapshot. We proceed in two steps to do so. First, an orthographic projection is used because it incurs no distortion and actual sizes of objects are maintained when they are projected. Second, a fixed point named **Ta** is chosen in the body (it corresponds to the spine base) so that it is always projected onto the middle of the texture window. Practically, **Ta** is determined to be the "middle" point of the virtual human assuming a standing posture in which its arms and hands are fully stretched above its head. Note that this posture is the one in which the virtual human's apparent size is maximal. The orthographic camera is placed at distance D from **Ta** (D is a scalar). During the simulation, the camera is then moved at **To** = **Ta** – D.**Vo**. Hence **Ta**'s projection necessarily coincides with the center of the texture window. On account of the orthographic projection, D actually does not influence the virtual human's projection size. On the other hand the viewing frustum does. Consequently, it must be carefully chosen so that no parts of the virtual character are culled away. This is done in a pre-processing stage in which the viewing frustum's dimensions (in the texture window) are set to the maximal size of the virtual human (i.e. with arms raised above its head).

4.3 Several Texture Resolutions

All the work has been realized on Silicon Graphics workstations using the Performer graphics toolkit. Because of hardware/software restrictions concerning textures, texture windows have dimensions that are powers of two. Several texture windows of decreasing size can be associated with every virtual human. As the virtual human moves farther, which leads to smaller image-space size in the scene window, a smaller texture window can be used thus reducing texture memory consumption. Practically, we allocated 256x256, 128x128, 64x64 and 32x32 pixel texture windows for a simulation running at a 1280x1024 resolution. The largest windows were only used for close-up views. As always, it can be a bit difficult to strike the right balance between texture memory consumption and visual realism. In addition to better managing texture memory, using several texture windows of decreasing size also helps to reduce visual artifacts. As a matter of fact large textures of virtual humans that are mapped onto very small (far) planes might shimmer and flash as the impostors move. When several texture resolutions are employed, these artifacts tend to disappear because the appropriate texture resolution is selected according to the impostor image-space size (in pixels). In a certain way this mimics the well-known effect obtained with "mip mapping". Finally, when a texture is generated the appropriate LOD of the geometry can be chosen based on the texture window size.

4.4 Main Current Limitation

Replacing a polygonal model of a virtual human with a single textured plane may introduce visibility problems: depth values of the texels are unlikely to match those of the actual geometry, which may lead to incorrect visibility, as illustrated in figure 5. We did not address this issue in this paper.

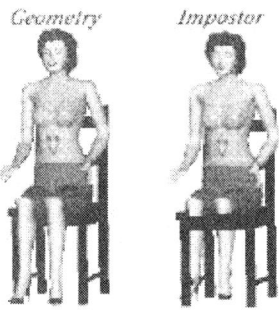

Fig. 5. Incorrect visibility

5 Image Cache Duration

For static objects camera motion is the one and only factor to take into consideration for cache invalidation [9,11]. The algorithm that decides whether a snapshot of a virtual human is stale or not is obviously a bit more complex. However, that algorithm has to execute very quickly because it must be performed for every virtual human at each frame. In our approach we distinguish two main factors: self-deformation of the virtual actor and its global motion with respect to the camera.

5.1. Virtual Humans as Self-Deforming Objects

Virtual humans can be considered as self-deforming objects in the sense they do not keep a static shape, i.e. they can take different postures. The basic idea for a cache invalidation algorithm is that the viewer need not see every posture of the virtual humans to fully understand what action they are performing. A few key postures are often meaningful enough. We propose a simple algorithm that reflects the idea of sub-sampling the motion. The idea is to test distance variations between some pre-selected points in the skeleton. Using this scheme the virtual human is re-rendered if and only if the posture has changed significantly.

Once we have updated the skeleton hierarchy we have direct access to joints' positions in world space. It is therefore quite straightforward to compute distances (or rather squared distances to avoid unnecessary square roots) between some particular joints. In concrete terms we compare four distances (Fig. 6) with those stored when the texture was last generated. As soon as the variation exceeds a certain threshold the texture is to be re-generated. Of course the thresholds depend on the precision the viewer demands. Furthermore, length variations are weighted with the distance to the viewer to decrease the texture refreshment rate as the virtual human moves away from the viewpoint.

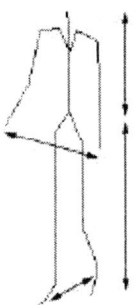

Fig. 6. Posture variations to test

We found out that four tests suffice to reflect any significant change in the virtual human's posture. Nevertheless, other tests should be performed if the simulation is meant to underscore some peculiar actions e.g. grasping of an object requires additional testing of the hand motion. Similarly, it might be necessary to increase or decrease the number of tests when using non-human characters. As a rule the number of limbs gives the number of tests to make.

5.2. Relative Motion of the Actor in the Camera Frame

Instead of testing independently camera motion and actor's orientation we have come up with a simple algorithm that checks both in a single test. The algorithm's main idea stems from the fact that every virtual human is always seen under a certain viewing angle which varies during simulation whether because of camera motion or actor's motion. Yet, there is basically no need to know what factor actually caused the variation.

In practice we test the variation of a "view" matrix, which corresponds to the transformation under which the viewer sees the virtual human. This matrix is plainly the product of the subjective camera matrix (camera in the scene window) and that of the articulated character. The cache invalidation algorithm then runs in pseudo-code as follows:

```
For every virtual human at frame 0   /* Initialization stage */
  Generate texture
  Store View Matrix
End for
For every virtual human at frame N>0   /* Simulation */
  Compute new View Matrix
  Compute View Variation Matrix M (from previously stored
                      view matrix to the newly computed one).
  Compute the amplitude of the corresponding axis/angle
  If angle>threshold
    Generate texture
    Store current View Matrix
  End if
End for
```

Building the axis-angle representation of a rotation matrix **M** consists in finding its equivalent rotation axis as well as the angle to rotate about it [16]. Finally, the threshold that indicates when the texture is to be regenerated can be weighted once again with the euclidian distance from the impostor to the viewer.

6. The Human Flow Test Bed

Our work on impostors originates from earlier research on human crowd simulation that was carried out in our laboratory. However, simulating a human crowd introduces many parameters that alter the frame rate results. We preferred to use a simpler environment in order to assess reliably the gain of impostors on geometry. In our simulation twenty walking virtual humans keep circling. They all move at different yet constant speeds, along more or less long circles (Fig. 7). A fast walking engine handles the motion of the actors, collision between characters are not detected and finally every articulated character always lies in the field of vision so that visibility culling does not play a role.

The first graph shows the influence of the posture variation thresholds used in the texture cache invalidation mechanism. The other factor, that is the viewing angle, was deactivated throughout this test. Along the horizontal axis are noted the posture variation thresholds beyond which a texture is re-generated while the vertical axis shows the amount of time required for rendering the complete scene. The vertical axis is normalized with respect to the amount of time needed to render the whole scene using the real geometry. When the threshold is set to zero every change in the posture triggers a re-computation of the texture, in which case the rendering time logically exceeds the reference rendering time. Note that there is only a marginal difference of 15% though, which clearly shows that impostors are hardly slower than the actual geometry even in the worst cases. Rendering time plummets when the variation threshold is increased: a threshold of 40%, 60% and 80% cuts respectively by two, three and five the rendering time. In practice there is no noticeable difference in the animation of the actors as long as the threshold is smaller than 15%. However, it makes perfect sense to set the threshold to a much higher limit (between 40% and 80%) because the motion remains absolutely understandable. On the other hand it becomes hard to grasp that the actors are walking beyond 90%.

Fig. 7. Simulating two football teams (left: impostors, right: real geometry)

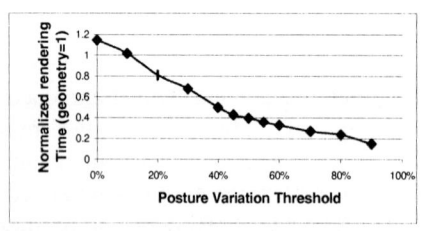 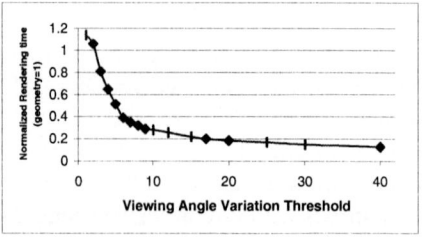

Graph 1.: Rendering speedup as a function of posture variation threshold

Graph 2.: Rendering speedup as a function of the viewing angle variation threshold

The second test focuses on the impact of the viewing angle on the rendering time. Like previously, the vertical axis is normalized with respect to a reference rendering time (that needed to render the whole scene with the actual geometry). On the horizontal axis are marked the viewing angle thresholds in degrees. Similarly to the first test we disabled the other factor in the cache invalidation mechanism. The critical threshold is reached for a viewing angle variation of two degrees only. Viewing angle thresholds of 5, 8 and 17 degrees cut respectively by two, three and five the rendering time. We consider that there is no real degradation of the animation up to 20 degrees. Refreshment of the actors' texture becomes too obvious beyond 30 degrees.

7. Conclusion

This paper shows that image-based rendering can be applied successfully to virtual humans. In particular, we have explained how to generate a texture representing a virtual human and proposed an image cache invalidation algorithm that works for any articulated character and executes reasonably fast. Two major issues, which were beyond the scope of this paper, could be addressed in future work:

1. Our texture refreshment algorithm performs on an individual basis. From the application point of view, the image cache invalidation mechanism should also consider virtual characters as a whole. Above all this would help achieve a quasi-constant frame rate, which is often regarded in virtual reality applications as more important than a high peak frame rate.

2. Because depth information is lost when complex 3D geometry is replaced with an impostor, especially with a plane, visibility may not be correctly resolved. Schaufler recently showed how to correct the visibility by directly modifying the depth value for every texel [17]. However, faster techniques could be investigated in the specific case of virtual humans. For example, the concrete problem depicted in figure 5 could be solved by decomposing the impostor's plane into several planes e.g. one for each major body part.

Acknowledgements

We wish to thank Soraia Raup-Musse for preliminary tests on the use of billboards for the representation of virtual humans. Part of this work has been sponsored by the European ACTS project COVEN.

References

1. Capin, T.K., Pandzic, I., Noser, H., Magnenat-Thalmann, N., Thalmann, D.: Virtual Human Representation and Communication in VLNET. In: IEEE Computer Graphics and Applications, Vol. 17, No. 2, March - April 1997 42-5
2. Regan, M., Post, R.: Priority Rendering with a Virtual Reality Address Recalculation Pipeline. In: Computer Graphics (SIGGRAPH '94 Proceedings) 155-162
3. Luebke, D., Georges, C.: Portals and Mirrors: Simple, Fast Evaluation of Potentially Visible Sets. In: 1995 Symposium on Interactive 3D Graphics 105-106
4. Heckbert, P., Garland, M.: Muliresolution modelling for fast rendering. In: Proceedings of Graphics Interface'94, 43-50
5. Popovic, J., Hoppe, H.: Progressive Simplicial Complexes. In: Computer Graphics (SIGGRAPH '97 Proceedings), 217-224
6. Garland, M., Heckbert, P.S.: Surface Simplification Using Quadric Error Metrics. In: Computer Graphics (SIGGRAPH '97 Proceedings), 209-216
7. Torborg, J., Kajiya, J.T.: Talisman: Commodity Real-time 3D Graphics for the PC. In: Computer Graphics (SIGGRAPH '96 Proceedings), 353-363
8. Maciel, P.W.C., Shirley, P.: Visual Navigation of Large Environments using Textured Clusters. In: 1995 Symposium on Interactive 3D Graphics, 95–102
9. Schaufler, G., Stürzlinger, W.: A Three Dimensional Image Cache for virtual reality. In: Proceedings of Eurographics'96, C-227 -C-234
10. Shade, J., Lichinski, D., Salesin, D.H., DeRose, T., Snyder, J.: Hierarchical Image Caching for Accelerated Walkthroughs of Complex Environments. In: Computer Graphics (SIGGRAPH'96 Proceedings), 75-82
11. Schaufler, G.: Exploiting Frame to Frame Coherence in a Virtual Reality System. In: Proceedings of VRAIS'96, Santa Cruz, California (April 1996), 95-102
12. Boulic, R., Capin, T.K., Huang, Z., Kalra, P., Lintermann, B., Magnenat-Thalmann, N., Moccozet, L., Molet, T., Pandzic, I., Saar, K., Schmitt, A., Shen, J., Thalmann, D.: The HUMANOID Environment for Interactive Animation of Multiple Deformable Human Characters. In: Proceedings of Eurographics'95, Maastricht (August 1995) 337-348
13. Shen, J., Chauvineau, E., Thalmann, D.: Fast Realistic Human Body Deformations for Animation and VR Applications. In: Computer Graphics International'96, Pohang, Korea (June 1996) 166-173
14. Pratt, D.R., Pratt, S.M., Barham, P.T., Barker, R.E., Waldrop, M.S., Ehlert, J.F., Chrislip, J.F.: Humans in Large-scale, Networked Virtual Environments. In: Presence, Vol. 6, No. 5, October 1997, 547-564
15. Funkhouser, T. A., Séquin, C.H.: Adaptative display algorithm for interactive frame rates during visualization of complex virtual environments. In: Computer Graphics (SIGGRAPH'93 Proceedings), 247-254
16. Pique, M. E.: Converting between Matrix and Axis-Amount representations. In: Graphics Gems (Vol. 1), Academic Press, 466-467
17. Schaufler, G.: Nailboards: A Rendering Primitive for Image Caching in Dynamic Scenes In: Proceedings of 8th Eurographics workshop'97. St. Etienne, France, June 16-18 1997, 151-162
18. Sillon, F., Drettakis, G., Bodelet, B.: Efficient Impostor Manipulation for Real-time Visualization of Urban Scenery. In: Proceedings of Eurographics'97 (1997) C-207-C-217

Can We Define Virtual Reality? The M_RIC Model

Didier Verna and Alain Grumbach

ENST, Dpartement Informatique,
46, rue Barrault
75634 Paris cedex 13, France
{verna, grumbach}@inf.enst.fr
This work benefits from the financial support of DRET/DGA

Abstract. In this paper, we propose a reasoning model aimed at helping to decide on the virtual status of a given situation, from a *human* point of view rather than from a technological one. We first describe how a human and his environment interact. The notion of "reality" will be seen through this description. Then, we propose a set of possible "cognitive deviations" of reality leading to situations of virtual reality. This model provides three major benefits to the field of Virtual Reality: first, a global definition and a systematic mean of categorizing related situations; secondly, the ability to discuss on the virtual status of *real* situations and not only synthetic, computer generated ones; thirdly, a demonstration on how the field of Tele-Operation is heavily related to virtual reality concepts, and some perspectives on future tele-operation intelligent user interfaces.

1 Introduction

Facing the constant growth of activity in the field of Virtual Reality, it is important to notice that 1/ although virtual reality systems are designed for use by humans, technological research is much more advanced than studies on the cognitive aspects, and 2/ the field of Virtual Reality lacks a general agreement on the terms to use and the meaning to give to them.

We hence propose a model called *M_RIC*[1], which comprises a description of "reality" as a set of interactions involving a human being and his environment, and a set of possible "cognitive deviations" allowing a real situation to become virtual. Provided with this model, we are able to decide whether such or such situation (even real ones) can be labeled Virtual Reality. Furthermore, this model shows that the field of Tele-Operation is actually heavily connected to Virtual Reality, and give us perspectives on what could be the future intelligent user interfaces for tele-operation.

---

[1] *M_RIC* is a French acronym for "Model Representing Cognitive x Interaction"

2 Reality as a Set of Cognitive Interactions

2.1 The $M_RIC\text{-}r$ Descriptive Model

Our model concentrates on a single human being, called the **operator**, interacting with his environment. Any other humans are considered part of the environment.

Model Agents
- In a first step, we separate the situation in a **Mental Agent** and a **Physical Agent**. The mental agent corresponds to the operator's mind. The physical agent is the set comprising the operator's body (which is indeed a physical object), the environment and the laws of physics governing them.
- In a second step, we separate the physical agent in an **Operating agent** and an **External Agent**. The operating agent corresponds to the operator's body. We call it so because any human action on the environment is actually performed primarily through the body, and not directly from the mind to the environment. The external agent is the rest of the physical world.
- In a third step, we separate the mental agent in a **Control Agent** and a **Transitional Agent**. The control agent is related to the operator's awareness, intelligence and decision processes. The transitional agent represents implicit processes like reflex actions or perceptions, not reaching the level of consciousness.

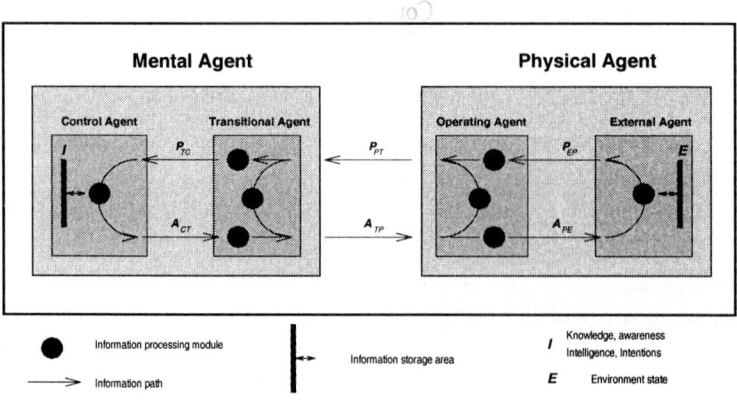

Fig. 1. $M_RIC\text{-}r$: Model of Reality

Information Processing
The complete descriptive model is presented in figure 1. The different information paths are noted A or P according to their direction (Action or Perception), and indexed with their origin and destination agents. Each agent is in charge of

several information processing tasks, mainly devoted to translating the output of the previous agent into input for the next one. For example:
- $A_{CT} \to A_{TP} \to A_{PE}$ The intention of walking is translated into a sequence of nerve impulses, which in turn produce a real body motion.
- $P_{EP} \to P_{PT} \to P_{TC}$ The light emitted by an object produces optical nerve activity, which in turn is interpreted as the "presence" of the object.

Notion of Interaction

In addition to those straight connections, the figure 1 shows four loop-backs in the information paths:
- $P_{TC} \to A_{CT}$ This represents the operator's decision processes. For instance, the operator can decide to grab an object because he *knows* the object is there, maybe because he can *see* it.
- $A_{PE} \to P_{EP}$ This represents the reaction of the environment. For instance, we can get an image of our own body, colliding with an object prevent us from moving the way we want.
- $A_{TP} \to P_{PT}$ This represents the proprioceptive feedback. For instance, independently from the environment itself, we know our orientation in space.
- $P_{PT} \to A_{TP}$ This represents reflex (re)actions, that is, actions undertaken without any control of will.

From *M_RIC* point of view, we will say that two agents are in **interaction** if and only if there is an information loop linking them, and those agents are the extremities of this loop.

This means in particular that agents in interaction must connect back to each other through an information processing module. In our model, we hence have four kinds of interaction: the Control Agent or the Transitional Agent, with both the Operating Agent and the External Agent. An interaction thus implies some kind of "dialog" between the concerned agents, in which the information sent back depends partly on the information received. This is why we do *not* state that the Operating Agent interacts with the External Agent. Rather, we could say that they are in **mutual action**.

2.2 Notion of Reality

Trying to define "reality" is not our purpose, since it would be more of a philosophical matter. Instead, we will state that reality can be seen through the model we just described. In other words, we consider that the *M_RIC-r* model is a *cognitive model of Reality*. This point of view brings out two important aspects of the notion:
- **Agent classes.** Each agent in the model has a special duty, a precise internal architecture and a particular set of connections with the other agents. These features define the agent class.
- **Agent Instances.** For each agent class, several instances can be provided without altering the model integrity. For instance, a human body and a robot could be two different instances of an Operating Agent.

3 What is Virtual Reality?

3.1 Sources of Virtuality

We propose a dual interpretation of the expression "virtual reality", leading us to the following definitions:
- First, we consider the terms separately. Here, the term "reality" is to be seen as described in the previous section, that is, through the M_RIC-r model. A *virtual* reality is then a reality which looks like the operator's, but which is not actually his. Virtualizing reality hence means replacing or modifying one or several components of the real situation, but still preserving a common behavior. Such virtualization processes are called **Type 1 Virtuality Sources**.
- In a dual approach, we state that the expression "virtual reality" cannot be split. From this point of view, the virtualization processes are no longer aimed at imitating the real components of the situation, but rather at proposing totally new ones, behaving differently, and in particular, not the usual way. Such virtualization processes are called **Type 2 Virtuality Sources**.

3.2 Type 1 Virtuality Sources

Augmented Reality For one interpretation of the term, Augmented Reality means mixing real and virtual objects in the same scene, for instance[4], a system designed to include in real time virtual objects onto a live video. The purpose is also to allow participants to interact with these objects as well as with the real environment. This kind of virtualization process complies with our definition of the type 1 virtuality sources: the resulting situation is not exactly the real one but is an imitation of a real environment (the virtual objects could perfectly well be real). Moreover, the aim being to allow interaction with the virtual objects too, the resulting environment is expected to behave the same way as a real environment would. We thus *modify* the situation by adding new objects that behave the same way real objects would, hence preserving a common behavior.

Artificial Reality Artificial Reality is often referred to as the ability to create worlds that do not exist, such as statistical worlds, and to display them like 3D objects. Following this terminology, the two categories of Virtual Reality applications would be: 1/ simulating the real world and 2/ creating such abstract worlds. This classification is not relevant according to our cognitive vision of the concept. Representing abstract data is something older than virtual reality technologies. What is now permitted with these technologies is to navigate in such worlds. However, this kind of virtualization processes falls into the category of type 1 virtuality sources: consider that such a virtual statistical world could exist as a real world, for instance if we built a physical set of cubes representing the statistical values and put them together in a room. From a cognitive point of view, Artificial Reality actually consists of imitating a special case of real environment. Therefore, we are just in front of another case of type 1 virtualization process.

3.3 Type 2 Virtuality Sources

Augmented Reality Previously, we spoke of Augmented Reality in terms of adding virtual *objects* to a real scene. Here we consider a second aspect: adding virtual *information* to the real scene. In a recent paper from Nagao [7], an augmented reality system gives to the operator "[...] the feeling of talking to the object itself [...]". When the operator looks at a book, he is not only given certain information about the book, but the ability to talk directly to the book and ask it a few more questions. This example of augmented reality corresponds exactly to what we call a type 2 virtualization process. Here the environment is not just imitated, but its behavior is modified. More and more similar processes are added to current systems, e.g. in computer aided surgery[6], where for instance, the operator is given the ability to see through the patient's skull and brain, thanks to a virtual schema added on the real image of the operating zone.

Released Reality The general purpose of Augmented Reality is namely to augment objects abilities, perceptions, informations etc. Similarly, the counterpart of augmenting abilities, is diminishing disabilities. This means that another possibility for type 2 virtualization processes lies in the ability to "release" real world constraints, for instance, the inability to reverse time, to escape from laws of physics etc. Several related ideas can already be seen in some systems known as augmented reality systems. We prefer the expression "Released Reality". Here are some examples: in several VRML (Virtual Reality Modeling Language) viewers, the user can enable/disable collision detection, toggle walk/fly navigation mode. Those options, like going through walls or flying across the scene correspond to releasing several physical constraints. Similarly, in several virtual reality video games or virtual museum visiting systems, the user can jump directly from one room to another, releasing this way the temporal constraint of movements. Those processes are type 2 virtualization processes, since the real behavior is not imitated but modified.

3.4 Definition of Virtual Reality

Having some virtuality sources in a given situation is necessary to speak of virtual reality, but not sufficient. Our model of reality features a set of agents, each one belonging to its own class. In our point of view, the term "reality" is essentially associated with the notion of agent class. This means that all *realities*, whether virtual or not, should follow the model structure, and thus respect the agents classes. Similarly, the term "virtual" has more to do with the agent instances. A *virtual reality* would then be a reality that conforms with the M_RIC model, but with virtual agents instead of real ones. These considerations lead us to propose the following definition:

> Let us take a situation V to be examined. This situation must conform with the M_RIC model, and will be called a situation of Virtual Reality

if and only if one or more of its agents differ from the corresponding real one(s) and if all such agents (then called "virtual agents") can be obtained from real ones thanks to virtuality sources of type 1 and/or 2.

Since in any case, the agents classes are required to be the same, the topography of the connections between the agents must be preserved as well. As a consequence, the four types of interaction described earlier are a necessary component of any Virtual Reality system. This point of view, although our acception of the term "interaction" is specialized, is commonly agreed on.

4 Immersion and Virtual Reality

Amongst all concepts and ideas involved in current virtual reality systems, the notion of "immersion" is the most widely used. In this section, we show how the concept of Immersion fits with our definition of Virtual Reality, and we demonstrate how our model enables us to decide on the virtual status of real worlds too.

4.1 Immersion and M_RIC

Overview The most well-known case of immersion is the one in which the operator evolves in a computer generated world thanks to data suit, Head Mounted Display (HMD), data gloves ... and feels physically present in this virtual environment.

In such a situation, the human body, as an Operating Agent, is in contact with a new external agent imitating the real environment. In order to keep a coherent physical feeling of presence, ideal immersive systems should consequently disconnect the mental agent from his real environment, but still handle a perfect model of the human body and its "mutual action" with the simulated environment (physical constraints, collisions, visual body feedback ...). Hence, from M_RIC point of view, the mental agent should be completely disconnected from its own physical agent, and linked to a completely virtual one instead. This ideal situation can be modelized as shown in figure 2. In this model, the virtual situation is obtained by "deviating" the information paths A_{TP} and P_{PT} towards an imitation of the real physical agent. This modelization complies with our definition of Virtual Reality, since the whole physical agent is a virtual one (it differs from the real one), and this agent is obtained thanks to type 1 virtuality sources.

Let us precise that we are **not** suggesting (and we do **not** think) that it should be possible to separate mind from body. But when a system provides an efficient immersive feeling to the operator, and for instance produces realistic synthetic images of the body, then the operator becomes likely to "believe" the image (s)he sees, and accept the feedback (s)he gets as a real one. This is what our model represents.

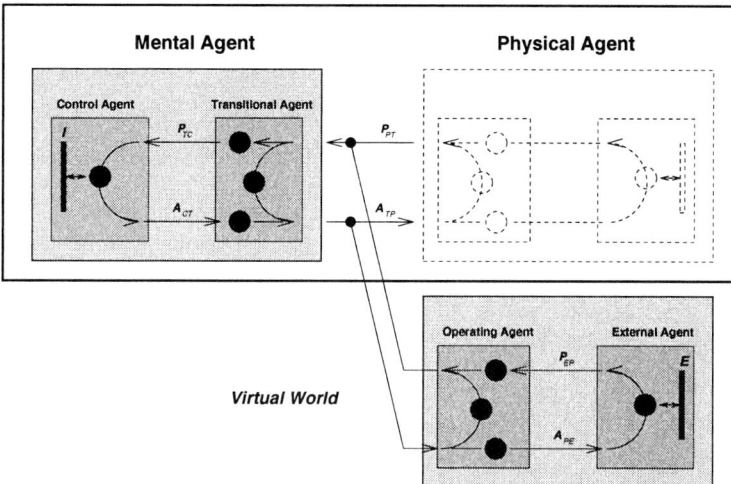

Fig. 2. M_RIC-i: Model of Immersion

Limitations At this time, current immersive systems are far from being ideal, because they break two important information paths of the M_RIC-i model:
- We can not completely disconnect the operator from his own environment. In a virtual soccer game[5], the soccer player is in contact with the real ground, even if he believes it is the soccer court, but this situation is acceptable only as long as the virtual ground corresponds to the real one. In this situation, the information paths comprising A_{PE} and P_{EP} are not completely deviated as required by our definition of Virtual Reality.
- There are situations in which the proprioceptive feedback is important: in flight simulation, rendering the effects of gravity or acceleration is difficult to achieve, but should be present for a realistic rendering. The information loopback A_{TP}-P_{PT} (inside the control agent) is currently broken. The idea that any virtual reality system should handle properly all interaction components, including proprioception, complies with the point of view of Quéau[8].

As far as the M_RIC reasoning model is concerned, we cannot oppose a technological argument to a theoretical model. Therefore we think that the simulation systems cited above do develop towards virtual reality systems, but are yet imperfect due to technological constraints.

4.2 Can Real Worlds be Virtual?

Whereas we have only spoken of synthetic environments until now, an important feature of our model is to give us the ability to extend the reflection to real worlds too. In the next paragraphs, we will explain why and how real worlds can be virtual under certain circumstances, and again we will position the traditionally ambiguous case of Augmented Reality.

Real Immersion In the previous section, we dealt with immersion in *synthetic* environments ("virtual immersion"). Now we would like to show that the *synthetic* aspect of the simulation is not necessary to have an immersive virtual reality system. Consider a situation of immersion in a synthetic environment, which is aimed at reproducing the exact reality. Say, a guided tour in a virtual museum where the operator can navigate in rooms (but still collide with walls) and look at the paintings. Now, consider a situation in which an operator is given exactly the same interface (head mounted display, joystick ...) but is interacting with a real (distant) museum. It is clear that from the operator's point of view, the situation remains the same. The real situation can be called "virtual reality" because like in the simulated case, we provide a completely new physical agent (real instead of synthetic this time) with its own control and external agents. This new agent is indeed virtual because none of the actual physical agent components are supposed to be preserved. Moreover, since this virtual physical agent is actually a real one, it falls in the category of type 1 virtuality sources. The informations paths $A_{TP}P_{PT}$ are thus deviated the same way in both cases, and the model presented in figure 2 is still a valid representation of this situation.

This is why we think that the distinction synthetic/real is not relevant to label a situation "virtual reality". Cognitively speaking, Virtual Reality must not be restricted to computer based simulation. This point of view differs from the one of Burdéa[1] and Quéau[8] for whom a virtual reality system must be based on computer graphics before anything else.

Augmented Reality Augmented Reality situations are interesting because they often mix real and synthetic components. Since we just saw that a real scene can, under certain circumstances, be a virtual reality situation, the question of the virtual status of Augmented Reality arises. We think that this status depends on the situation:
- If the operator *is not* in direct contact with the real scene (such as tele-operating a distant robot or visiting a distant museum), the situation may actually be a mix of real and synthetic immersion, obtained thanks to type 1 virtuality sources. Hence, it is acceptable to label the situation Virtual Reality. It would actually be more appropriate to speak of **Augmented Virtual Reality** since real immersion alone is already a situation of virtual reality as we just saw.
- If the operator *is* in direct contact with the real scene and the goal is not to change this (like evolving with translucent glasses which superimpose objects onto the real scene), we can no longer talk of immersion, since the operator is explicitly required to stay in contact with his real environment. This fact hence doesn't comply with our definition of Virtual Reality. Here we can speak of Augmented Reality but not of Virtual Reality.

5 Examples

To illustrate further how we can use the *M$_R$IC* model to decide on the "virtual reality" status of such or such situation, let us give the outlines of the reasoning on two contradictory examples.

5.1 Example 1

In this example[2], an operator is immersed in a virtual nuclear plant, and is given the ability to navigate in the plant and perform several operations. The corresponding real situation is the one in which the operator acts in a *real* an similar nuclear plant. With respect to the *M$_R$IC-r* model, the new agents are as follows:
- The control agent remains the same as in the real situation. Indeed, the operator still decides what to do and controls the virtual body.
- With a little training (less training means better system), the operator will be able to use the joystick by reflex to move around. This implies that the transitional agent remains the same as in the real situation when the system interface is perfectly assimilated by the operator. Moving around in the virtual environment should indeed become as obvious as walking in the real room.
- The External Agent becomes the nuclear plant computer model. This is an imitation of a real environment. We are thus in front of a type 1 virtualization process.
- The Operating Agent becomes the human body computer model. Although this model is not perfect (e.g. only the operator's hand is visually represented) the ultimate goal is clearly to imitate the operator's body, which is a type 1 virtualization process.

We now have determined the corresponding real case along with the new agents involved in the situation. Let us check the validity of these agents according the the class specifications imposed by the *M$_R$IC* model.
- The operator is given both the ability to move his virtual body, and to perceive it (at least the hand), hence respecting the A_{TP} and A_{PT} information paths.
- The new Operating Agent has the ability to grab objects in the virtual plant, and collision detection is implemented, hence handling correctly the A_{PE} and A_{EP} information paths.

We hence have a situation in which a new (virtual) physical agent is provided. This agent and its interaction with the mental agent conforms with the *M$_R$IC* model requirements. Moreover, this agent is obtained thanks to type 1 virtuality sources. We are thus in front of a situation of virtual reality, and more precisely a situation of "virtual immersion".

5.2 Example 2

Let us take again the example proposed by Nagao[7]. A user with a translucent screen wanders in a library, and each time he looks at a book through the screen, he can verbally interact with it directly. Here, the user is already in a real library, so there is no other corresponding real situation. The system does not actually provide any new agent, since the operator is explicitly required to stay in his own environment. Hence, we can already conclude that this situation wouldn't be called Virtual Reality. Our definition specifies that at least one of the model agents should be replaced, which is not the case here. However, this example illustrates the fact that we can have virtuality sources in a situation without it being a Virtual Reality situation properly speaking. Indeed, giving the "feeling of talking to the book itself" constitutes a type 2 virtuality source. From the operator's point of view, an object (the book) is virtualized by modifying its normal behavior. This situation belongs to the category of Augmented Reality (type 2), but according to our definition, not to Virtual Reality systems.

6 Virtual Reality and Tele-Operation

In this section, we demonstrate that the fields of tele-operation and virtual reality are strongly related, and we show how our model can bring out several interesting perspectives on what could be future interfaces for tele-operation systems,

We call "tele-operation" a situation in which an operator is remotely working in a distant[2] or inaccessible area. Such situations use artificial tools to both transmit orders to the manipulation device (e.g. a robot), and receive feedback from it.

6.1 Sources of Virtuality in Tele-Operation

Immersion It is important to notice that more and more tele-operation systems use virtual reality interfaces at the perception level. After using screens to display the distant scene, tele-operators are provided with HMD's allowing them to get a spatial view of the area, and even to move their point of view. In such systems, the idea is actually to provide an immersive environment to the operator. Giving the operator the feeling of being present in the distant area makes such systems fall into the category of virtual reality system, because they actually implement a case of real immersion, which we proved to be a case of Virtual Reality. This constitute the first relation between the fields of Virtual Reality and Tele-Operation.

Augmented/Released Reality The process of virtualizing tele-operation situations does not stop at the immersion level. Many recent applications have shown the utility of Augmented Reality concepts (such as providing symbolic information superimposed on the visual field) for tele-operation[6]. However, the concepts of Augmented Reality extend farther than just the perception level: the main difference between real operation and simulated operation is that in a real case, the operations are usually irreversible. This constraint led researchers to develop training systems as well as autonomous (and hopefully robust) robots.

---

[2] What we call "distance" here means spatial distance as well as temporal distance.

When using training systems, the tele-operator is actually given a chance to "reverse time" in case of mistakes. This idea falls into the category of Released Reality, and type 2 virtualization processes.

6.2 Virtualizing the Mental Agent

Until now, we have demonstrated how virtualization processes can affect the external agent, the operating agent, and at most the whole physical agent. Logically, the question of determining whether virtualizing the other agents in the model is sensible arises. This question makes sense if considered relatively to the field of tele-operation.

Virtual Control Agent By adding autonomous decision processes in a tele-operation system, we enter a new field of virtuality: we actually provide a new (and virtual) control agent in the system, collaborating with the operator's. From M_RIC point of view, this is the first time that a virtuality source has dealt with the mental agent itself. The operator actually gets the feeling of controlling not only an operating agent, but an operating augmented with a minimum of intelligence, thus modifying the common behavior of real operating agents. This is a case of (Type 2) Augmented Virtual Reality, not only by perception, not only by action, but by *reflection*.

Virtual Transmutation Until now, we considered two main situations: Immersion, in which the operator is manipulating the environment with "his own hands", and Tele-Operation, in which the environment is modified indirectly, through robot directives. In this last case, an important problem is to provide systems easy to learn, with a training period as short as possible. We saw precedently that as long as the operator doesn't act directly with his own body, or with an isomorphic synthetic avatar like in an immersive situation, a period of adaptation is necessary to be able to use the interface (joystick, data gloves ...) without having to think about it. Faced with such a constraint, the ultimate goal of tele-operation systems could be to provide a device for which there would be no more training period, where the operator could give orders only by moving his own body. Consider a car assembly robot, say, capable of drilling and screwing operations. The operator is given a synthetic vision of his arm, superimposed on the image of the real scene. This way, (s)he doesn't actually notice the presence of a robot, but instead gets the feeling of working with his own hands. When a drilling operation is needed, the operator just points a finger to the drilling zone, and the robot immediately takes a real driller and operates as requested (grabbing the driller may not be displayed since it is not the essential part of the operation). Similarly, virtually grabbing a screw, and pulling it up to the hole would make the robot leave the driller, grab a screwer and perform the operation directly. What is interesting in this zero-training interface is that the operator only needs to know the natural movements he has been doing all his life. Hence, everything occurs as if the robot became the operator's new operating agent.

This virtualization process is thus a "virtual transmutation" for the operator. Substituting a robot to the human body is a type 2 virtualization process, since the behavior of the operating agent is completely changed.

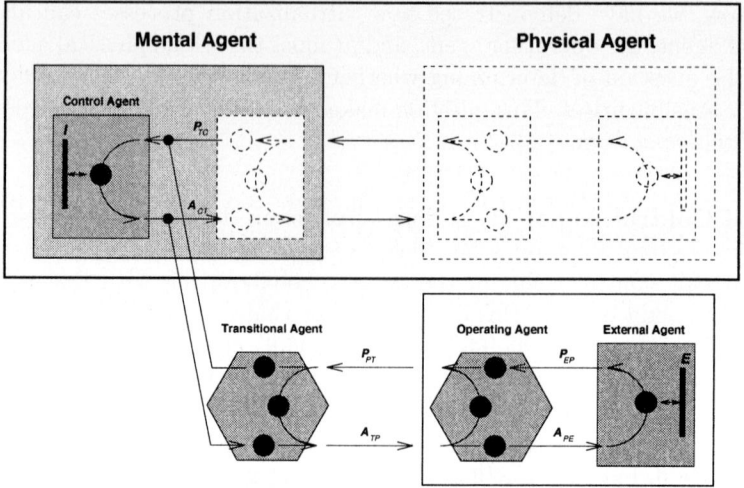

Fig. 3. M_RIC-d:Intentions Detection

Intentions Detection In an even more ultimate view, the ideal situation is the one in which the operator does not have to work any more! This means that if we want the operator to keep control over the events, the aim of the system would be to detect as fast as possible the operator's intentions, and proceed automatically. While the very futuristic view of such a situation is a mental communication between the operator and the system, this goal can still be approached with an "intentions detection system"[9] minimizing the physical work of the operator. For instance, given the presence of an object in the environment, and given that the operator is currently moving his arm towards the object, an intention of grabbing the object is becoming more and more likely, and could in turn be detected. In terms of deviation from the M_RIC model, the system communicates here with the operator at the highest possible semantic level, that is, directly with the control agent. This situation is modelized on figure 3, and represents the highest level of virtuality attainable, while keeping an operator in the situation.

7 Conclusion

In this paper, we built a cognitive model of interaction through which the concept of Reality is seen. We proposed the notion of "virtuality source", aimed at modifying real components of a situation in order to make them become virtual.

The notion of Virtual Reality was then defined as the virtualization of one or more agents of the model. We think that our vision of Virtual Reality has three major benefits:
- Our model provides a systematic way of deciding on the virtual status of any particular situation. This will hopefully help clarifying the notion and its related concepts.
- This categorization process is not limited to synthetic worlds, but also extends to real worlds.
- Our model demonstrates to which extend the fields of Tele-Operation and Virtual Reality are connected, and provides several interesting perspectives on future intelligent tele-operation interfaces.

In our opinion, the main distinction between different Virtual Reality situations does not lie in the synthetic or real aspect of the situation, but rather in the *immersive* or *tele-operatory* aspect. While type 1 virtuality sources are mainly related to the notion of immersion, it seems that type 2 virtuality sources would be far more helpful in tele-operation systems. However, the illustrations cited along this paper tend to show that type 1 virtuality sources are currently much more developed than type 2. An in-depth research on the notion of Tele-Operation Assistance[10] may be of some help to correct this imbalance.

References

1. Burdea, G., Coiffet, P.: La Réalité Virtuelle. Hermès, Paris (1993)
2. Fertey, G., Delpy, T., Lapierre, M., Thibault G.: An industrial application of Virtual Reality: an aid for designing maintenance operations in nuclear plants. In proceedings of: L'interface des mondes Réels et Virtuels, pp. 151-162. Montpellier, France (1995).
3. Grumbach, A., Verna, D.: Assistance cognitive à la téléopération en monde virtuel. In proceedings of: Journées Nationales Réalité Virtuelle, GT-RV, GDR-PRC, pp. 38-46. Toulouse, France (1996)
4. Kansy, K., Berlage, T., Schmitgen, G. Wikirchen, P.: Real-Time Intergration of Synthetic Computer Graphics into Live Video Scenes. In proceedings of: L'interface des mondes Réels et Virtuels, pp. 151-162. Montpellier, France (1995).
5. Mazeau, J.-P., Bryche, X.: Un espace interactif dispersé destiné à supporter des rencontres sportives. In proceedings of: L'interface des mondes Réels et Virtuels, pp. 189-198. Monpellier, France (1995)
6. Mellor, J.-P.: Enhanced Reality Visualization in a Surgical Environment. M.I.T. Technical Report No. 1544.
7. Nagao, K., Rekimoto, J.: Ubiquitous talker: spoken language interaction with real worlds objects. (1995)
8. Quéau, P.: Le Virtuel. Champ Vallon, Seyssel (1993)
9. Verna, D.: Téléopération et Réalité Virtuelle: Assistance à l'opérateur par modélisation cognitive de ses intentions. In proceedings of: IHM'97. Poitiers, France (1997).
10. Verna, D.: Smantique et Catgorisation de l'Assistance en Ralit Virtuelle. In proceedings of: Journées Nationales Réalité Virtuelle, GT-RV, GDR-PRC. Issy-les-Moulineaux, France (1998).

Distortion in Distributed Virtual Environments

Matthew D. Ryan, Paul M. Sharkey

Interactive Systems Research Group
Department of Cybernetics, The University of Reading, Whiteknights, Reading RG6 6AY, UK, tel: +44 (0) 118 9875 123, fax: +44 (0) 118 9318 220
{M.D.Ryan, P.M.Sharkey}@reading.ac.uk
http://www.cyber.reading.ac.uk/ISRG/

Abstract. This paper proposes a solution to the problems associated with network latency within distributed virtual environments. It begins by discussing the advantages and disadvantages of synchronous and asynchronous distributed models, in the areas of user and object representation and user-to-user interaction. By introducing a hybrid solution, which utilises the concept of a causal surface, the advantages of both synchronous and asynchronous models are combined. Object distortion is a characteristic feature of the hybrid system, and this is proposed as a solution which facilitates dynamic real-time user collaboration. The final section covers implementation details, with reference to a prototype system available from the Internet.

Keywords: distributed virtual environments, network latency, collaboration, interaction, multi-user, virtual reality.

1 Introduction

Within a distributed virtual environment users interact with objects and state change events are generated. These events are normally transmitted to other users within the virtual environment across a network. The timing of events can be managed using either synchonised or asynchronous clocks.

1.1 No Clock Synchronisation (Asynchronous)

In this model, the environment contains no uniform, global time. Each host has a local clock, and the evolution of each event is described with respect to this local time. Because there is no global time, all event messages are sent without reference to when they occurred, and so events are replayed as soon as a user receives them. In this way, users always perceive remote users as they were some time in the past.

1.2 Global Time (Synchronous).

When using synchronous time, as events are transmitted, they are time-stamped according to a global time that is synchronised between all users [1]. When events are received by a user, they are replayed at the correct global time. This usually requires the model to be rolled back to the correct time of the event – time must then be advanced quickly to the current time, to allow real-time local interaction.

1.3 Network Latency

The network connecting users within the virtual environment induces latency of information interchange, which causes problems in the areas of user and object representation. The following two sections and Fig. 1 describe the problems, and suggest that different time management techniques are best for the two areas.

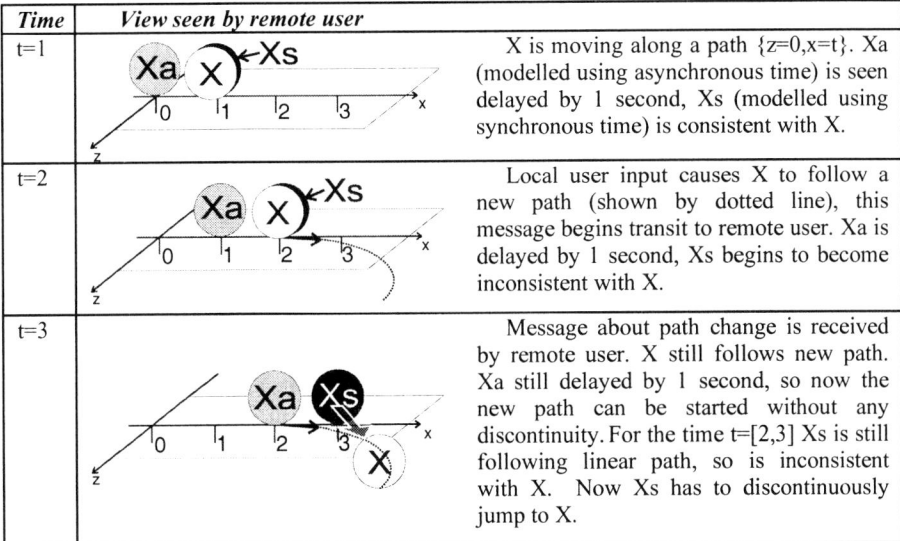

Time	View seen by remote user	
t=1		X is moving along a path {z=0,x=t}. Xa (modelled using asynchronous time) is seen delayed by 1 second, Xs (modelled using synchronous time) is consistent with X.
t=2		Local user input causes X to follow a new path (shown by dotted line), this message begins transit to remote user. Xa is delayed by 1 second, Xs begins to become inconsistent with X.
t=3		Message about path change is received by remote user. X still follows new path. Xa still delayed by 1 second, so now the new path can be started without any discontinuity. For the time t=[2,3] Xs is still following linear path, so is inconsistent with X. Now Xs has to discontinuously jump to X.

Fig. 1. User positions as seen by a remote user. X is the local user, Xa is the user modeled asynchronous time, Xs is the user modeled using synchronous time. The network delay, $\overline{\Delta}$, is 1 second

1.4 Asynchronous Time for User Representation

As Fig. 1 shows, user representations will appear discontinuous if a synchronous model is used. The asynchronous model, however, does not lead to discontinuities so is advantageous for user representation.

1.5 Synchronous Time for Object Representation

If asynchronous clocks are used, a local user will always see the past state of remote users and objects, as Fig. 1 shows. The model of objects at the local site will therefore be different to the model at the remote site. If objects appear in different places to different users, the users cannot interact with those objects. The only experimentation showed that standing waves occurred at multiples of the resonant frequency (an expected result from the control theory [6]).

3.2 Distortion in the Virtual World

The delay associated with propagation of force along objects in the real world is derived from length and stiffness of the material. In the virtual world, however, the delay is derived from the network. The propagation of force as waves of distortion through objects in the real world is therefore analogous to propagation of event messages through the network. By showing the force propagation through objects in the form of distortion, users are made aware of the delay that is present, and can adapt to the maximum achievable rate of interaction.

3.3 Collaborative Interaction

As a user changes the state of objects within their vicinity, those state changes will be reflected immediately on parts of the object close to that user. As the state change messages are transmitted across the network, the state changes initiated by the user will be seen to propagate along the object. When the state changes reach the remote user, the remote users interaction is taken into consideration, and resultant actions are determined [7]. These actions are sent continually as state changes back along the object (and also the network) to reach the local user again. This interaction occurs as a dynamic closed loop feedback system.

4 Implementation

4.1 Object States

Each object in the view seen by a local user will be displayed at a time $t-\Delta$, obtained from the causal surface function $\Delta = S(x,y,z)$. The causal surface is continuous and dynamically changes as users move and as network delays vary, such that the value of the causal surface is always greater than the actual network delay at each user. Given that $\overline{\Delta}$ is bounded within the range $[0, \max\{S\}]$, all the states of each virtual object must be defined over the range $[t-\max\{S\}, t]$, where t is current time. The trajectory of each object state can be implemented as a function or set of n functions:

$$X(t) = f_i(t) \quad t_i < t < t_{i+1} \quad (2)$$

for $i = 1, 2, \ldots n$, where t_i is the start time of the ith function, and $t_1 \leq (t-\max\{S\})$. The functions $f_i(t)$ are stored in a temporally ordered list of functions, the most recent function being held at the head of the list. A function $f_i(t)$ can be removed from the list if a function $f_j(t)$ exists in the list such that $t_j < (t-\max\{S\})$.

Every defined parameter of each object (the states of the objects) must be specified over the interval $[t-\max\{S\}, t]$. The states of object may include, for example, position, orientation, colour, temperature, but all types of interaction available to the users must be defined parametrically. A separate list of functions is used for each object state.

4.2 Virtual States

The previous sections have concentrated on distortion of *shape*. Object states define *all* dynamic parameters of the object, including all the states that can be influenced by interaction. Therefore, as each point on the object is delayed by a different amount, *all* dynamic states of the object will change across its surface. For example, if the temperature of an object is increasing over time, a delayed part of the object will be at a lower temperature than a part closer to the (local) heat source.

4.3 Demonstration Program

A simple demonstration program, showing the use of the causal surface is available from the ISRG website. The program allows two users to interact with objects within the same world. A simulated communication channel between the users allows variable network latencies.

5 Conclusion

This paper discusses an alternative solution to prediction for many of the problems associated with network latency within distributed virtual environments. Remote users, and objects close to them are viewed by local users as they were some time in the past, thereby removing state discontinuities, and allowing visualisation of remote interaction. Objects close to local users are displayed in real-time, such that interaction is possible. Objects are delayed by a smoothly varying amount between the local and remote users. Distortion occurs due to the varying delay, and this has strong parallels in the real world – state changes are propagated through objects at a finite rate. In the virtual world, this rate is derived from the network delay, and the distortion allows visualisation of information transfer to allow real-time dynamic interaction.

Acknowledgement. This work is supported by a Postgraduate Studentship Award from the UK's Engineering and Physical Sciences Research Council.

References

1. Roberts, D. J., Sharkey, P. M.: Maximising Concurrency and Scalability in a Consistent, Causal, Distributed Virtual Reality System, Whilst Minimising the Effect of Network

scripting language. The data element definitions and model objects can be directly mapped to Javascript or C++ data structures.

Previous research on physical properties for distributed network simulation required by general model algorithms has included the DIS (Distributed Interactive Simulation) protocol [1]. VRML research related to DIS is being carried out by the DIS-VRML-JAVA working group associated with the VRML Architecture Group. An alternative to DIS based VRML is the virtual reality transfer protocol [2]. The research presented in this paper is about VRML simulations that are completely generic. It provides an extensible framework for the editing of physically based properties used by multifunctional sets of model algorithms.

Data Definitions for VR Simulation

This research is based upon the following metaphor. Physically based simulations require models and algorithms to implement the simulation. Large numbers of models exist whose algorithms involve physical properties that are well understood, standardized and can be approximated by a Level Of Detail (LOD) paradigm. Such a „simulation LOD" paradigm allows VR simulation models to use approximate algorithms to manage the computational complexity of simulations within a virtual environment. Managing simulation complexity is critical when immersed inside a VRML base virtual environment that includes multi-user behaviors.

Consider the following example of the simulation LOD paradigm applied to a VR/VE or VRML sensor simulation. In the case of a Radar sensor simulation, the coarsest simulation LOD involves the solution of the generic radar equation. The next finer LOD for radar simulation involves a more physically based model of ground clutter, weather and multipath effects. Finer radar model LOD's can be generated by considering more realistic models of system losses, electromagnetic interference, aspect dependant cross sections, antenna directivity, statistical techniques and even hostile actions among role playing fanatics. Descriptions of the equations for various radar model LOD's and their associated model properties can be found in various sources [3 , 4, 5].

These various radar model LOD's require well defined properties that need to be initialized to realistic values and updated as the VE simulation progresses. The SimVRML editor provides a VRML based interface that addresses the need to initialize and update VR/VE physical properties. These properties involve sensor models along with a set of models that provide for the simulation of common behaviors in a VR/VE/VRML universe.

The models that have properties defined for the SimVRML editor described in this paper are models for vehicles, ships, subs and aircraft motion, along with models for communications, sensors, role playing, combat operations, industrial, chemical and biological. The data element definitions for the properties simulated in the above models are defined as a series of Java classes.

The base class for the SimVRML editor deals with the variables and methods needed to manage data extraction, insertion, descriptive names for the JDBC objects and pointers to default geometries and model algorithms for a set of user defined LOD's. The SimVRML editor has a class that deals with the variables and methods needed to manage data extraction and insertion of dynamic data such as simulation time, pointers to the methods and models used in the simulation, along with status, position, motion parameters and other common simulation housekeeping data.

The SimVRML editor operates on many common Objects that are hierarchical in structure. Such hierarchical objects consist of data elements describing physical properties and also data elements that describe equipment that in turn are described by data elements within other subclasses. Thus, a Vehicle object may have a radio object and an engine object as components of its hierarchical structure.

The SimVRML base class and its subclasses have a public variable that is an enumerated type. The enumeration's are simply ASCII descriptions (less than 33 characters) of the various properties that are shared by the common objects that are simulated via the above models. There are also methods that are used to extract and insert valuations for the properties in the SimVRML base class and its subclasses. Using derived classes and virtual functions and providing an API for the JDBC fields, the SimVRML editor can be made extensible. Thus, a bigger and better model algorithm that needs more sophisticated properties can be „plugged" into the SimVRML editor. Other designers could then just publish their enumerations and „get and put" virtual functions.

Subclasses of the SimVRML base class consist of classes related to physical properties for the following object categories. Hierarchical high level objects like aircraft, ships and submarines, vehicles and people. Low level object categories of the SimVRML editor are sensors, weapons, facilities (Architectural objects), machinery, structural elements of objects, computer hardware and software, chemical and biological. There is also an interaction class that is used by the engagement model and to also keep track of static properties that can be applied to current behavior interactions between objects. The SimVRML base class has common physical properties that are used by all the model algorithms.

Model Related Data / Implementation for VR Simulations

In the SimVRML editor system, the number and sophistication of the properties in the enumeration public variable in the various classes is driven by the sophistication of the model algorithms. The simulation LOD for the SimVRML system is different for the various models.

The sensor models and the SimVRML sensor classes representing the various sensor properties have a highly realistic LOD. The sensor model requires properties related to the advanced radar, active and passive sonar, jamming, electrooptical and lidar equations. The radar model requires properties for the basic radar equation, plus properties related to advance features including electromagnetic interference, ground clutter, antenna configuration, variable cross section, countermeasures and multipath effects. The radar model produces a signal to noise ratio that is generated from a discretization of probability of detection curves versus false alarm rate and number of pulses illuminating the detected object. Physical properties are needed for all the input parameters of the various LOD's of the radar equation. Some radar equation parameters for low level radar calculations lump multiple physical functions into one parameter and approximate the parameters physical value. Realistic radar calculations for high level LOD radar models deaggregate the lumped physical properties for advanced radar model features. These high level radar models require appropriate properties for input into the radar algorithms.

The sonar model requires properties for input into the active and passive sonar equations, sonobuoys, towed arrays and variable depth sonar's [6]. Sonar calculations depend upon the marine environment as much as they depend upon the sonar equipment physical properties. For sonar calculations, the environment is divided into 3 sound propagation zones. Environment effects due to transmission / reverberation loss properties are arrays of values for various ocean conditions and target position relative to the 3 sound propagation zones. The simplest sonar model LOD has table lookup properties for good, fair and bad ocean environments. Sonar classification models require individual target noise properties for subcomponents of an object. Likely subcomponents are machinery (primarily engines and propellers), underwater sensors (especially active and towed) and architectural structures (hull). Target noise properties are required for various speed values. Probability of detection is calculated for individual noise components by dividing the calculated signal to noise ratio by a standard deviation of a normal distribution related to the noise component and then comparing to a normal distribution with mean 1. The primary problem in sonar modeling is generating reasonable physical values for sonar environment and target noise.

The basic Visibility model operates on object detectability properties. Sufficient weather effects are built into the VRML specification for very simple visual calculations. An advanced visibility model based upon electrooptical algorithms [7] requires calculation of the number of sensor pixels encompassing the detected object. Detection probability is generated via an exponential probability distribution that can be discretized into a table look up. The table look up function of the model is based upon optical signal to noise thresholds for the various categories of objects in the virtual environment. If an Infrared or FLIR model is needed then the thresholds require temperature dependence factors.

The Communications model has a moderately realistic LOD. The communications model requires properties related to the basic communications and jamming equations, which are similar to the radar equations without a cross section factor. Properties related to advanced communications features that depend upon clutter, antenna configuration, interference, multipath and terrain are similar to those properties needed by the radar equations to calculate similar radar effects. The Communications network model has a low LOD to calculate path delays. Path delays are calculated by assuming that delay points behaves according to M/M/1 single server queue with exponentially distributed service rate and interarrival time [8]. Properties needed by the communications network models are mostly dynamic properties related to compatibility of network nodes and communications equipment operational status. Such properties reside in the classes used for simulation housekeeping.

The motion model is a low to medium LOD model that requires properties related to basic ballistics, navigation, navigation error, along with maximum and minimum properties (weight, speed, altitude...). The Flight, ship and submarine operations models are similar to the queuing and probabilistic elements of the communications network model but require interaction with the motion model, fuel consumption properties and specific motion constraints. Fuel consumption algorithms require speed and fuel factors for minimum fuel use and also fuel factors to interpolate fuel use at speeds other than the minimum fuel usage velocity. Ship and submarine operations are similar to aircraft flight operations but with different constraints. Motion constraints can be thought of as a set of rules depending on the type of simulation object and the model applied to the object. Navigation errors are drawn from a normal distribution with mean zero and standard deviation specific to the navigational sensor object. The motion model and all the other models require system failure calculations. For failure calculations, we have equation 1 where A is mean time before failure and B is probability of failure. If $B = 0$ then the failure time is the current time plus some appropriately large constant.

$$\text{Failure time} = A \left[(\text{Log}(1-\text{rand}(x))/(\text{Log}(1-B)) \right] + \text{current time} \qquad (1)$$

The engagement model is a combat operations model. The engagement model requires properties related to engagement probabilities (failure, detection, acquisition, hit) and equipment characteristics. Air related engagements are based upon simple probabilistic equations. Other properties related to air engagements and air to ground engagements are sensor activation time, sensor scanning arc, lists of target sensors, lists of targets and weapon lifetime. Ground based direct fire engagements are related to a discretization of the Lancaster equations [9] based upon lookup tables. The lookup tables are indexed based upon the characteristics of the objects engaging. Ground engagements between hierarchical objects, such as groups of vehicles are indexed based upon group characteristics. The results of the lookup table searches are passed to a simple probabilistic model. Ground based indirect fire, which is engagement between objects separated farther than a user specified threshold, is modeled via a probabilistic model. Indirect fire assets such as artillery are also included in the direct fire model.

Engagement damage is related to a set of probability factors for failure, deception and repair along with defensive and offensive characteristics. Damage factors are calculated for the following categories of an object: structural, fuel, equipment, and operational status. Damage factors are simple multipliers that are compared to thresholds that enable/disable/ or repair/destroy components of the object.

It is very hard to generate standard properties for people. This is due to the complexity of people and diversity of opinion on how to approximate human behavior. In the SimVRML system, basic person physical properties would be compared to environmental constraints that would be managed by a basic simulation housekeeping process. Beyond constraint checking, such social models would be relegated in the SimVRML system to managing verbal communication within the VR scene and input / output of commands within the VR simulation.

In the SimVRML system, models for structural, chemical, biological processing and any other remaining behavior functions are queuing models augmented by very low level algorithms. These low level algorithms use the current set of properties as thresholds that either disable / enable the object or switch from one geometry LOD to another. As an example, if the melting point is exceeded then the object consisting of a solid geometry would be replaced by an indexed face set of the melted object. Another example would be the failure of an object that would be used by a damage model to affect the state of other objects in the virtual environment.

Model Interaction and Object Interrelationships

In order for the extendable features of the SimVRML editor to function optimally, the interaction of the model algorithms and the object interrelationships need to be defined. The level of complexity of the interrelationships of the object physical properties in an extendable and hierarchical VE generated by SimVRML class schemas is just the local complexity of the data / model interaction. If the virtual environment is distributed or if control is shared in a local virtual environment then several factors influence the complexity of the object / model interactions. The primary factors are time, transfer / acquisition of control, transfer / acquisition of editing rights to the properties and control / acquisition of model algorithms and model LOD's. Time synchronization depends upon agreement on how to broadcast time, when to declare a time stamp valid and how to interpolate time stamps. Much of the preliminary agreement on time is present in the VRML 97 specification [10] as it applies to nodes and simple behaviors.

In a complex VRML simulation one method of agreement about the overall virtual environment within a distributed simulation is to adopt the rules inherent in the DIS specification. The SimVRML editor adopts a hybrid approach consisting of the

DIS rules and methods to override the rules or disallow overriding based upon model / object „rights". The SimVRML base class has methods to extract data sets from multiple object schemas and to set the structure of the data requirements based upon the model algorithms and model interactions.

The results of the model and data interactions requires that model execution, data storage and data extraction be synchronized. One way to affect global control of various model and physical property interactions is to treat the system as though it was a parallel simulation environment. The housekeeping management scheme chosen for the Virtual Environment generates a set of simulation semaphores. These simulation semaphores are used to make sure that data is extracted or stored at the correct times and that models for the physical behaviors execute in a realistic sequence that produces common sense results.

The SimVRML system is designed to be an extendable system with user defined models and physical properties added to a „base system" of models and physical properties. In this case there can be multiple simulation semaphore sets that can be activated or deactivated based upon virtual environment rights possessed by controlling avatars or simulation umpires. Suppose you have a VR simulation that has user defined models appended to a base collection of models and their associated physical properties along with their defined interrelationships. If you start with a realistic simulation semaphore set that produces realistic simulation results, how do you produce a realistic simulation semaphore set for the extended VE containing the user defined models. One way to satisfy the requirement that the extended system produce realistic results is to require a sanity check on the results. The simplest form of sanity check would require the simulation state to be outside of obvious error states. Further sanity checks would compare the simulation state for conformation to test parameter limits. Such sanity checks require well defined test simulations within test virtual environments.

Consider the model and physical property interactions for simple linear motion. First, consider scale. Aircraft and ship positions are best stored in geodetic coordinates while ground motion is best served by Cartesian or Universal Transverse Mercator (UTM) coordinates. Motion inside a building is most likely to be Cartesian. Motion over several kilometers is probably best represented by UTM coordinates. Next, consider weather and environmental conditions. Object states are needed for daylight calculations. Navigation properties have to be combined with object motion characteristics. Motion requires awareness of the surrounding objects that exceeds simple collision detection. Motion requires collection of data regarding the visibility status of objects and the properties of the collecting sensors. Thus, data must be extracted from multiple object classes. Motion requires execution synchronization between the motion, navigation and detection algorithms at the minimum. If objects are interacting in a manner that alters the properties and geometry of the interacting objects then interaction algorithms must execute. Results of physical object interactions need to be propagated to the other motion algorithms under the control of motion semaphores.

One solution for the simplification of synchronization of model algorithms is to separate behaviors that must be event driven and simulation cycle based. Cycle based algorithms can be applied to all objects in a simulation subject to pre defined conditions. Processing VR behaviors via a Simulation cycle and then broadcasting the results to the VR objects affected by the behaviors solves some of the problems introduced by object and model interactions. Processing via simulation cycles introduces other problems. One problem is related to a requirement that user actions should be able to trigger model execution asynchronously. Event based algorithm execution requires awareness of all other active and possibly planned events and a set of rules and rights to umpire simulation logjams. Very simple model LOD's can be implemented so that events can be reliably precomputed and queued. Complex model LOD's with significant numbers of property and model interrelationships require constant updating of the event queue.

Consider the detection phase of the motion calculation in the event based portion of the VR simulation. The object in motion would have an instantiation in the VR world along with an instantiation of the detector such as eyes or a night vision goggle. There would also be an instantiation of an object that represents the model that is being executed to process the detection. The methods of the „detection model" object would extract the relevant physical properties from various object classes and spawn events to manage and localize the effects of the interactions between the models and physical properties. Users can make their own constructors / destructors and methods for model objects. Thus the user can attempt to manage the problems posed by model and property interrelationships by incorporating management of the interrelationships in the objects representing the models.

One paradigm for managing the relationships between physical properties and also the simulation model algorithms is to use standard object oriented design (OOD) methodologies such as OMT [11] and Shlaer-Mellor [12]. OMT and other OOD methodologies attempt to generate correct relationships between physical properties, events and simulation model algorithms. By applying OMT or other such OOD methodologies to the SimVRML base classes and simulation model algorithms, a reasonable management scheme for the property / model interrelationships of a baseline SimVRML system can be produced.

By using OMT and other equivalent OOD methodologies, users planning to extend the baseline SimVRML system can minimize effects of their user defined physical properties and models upon the SimVRML baseline system. Similarly, baseline rules for simulation cycle based execution within the SimVRML system can be produced by standard methods of semaphore design. The Shlaer-Mellor Methodology has been analyzed mathematically to examine the question of correctness of OOD for event driven simulations [13].

The SimVRML editor can be used to initialize the state of a Virtual Environment containing realistic general behaviors. This initialization procedure is performed by editing the physical properties that are dynamic. The default VRML description of a virtual environment contains a wealth of geometry, position and VR sensor information. Beyond geometry and standard VRML sensors and interpolators, what do you put in the housekeeping classes to attempt to produce a simulation semaphore set that provides accepted results under test conditions? The housekeeping properties should include enough simulation state data to keep track of object states used by the models, simulation rights and the defined semaphore sets. In addition to the geometry inherent in VRML nodes, these housekeeping properties keep track of simulation commands and data that can be used to map the model algorithms to the physical properties.

In addition to managing data and model relationships, housekeeping properties are used to store descriptions of multi-user interactions and pointers to static physical properties for interactions. These interactions are different from the model and physical property interactions described above. Multi-user interactions describe behavior effects between objects that are actually engaging in simulated virtual behavior. One of the fundamental multi-user interactions between objects in a virtual environment is information communication. Housekeeping properties are used to track communications text and dynamic data communications within the virtual environment. One function of the Housekeeping properties is to track the simulation state of speech simulations and to track spoken simulation command input. By keeping track of simulation LOD's in the housekeeping properties, the correct set of static physical properties can be extracted by a generic virtual getModel method. By combining low level state information with high level interaction and model LOD state information a virtual environment simulation can truly become more than the sum of its parts.

SimVRML Editor Interface

The SimVRML editor was created using 3D Website Builder [14] and Cosmo Worlds [15]. Although there is still no integrated development environment for VRML behaviors that is affordable, acceptable components are now becoming available. 3D Website Builder is used to create the geometry of the SimVRML editor interface. Cosmo Worlds is used for polygon reduction, VR/VE/VRML sensor creation, VRML routing and scripting within the script node. VRML scripting was done in Javascript [16, 17] and Java [18, 19].

The SimVRML editor interface is a compromise between the goals of a 3D anthropomorphic VR/VE/VRML interface and the cardinal goals of webcentric virtual reality: speed, speed and more speed. A fully anthropomorphic virtual reality behavior editor interface could be realistically composed of 3D subcomponents constructed using thousands of polygons. For example, the average power property used by the sensor model algorithms could have a realistic model of a generator unit with clickable parts in an anthropomorphic version of the editor interface.

The design paradigm applied to the SimVRML editor interface reduces the anthropomorphic aspect of the interface to texture maps. Photo images or rendered images of 3D models representing the various simulation model properties are applied to 3D palettes constructed using simple solid primitives. For properties representing high level hierarchical subcomponents of an object, such as equipment, this texture map strategy works very well and is illustrated in Figure 1.

Fig. 1. Equipment Palette SimVRML Interface for Hierarchical Object

For more esoteric and abstract properties with no isomorphism's between anthropomorphism and algorithmic functionally, a different reduction strategy was developed. In the case of abstract properties, an anthropomorphic texture map or maps, representing an aggregate of related properties was generated. Hot spots representing the individual properties of the aggregate texture map are used by the editor to edit property values. Consider the basic radar equation. Sets of texture maps of generic radar properties are placed near to a texture map of a text version of the generic radar equation. The equation texture map is subdivided and overlain upon 3D primitives. Subdivision is necessary to avoid browser environments that do not support the VRML image texture or material nodes transparency features. Since the Virtual Reality Modeling Language is extensible, extending the SimVRML editor interface by users who have added extra model properties is a simple task. Extending the SimVRML editor interface is primarily a case of image processing and 3D geometry building

User input is through a series of knobs and sliders. This input strategy is made necessary due to the lack of a keyboard sensor in the VRML specification. The 3D Input interface for both sliders and knobs is similar. The interface consists of a VRML model of a slider or knob constructed from primitives and indexed face sets, along with a 3D indicator and a 3D control. 3D indicators are used to display the current value of the property. The user modifies the property values using the movable portions of the slider or knob by clicking or dragging. The user can also use the 3D control to edit property values by clicking on subcomponents of the control, such as arrows. The radar equation texture map palette is illustrated in Figure 2.

Fig. 2. Aggregate Texture Maps for Radar Parameters in SimVRML Editor

Sliders, knobs, controls and indicators have their own standard set of „SimVRML editor properties". These interface properties are properties for minimum / maximum input values, data type of values, current value, type / size / color of 3D text for display of the current values, scaling factors and position / orientation relative to the slider / knob interface components. Just as the simulation models require a set of standard properties, there is a need for some sort of standard set of input properties

60 John F. Richardson

for virtual environments. The geometry of the input widgets is up to the input interface designer. The SimVRML editor interface implements what I consider a minimal set of input properties. Figure 3 illustrates scalar data types. Arrays and other structures could be displayed by duplicating and offsetting VRML group nodes representing the various types of scalar data types displayed via geometry primitives and VRML text.

The SimVRML editor has an option for 2D operation. This option is enabled from within the 3D virtual environment and is based upon Java applets. The 2D option has a SimVRML applet for each of the various object classes. The 3D user input virtual environment is also illustrated in Figure 3

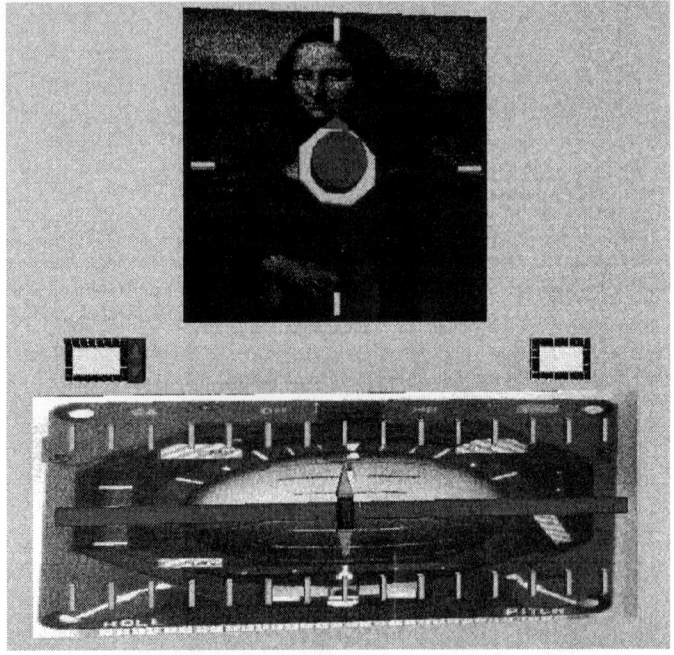

Fig. 3. Slider and Knob Input Interface With Control (arrows) and Indicator

One of the most important considerations related to editing properties for VR simulations is the realism of the data values. The majority of properties in the subclasses of the SimVRML base class have well known published reference sources. Commercial instances of the various abstract objects are particularly well documented. Military and adventure instances of simulation objects are not well documented. Potential sources for such adventure data are user guides for various game simulators, documents published by Jane's Information Group and manufacturers advertising brochures, repair manuals and user's manuals. Many physical properties can be obtained through standard scientific reference works such as those published by the Chemical Rubber Company. Fascinating and generally correct sources of physical properties are newsletters and publications of hobby organizations such as the American Radio Relay League.

6 Future Work

The SimVRML editor is used to edit static characteristics for physical properties used by VRML behavior models. The next obvious extension is to create a SimVRML layout editor to operate on the variables and methods of the dynamic properties. As an example, consider a Yacht with no engine, antennas, communications or navigation equipment. Using such a layout editor, the user could drag and drop engines, radio and other equipment onto the VRML yacht. The equipment would be from palettes containing thumbnails created by querying the VRML simulation behavior database.

The Model algorithms and the methods for extracting data need for the algorithms have to be implemented through a SimVRML behavior editor. There is also a need for a SimVRML command editor to dynamically input parameters into the VR behaviors. One obvious enhancement to the various model algorithms is to use the fact that a VR/VE/VRML simulation is intrinsically in 3 dimensions. The current damage model simply decides on the fate of a particular VR object. An enhanced damage model could also change the geometry of the object using the createVRMLFromURL method or by inserting and deleting nodes. Physically relevant 3-D dials and indicators would replace two-dimensional textual status boards. In addition a set of OMT diagrams for the baseline SimVRML editor and related models have to be generated.

References

1. Wicks, J., Burgess, P.: Standard for Distributed Interactive Simulation – Application Protocols. IST-CR-95-06, Institute for Simulation and Training (1995)
2. Dodsworth, C.: Digital Illusions. Addison-Wesley (1997)
3. Skolnik, M.: Radar Handbook (2nd Ed.). McGraw-Hill Publishing Company (1990)
4. Interference Notebook. RADC-TR-66-1, Rome Air Development Center (1966)
5. Wehner, D.: High-Resolution Radar (2nd Ed.). Artech House (1995)
6. Horton, J.W.: Fundamentals of Sonar (2nd Ed.). United States Naval Institute (1959)
7. Holst, G.: Electro-Optical Imaging System Performance. JCD Publishing (1995)
8. Kleinrock, L.: Queuing Systems (Volume 1). John Wiley & Sons (1975)
9. Przemieniecki, J.S.: Introduction to Mathematical Methods in Defense Analyses. American Institute of Aeronautics and Astronautics, Inc. (1990)

10. VRML 97 ISO/IEC 14772-1:1997
11. Rumbaugh, J., Blaha, M., Premerlani, W., Eddy, F., Lorensen, W.: Object-Oriented Modeling and Design. Prentice-Hall (1991)
12. Bowman, V.: Paradigm Plus Methods Manual. Platinum Technology (1996)
13. Shlaer, S., Lang, N.: Shlaer-Mellor Method: The OOA96 Report. Project Technology, Inc. (1996)
14. Scott, A.: Virtus 3-D Website Builder Users Guide. Virtus Corporation (1996)
15. Hartman, J., Vogt, W.: Cosmo Worlds 2.0 Users Guide, SGI Inc. (1998)
16. Bell, G., Carey, R.: The Annotated VRML 2.0 Reference Manual. Addison-Wesley (1997)
17. Ames, A., Nadeau, D., Moreland, J.: VRML 2.0 Sourcebook (2nd Ed.). John Wiley & Sons, Inc. (1997)
18. R., Matsuda, K., Miyashita, K.: Java for 3D and VRML Worlds. New Riders Publishing (1996) Lea,
19. Brown, G., Couch, J., Reed-Ballreich, C., Roehl, B., Rohaly,T.: Late Night VRML 2.0 with Java. Ziff-Davis Press (1997)

The Scan&Track Virtual Environment

Sudhanshu Kumar Semwal[1] and Jun Ohya[2]

[1] Department of Computer Science, University of Colorado at Colorado Springs,
Colorado Springs, CO, 80933-7150, USA
`semwal@redcloud.uccs.edu`
[2] Head, Department 1, ATR MIC Laboratories,
ATR Media Integration and Communication Research Laboratories, Japan,
2-2 Hikaridai, Seika-cho, Soraku-gun, Kyoto, Japan 619-02
`ohya@mic.atr.co.jp`

Abstract. We are developing the *Scan&Track* virtual environment (VE) using multiple cameras. The Scan&Track VE is based upon a new method for 3D position estimation called the *active-space indexing method*. In addition, we have also developed the *geometric-imprints* algorithm for significant points extraction from multiple camera-images. Together, the geometric-imprints algorithm and the active-space indexing method, provide a promising and elegant solution to several inherent challenges facing camera-based virtual environments. Some of these are: (a) correspondence problem across multiple camera images, (b) discriminating multiple participants in virtual environments, (c) avatars (synthetic actors) representing participants, (d) occlusion. We also address a fundamental issue: can virtual environments be powerful enough to understand human-participants.

1 Motivation

Virtual environments (VEs) pose severe restrictions on tracking algorithms due to the foremost requirement of real-time interaction. There have been several attempts to track participants in a virtual environment. These can be broadly divided into two main categories: encumbering and non-encumbering [1,2,3,4]. A variety of encumbering tracking devices have been developed, for example acoustic [1], optical [5,6], mechanical [7,8,9,10], bio-controlled, and magnetic trackers [23,11]. Most of the camera-image based systems are examples of un-encumbering technology [12]. The degree of encumbrance also matters: outside-looking-in systems for optical tracking are less encumbering than the inside-looking-out systems because the user wears a set of receiving beacons instead of four cameras placed on the user's head. The set of beacons are lighter in comparison to wearing four cameras [1,5]. In addition, optical and camera-based VEs have problems of occlusion [1,24].

As indicated by [13], mostly magnetic trackers have been used in virtual environments as they are robust, relatively inexpensive, and have a reasonable working volume or active-space. However, magnetic trackers can exhibit tracking errors of upto 10 cms, if not calibrated properly [13]. Magnetic trackers are also affected by magnetic objects present in the surroundings. Magnetic sensors, placed on several places on the body of the human participant, can be used for detecting the motion of the participant. The motion is then used to control a synthetic human-form or an avatar of the participant. Some solutions to drive an avatar using minimal sensors are in [11,22,23].

The resolution and accuracy of camera based systems is dependent upon the size of the pixel. It is difficult to differentiate between any two points if the size of the pixel is large and the projection of both points falls on the same pixel. Sometimes application determines the mode of tracking. Medical applications require trackers to be more precise and accurate. For human-centered applications [18], non-encumbering tracking methods are particularly suitable as no wires or gadgets are placed on participants.

1.1 Unencumbered Virtual Environments

Camera-based techniques are well suited for developing unencumbering applications. Inexpensive video-cameras are also readily available. This area is well studied, and Krueger's work [12,20,21] is well known for virtual environment interaction using 2D contours of silhouette of human participants, and interpreting them in a variety of ways. When 2D camera-images are used, there is no *depth* information available with the image. Much research has been done in the area of computer vision [14,15,16,17], stereo-vision [14,19], object-recognition [15], and motion analysis [16,25] to recover the depth information.

The problem of occlusion is inherent in camera-based systems [1]. Since 2D-camera images are used to determine the participant's position, it is difficult to infer whether the participant's hand is hidden behind their body, or is in their pocket. The occlusion problem is more severe when multiple participants are present in a camera-based virtual environment. To the best of our knowledge, there are no camera-based virtual environment where the occlusion problem has been successfully solved. Color based discrimination which tracks the change in color are not robust, as shadows and lighting changes make empirical algorithms fail. Another method to solve the occlusion problem is to consider previous frames to infer that the hand is *now* in the pocket.

The well known correspondence problem is ever-present when purely vision-based systems are used. As mentioned in [13], there are several compromises made to resolve the issue of correspondence and recognition. Even then, it is difficult to find a topological correspondence between the multiple contours extracted from the multiple camera-images of the same scene. In the field of computer vision and photogrammetry, there is a wealth of research on motion tracking [14,15,16,17]. There has been much research effort in the area of understanding and recognition of facial expression, body movements, gestures and gaze of the participants [4,20,21].

The Virtual Kabuki system [26] uses thermal images from one camera to estimate the participant's planar motions in a 3D environment. Non-planar 3D motion is not tracked. An estimate of the joint positions is obtained in real-time by applying 2D-distance transformations to thermal images. Other points such as the knee and the elbow are estimated using genetic algorithms [26]. Once extracted the motion is mapped on to a kabuki-actor. The system tracks planer motions of a participant in real time.

Blob models [24] are used in the MIT's Pfinder system developed at the MIT Media Lab. The system uses one camera and works with one participant in the environment using a static scene, such as an office. Interestingly, depth perception is limited to 2D, for example when the participant jumps it is considered a move backwards. So essentially, the system estimates only the 2D information.

Most of the camera-based VEs base their judgement upon the color information and estimate the 3D position of the participant by using the information available from multiple cameras. The process involves solving the contouring problem, correspondence problem, and significant point extraction [13].

Camera based systems also face the inherent ambiguity of 2D-camera projections. This can be illustrated by arranging fingers so that the shadow projected on the wall can, for example, look like a goat. When multiple cameras are used, the ambiguity problem is somewhat reduced as we have multiple views available. However, the correspondence problem across multiple images must be resolved. Extraction of only a few key-features or significant points from an image, has been investigated in great detail for this purpose. The idea behind significant point extraction is that a small collection of points may provide enough information about the intent or pose of the participant. Tracking the trajectory of an object is the focus of research in [25]. In Multiple Light Display experiment, multiple beacons of light are used to analyze the motion of human participants [6]. Simple light displays placed on the participants are tracked. It is argued that twelve points are sufficient to give an impression of actual motion. This is interesting as it may also provide an answer to the minimal significant points on the human-body that are sufficient to understand the motion of the participant.

A variety of contour-extraction methods have been developed for gesture understanding [27]. The Immersive-video [29] application uses color averaging of multiple camera-images to determine the color of 3D grid-points. Snakes [28] use minimization and spline-based contouring to lock onto an object of interest in the image.

Recently, there has also been a growing interest in using successful 2D and 3D data structures for recovering the depth information. Jain et. al. [29] combine the vision and graphics techniques for processing the video-streams offline, non-interactively, so that multiple participants can view the processed scene from different angles after preprocessing has been completed. In immersive video, the color-based discrimination is used between frames to identify pixels of interest, which are then projected to find the voxels in a 3D-grid space based on the color of the region (pixel) of interest. The marching cubes algorithm is then used to construct the iso-surface of interest [29]. This method does not track the participants interactively in a virtual environment. Instead it processes the video-sequences from multiple cameras, and allows participants to view the processed data.

2 The Scan&Track System

We are developing the Scan&Track virtual environment using the geometric-imprints algorithm and active-space indexing method. The geometric imprints algorithm is based upon the approach that end-points of the cylindrical body-parts are most likely to be visible across multiple cameras, and therefore, are more likely to be identified using the contours of the images. The main difference between the proposed Scan&Track system and other existing camera-based virtual environments is that (a) color is not the main focus for identifying significant points on the participant's body in the Scan&Track VE, and (b) Significant points change with the pose in the geometric-imprints algorithm, and therefore may be different depending upon the pose. In each frame we ask where are the tips of the cylindrical 2D-shape in the camera-image. So the geometric-imprints approach is fundamentally different than the vision based system where the same significant points are sought in every frame. A major advantage of the active-space indexing method is that position estimations are provided *without* any knowledge of camera-orientation. Exact camera orientation is critical for other existing camera-based systems to-date [29].

The active space indexing method is a novel method for estimating the 3D position using multiple camera-images. During preprocessing, the system uses three cameras to record a planar-slice containing a simple pattern arranged on a regular grid. The planar slice is then moved at regular intervals and the corresponding camera-images are stored. In this manner, *active-space* or the 3D-space between these parallel slices is scanned. During preprocessing, the scanned camera images are processed to create an active-space indexing mechanism which maps 3D points in the active-space to the corresponding projections on the camera-images.

Once the active-space indexing mechanism has been created, the location of a 3D point can be estimated by using the point's projections on multiple camera-images. The active-space indexing method is scalable as the *same* 3D-space could be scanned for both the low and the high-end systems. Since the size of the 3D active-space can also vary, the 3D active-space working volume itself is scalable. In comparison to other tracking methods, the active-space indexing method avoids the complicated camera calibration operations. As the active-space indexing method provides 3D space-linearity for position estimation, the distortions due to camera projection are automatically avoided.

In the following sections, we explain both the geometric-imprints algorithm and the active-space indexing method.

3 The Geometric-Imprints Algorithm and Associated Results

Body postures express emotions and reveal our inner-self. For example, the contour-drawing in Figure 1a could be interpreted as a dance pose. Similarly,

Figure 1b could mean that the person has just been victorious. The characteristics of both these poses can be captured by some key-points on the contour, as shown in Figure 2. Our geometric-imprints method is based on the observation that human body parts are mostly cylindrical in nature, especially those which are the basis of articulated motion. When we look at participants from multiple camera-images, the *tip* of the cylindrical body-shapes is expected to be visible from many cameras. These tip-points define the *geometric-imprint* of a contour in the Scan&Track system. The geometric-imprints method extracts information about these cylindrical shapes from a contour. In case of Figure 1a, finger tips are the logical endings of the cylindrical human arm, and the bend at the elbow is quite obvious and should be detected. Similarly, we have shown some points in Figure 1 to indicate the geometric curve bending and the logical-ends of cylindrical body parts.

We wish to capture the points of the cylindrical endings of a 2D contour from the human-silhouette as shown in Figure 3a-b. Some other points may be included depending upon the curvature of a given contour. We consider this set of points as the *geometric-imprint* of the image. This is because these points and their topology facilitates determination of the pose of the participant. Our motivation for developing the geometric-imprints method was to also reduce the complexity of the correspondence problem. Consider 2D-contours extracted from multiple camera-images looking at a cylindrical object (Figure 2). The tip of the cylindrical object would project as a tip of a 2D-cylindrical curve in most of these 2D-contours. It is much easier to correspond extremities of curves across multiple camera images [38]. Geometric-imprints are dependent primarily upon the analysis of contours of an image, thus our approach is different than other existing methods where same key-feature of the image in every frame must be estimated. For example, in many approaches, as well as our earlier efforts [26], the same joints are estimated in every frame. This is certainly useful when the display program is skeleton-based and the joint information is needed for placing a synthetic human-actor in a desired pose. In the geometric-imprints algorithm, when the participant assumes different positions, the shape of participant's silhouette on the camera-images also changes. Therefore we expect the geometric-imprint set to vary, from one frame to another, depending upon the shape of the curve in the camera-images from one moment to another.

We have implemented an *automatic* recursive splitting algorithm which can successfully deal with arbitrary (multiple foldings) curves. Figure 3 shows the expected correspondence between geometric-imprint of one pose to another. Figure 4 shows three camera-images (4a-c) of the same pose, and their geometric-imprints. More details of this algorithm are in [39].

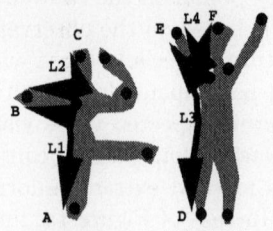
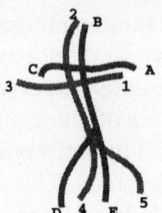

Figure 1: Postures express emotions

Figure 2: The Correspondence Problem

(a) starting point   (b) starting point

Figure 3: (a) Spread out pose. Five geometric imprints. (b) Dancing pose. Seven geometric imprints.

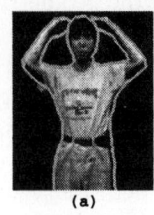

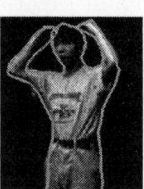

(a)   (b)   (c)

(d)   (e)   (f)

Figure 4: Geometric-imprint points of three camera images for the same pose. (a-c) three camera-images for the same pose, (d) 4 (e) 4 and (f) 5 geometric-imprint points.

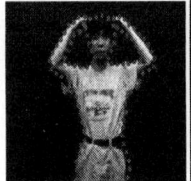
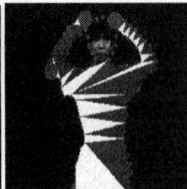

Figure 5: (a) Scan-line algorithm for automatic extraction of the contour. (b) Geometric-imprints algorithm using the automatically extracted contour

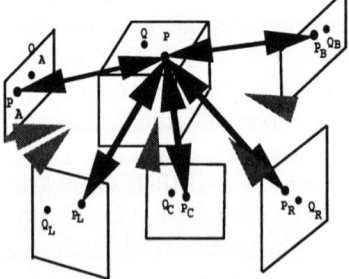

Figure 6: The relationship of points P and Q changes depending upon the view as the cameras move around them.

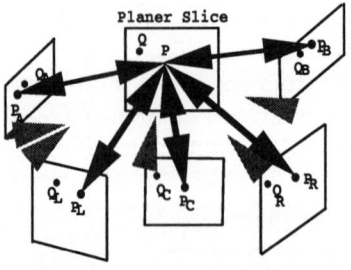

Figure 7: The relationship of the point on a slice remains same for a variety of planar views in the same hemisphere w.r.t. to the slice.

Only one shoulder point in Figure 4c has been identified as the geometric-point. The implementation identifies five cylindrical end-points on this complex curve in Figures 4b and 4c. In Figure 4, we have used the same pose for the images captured from three cameras. Notice that all the significant points, marked one to five in Figure 4d-f, are common in the three figures. One extra elbow-point is also a geometric-imprint point in Figure 4f. In our implementation we have mainly shown the tips of cylindrical shapes, however, the places where folding occurs can also be the geometric-imprint point as explained in [39]. As shown in Figure 4, similar topological curves generate a similar geometric imprint set. Once the geometric imprint has been obtained it is much easier to find a correspondence. Note that geometric-imprint points marked 1 in Figure 4d-f correspond to the same 3D-point (right-hip). Similarly, points marked 2, 3, 4 correspond to the tip of the right hand, head position, and the tip of the left hand, respectively. Note that the sixth point can be discarded by using the active-space indexing method explained below. The image-imprint of the sixth point in Figure 4f, matched with any image-points in the other two camera-images, will results in no 3D point correspondence using the active-space indexing method. Thus, the correspondence problem in the Scan&Track system is simplified. Figure 5 shows geometric-imprint obtained by using an *automatic* scan-line algorithm [40]. Colored images are at http://www.cs.uccs.edu/~semwal/VW98.

4 The Active-Space Indexing Method and Associated Results

4.1 Camera Calibration, Space-Linearity and Over-Constrained Systems

There have been many attempts to estimate the 3D motion of the participants with minimal number of points used for camera-calibration, for example, three points are sufficient as suggested by Ullman [6]. Recently, there have been many studies where five or more points are used for stereo-matching and creating novel views [20,21]. Most of the systems which use a minimal number of points are usually under-constrained, in the sense that any error in camera-calibration or camera orientation estimates may result in severe registration and accuracy errors [13].

In implementing the active-space indexing method, we use several points, during preprocessing, and create a spatial 3D-data structure using these points. Our motivation to use several points is to subdivide the active-space, so that only a few points are used locally to estimate the position during tracking, similar to the piece-wise design for surfaces and contours. In systems using a minimal number of points, a global calibration is used, and therefore it creates an under-constrained system [13]. The non-linearity and tracking errors are more profound due to the use of an under-constrained system.

In our approach, by subdividing the 3D active-space into small, disjoint, voxels or 3D-cells, we use only a small number of points, which are the vertices of the 3D-voxel, for estimating a 3D position inside that voxel. In this way, only a few points estimate the 3D position. The major advantage of using a large number of points is that the non-linearity due to camera calibration is reduced. In particular, we can assume that a linear motion inside the small, 3D-voxel space will also project linearly on a camera-image. Thus, the effects of camera-distortion are avoided. More accurate estimation within the 3D-cell or voxel are possible as this assumption also allows the use of linear interpolation within the 3D-cell or voxel.

4.2 Estimating Depth Using Multiple Cameras and Slices

Consider the projections of two points P and Q in Figure 6. Depending upon the viewpoint and multiple cameras facing the two points P and Q, the projections of these two points change, particularly their relationship changes as we move from left to right, from image plane A to image plane B via planes L (Left), C (center), and R (right) as shown in Figure 6. The spatial information between the two points is lost. How can we infer that points Q_A and Q_B are actually the same point Q in 3D space? Next, consider two points P and Q on a planar-slice and the same set of multiple cameras, as shown in Figure 7. Note that the spatial relationship of projections of points P and Q, in all the planes in the same hemisphere w.r.t. the planer slice, remains same. Thus, it is much easier to deal with points in a planer-slice. In addition, zoom-in or zoom-out also does not change the relationship of the visible points. In particular, w.r.t. to two lines L1 and L2 on a plane, arbitrary zooming of the camera or changing the orientation of the cameras in the same hemisphere, as shown in Figure 8, does not have an effect on this relationship. In particular, point Q remains to the right of projected-line PL1, and point P to the left, in both the projected-images. Both points are above the projected-line PL2 as expected. We can now extend the idea to many lines. A grid of lines partitions the slice into several disjoint grid-cells in Figure 9. Figure 9 also shows a camera image which is facing a planar slice at an angle pointing slightly upwards. There is a perspective deformation of the lines, yet the relationship of point P and Q is consistent with the planer slice, and the 2D cell-index of both points is same.

All three cameras are placed in such a way that they are in the same hemisphere w.r.t. the active-space slices. Let S1, S2, and S3 be the projection of a 3D point S on the left, center, and right camera images respectively. This is shown in Figure 9. We call the triplet (S1, S2, S3) an imprint-set for point S. Here S1, S2, and S3 are the 2D pixel coordinates of the projection of point S on the left, center, and right camera-images respectively. If a 3D point is visible from multiple cameras, then the location of the imprint of the 3D point in multiple camera-images can be used to estimate the 3D position of S. Given the image-imprint (S1,S2,S3), the *active-space indexing method* finds the 3D-cell or voxel containing the point S. In our present implementation, these triplets are provided by the user.

4.3 Preprocessing to Create Active-Space Indexing

Multiple planar slices can now be stacked for estimating the depth information. These active-space slices occupy space called an active-space volume, or simply an *active-space*. The slices divide the active-space into a set of disjoint 3D-cells or voxels. Camera-images for every slice are processed one by one. During preprocessing, one camera is placed such that the view-normal is perpendicular to the white-board used for our experiments. The other two cameras are to the left and right of the first camera as shown in Figure 9. We have chosen a 12 by 12 grid pattern, where grid intersections are highlighted by small black circles. The grid-pattern occupies a 55cm by 55cm space on a white-board. Each square of the grid is 5cm by 5cm. The white-board is physically moved and recorded by three cameras at the same time. Eight such recordings result in eight slices for every camera. The inter-slice spacing is 10 cm. The white-board and the grid-pattern on it are visible from all the three cameras. The active-space volume is a cube of 55cm by 55cm by 70cm. The active-space is large enough to track the face and upper body of the participants for two sets of experiments we have conducted so far. A larger active-space can be easily constructed by using a larger panel instead of the smaller white-board used for our experiments. All the 12 by 12 dots on eight of these slices are shown in Figure 11a-c for all the three cameras. Because of the space limitation, we do not explain the preprocessing algorithm here. For details, please refer to [38].

4.4 Position Estimation

To estimate the location of a 3D point given its imprint-set (S1,S2,S3), we have implemented the following algorithm. The active-space indexing mechanism finds the 3D location based on the imprint set triplet. The triplet in our implementation is provided by the user by using mouse-picks on the respective camera-images. For example, if the tip of the nose is visible in all the three camera images for our experiment, then we can click on the tip of the nose in all the three images to obtain a triplet (S1,S2,S3) for the nose. This is shown in Figure 10a-c where S1, S2, and S3 are the projections on the left, center, and right cameras for the point S.

Given a image-imprint (S1,S2,S3) corresponding to a 3D-point S, we search all the eight slices and find the voxel containing point S. Due to space limitation, we have not explained the details of this algorithm here. Details are in [38].

Figure 10d-e shows the result of our implementation using six imprint-sets. Corresponding 3D voxels are also shown by visualizing them as a connected skeleton figure. We have highlighted the corresponding points in the image in Figure 10c and 10d. Another, slightly different set of points is shown in Figure 10e. Figure 10f shows the participant's pose by using an in-house synthetic actor developed in our laboratory. We have also tested our active-space indexing method by using two different camera settings, thus creating a different set of slices and indexing mechanism, and have obtained similar results.

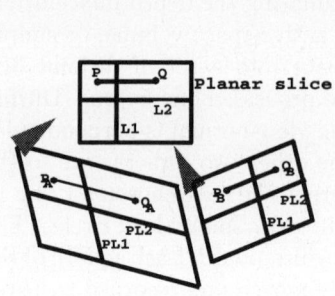

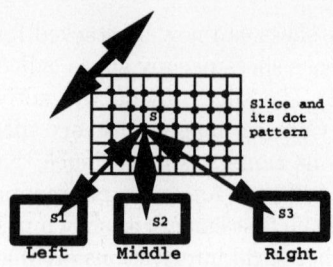

Active space creation

Figure 8: Projection of two points on two planes.

Figure 9: Imprint-set (S1,S2,S3) for point S. S1, S2, and S3 are 2D points on the respective camera-images.

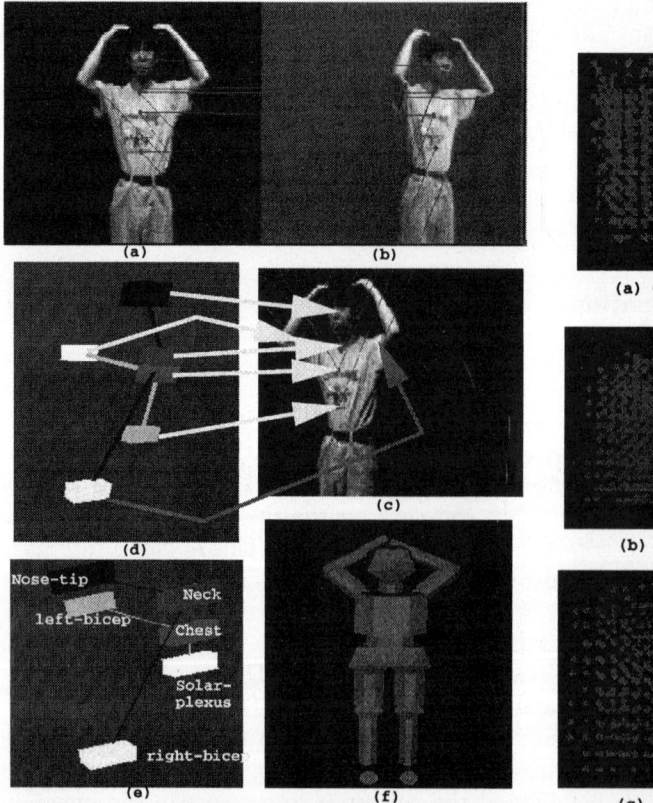

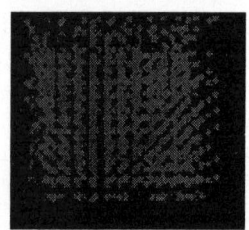

(a) Center camera

(b) Left camera

(c) Right camera

Figure 10: a-c: Selecting six image-imprints on the middle, left and right camera images. (d) associated 3D-cells connected by a simple skeleton. (e) Another skeleton representing a different set of six points. (f) A simple synthetic actor mimics the pose of the participant.

Figure 11: Active-space points for the three images.

The Scan&Track Virtual Environment   73

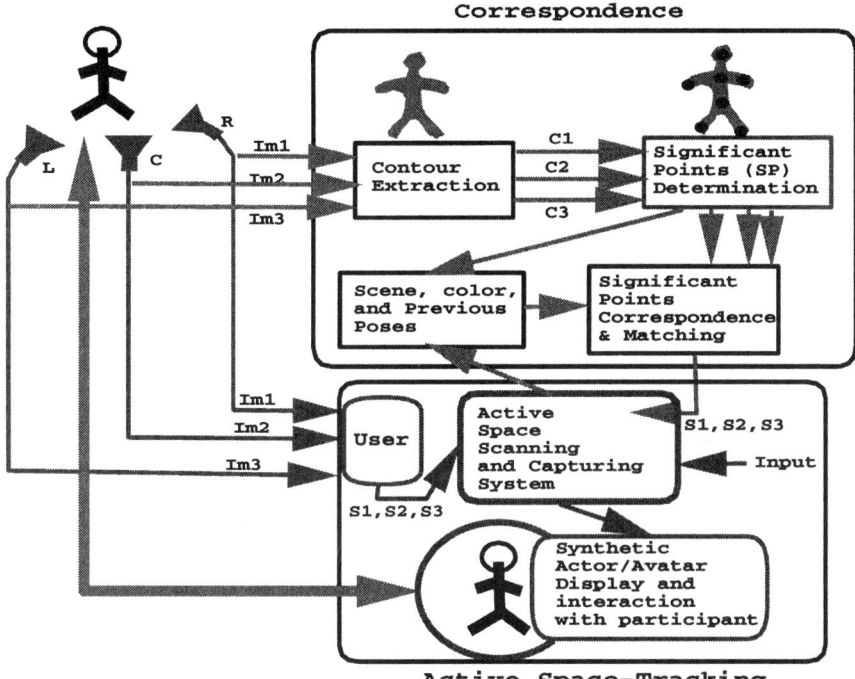

Figure 12: Block Diagram for the Scan&Track System

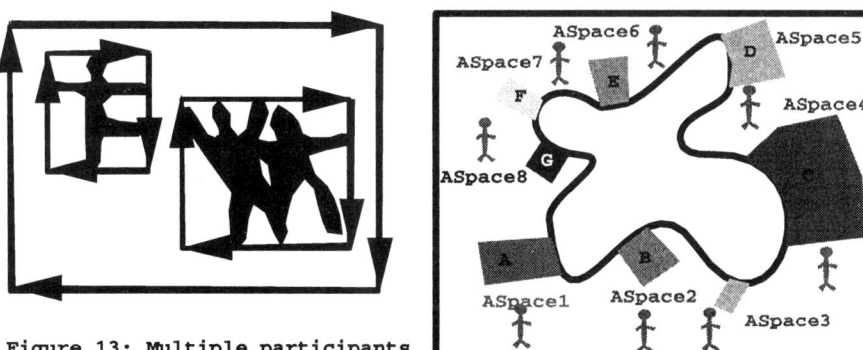

Figure 13: Multiple participants

Figure 14: World of active-spaces

The technique works because there is enough shift in the projection of the points due to the camera positioning that the depth discrimination is possible. Unless the three camera angles are identical or the grid is very wide, it is highly unlikely that more than two slices have the same area formed by I1, I2, and I3. In fairness to our method, this would mean that the resolution of the sliced active space needs to be finer, or camera angles need to change. It can be concluded that, given three imprint-points, a unique 3D cell-index can be found. As indicated before, colored-images are at http://www.cs.uccs.edu/~semwal/VW98.

5 Block Diagram of the Scan&Track System

The block diagram of the system is shown in Figure 12. The Scan&Track system is an outside looking-in system [1]. It consists of *(a) the Correspondence* system, and *(b) the Active Space Tracking* system.

There are four sub-systems to the Correspondence system:

(i) **Contour extraction**: Images are to be analyzed and an outline of the silhouette is extracted from the images. Let contours C1, C2, and C3 represent the human-silhouettes from three camera-images Im1, Im2, and Im3, respectively. This is well researched area of computer vision. We have developed a scan-line algorithm for automatic extraction of contours [40,30,31].

(ii) **Significant points determination**: As explained earlier, the geometric-imprint is extracted by the geometric-imprints algorithm.

(iii) **Significant points correspondence and matching**: The geometric-imprints of one contour are corresponded to the geometric-imprints of contours from other camera-images capturing the same pose. The outcome of the matching algorithm is to provide an imprint-set, a triplet (S1,S2,S3), for every point in the geometric-imprint extracted from the camera-images.

(iv) **Scene, color, and previous poses database**: The scene information, color of geometric-imprints points, and previous poses are to be used for refining the correspondence and matching of the geometric-imprints across multiple camera-images.

The Active Space Tracking system is used to estimate the position of point S given the triplet (S1,S2,S3). The Active Space Tracking system has the following two main sub-systems:

(i) **Active-space scanning and tracking system**: As explained earlier, we use the active-space indexing mechanism, which allows us to determine the location of a 3D point S, given its geometric-imprint (S1,S2,S3). At this time, we specify the corresponding points on multiple-camera images using mouse-picks. In future, these points would be *automatically* generated by the Correspondence system as shown in Figure 1. We are investigating novel patterns (e.g. checkered board patterns) to automatically find the grid-points on the planer slice during preprocessing.

(ii) **Synthetic actor and/or avatar display**: Using the active-space indexing method we have been successful in positioning a human-model for our feasibility experiments. In future, an avatar or synthetic human actor is expected to replicate the motion of the participant. In future, we plan to completely automate the Scan&Track system so that a person in a 3D environment can be tracked and be represented by an avatar. This is the goal of our proposed research.

Multiple participants: We also expect the Scan&Track system to work when multiple participants are inside the active-space as shown in Figure 13. Presence of multiple participants and their images, are grand challenges in purely vision-based systems. For example, it is highly likely that the geometric-imprint for each camera image will not have an identical number of points even though cameras are viewing the same scene. This could be due to occlusion by other participants in the VE. As explained earlier, correspondence is much easier for the Scan&Track system as the active-space indexing provides valuable 3D information. As shown in Figure 14, mesh-splitting may be necessary when multiple participants are present [32].

Ratio-theory: To resolve frame-to-frame correspondence, as well as correspondence across multiple images of the same scene, we plan to use the concept of ratio theory related to body parts. The idea behind the *ratio theory* can be best understood by imagining a tailor's measurement. The extremities of a contour can be related easily if we start with the dimensions of the participant as shown in Figure 1a and 1b. From one frame to another, the length of the body-extremities of the participant can not change. Let us assume, that the geometric-imprints of two poses have been obtained as shown in Figure 1. We now need to correspond point A with point 1, point B with point 2, and so on. Then the points are connected i.e. 1 to 2 to 3 and so on. In Figure 1, the curve length L1 between extremity A and B corresponds to the curve length L2 between D and E, and so on. In particular, it can be said that the ratio L1/L2 would approximately equal L3/L4. So the correspondence problem reduces to matching and finding a best fit in a small search-space dependent upon the number of geometric-imprint points on curves from camera-images.

Double verification: The Scan&Track system allows a *double verification* for validity of correspondence. For example, if it is found that a triplet (S1,S2,S3) are a match, we can also verify it by matching the color of S1, S2 and S3 from the images. If they are different then we do not have a match. In addition, we can have a variety of other measures. For example, if the estimated pose of an avatar is drastically different than the pose in the previous frame, then it might indicate correspondence error unless the participant is moving extremely fast in the VE.

Avatars and Human Actors: Since virtual environments are expected to be populated by both avatars or human forms which replicate the movement of participants, and virtual synthetic actors whose autonomous movement is directed by computers [23,19]. In the Scan&Track system, the actions of the participant are to be tracked and mapped to the synthetic human form [33,34,35,36,37].

6 Expected Significance of the Scan&Track System

As is true of any vision-based system, the discrimination capability of our system is limited by the physical-size of the pixel in the camera-images. However, the system allows the use of multiple cameras, and thus multiple indices and a more accurate prediction of depth. Once we have determined a 3D-cell or voxel value and an approximate location, then we could automatically use another set of cameras for a much closer and precise look at the 3D-space near the 3D-point. In other words, the active indexing method can be applied twice or more. The first time, it would be used to find a high-grained index, and later we would find a more precise index by using those cameras which have the most detailed view of the slice and nearby areas. The information about a more detailed view would be recorded during preprocessing, as the camera arrangements do not change during tracking. Thus, we are suggesting the use of local and global cameras. Note that one camera could be local for one point, and could be listed as global for some other point in 3D space. Active indexing is extendible and amenable to hardware implementation; special purpose chips can be designed for position-estimation calculations. In addition, different slice-patterns could be available for low and high-end users for automatic preprocessing. The *active-space indexing mechanism* maps 3D points inside the active-space, to corresponding projections on the camera-images.

We must answer one obvious question: how would we deal with the situation when the camera is placed with such an acute angle that all the slices project as lines. In this situation, grid-lines may be barely visible for a very acute camera angle, and the slice will project as a line when the camera-image plane is perpendicular to the slices. We note that it is a highly unlikely situation as cameras are *placed by us*, and we can ensure that none of the slices are parallel to the view-normal of any camera.

The second, related, question is: can we still track all of the active space with the restriction that cameras can not be placed at acute angle w.r.t. slices. The answer is that all the details of that region can be obtained by using cameras slightly away and closely zooming on the area of interest. In addition, if for some reason the camera can not be moved, then the orientation of the slices can also be changed during preprocessing to create a new active-space indexing mechanism. It is this freedom to change the orientation of cameras and/or slices which makes the active-space indexing method versatile. More comments related to resolution, accuracy, responsiveness, robustness, registration, and sociability are in [38]. The Scan&Track is expected to be *accurate* and have extremely high *resolution* because several cameras can potentially zoom-in and provide high resolution active-space as desired. The active-space indexing is constant time when the number of slices and lines are constant. The *responsiveness* of the Scan&Track system would also depend upon the time it takes to calculate imprint-points from the camera-images. This needs to be further investigated but we note that the correspondence problem is much simplified due to the active-space indexing and the geometric-imprint algorithm. It is believed that the correspondence sub-system (Figure 1) will be the key to real-time interaction and should be implemented in hardware as much as possible [39]. The active-indexing system is extremely *robust* as it can always find a 3D-cell for given imprint-points within the active-space. As discussed in [38], the Scan&Track system uses camera-images which are better in resolving the *swimming* problem encountered in virtual environments. Virtual objects tend to swim because of the slight variations in estimating the 3D position of the tracked-position. Because of the active-space indexing, the same corresponding points on the image will always produce the same result and therefore the swimming problem is expected to be considerably reduced.

During preprocessing, cameras can be zoomed in and out, and placed depending upon the user's wish. Multiple user's can track the same 3D space based upon their own choice of slices and dot patterns. New cameras can be used to add more active-spaces as desired.

The active-space indexing method is unique and new, and it is an attempt to solve the corresponding problem across multiple mages, and is also a new method to estimate 3D position. Contour extraction method in the proposal finds those points on the human body which are "most" visible, and therefore are more likely to be present as end-points in contours extracted from camera-images.

Occlusion: In the Scan&Track system, we plan to look into past video-frames to resolve or at least know that the something which was visible before is not visible now. In this case, the propose Scan&Track system will continue to track those end-points which are visible (e.g. head and feet). The point is this that the Scan&Track system is robust as the Geometric-imprint changes from frame-to-frame.

7 Can VEs Really Understand Humans

The Scan&Track VE is expected to be a highly distributed system with several Scan&Track active-spaces physically distributed. Figure 14 shows several active-spaces. Although active spaces can be arbitrarily large, enough privacy to the human-participants is provided as no tracking can be done outside the active-space. Since we expect, several human-participants to be interacting in this highly distributed VE, it is appropriate to ask: (a) Can a VE be more powerful that a Turing Machine (TM)? (b) Can a VE really understand the human participants?

We have the following observations: (i) We feel VEs are essentially more powerful than the Turing Machine model, because of the non-linearity introduced by human-participants. By allowing multiple humans to interact in the physically distributed manner, VEs are expected to behave in a non-linear way because human behavior is essentially non-linear. (ii) Although VEs are non-linear and therefore expected to be more successful than TMs in dealing with human-interaction, it is our opinion that VEs may *not* be able to *completely* understand the *human participants*. Although we can not underestimate the human-brain, we have a simple, yet compelling argument: humans are best in *non linear abstraction*. A good example of non-linear abstraction can be found when we travel. How many of us really invest any time thinking about the plane flying? As soon as we board the plane, we are already making plans as to what we will do when we arrive at our destination. In other words, we have already abstracted the actual travel (we assume that we will arrive at the destination safely). To clearly state our observation: VEs may allow us to perform a non-linear task, however, they may not understand the human-participant and be able to predict with certainty what the human-participant wants to do at the very next moment.

8 Conclusions and Final Comments

The Scan&Track system avoids the complicated camera calibration operations, and the distortions due to camera projection are automatically avoided. The system, when implemented, would be scalable, as active-indexing for the same 3D-space could be developed for both the low and the high-end systems. In addition, the active-space volume is also scalable. These qualities make the Scan&Track system ideal for future human-centered applications.

The active-space indexing method provides a framework for unencumbered 3D tracking based upon multiple video sequences. The active-space indexing method does not require any camera calibration or camera orientation parameters for estimating the position. Given the imprint-set of a point, the active-space indexing method determines the 3D-cell or voxel of the active-space, containing that point, in constant time. The method provides space-linearity within the 3D-cell, and allows linear interpolation to be used for better position estimates. The preprocessing algorithm is simple, and can be easily automated. Planer slices can be arbitrarily large or small, and can have finer or coarse grid patterns. In future, we plan to use a much larger, 8 feet by 10 feet planar slice (wall) with a finer dot pattern.

The proposed Scan&Track system is useful for distributed VEs. Multiple user's can track the same 3D space based upon their own choice of slices and dot patterns. New cameras can be used to add more active-spaces as desired. The Scan&Track system can be used for personal active-space in front of the user's screen by placing three cameras at the top of the monitor. The preprocessing algorithm is simple, and can be easily automated. The Scan&Track system can also be used along with other existing tracking technologies. As cameras are expected to be mounted on the wall, and out of the way of the participants, the active-space indexing method is suitable for human-centered applications.

References

1. Meyer K., Applewhite H.L., and Biocca F.A.: A Survey of Position Trackers. PRESENCE, MIT Press 1(2) (1992) 173-200
2. Sturman D.J., and Zeltzer D.: A Survey of Glove-based Input. IEEE CG&A (1994) 30-39.

3. Speeter T.H.: Transforming Human Hand Motion for Tele-manipulation. PRESENCE, MIT Press 1(1) (1992) 63-79
4. Newby G.B.: Gesture Recognition Based upon Statistical Similarity, PRESENCE, MIT Press, 3(3) (1994) 236-244
5. Gottschalk S., and Hughes J.F.: Autocalibration for Virtual Environments Tracking Hardware. Proceedings of SIGGRAPH (1993) 65-71
6. Rashid R.F.: Towards a system for the Interpretation of Moving Light Displays. IEEE Transaction on PAMI, 2(6) (1980) 574-581
7. Sutherland I.E.: A head-mounted three dimensional display. ACM Joint Computer Conference, 33(1) (1968) 757-764
8. Brooks F.P., Ouh-Young M.J., Batter J.J., and Kilpatrick P.J.: Project GROPE – Haptic Displays for Scientific Visualization. Proceedings of SIGGRAPH (1990) 24(4) 177-185
9. Burdea G., Zhuang J., Roskos E., Silver D., and Langrana N.: A Portable Dextrous Master with Force Feedback. PRESENCE, MIT Press, 1(1) (1992) 18-28
10. Iwata H.: Artificial Reality with Force-Feedback: Development of Desktop Virtual Space with Compact Master Manipulator. Proceedings of SIGGRAPH (1990) 24(4) 165-170
11. Badler N.I., Hollick M.J., and Granieri J.P.: Real-Time Control of a Virtual Human using Minimal Sensors. PRESENCE, MIT Press, 2(1) (1993) 82-86
12. Krueger M.W.: Artificial Reality II. Addison Wesley Publishing Company, Reading, MA, 1-277 (1991)
13. State A., Hirota G., Chen D.T., Garrett W.F., Livingston M.A.: Superior Augmented Reality Registration by Integrating Landmark Tracking and Magnetic Tracking. Proceedings of SIGGRAPH (1996) 429-438
14. Faugeras O.: Three-Dimensional Computer Vision: A geometric Viewpoint. MIT Press, Cambridge, Massachussets (1996)
15. Grimson W.E.L.: Object Recognition by Computer: The Role of Geometric Constraints. MIT Press, Cambridge, MA (1990)
16. Maybank S.: Theory of Reconstruction from Image Motion. Springer-Verlag (1993)
17. Serra J.: Image Analysis and Mathematical Morphology. Academic Press, vols 1 and 2 (1988)
18. Talbert N.: Toward Human-Centered Systems. IEEECG&A, 17(4) (1997) 21-28
19. Cruz-Neira C., Sandlin D.J., andDeFanti T.A.: Surround-Screen Projection-based Virtual Reality: The Design and Implementation of the CAVE. Proceedings of SIGGRAPH, (1993) 135-142
20. Proceedings of the Second International Conference on Automatic Face and Gesture Recognition (1996) 1-384, Killington, Vermont, USA, IEEE Computer Society Press
21. Proceedings of the Second International Workshop on Automatic Face and Gesture Recognition (1995) 1-384, Zurich, Switzerland, IEEE Computer Society Press
22. Capin T.K., Noser H., Thalmann D., Pandzic I.S., Thalmann N.M..: Virtual Human Representation and Communication in VLNet. 17(2) (1997) 42-53
23. Semwal S.K., Hightower R., and Stansfield S.: Closed form and Geometric Algorithms for Real-Time Control of an Avatar. Proceedings of IEEE VRAIS (1996) 177-184
24. Wren C., Azarbayejani A., Darrell T., and Pentland A.: Pfinder: Real-Time Tracking of the Human Body, Proceedings of International Conference on Automatic Face-and-gesture Recognition, Killington, Vermount (1996) 51-56

can retrieve information (Rekimoto, 1995). We are currently focusing on the second problem, namely, detecting a device's ego motion.

As described above, our final goal is to record our trajectory in a visiting place and to replay it using a VRML 2.0 browser with an appropriate 3D model of the visiting place. Through our work towards this goal, we have recognized that ego-motion detection itself provides a good user interface for VRMK 2.0 browser. In general, a gyroscope is better hardware for identifying an ego motion of devices such as head-mounted displays (HMD) in virtual reality environments. We chose a CCD camera, however, mainly because we do not want to add more hardware to a small computing device for simplicity. Again, our final goal is to use a portable device in a real world to record the changes of our viewpoint in a visiting place. A CCD camera could be used to detect a global landmark. Thus, our challenge here is to see how well we can solve our problem using a CCD camera only.

2 CyberGlass: Design Issues for Portable Interfaces

We designed CyberGlass for users of portable computers, which are, in general, smaller, slower, and have less storage than desktop systems. In order take full advantage of these computers, we identified the following design issues:

- intuitive operation for examining the world: CyberGlass is a user interface designed to help us examine the world. When we look around the world, we normally turn our head or move our eyes. In a desktop environment, however, because of this restriction in the position of the display, that type of motion is impossible. Instead, we change our viewpoint by using pointing devices such as mice or touch sensors. When we carry a device with a display, the restriction disappears. We can move it to right or left while looking at its display. This is typical in video recording. We move a video camera so as to keep the things we want to record in the center of the display. Since we are already familiar with the action of filming a video, we can use this action as a metaphor for the user interface. We shall call this the "video recording metaphor." In fact, the main idea of CyberGlass is to capture images in a 3D virtual space as if through a video camera or a water glass in the real world. Note that this is not unusual in VR environment, but we are trying to apply the same type of idea to portable computers using computer vision techniques, rather than gyroscope.
- inexpensive movement detection: One of characteristics of portable computers is their ease of use – we can use them anywhere and anytime. Nevertheless, they have a serious deficiency. In general, to save battery consumption, portables have less CPU power and less memory. For this type of computer, simpler algorithms are preferable in order to reduce computation time. With respect to ego-motion detection, several computer vision algorithms are available. One is the optical flow algorithm. Several studies are based on optical flow (e.g. (Horn and Schunck, 1981) (Sundareswaran, 1991) (Barron, Fleet, and Beauchemin, 1994)). One particular example of the optical flow algorithm is shown in (Ancona and Poggio, 1993). This algorithm is said to be well-suited to VLSI implementation. Therefore,

compared with other optical flow algorithms, this algorithm is worth considering for portable computers. Optical flow computation, despite its complex calculation, can never reduce errors to a negligible level. If we can limit the working environment, we can expect that simpler methods such as frame difference could work well. Simple frame difference is much less expensive than optical flow algorithms. Fortunately and strikingly, in our experiment, the simple frame difference algorithm works very well when target images have a clear contrast in color depth a condition that we can generally expect around picture frames in museums. Therefore, we decided to use simple frame difference for a prototype system while we continue to investigate the other algorithm for further developments.
- approximation of rotation angle: Movement of a device is perceived as linear movement, even if we rotate the device. We are interested in rotation here. Therefore, we need to project linear movement to rotation.

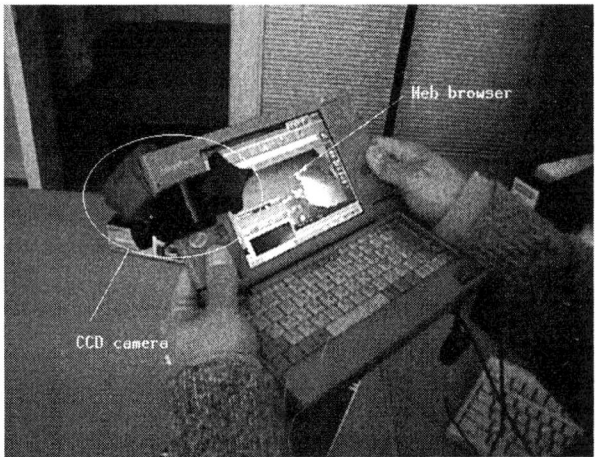

Fig. 1 A Prototype of CyberGlass.

3 Implementation

A prototype system of CyberGlass was developed based on the SONY CCD camera MC-1 and TOSHIBA portable computer Libretto50 (Pentium 75 MHz, 32MB). The CCD camera is arranged so as to match its direction with user's gaze. A picture of this system is shown in Fig. 1. This system consists of two software modules: a motion detection module and a 3D virtual world's viewpoint control module. A block diagram is shown in Fig. 2. Hereafter, I will explain how this system works.

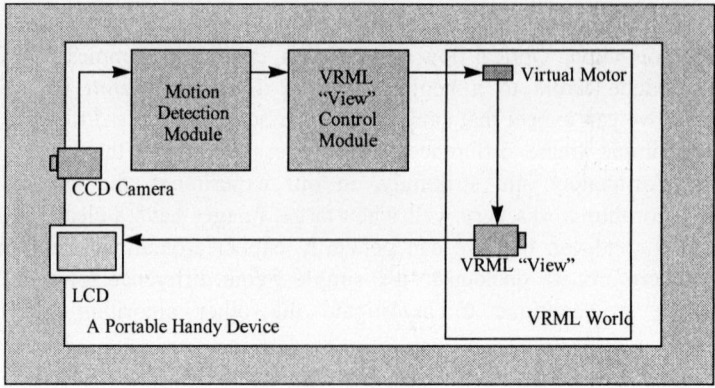

Fig. 2 A block diagram of CyberGlass

3.1 Motion Detection Module

The image captured by the CCD camera is stored in a frame buffer. After grabbing two successive frames, we perform an optical flow calculation. As I mentioned above, the method used is a frame difference algorithm. We can calculate a center of gravity for changes of all the pixels at time t by comparing two serial frames of images from a CCD camera. Let us call the center of gravity (x, y). After the next frame is received, we perform the same calculation to obtain the center of gravity at t +1. We call this (x', y'). From these centers of gravity, we can obtain (Δx, Δy), where Δx = x'- x, Δy = y'- y.

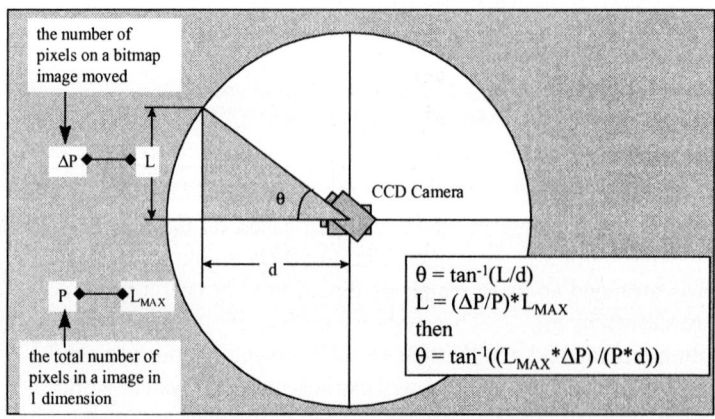

Fig. 3 Approximation of rotation angle of a device

3.2 3D Virtual World's Viewpoint Control Module

Once we have obtained the movement of the center of gravity (Δx, Δy), the 3D virtual world's viewpoint control module can rotate the viewpoint in a 3D virtual world by the following angle θ:

$$\theta = \tan^{-1}((\Delta P * L_{MAX}) / (P * d)). \tag{1}$$

where ΔP is either Δx or Δy in pixels and P is either the bitmap width or height in pixels. L_{MAX} is a distance in meters corresponding to P and d is a distance in meters to a target object in front of the device (See Fig. 3 in detail). The result is then represented on the display.

As described in the introduction, our final goal is to use a portable device in a visiting place. Therefore, d must be a correct distance from a CCD camera to a target object. In a real environment, by adding a special sensor hardware (e.g. an ultrasonic sensor) to the CyberGlass, it might be possible to obtain an exact distance d. In the case of a VRML 2.0 browser, however, we do not have any target. D, in this case, is the distance from our eyes to a virtual referential object in a virtual space. Thus, we need to set d to a constant.

4 Characteristics of an Experimental System

We conducted experiments with the CyberGlass equipped with both a CCD and a gyroscope for comparison. Fig. 4 shows traces of horizontal and vertical movement of the viewpoint according to the movement of a CyberGlass. The gyroscope provides almost the exact angle from an initialized position, whereas the CCD uses approximation calculated by equation 1. Even so, it should be noted that the approximated moving angles have nearly the same tendency as of the gyroscope. In particular, the approximated moving angles successfully return to 0 degrees whenever the gyroscope says that it is 0 degrees.

Unfortunately, when we consider both the horizontal and vertical axes, and we move a CyberGlass only in horizontal direction, a problem arises as shown in Fig. 4 (b). Although we did not move it in vertical direction, the angle approximation module automatically accumulates erroneous movement caused by noise. As the result, the angles went down towards the ground. We can avoid this by a forced solution. Namely, a CyberGlass can suppress updates of angles of either direction by detecting which direction has a major movement. If we need more degrees to be detected at one time, we will need to consider a more complex algorithm presented in (Roy and Cox, 1996).

5 Conclusion

We designed a VRML 2.0 interface for a portable device and developed a prototype system, called CyberGlass. This system is designed based on a "video recording metaphor". Namely, we can look around a 3D virtual world as if we were looking around the real world using a video camera. The current implementation has been tested in an environment where lighting is relatively moderate and objects are evenly distributed all around the environment so that any movement can be detected according to the motion of the handheld device.

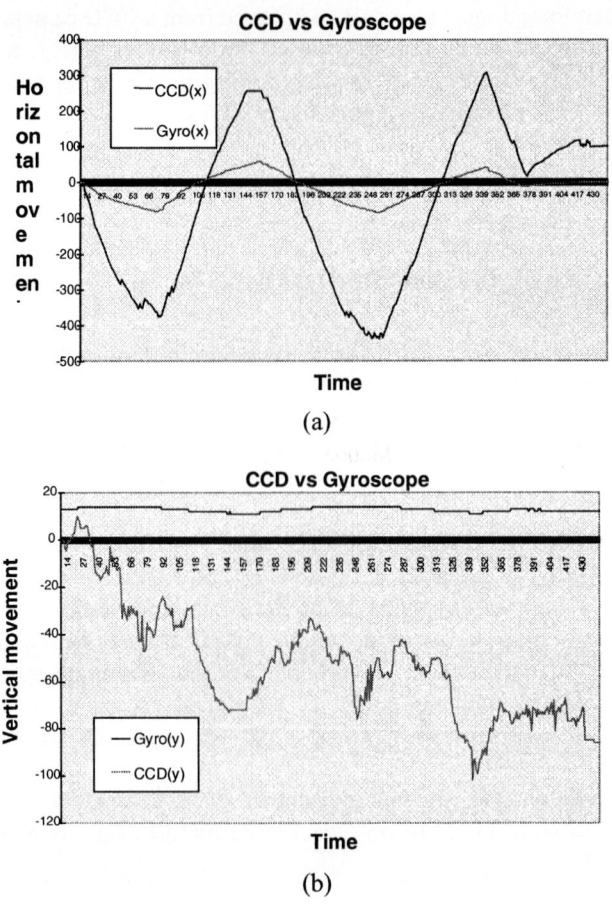

Fig. 4 A Trace of Horizontal/Vertical Movement.

One frequently asked question is why we do not try to detect forward or backward movements in this interface. It may be interesting to note that, according to our forward/backward movement with CyberGlass, the viewpoint inside a 3D virtual world changes. Nevertheless, I believe that, with respect to forward/backward movement, it would be better to use a push button interface rather than to change our standing position. One reason is the limited space available for the user to move. The other reason is that we are familiar with the metaphor of "driving a car" using an accelerator.

This is a report of work in progress. In future work, we would like to integrate this system with NaviCam so as to determine a global position of CyberGlass in order to produce a platform for more advanced applications.

References

1. Rekimoto, J. 1995. Augmented interaction: Interacting with the real world through a computer. In Proceedings of the 6th International Conference on Human-Computer Interaction (HCI Intenational'95): 255-260.
2. Ancona, N. and Poggio, T. 1993. Optical Flow from 1D Correlation: Application to a simple Time-To-Crash Detector, MIT AI Memo No. 1375.
3. Barron, J. L., Fleet, D. J., and Beauchemin, S. S. 1994. Performance of optical flow techniques. Int. J. Computer Vision, 2(1): 43-77.
4. Horn, K. and Schunck, B. 1981. Determining optical flow. Artificial Intelligence, 17; 185-203.
5. Sandareswaran, V. 1991. Egomotion from global flow field data. In Proceedings of IEEE Workshop on Visual Motion: 140 - 145, Princeton, NJ.
6. Roy, S. and Cox, I. J. 1996. Motion without Structure. In Proceedings of IEEE International Conference on Pattern Recognition, Vol 1:728-734.

Work Task Analysis and Selection of Interaction Devices in Virtual Environments

Thomas Flaig[1]

[1] Fraunhofer-Institute for Manufacturing Engineering and Automation IPA,
Demonstration Center Virtual Reality, Nobelstraße 12,
D-70569 Stuttgart, Germany
flaig.t@IPA.FhG.de

Abstract. The user interfaces in virtual environments depend on the work task given by specific applications and the adaptation to the human senses. This paper describes a method for work task analysis and selection of interaction devices for the design of user interfaces in virtual environments. The method takes into consideration degrees of freedom in the interaction process and the human senses. Characteristic is the systematic process for the designer. The method will be described and the results in an experimental environment discussed.

1 Introduction

Over the past few years, Virtual Reality (VR) has grown from an experimental technology to an increasingly accepted standard part of the business process. VR offers significant benefits as a problem-solving tool in various applications. It gives the user the feeling of being a part of the application to see and examine products, plans or concepts before they are realized [1].

The starting point for problem-solving in Virtual Environment (VE) is choosing the technological configuration for a VR system. It is mainly the application, which drives the need for particular technology requirements. These requirements are the computer hardware, VR software and the configuration of interaction devices. Especially the adaptation of interaction devices has a close influence on the human performance in problem-solving processes.

From the beginning, VR technology has produced a broad variety of interaction devices. Some, like force-feedback systems, for use in specific work fields and others for more universal use. Therefore the designer has no easy choice. The result is, that in expert interviews the user-interface of VR systems is rated unsatisfactory because of its user-hostility [2].

2 Conditions

One characteristic of VR technology is multi-modal communication between a user and a Virtual Environment. A wide variety of VR interaction technology for perception and manipulation in VE is available for use in practical applications. They differ in performance, information throughput rate or user-friendliness. For example the visual sense can be served by a common monitor, a head-mounted display (HMD) or a CAVE™-system. The choice depends on the necessary degree of perception and the work tasks in VEs. To balance both factors is the job of the designers of the user interface. VR applications commonly disregard human factors. Most designers have not examined the requirements of psychology and perception [3].

The main requirements for the interaction devices are driven by work tasks for system and application control. The required interactions are so-called necessary interactions in VE at configuration and run time. The task of the designer is to fulfill these necessary requirements with the available interaction devices and to take into consideration the human factors for perception and manipulation processes. Several researches have reviewed the important ergonomic issues in VR. But it is rare to find ergonomic guidelines for designing VEs and especially the configuration of interaction devices. The goal is to gain a maximum in human performance for a given work task. Experiments show, that the terms of interaction, presence and interaction devices are very important issues in human performance [4]. Sheridan stated that the determinants of sense of presence are: the richness of sensory stimuli, simultaneous viewpoint changes with head movements, the ability to handle objects inside the virtual environment and the dynamic behavior of the moveable objects [5], [6]. A breakdown of sense of presence can occurs because of the weight of the HMD, time lags or poor balanced configuration of interaction devices in VE. The result is a reduce in human performance. To gain an optimum in performance a method for configure interaction devices has to take into consideration the factors of perception by given requirements.

3 Method

The configuration of interaction devices has to take into consideration the requirements of the work tasks (necessary interaction of the user), the degrees of freedom (DOF) of the interaction devices in VE (possible interactions) and the combinations of interaction devices [7], [8]. The necessary interactions of users will be separated from the specific work tasks of system and application control and classified by the method of Ware-MacKenzie [11]. Here the interactions will be classified by DOFs. Multiple DOF devices such as 3D or 6D trackers and glove input devices are excellent choices for multiple DOF tasks such as viewpoint or object placement by gestures. Similarly, 2D devices are well suited for 2D tasks such as drawing or pointing on a CRT. The same classification of the interaction devices allows a first assignment of interaction devices to the work tasks by DOFs. By the use of grading and comparison the final combination of interaction devices will be chosen by taking the allowed combinations of interaction devices with their mutable combinations into consideration (Fig. 1 shows the methodical steps to find an optimized combination of interaction devices).

(1) Classification and grading of necessary interactions for controlling and observing the VR system based on DOFs.
(2) Classification and grading of necessary interactions for the application in the VE based on DOFs.
(3) Classification and grading of the interaction devices based on DOFs.

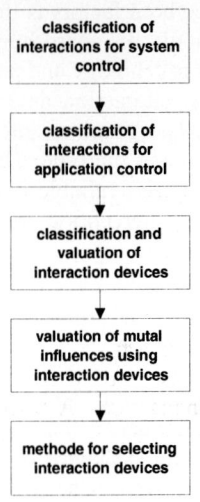

Fig. 1. Method for task-analysis and selection of interaction devices

Problems arise, when using interaction devices for tasks that do not have the same number of DOF. For instance, specifying the 3D position and orientation of an object with a mouse is difficult because one can only modify two DOFs at a time. Conversely, using higher DOF devices for lower DOF tasks can also be confusing if the interaction device is not physically constrained to the same DOF as the task.

(4) Grading of the combination of interaction devices with input/output functions.

Not all combinations of interaction devices are meaningful. For instance the use of a computer mouse in combination with a HMD make no sense.

(5) Choice of interaction devices by the use of the grading and comparison.

The choice of interaction devices begins with the comparison and grading of input and output devices with the necessary interaction for each DOF. The result is a table of interaction devices with a grading depending on system and application relevant work tasks. Further the tables will be used to build up matrices with the combinations of input and output devices for system and application work tasks. A first rough ranking will show, how use-full each interaction device is for a specific work task separated for system and application work tasks). Because not all combinations are useful, the matrices have to be compared and valued with the possible combinations of interaction devices, described in step 4. The result is a ranking, which interaction device fits best the given system or application requirements. The separate ranking for system and application work tasks could lead to an overlap of two different work tasks to the same human sense. This is sometime very disturbing for a user. For instance, printing system information in the view field of the user can be very disturbing in an immersive environment. Such overlaps can be solved by the mapping one function to another human sense. Here, system information can be presented as acoustic signals or as a speaking voice.

4 Experimental Environment

The method will be evaluated in an experimental environment for virtual prototyping [12]. A VE has to be designed to fulfill design, validation and training requirements in safety engineering. Safety systems are very complex and the development a difficult task for design engineers [9]. A lot of rules and laws have to be regarded. Mechanical and electrical know-how is necessary for the technical design, ergonomic and psychological know-how for the control design. Most accidents occur because of errors in the control design. Missing ergonomic aspects lead to high workload and low concentration. The test environment for the virtual prototyping of safety systems consists of a robot working cell with two drilling machines and two separate working stations. A worker has to interact with the system by programming or reprogramming the robot system, by exchanging the storage systems and by the repair of male-functions of the robot system, the drilling machines and the working stations (Fig. 2 shows the geometrical model of the robot working cell with the safety system components).

Fig. 2. Geometric model of the experimental environment

5 Results

The process of virtual prototyping consists of an order of work tasks with different tools. Each tool is well adapted to the problem-solving process [10]. In a VE the user controls these tools by the use of interaction devices. The use of interaction devices for problem-solving is not constant but differs from the work task and the DOF the device in VE.

The method for work task analysis and selection of interaction devices has been tested in the experimental environment. The first step is to define the work tasks for VR-system and application control and observation. Table 1 and 2 show the work task separated into the required DOFs, input and output interactions. The grading of the tasks is a subjective ranking with 5 levels of importance.

Table 1. Classification and grading of required interactions for system control and observation in virtual environments based on degrees of freedom

degrees of freedom		input interactions		output interactions	
	1	text input	o	text output	o
		binary input	++	binary system condition	+
	2	point at objects	++	menue output	+
		selection in virtual menues	++	system conditions	+
				system parameter output	o
	6	pointing input	++		
		spatial navigation	++	menue output	++
		selection in virtual menues	++		

-- very unimportant / - unimportant / o not affecting / + important / ++ very important

Table 2. Classification and grading of required interactions for application control based on degrees of freedom

degrees of freedom		input interactions		output interactions	
	1	input object parameter	-	output object parameter	-
		input object relations	-	output object relations	--
		binary inputs	+	binary object conditions	-
	2	input object parameter	++	output menues	++
		input object relations	o	output object parameter	+
		object selection	+	output object realiations	+
		selections in virtual menues	++	simulation results	++
	6	input object parameter	+	ouput menues	++
		input object relations	++	output object parameter	++
		object selection	++	output object relations	++
		input spatial navigatin	++	simulation results	++
		selectins in virtual menues	+		
	n	communication between users	+	communication between users	+
				simulation results	++

-- very unimportant / - unimportant / o not affecting / + important / ++ very important

This method guarantees, that important work tasks will be mapped to high ranked interaction devices (Table 3). Classification by DOF of the interaction devices is shown in Table 3. The process is the same as for the work tasks before. The grading ranks how suitable the interaction device is for the required immersion and presence in the VE.

Table 3. Classification and grading of interaction devices based on degrees of freedom

degrees of freedom		input devices		output devices	
	1	bio signal key switch keyboard	+ o o +	vibration output signal light buzzer	+ + +
	2	eye tracking computer mouse	+ +	monitor	++
	6	tracking system space ball Space Mouse™ flying joystick 3D-pencilt Immersion Probe™ mechanical kinematic	++ + ++ ++ + + +	monitor with shutter glasses projection with shutterglasses CAVE™ system with shutter glasses headmounted display BOOM™ system retina projektion system stereo headphone speaker system mechanical kinematic motion plattform	+ + ++ ++ ++ ++ ++ ++ ++ +
	n	data glove exoskeleton micropnone video camera	++ ++ ++ ++	exoskeleton	++
-- very unfit / - unfit / o not affecting / + suitable / ++ very suitable					

The classification of interaction devices will be rated by the highest possible DOF. The use of interaction devices with a higher DOF than the linked work task is possible. All DOFs of a dataglove are for instance hardly ever used. Further is it possible to combine different interaction devices with lower DOF than required form the work task. Not all combinations are however useful. Table 4 shows the combinations of input and output devices with their subjective grading.

The final selection of the interaction devices will be done by grading and comparison. The steps are as followed:

(1) To select interaction devices, the designer has to combine and value the interaction devices with the necessary interactions of the work tasks for system and application control and observation. The results are tables with ranked input and output devices sorted by system tasks, application tasks and DOF.
(2) As not all combinations of interaction devices are useful, all interaction devices have to be valued with the results of Table3 (mutual influence of combinations). The result are rankings for all interaction devices sorted by system tasks, application tasks and DOF.
(3) The last step is a check if there is an overlapping of two different work tasks to the same human sense. If there is a collision, one work task have to be mapped to another human sense.

For a virtual prototyping VE in safety engineering the described method leads to the following combinations of interaction devices (Table 5). The result is a rank list for the interaction devices sorted by the DOF, system (sys) and application (app) related requirements.

The VE for virtual prototyping is a immersive environment based on HMD and stereo speaker or headphone as the main output devices. The main input devices are the dataglove or flying joystick combined with a tracking system. An exoskeleton would add tactile and force perception to the VE. The rank for input devices shows that immersive environment is not very useful for the system relevant tasks . To solve this problem a second person should guide the person who does the validation. This second person controls the environment with conventional input devices. The monitoring of system relevant information is possible and helpful in immersive VE.

Table 4. grading of mutual influences between interaction devices

		monitor with shutter glasses	projection with shutter glasses	CAVE™ system	headmounted display	BOOM™ system	retina projektion system	stereo headphone	speaker system	exoskeleton	vibration output	motion platform	signal light	buzzer	mechanical kinematic
							output devices								
input devices	tracking system	+	+	+	+	-	+	+	+	-	-	0	0	0	0
	space ball	0	0	0	+	0	0	+	+	-	-	0	+	+	+
	flying joystick	0	0	0	+	0	+	+	+	-	-	0	+	+	0
	3D-pencil	0	0	0	+	0	0	+	+	-	-	0	+	+	-
	data glove	0	0	0	+	0	+	+	+	-	-	0	+	+	-
	exoskeleton	0	+	+	+	0	+	+	+	+	-	-	+	+	-
	computer mouse	+	-	-	-	-	+	+	+	+	0	+	+	+	0
	eye tracking	0	-	-	-	-	+	+	+	+	0	+	+	+	0
	bio signal	+	+	+	+	+	+	+	+	0	0	0	+	+	+
	microphone	+	+	+	+	+	+	+	+	+	+	+	+	0	+
	key	0	0	0	+	+	+	+	+	0	-	0	+	+	-
	switch	0	0	0	+	+	+	+	+	0	-	0	+	+	-
	keyboard	+	0	0	-	0	+	+	+	-	-	-	+	+	+
	video camera	+	+	0	-	0	+	+	+	0	-	-	+	+	0
	Immersion Probe™	+	0	0	+	0	-	+	+	-	-	0	+	+	-
	Space Mouse™	+	0	0	+	0	-	+	+	-	-	0	+	+	-
	mechanical kinematic	+	0	0	+	0	-	+	+	-	-	0	+	+	-

- not usefull / o limited use / + usefull

The ranking of the devices with DOF 1 and 2 in Table 5 shows a correlation. This is not surprising because the exercises can be solved with non VR related devices. DOF 6 and n show a significant difference. In this cases the exercises are related to spatial perception and action. The tendency to VR related devices is reasoned by the application related exercises for virtual prototyping in safety engineering.

Table 5. Rank of interaction devices for system and application control

degrees of freedom		input devices	rank sys	rank app	output devices	rank sys	rank app
	1	bio signal key switch keyboard	3 2 2 1	3 2 2 1	vibration output signal light buzzer	2 1 1	2 1 1
	2	eye tracking computer mouse	2 1	1 0	monitor	1	0
	6	tracking system space ball Space Mouse™ flying joystick 3D-pencil Immersion Probe™ mechanical kinematic	4 5 1 2 6 7 3	1 3 3 2 5 7 6	monitor with shutter glasses projection with shutter glasses CAVE™ system headmounted display BOOM™ system retina-projektion system stereo headphone speaker system mechanical kinematic motion platform	5 10 6 3 9 4 1 1 8 7	4 9 6 3 9 5 2 1 8 7
	n	data glove exoskeleton microphone video camera	0 0 0 0	1 4 2 2	exoskeleton	0	1

6 Conclusion

The use of the method for task-analysis and selection of interaction devices have been tested in an experimental environment at the Fraunhofer IPA. Therefore a VE has been designed for the specific requirements of virtual prototyping work tasks in safety engineering. Design, validation and training work tasks selected work tasks.

The method takes into consideration the classification of work tasks (system and application relevant), classification of interaction components and the mutual influences of combinations of interaction devices. Its uniqueness is a straight forward process to select interaction devices depending on immersion and physiology of the human senses.

References

1. Leston, J.; Ring, K.; Kyral, E.: Virtual Reality; Business Applications, Markets and Opportunities. London: OVUM Reports, Ovum Ltd., 1996.
2. Niedetzky, H.-M.; Triller, M. T.: Virtual Reality; Ein Marketinginstrument der Zukunft?. Pforzheim: Fachhochschule Pforzheim (Hrsg.); Delphi-Erhebung, 1995.
3. Durlach, N.: VR Technology and Basic Research on Humans. In: IEEE Computer Society Press: Virtual Reality Annual International Symposium '97: Conference Documentation; Albuquerque, 1-5 March 1997. Washington, Brussels, Tokyo: IEEE Computer Society Press, 1997, S. 2-3.
4. Lee, N., S.; Park, J., H.; Park, K., S.: Reality and human performance in a virtual world. In: Industrial Ergonomics 18 (1996), p 187-191.
5. Ellis, S. R.: Presence of Mind. In: Presence, Vol. 5 No. 2, 1996, pp. 247-259.
6. Sheridan, Th. B.: Further Musings on the Psychophysics of Presence. In: Presence, Vol. 5 No. 2, 1996, pp. 241-246.

7. Flaig, T.; Wapler, M.: The Hyper Enterprise. In: Roller, Dieter (Hrsg.): Simulation, Diagnosis and Virtual Reality Applications in the Automotive Industry: Dedicated Conference on ..., Proceedings, Florence, Italy, 3rd-6th June 1996. Crydon, London: Automotive Automation, 1996, S. 391-398.
8. Bauer, W.: Virtual Reality as a Tool for Rapid Prototyping in Work Design. In: Koubek, R. J.: Karwowsky, W. (Editors): Manufacturing Agility and Hybrid Automation I. Proceedings fo the 5th International Conference on Human Aspects of Advanced Manufacturing HAAMAHA'96. Maui. August 7-9 1996. Louisville: IEA Press, 1996, pp 624-627.
9. Flaig, T.; Grefen, K.: Auslegung sicherheitstechnischer Einrichtungen mit Virtueller Realität. In: Fachtagung SA, Simulation und Animation für Planung, Bildung und Präsentaion; 29. Februar - 01. März 1996, Magdeburg, Deutschland.
10. Kuivanan, R.: Methodology for simultaneous robot system safety design. VTT Manufacturing Technology, Technical Research Centre of Finland, ESPOO 1995.
11. Herndon, K., P.; van Dam, A.; Gleicher, M.: The Challenges of 3D Interaction; A CHI'94 Workshop. In: SIGCHI Bulletin Literatur zur Kollisionserkennung (1194) Volume 26, Number 4, S. 36-43.
12. Westkämper, E., Kern, P.: Teilprojekt D1; Virtuelle Realität als Gestaltungs, Evaluierungs- und Kooperationswerkzeug. In: Univerität Stuttgart (Hrsg.): Ergebnisbericht 01. 10. 1994 - 31. 12. 1997; Sonderforschungsbericht 374 Entwicklung und Erprobung innovativer Produkte - Rapid Prototyping. Stuttgart, Germany, 1997. S. 369-424.

Effect of Stereoscopic Viewing on Human Tracking Performance in Dynamic Virtual Environments

Paul Richard[1], Philippe Hareux[1], Philippe Coiffet[1], and Grigore Burdea[2]

[1] Laboratoire de Robotique de Paris
UPMC-UVSQ-CNRS
10-12 avenue de l'Europe, 78140 Velizy, France
{richard, hareux, coiffet}@robot.uvsq.fr
http://www.robot.uvsq.fr
[2] CAIP Center
Frelinghuyssen Rd, P.O. Box 1390, NJ, USA
burdea@telephone.edu
http://www.caip.edu

Abstract. In this paper, we present the results of a human factor study aimed at comparing the effect of stereoscopic versus monoscopic viewing on human tracking performance. The experimental paradigm involved tracking and grasping gestures toward a 3D moving object. This experiment was performed using different frame rates (from 28 frames per second (fps) down to 1 fps). Results show that monoscopic viewing allowed stable performance (grasping completion time) down to 14 fps. Stereoscopic viewing extended this stabilty to 9 fps, and decrease task completion time by 50 % for frame rate under 7 fps. We observed that stereoscopic viewing did not much increase performance for high frame rates.

1 Introduction

Virtual Reality (VR) is emerging as an important technology that will have a profound influence on a wide variety of fields such as training, entertainment, data visualization, and telerobotics. VR interactions are based on the ways we interact with the real world.

Human interaction with its environment is primarily visuo-motor, and vision is the dominant source of feedback concerning the effects of actions. For instance, over the course of a normal day, an average person makes hundred of limb movements to objects in space. To produce such movements one must use visual information about the position of the object in space. When reaching for a moving object, one should also use information about object's velocity [1], [2].

In a Virtual Environment (VE), both perceived position and velocity of objects in respect to the observer are subject to perceptual distorsions. One of the most important parameters that may cause such perceptual distorsions is temporal resolution - the number of updated images per unit time. The temporal resolution is affected by a number of hardware and software factors. Three separable factors need to be considered in assessment of the temporal resolution of virtual reality visual display systems: (i) frame rate, (ii) graphics update rate, and (iii) delays.

The frame rate is a hardware-controlled variable that determines the number of images rendered by the computer graphics system per second. The update rate of virtual reality visual display systems is a more important temporal variable than frame rate. For instance, if a display system has a frame rate of 60 Hz, but an update rate of 4 Hz, then the system presents 15 consecutive identical images of the scene before it changes any of the elements in the scene, and then presents 15 consecutive images of the new scene. Thus this system can present only four images per second. A major factor in determining the update rate is the computational complexity of the virtual world.

Delays in the virtual reality systems are of two types: computational and sensor. Computational delay is a major factor in determining the update rate of a display system. Sensor delay is the time required for the sensor system to perceive a movement made by the user that requires updating the display. Sensor delay and computational delay are additive. For instance a system which has a 10 Hz update rate and a 150 ms sensor delay, would produce a maximum delay of 250 ms whenever the user's head moved enough to require the synthesis of a new image of the virtual world.

For low graphics update rate, virtual objects appear to move in discrete spatial jumps separated in 3-D space by the inter-station distance and in time by the inter-station interval. Then, the human visual system has to bridge the gaps between the stations where an object is actually presented, by using spatio-temporal interpolation (spatio-temporal interpolation creates the impression of motion from a sequencence of stationary images by reconstructing the motion path in between the stations actually presented).

Beyond the basic phenomenon of apparent motion itself, there have been few psychological investigations of the implication of this apparent continuity for other aspects of visual perception. In particular, if an object moving in discrete spatial jumps is perceived as if in continuous motion, what does it imply about the perceived visual direction of the object at any one instant of time? Several distinct lines of evidence point to the conclusion that the visual direction of the object in these circumstances may be the one that it would be occupying if it were really in continuous motion. Thus, apparently moving objects can lead to smooth tracking eye movements in which the eye continuously changes its position in the same way that it does to keep a continuously moving target. Moreover, Thomson showed that intermittently sampled visual information may be used continuously in the control of movements [3], [4]. However, as the information from an apparently moving target is degraded by increasing the spatio/temporal interval between successive target presentations, there will come a point where the eyes will no longer follow the target continuously, but will move from position to position in a serie of saccades. Moreover, there will come a point where the hand will no longer follow the target continuously, but will also move from position to position.

Ranadive investigated the effect of the update rate on human performance in manipulation tasks using monoscopic display. Subjects were asked to perform two remote manipulation tasks using an Argonne E-2 seven-degree-of-freedom servo manipulator. Performance on each task was defined as the inverse of the time required to do that task correctly. The graphics update rate was adjusted to 28, 16, 8, or 4 fps. Ranadive observed that performance fell when the update rate was below 14 fps [5]. Massimino and Sheridan compared manipulation capability for direct vision versus monoscopic video display in simple block-insertion tasks. They found that mean completion times dropped dramatically as the update rate fell below 14 fps [6]. However these studies used only monoscopic displays.

Yeh and Silberstein suggested that visual presentations of perspective displays updated at slow rates may benefit signifiquantly for the inclusion of binocular disparity [7]. Regan and Beverley observed that depth judgments are more accurate with dynamic disparity at update rates slower than 2 fps [8]. This suggests that stereoscopic display may be superior to monoscopic display at slow update rates.

Some earlier studies with television displays showed that stereoscopic displays, as compared to monoscopic ones, did not provide significant advantage in performing some telemanipulation tasks [9],[10],[11]. More recent studies, however, indicated that stereo performance was superior to monoscopic under most conditions, while the amount of improvement varied with visibility, task, and learning factors [12], [13]. These results showed that the advantage of the stereoscopic television display become pronounced with increased scene complexity and decreased object visibility.

Monoscopic and stereoscopic graphics displays were compared by employing three-axis-manual tracking tasks [14], [15]. Results were consistent with previous television display results, indicating that stereoscopic graphic displays did generally permit superior tracking performance, while monoscopic displays allowed equivalent performance when they were defined with adequate visual enhancement depth cues such as perspective grids.

2 Experiment

In this experiment we investigate the effect of stereoscopic viewing on human performance in a tracking/acquisition task of a 3-D moving virtual object for different graphics update rates.

The experimental VR system architecture is illustrated in (Fig. 1). A loosely-coupled, client-server architecture allows for the distribution of computation for the simulation on two workstations. One Sun 4 workstation is dedicated to reading and calibrating glove data, and maintaining state information on all objects in the virtual world. An HP755 workstation is dedicated to graphics rendering and display at a frame rate of 28 fps. The HP755 monoscopic display (1280x1024 pixel resolution) was replaced by a special stereo monitor with 120 Hz

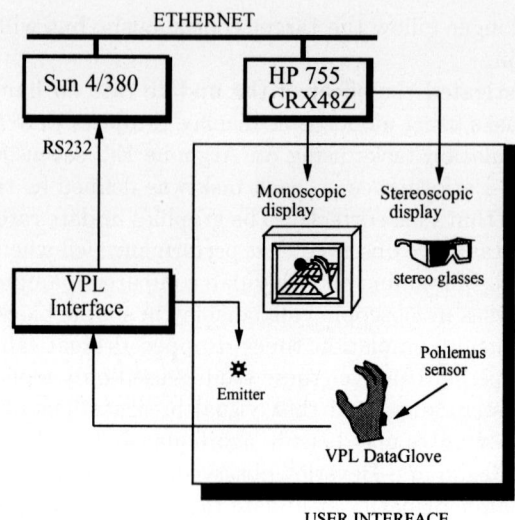

Fig. 1. Experimental system architecture

frame rate (required for the use of stereo glasses). A VPL DataGlove^{TM} is used to measure hand gestures [16]. A Polhemus^{TM} sensor which is mounted on the back of the glove transmits 3-D wrist position and orientation [17]. The accuracy of the Polhemus^{TM} sensor (Isotrack^{TM} model) is about 2.5 mm translation, and $1°$ in rotation.

2.1 Visual Display

In stereoscopic vision our brain fuses two slightly different views of the world (seen by both eyes) into one coherent 3-D image. In a monoscopic graphics display, a single 2-D image is presented to both eyes.

The human brain interprets the 2-D monoscopic image as a 3-D image by utilizing depth cues (perspective, occlusions, motion parallax, and so on). In a stereoscopic graphics display, two separate images generated with slightly different viewpoints are presented to both eyes.

There exist different techniques to present two separate images to both eyes [15]. Our experiments use a single screen with alternating (time-multiplexed) left and right views, and LCD shutter glasses. Alternating left and right images are synchronized with the opening and closing action of the shutters through an infrared (IR) controller (Fig. 2).

2.2 Virtual Environment

The experimental virtual environment (Fig. 3) is composed of black walls in perspective, a virtual hand, and a deformable red ball (target). Visual depth

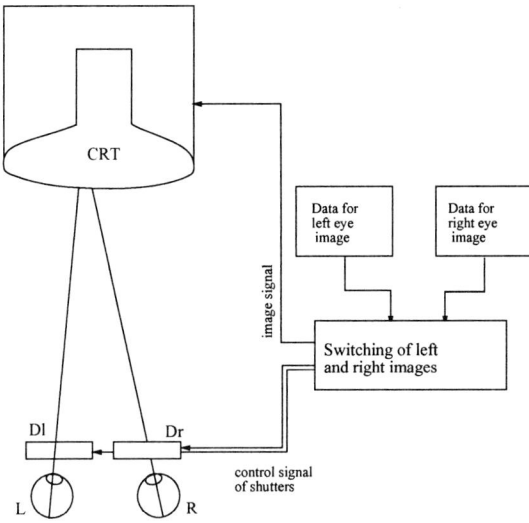

Fig. 2. Binocular viewing system using a time shared display of left and right images

cues such as vertical projection of object "shadows" and a grid background can be introduced in the environment to improve depth perception. The volume of the virtual room is about 1 m^3. The virtual hand is made of 129 polygons and has the same kinematics as the human hand. The ball is made of 72 polygons. Both objects are programmed into a "display list" using the Starbase Graphics Library [18], double buffering, and Gouraud shading with one light source.

2.3 Protocol

Each trial was run as follows: The target ball appeared in the virtual room with the same velocity (25 cm per second). The subject was then instructed to track the moving target and grab it as quickly as possible. For a given experimental session, subjects performed with a 15 seconds rest period between trials. Each session consisted of 10 trials.

Subjects were seated so that the eye-visual display distance was approximately 60 cm. In the stereoscopic viewing mode, stereo glasses were worn. The DataGlove^{TM} was fitted to their right hand, then a quick calibration was done. Subjects performed one trial session to familiarize themselves with the limits of the virtual room and the grasping (gesture recognition) technique (Fig. 4). Grid lined perspective walls were superimposed on the virtual walls. Laboratory room illumination was kept low in order to increase the contrast between the display and the immediate surroundings. During the task, the moving target was introduced in the virtual room always at the same location but with a random trajectory in a 45° cone. Task completion time was recorded after each trial.

Fig. 3. Experimental virtual environment

Two groups of 42 subjects each (42 males and 42 females) were used for the experiment. The first group performed the tracking task using the monoscopic display, while the second group performed the same task using the stereoscopic display. Each group was divided in 6 subgroups (G1, to G6) of 7 subjects each. G1 practiced capturing the target at a frame rate r1=28 fps, G2 at r2=14 fps, G3 at r3=7 fps, G4 at r4=3 fps, and G5 at r5=2 fps, G6 at r6=1 fps.

3 Results

Task completion time was used as a measure of performance. For each value of the graphics update rate, we recorded the task completion over trials and over subjects for both viewing conditions (monoscopic and stereoscopic). This allows a comparison between viewing conditions for each update rate and for each trial.

Results show that performance was stable from 28 fps down to 14 fps when using the monoscopic visual display (Fig. 5), and from 28 down to 7 fps when using the stereoscopic display. Performance is not statistically different between 28 fps and 14 for both viewing conditions (Fig. 6). However, stereo mode increased performance by 50% for update rates lower than 7 fps. It also appeared that stereo mode provides more reliable results (STD are 50% smaller for update rates between 1 fps and 7 fps, and 30% smaller for update rates between 28 fps and 7 fps). We observed that the learning process stops after 9 trials for all update rates for monoscopic viewing (Fig. 7). For stereoscopic display there is very little learning for update rates above 7 fps. For low update rates, the learning process continues up to 10 trials (Fig. 8).

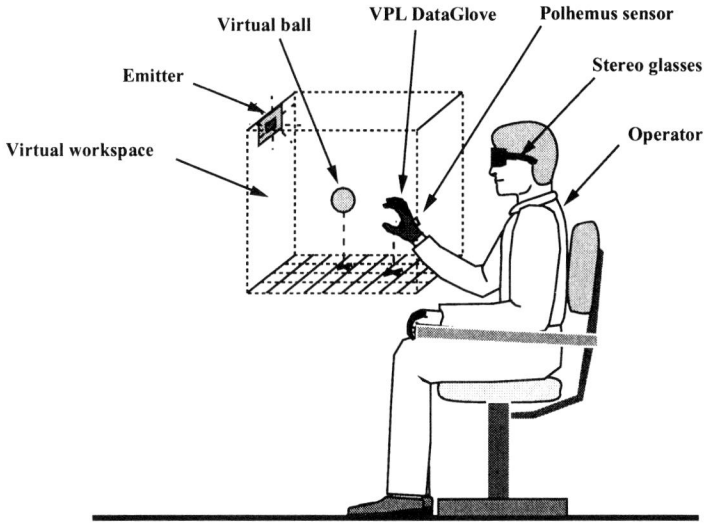

Fig. 4. Experimental configuration.

4 Discussion

We observed that for update rates equal or higher than 14 fps, subjects moved their hand continuously in space, while for update rates less than or equal to 3 fps, they exerted rather saccadic movements for both viewing conditions. In the latter case, the strategy used was to move the hand from position to position. This suggests that spatio-temporal interpolation was impossible to perform. More data are required to assess the maximum update rate that makes possible spatio-temporal interpolation for a 3D moving target.

Stereoscopic viewing proved superior to monoscopic viewing for low update rates. The reason is probably that for low update rates, operators were provided with a series of persistent static images rather than a perceptible motion of a target on a static background. Thus, depth information directly available through motion of the objects in the visual scene was not available in this case. These results confirm those previously obtained by Regan and Beverley who observed more accurate depth judgments with dynamic disparity at slower rates that 2 fps [8]. For faster update rates, spatio-temporal interpolation allowed the use of object motion for depth perception.

The results obtained from this experiment should be complemented by taking into consideration particular conditions where other tasks involving grasping gestures are to be performed with complicated movements. However, our results can be used as guidelines for investigations and design of simple manual interaction with virtual objects.

References

1. A.P. Georgopoulos, J. Kalaska, and J. Massey, "Spatial trajectories and reaction times of aimed movement: effects of practise, uncertainty, and change in target location", *Journal of Neurophysiol.*, 46:725-743, 1981.
2. C.G. Atkeson and J. Hollenback, "Kinematic features of unrestrained vertical arm movement", *Journal of Neuroscience*, 5:2318-2230, 1985.
3. J.A Thomson, "How do we use visual information to control locomotion ?" Trends in Neuroscienc es 3, 247-250, 1980
4. J.A Thomson, "Is continual visual monitoring necessary in visually guided locomotion ?" Journal of Experimental Psychology: Human perception and performance9, 427-443, 1983.
5. V. Ranadive, "Video Resolution, Frame-rate, and Grayscale Tradeoffs under Limited Banwidth for Undersea Teleoperation", SM Thesis, M.I.T, September 1979.
6. M. Massinimo and T. Sheridan, "Variable force and visual feedback effects on teleoperator man/machine performance" *Proceedings of NASA Conference on Space Telerobotics*, Pasadena, CA. Vo.1, pp:89-98, January 1989.
7. Y.-Y. Yeh and L.D. Silberstein, "Spatial judgments with monoscopic and stereoscopic presentation of perspective displays." *Human Factors*, 34(5), 583-600, 1992.
8. D. Regan, K.I. Beverley, "Some dynamic features of depth perception", *Vision Research*, Vol:13, 2369-2379, 1973.
9. W.N. Kama and R. DuMars, "Remote Viewing: A Comparison of Direct Viewing, 2-D and 3-D Television, AMRL-TDR-64-15, Wright-Patterson Air-Force Base, 1964.
10. P. Rupert and D. Wurzburg "Illumination and Television Considerations in Teleoperator Systems". Heer, E. (Ed.), *Remotely Manned Systems*, California: California Institute of Technology, pp. 219-228, 1973.
11. L.A. Freedman, W. Crooks and P. Coan, "TV Requirements for Manipulation in Space". *Mechanism and Machine Theory*, 12, 5, 425-438, 1977.
12. R.L Pepper, D. Smith and R. Cole, "Stereo TV Improves Operator Performance under Degraded Visibility Condition" *Optics and Engineering* 20, 4, 579-585, 1981.
13. R.L. Pepper, R. Cole, E. Spain and J. Sigudson, "Reseach Issues Involved in Applying Stereoscopic Television to Remotelly Operated Vehicles" *Proceedings of SPIE, 402-Three-Dimensional Imaging*, 170-173, 1983.
14. S.R. Ellis, W. Kim, M. Tyler, M. McGreevy and L. Stark, "Visual Enhancement for Telerobotics: Perspective Parameter". *IEEE 1985 Proceedings of the International Conference on Cybernetics and Society*, pp. 815-818, 1985.
15. W.S. Kim, S. Ellis, B. Hannaford, M. Tyler and L. Stark, "A Quantitative Evaluation of Perspective and Stereoscopic Display in Three-Axis Manual Tracking Tasks" *IEEE Transportation Systems, Man and Cybernetics*, SMC-17, 1, pp. 16-72, 1987.
16. VPL Research Inc., "DataGlove model 2 Operating manual", Redwood City, CA, 1987.
17. Polhemus Navigation Science Division, *Space Isotrack User's Manual*, Colchester, VT. 1987.
18. Hewlett-Packard, "Starbase Display List Programmers Manual", 1st Edition, January, 1991.

Interactive Movie: A Virtual World with Narratives

Ryohei Nakatsu, Naoko Tosa, and Takeshi Ochi

ATR Media Integration & Communications Research Laboratories
2-2, Hikaridai, Seika-cho, Soraku-gun, Kyoto, 619-0288, Japan
{nakatsu,tosa,ochi}@mic.atr.co.jp
http://www.mic.atr.co.jp/

Abstract. Interactive movies have emerged as a new type of media that implements interaction capabilities into movies. In interactive movies, people enter cyberspace and enjoy the development of a story by interacting with characters in the story. In this paper, we first explain the concept of interactive movies and briefly describe the prototype system we have developed. We then describe the construction of a second system, which we are currently developing, as well as several improvements incorporated in it.

1 Introduction

Ever since the Lumiere brothers created cinematography at the end of the 19th century[1], motion pictures have undergone various advances in both technology and content. Today, motion pictures, or movies, have established themselves as a composite art form that serves a wide range of cultural needs extending from fine art to mass entertainment. However, conventional movies unliterally present predetermined scenes and story settings, so audiences take no part in them and make no choices in story development. On the other hand, the use of interaction technology makes it possible for the viewer to "become" the main character in a movie and enjoy a first-hand experience. We believe that this approach would allow producers to explore the possibilities of a new class of movies. From this viewpoint, we have been conducting research on interactive movie production by applying interaction technology to conventional movie making techniques. As an initial step in creating a new type of movie, we have produced a prototype system[2]. Based on this system, we are currently developing a second prototype system with many improvements. This paper briefly describes the first prototype system and outlines its problem areas and required improvements. The paper also introduces the configuration of the second prototype system, which is now being refined by incorporating the described improvements.

2 Outline of Interactive Movies

2.1 Concept

Compared with existing media, interactive movies can be regarded as audience-participation, experience-simulating movies. An interactive movie consists of the following elements:

1. An interactive story that develops differently depending on the interaction of the audience;
2. An audience that becomes the main character and experiences the world created by the interactive story;
3. Characters who interact with the main character (audience) in the story.

2.2 Configuration of the First Prototype System

Based on the concept described above, we developed our first prototype system[2]. The following is a brief outline of this system.

(1) Software

Figure 1(a) shows the software configuration of the system. The interactive story consists of a collection of various scenes and a state-transition network between the scenes.

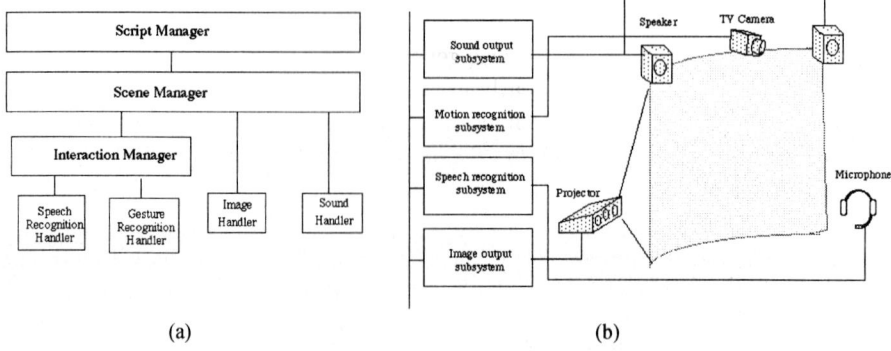

Fig. 1. Configuration of first prototype system: (a) software and (b) hardware.

The script manager stores the data of the state-transition networks and controls the scene transition according to the interaction result. The scene manager contains descriptive data of individual scenes and generates each scene by referring to the descriptive data of the scene specified by the script manager. The interaction manager is under the control of the script manager and scene manager, and it manages the interaction in each scene. The handlers are controlled by the scene manager and interaction manager. They control various input and output functions such as speech recognition, gesture recognition, output of visual images and output of sounds.

(2) Hardware

Figure 1(b) shows the hardware configuration. The system consists of an image output subsystem, a speech recognition subsystem, a gesture recognition subsystem and a sound output subsystem. In the image output subsystem, a high-speed CG-generating workstation is used for the visual image output. The speech recognition operations are executed by a single workstation. The gesture recognition function is also executed by a workstation. The sound output subsystem consists of several PCs. Background music, sound effects and character dialogs are simultaneously produced by this subsystem.

2.3 Evaluation and Problems

We tested the first prototype system with approximately 50 people during the half-year period following completion of system development. Based on their comments, we evaluated the system and identified areas for further research, as summarized below.

(1) Number of participants

The basic concept of the first system was a story with just one player acting the role of hero. However, the first system lacked the multi-user functions needed for the story to take place in cyberspace, since cyberspace will be created over a network and will require the story to develop from not just one player but from the interactions of several players participating at the same time.

(2) Frequency of interaction

Interaction in the first system was generally limited to change points in the story, so the story progressed linearly along a predetermined course like a movie except at these change points. There are certain advantages to this technique, such as being able to use the story development techniques and expertise accumulated by skilled cinematographers. However, the disadvantage of using fixed story elements created in the same way as for a conventional movie is that the player seems to end up a spectator who finds it difficult to participate interactively at points where interaction is clearly required. The limited opportunities for interaction create other drawbacks for the player, such as having little to distinguish the experience from watching a movie and having a very limited sense of involvement.

3 Description of Second System

3.1 Improvement

The following points were used to improve the second system as described below.

(1) System for multiple players

Our initial effort to develop a system for multiple players allowed two players to participate in cyberspace in the development of a story. The ultimate goal was to create a multi-player system operating across a network, but the first step in the present study was the development of a prototype multi-player system consisting of two systems connected by a LAN.

(2) Introduction of interaction at any time

To increase the frequency of interaction between the participants and the system, we devised a way for players to interact with cyberspace residents at any point in time. Basically, these impromptu interactions, called story unconscious interaction (SUI), occur between the players and characters and generally do not affect story development. On the other hand, there are sometimes interactions that do affect story development. This kind of interaction, called story conscious interaction (SCI), occurs at branch points in the story, and the results of such an interactions determine the future development of the story.

(3) Other improvements

Emotion recognition: To realize interaction at any time, an emotion recognition capability was introduced. When players utter spontaneous utterances, the characters react by using their own utterances and animations according to the emotion recognition result. Motion capture: We introduced a motion capture system based on magnetic sensors. There are two major reasons for such a system. One is to show avatars as alter egos of the players on screen, thus giving the players the feeling that they are really active participants with the system. The other is to improve gesture recognition. The first system's gesture recognition based on images obtained by a camera was ineffective due to low light. Therefore, we wanted to use motion capture data for gesture recognition.

3.2 Software System Structure

Figure 2(a) shows the structure of the software used in the second system.

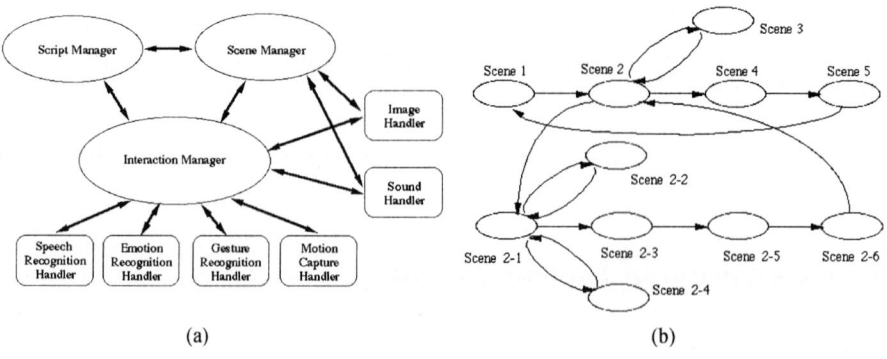

Fig. 2. (a) Software configuration of second system and (b) scene transition network.

(1) System structure concept

While the first system stressed story development, the second system had to achieve a good balance between story development and impromptu interaction by incorporating the concept of interaction at any time. This required building a distributed control system instead of a top-down system structure.

There is a variety of architectures available for distributed control systems, but we chose to use an action selection network [3] that sends and receives activation levels among multiple nodes. These levels activate nodes and trigger processes associated with the nodes at a point beyond the activation level threshold.

(2) Script manager

The role of the script manager is to control transitions between scenes, just as it did with the first system. An interactive story consists of various kinds of scenes and transitions among scenes. The functions of the script manager are to define the elements of each scene and to control scene transitions based on an infinite automaton (Fig.2(b)). The transition from a single scene to one of several possible subsequent scenes is decided based on the SCI result sent from the scene manager.

(3) Scene manager

The scene manager controls the scene script as well as the progress of the story in a scene. Action related to the progress of the story in a scene is called an event, and event transitions are controlled by the scene manager. Events for each scene consist of scene images, background music, sound effects, character animation and character speech, and player and character interaction.

The script for each scene is pre-stored ahead of time in an event network, and the scene manager generates each scene based on data from the script manager via a script.

The timing for transition from one event to the next was controlled by the scene manager in the first system, but absolute time cannot be controlled in the second system because it incorporates the concept of interaction at any time. However, relative time and time order can be controlled in the second system, so the action selection network was applied here as well. The following describes how this works.

1. Activation levels are sent or exchanged among events as well as external events.
2. An event activates when the cumulative activation level exceeds the threshold.
3. On activation of an event, a predetermined action corresponding to the event occurs. At the same time, activation levels are sent to other events, and the activation level for the activating event is reset. The order of events can be preset, and variation as well as ambiguity can be introduced into the order of events by predetermining the direction that activation levels are sent and the strength of activation levels.

(4) Interaction manager

The interaction manager is the most critical component for achieving interaction at any time. Figure 3 shows the structure of the interaction manager. The basis of interaction at any time is a structure that allots each character (including the player's avatar) an emotional state, and interaction input from the player along with interaction between the characters determine the emotional state as well as the response to that emotional state for each character. Some leeway is given to how a response is expressed depending on the character's personality and circumstances. The interaction manager is designed based on the concepts outlined below.

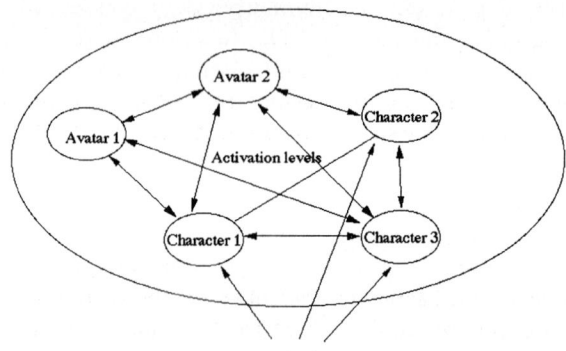

Fig. 3. Structure of interaction manager.

1) Defining an emotional state

The state and intensity of a player's ($i = 1, 2...$) emotion at time T is defined as

$$Ep(i,T), \; sp(i,T) \tag{1}$$

where $sp(i,T) = 0$ or 1 (0 indicates no input and 1 indicates an input).

Similarly, the state and intensity of an object's ($i = 1, 2...$) emotion at time T is defined as

$$Eo(i,T), \; so(i,T). \tag{2}$$

2) Defining the emotional state of an object

For the sake of simplicity, the emotional state of an object is determined by the emotional state when player interaction results from emotion recognition:

$$\{Ep(i,T)\} \rightarrow \{Eo(j,T+1)\}. \tag{3}$$

Activation levels are sent to each object when emotion recognition results are input as

$$sp(i,T) \rightarrow sp(i,j,T), \tag{4}$$

where $sp(i,j,T)$ is the activation level sent to object j when the emotion of player i is recognized. The activation level for object j is the total of all activation levels received by the object:

$$so(j, T+1) = \sum sp(i,j,T). \qquad (5)$$

3) Exhibiting action

An object that exceeds the activation threshold performs action $Ao(i,T)$ based on an emotional state. More specifically, action is a character's movement and speech as a reaction to the emotional state of the player. At the same time, activation levels $so(i,j,T)$ are sent to other objects:

$$\begin{aligned} &if\ so(i,T) > THi \\ &then\ Eo(i,T) \rightarrow Ao(i,T),\ Eo(i,T) \rightarrow so(i,j,T) \\ &so(j,T+1) = \sum so(i,j,T). \end{aligned} \qquad (6)$$

This mechanism creates interaction between objects and enables more diverse interaction than simple interaction with a one-to-one correspondence between emotion recognition results and object reactions.

3.3 Hardware System Structure

Figure 4 shows the second system's hardware structure, composed of image output, voice and emotion recognition, gesture recognition and sound output subsystems.

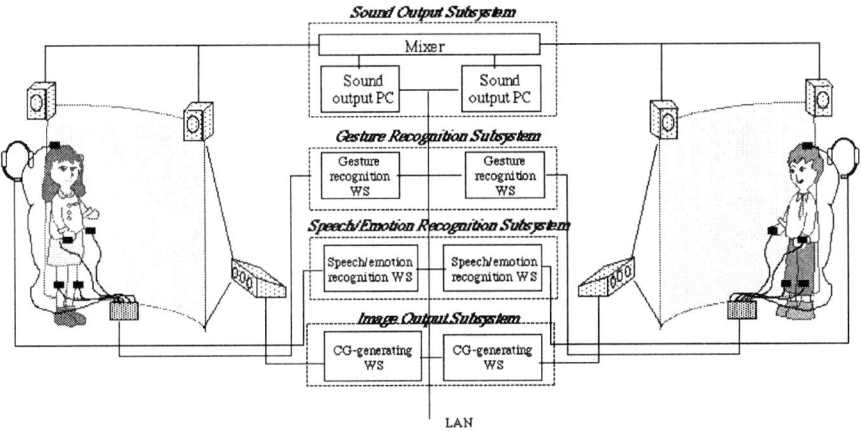

Fig. 4. Hardware configuration of second system.

(1) Image output subsystem

Two workstations (Onyx Infinite Reality and Indigo 2 Impact) capable of generating computer graphics at high speed are used to output images. The Onyx workstation is used to run the script manager, scene manager, interaction manager and all image output software. Character images are pre-stored on the workstations in the form of computer graphic animation data in order to generate computer graphics in real time. Background computer graphic images are also stored as digital data so background images can be generated in real time. Some background images are photographic images of real scenery stored on an external laser disc. The multiple character computer graphics, background computer graphics and background photographic images are processed simultaneously through video boards on both the Onyx and Indigo 2 workstations.

Computer graphics are displayed in 3-D for more realistic images, and a curved screen is used to envelop the player with images and immerse him or her in the interactive movie world. Image data for the left and right eye, previously created on the workstations, are integrated by stereoscopic vision control and projected onto a curved screen by two projectors. On the Indigo 2 end, however, images are output on an ordinary large-screen display without stereoscopic vision because of processing speed.

(2) Voice and emotion recognition subsystem

Voice and emotion are recognized with two workstations (Sun SS20s) that also run the voice and emotion recognition handlers. Voice input via microphone is converted from analog to digital by the sound board built into the Sun workstation, and recognition software on the workstation is used to recognize voices and emotions. For the recognition of meaning, a speaker-independent speech recognition algorithm based on HMM is adopted[4]. Emotion recognition is achieved by using a neural-network-based algorithm[5]. Each workstation processes voice input from one player.

(3) Gesture recognition subsystem

Gestures are recognized with two SGI Indy workstations that run the gesture recognition handlers. Each workstation takes output from magnetic sensors attached to a player and uses that data output for both controlling the avatar and recognizing gestures.

(4) Sound output subsystem

The sound output subsystem uses several personal computers because background music, sound effects and speech for each character must be output simultaneously. Sound effects and character speech are stored as digital data that are converted from digital to analog as needed, and multiple personal computers are used to enable simultaneous digital to analog conversion of multiple channels in order to output these sounds simultaneously. Background music is stored on an external compact disc whose output is also controlled by the personal computer. The multiple-channel sound outputs are mixed and output with a mixer (Yamaha 02R) that can be controlled by computer .

4 Example of Interactive Story Production

4.1 An Interactive Story

We have produced an interactive story based on the previously described Second System. We selected "Romeo and Juliet" by Shakespeare as the base story for the following reasons.

1. There are two main characters in the story and, therefore, this supplies a good example of multi-person participation.
2. "Romeo and Juliet" is a very well known story, and people have a strong desire to act out the role of hero or heroin. Therefore, it is expected that people can easily get involved in the movie world and experience the story.

The main plot of the story is as follows. After their tragic suicide the lovers' souls are sent to Hades, where they find that they have totally lost their memory. Then they start their journey to rediscover who they are and what their relationship is. With various kinds of experiences and with the help and guidance of characters in Hades, they gradually find themselves again and finally go back to the real world.

4.2 Interaction

There are two participants, one plays the role of Romeo and the other Juliet. The two subsystems are located in two separate rooms and connected by a LAN. Each participant stands in front of the screen of his/her respective system wearing specially designed clothes to which magnetic sensors and microphones are attached. In the case of Romeo, the participant wears a 3-D LCD-shutter glass and can enjoy 3-D scenes. Their avatars are on the screen and move according to their actions. They can also communicate by voice. Basically, the system controls the progress of the story with character animations and character dialogues. Depending on the voice and gesture reactions of the participants, the story moves on. Furthermore, as is described before, interaction is possible at any time. When the participants utter, the characters react according to the emotion recognition results. Consequently, depending on the frequency of the participants' interaction, this system can go anywhere between story-dominant operation and impromptu interaction-dominant operation. Figure 5 illustrates typical interactions between the participants and the system.

5 Conclusions

In this paper, we first explained the concept of interactive movies and briefly explained our first prototype system. Based on an evaluation of this system, we identified several problems in the system that needed to be improved. One is the lack of frequent interactions and the other is single-person participation. To overcome these deficiencies, we are developing a second system. We explained

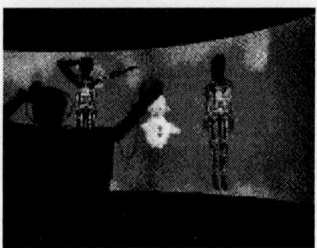 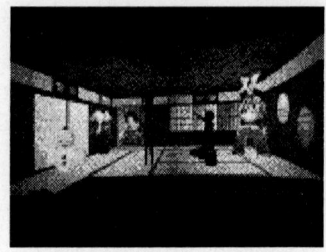

(a) "Romeo" controls his avatar (b) "Romeo" tries to touch object in Japanese curiosity shop

Fig. 5. Examples of interaction between participants and system.

two significant improvements incorporated into the second system: interaction at any time and two-person participation through a network. We described the software and hardware configurations of the second system while emphasizing these improvements. Finally, we illustrated the operation of our Second System with the example of our interactive production of "Romeo and Juliet".

References

1. C. W. Ceram, "Eine Archaologie des Kinos," Rowohlt Verlag, Hamburg (1965).
2. Ryohei Nakatsu and Naoko Tosa, "Toward the Realization of Interactive movies - Inter Communication Theater: Concept and System," Proceedings of the International Conference on Multimedia Computing and Systems'97, pp.71-77 (June 1997).
3. Pattie Maes, "How to do the right thing," Connection Science, Vol.1, No.3, pp.291-323, (1989).
4. Tetsu Shimizu et al., "Spontaneous Dialogue Speech Recognition Using Cross-Word Context Constrained Word Graph," Proceedings of ICASSP'96, Vol. 1, pp. 145-148 (April 1996).
5. Naoko Tosa and Ryohei Nakatsu, "Life-like Communication Agent - Emotion Sensing Character 'MIC' and Feeling Session Character 'MUSE' -," Proceedings of the International Conference on Multi-media Computing and Systems, pp.12-19 (June 1996).

Real-Image-Based Virtual Studio

Jong-Il Park and Seiki Inoue

ATR Media Integration & Communications Research Laboratories
2-2, Hikaridai, Seika-cho, Soraku-gun, Kyoto, 619-0288, Japan
{pji,sinoue}@mic.atr.co.jp
http://www.mic.atr.co.jp/

Abstract. In this paper, we propose a real-image-based virtual studio system where a virtual environment is generated by an image-based rendering technique and then a studio scene is put in the environment based on a 3D compositing technique. The system is implemented and the validity of the system is confirmed through experiments.

1 Introduction

The theme of constructing and displaying virtual environments has been extensively explored for decades in both research and commercial fields.

A key technology in the theme is to composite various image/video sources into an image/video. There has been considerable works on juxtaposing real images and computer graphics(CG) in the context of virtual reality. Krueger's VIDEOPLACE [4] focuses on interaction between a user and computer generated worlds. Hayashi *et al.*'s virtual studio system [1] rather emphasizes the image quality. The difference comes from their purposes. The former is aiming at providing users with interactively enjoying the virtual worlds while the latter is pursuing high quality integration of multiple image sources in the virtual world. In order to answer to both of the needs: interaction with virtual environments and generation of multimedia contents, we are developing an Image Expression Room(IERoom) [2]. In the IERoom, one can locate and observe oneself in a virtual environment and can create various images easily with high degree of freedom.

In this paper, we focus on pursuing reality in virtual worlds. The aim is to create multimedia contents. By constructing and displaying virtual environments and then inserting a studio scene in the environment, we merge a real studio scene and the virtual environment. The virtual environment can be real images as well as CG. If it includes only CG, the merging is so simple. Just setting the parameters of the CG to those of a real camera taking the studio scene would be enough. This is the approach taken in [1]. Here, we consider both of the image sources.

We propose a real-image-based video compositing system, *Real-Image-Based Virtual Studio*, in this paper. The most demanding feature of the system may be to generate an arbitrary view using real images because the viewpoint, orientation, and conditions of the virtual camera taking the virtualized real environment should be adjusted to those of the studio camera. An image-based rendering technique [8] is employed to meet the requirement.

The approach in this paper is first to take an environment scene with multiple cameras and then to extract a sharp and dense depth map based on multi-view stereo matching technology [7]. Then, an arbitrary view is generated using the images and the depth map [8]. Since the depth map of the arbitrary view is simultaneously generated, the method is well suited for Z-key composition. We can display the merged image on a large screen in front of the IERoom and interact easily with the virtual environment, which enables natural image expression.

2 Image Expression Room

We first briefly introduce the concept of the IERoom. Figure 1 shows its configuration.

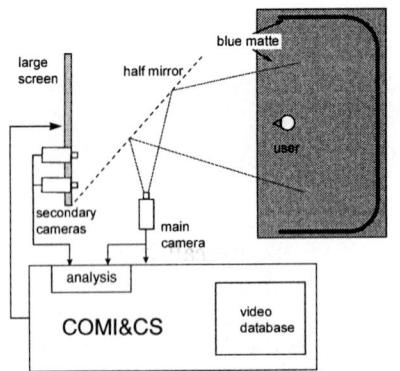

Fig. 1. The Image Expression Room.

The major components of the IERoom include a chroma-key studio, a large screen, a half mirror in front of the screen, studio cameras, and the COMI&CS (Computer Organized Media Integration and Communication System). The user can see himself/herself in a virtual scene and express himself/herself with interacting it through the COMI&CS. The main camera shoots the studio scene through the half mirror from the side of the screen. In this way, the user can interact with the output image as if he/she is seeing a mirror, which is one of the most convenient and friendly way of interaction to human. Furthermore, eye contact between the actor and the viewers can be realized with ease since gazing oneself also implies gazing assumed viewers in the configuration of the IERoom. The blue background region in the images from main camera is eliminated by passing them through a chroma-keyer. The secondary cameras can catch the human motions and the COMI&CS system analyses them to control various media components. Details can be found in [2].

3 Real-Image-Based Virtual Studio

3.1 3D Virtual Environments

An image-based rendering technique is employed for creating virtual environments. We attempt to build a virtual environment using multi-view real images and its disparity map. Five cameras are used in our implementation. One camera is located at the center and others are located symmetrically in the horizontal and vertical direction. A dense and sharp depth map of the center camera is extracted on the basis of multi-view stereo matching technique which is designed to overcome the effect of occlusion [7]. If we can generate an arbitrary view only using the available information: multi-view images and a depth map, we can say that a real scene is virtualized. In this way, we can construct virtual environments.

3.2 Arbitrary View Generation

We generate an arbitrary view and its depth map given multi-view images and the center image's depth map. The method is based on a 2-step approach. Suppose we have a virtual camera and move the camera to an arbitrary position and orientation.

First step is to cope with pure translation of viewpoint. This process depends on the depth of each pixel. Thus, we call it 3D processing. This step consists of, first, transforming the depth map into that of a new view position and then, mapping some colors from the images of proper secondary cameras.

The depth map of the center view is transformed into that of a new view position. The forward mapping technique with supersampling is used. For the folds where multiple pixels are mapped on the same grid, we choose the smallest among the superposed depth values assuming that objects are opaque. Color(or intensity for gray image) information is simultaneously mapped during the transformation. For the uncovered areas, we directionally interpolate the depth map. We make use of background depth values in interpolating depth of the uncovered areas. The reason to interpolate depth map for the uncovered area is two fold. One is to provide a way of guessing a proper color information from secondary cameras. The other is to output a depth map for further use in 3D video composition. Then, we interpolate the colors of the uncovered area by a backmapping using the depth value and a validity check.

Second step is to cope with zooming and pure rotation of the virtual camera. It is independent of the depth of each pixel and thus involves only 2D processing. Notice that, when we handle the orientation and scale, we also do the same job for the depth map to prepare for the 3D composition.

Details on the arbitrary view generation can be found in [8].

3.3 3D Video Composition

The video composition in the IERoom can be divided into 3 categories based on the level of exploiting 3D property. One is the 2D composition where multiple image sources are just juxtaposed in layers. The second is the 2.xD composition based on the layered representation of image sequence [9], which is beyond 2D but below 3D. We segment each image into some layers and handle each layer independently. The third is the 3D composition based on full 3D information of a scene, which we focus on in this paper.

Suppose we are to merge multiple image sources into one image. If all the image sources are taken by fixed video cameras, we can merge the images by a simple Z-key method [3]. The disparity values of each pixel of multiple images to be composed are compared and the image data of the largest disparity, equivalently, the nearest point from camera, at the pixel position are selected as the pixel value of the composed image.

If one of the cameras undergoes camera works, we should adjust other images according to the camera works [1][6]. In the IERoom, the main camera is allowed to move freely and to change the focal length. Thus, when we are to put the studio scene in a virtual environment, the virtual camera shooting the virtual environment should be able to vary according to the works of the main camera. Moreover, to utilize the Z-key method, the corresponding depth map should also be prepared. These can be implemented as we described in the Sect.3.2.

3.4 Implementation

The overall block diagram of the real-image-based virtual studio system in the IERoom is shown in Fig.2

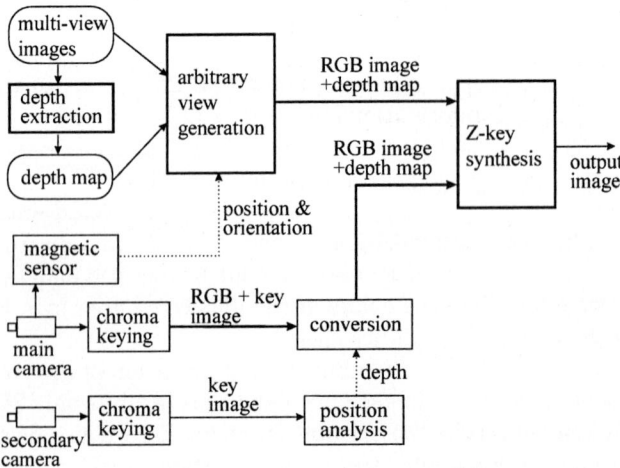

Fig. 2. Conceptual flow diagram of the real-image-based virtual studio system in the IE Room.

The position and orientation of the main camera are measured by a magnetic sensor and transmitted to the arbitrary view generating unit. The view generating unit produces a virtual view having the same position and orientation to those of the main camera. Because the view generation is purely software-implemented now, it cannot produce arbitrary views in the video rate. Thus, we prepare an arbitrary view and its depth map *a priori* for a number of sample view points within a volume of interest and store them in a frame memory, similar to the approach of Movie-Map [5]. When we want to explore the virtual environment, in other words, when we are to merge a studio scene in the virtual environment, the nearest virtual view position to the measured value are calculated first. Then the corresponding view and its depth map are called from the frame memory and transmitted to Z-key synthesis unit through a geometrical transformation unit. The geometrical transformation unit executes 3D image rotation and zooming in real-time. In this implementation, dynamic virtual environments, i.e. containing moving objects, cannot be handled. The most desirable solution toward dynamic environments may be to make the arbitrary view generation processed in the video rate, which is under extensive investigation.

The position of the user on the blue-background studio is detected by a secondary camera located on the top of the screen. A priori knowledge that the user is on a flat floor is exploited. The image from the main camera is now transformed into an RGB image with a constant depth measured by the secondary camera and transmitted to the Z-key synthesis unit. Since the image from the main camera is regarded as a flat panel at the specified depth, the true 3D composition is not allowed in the current implementation. It can be achieved only if we have a real-time dense depth mapper in the studio [3]. In most application, however, the flat panel approach gives sufficiently good results. Another limitation at the current implementation is that multi-actors are handled in one layer. To handle them separately, we should introduce an analysis unit possibly with more secondary cameras, which is currently investigated. Using a real-time dense depth mapper can also be a solution.

We show experimental results in Fig.3. The user is standing at a fixed position. The main camera is moved effectively to the right(actually to the left because we use a half mirror in the IERoom) and slightly zooming in. We see quite a natural-looking composition result. When we observed the scene in real-time, we felt the user was actually in the virtual environment. We have confirmed through many experiments that the view synthesis method could generate a variety of real-image-based virtual environments successfully and the 3D composition with a moving camera could produce natural-looking composition images.

4 Concluding Remarks

In this paper, we propose a real-image-based virtual studio system where a virtual environment is generated by an image-based rendering technique and a studio scene is put in the environment based on a 3D composition technique.

(a) (b)

Fig. 3. Experimental results: 3D composed images (a) before and (b) after camera operation.

A prototype system is implemented and the validity of the system is confirmed through experiments.

At the current implementation, dynamic virtual environments cannot be handled. Thus, much effort is exerted on generating the arbitrary view in real-time. Another limitation is that full 3D information on the objects in the studio is not available which can be overcome only by introducing a real-time dense depth mapper.

We are also considering another scenario in the virtual studio: taking a scene by a moving camera, estimating/measuring the motion, and then control the studio camera according to the estimated/measured camera motion.

Acknowledgment: The authors are grateful to Mr. Masaki Hayashi of NHK, for his valuable comments.

References

1. M.Hayashi et al., "Desktop virtual studio system," *IEEE Trans. Broadcasting*, vol.42, no.3, pp.278-284, Sept. 1996.
2. S.Inoue et al., "An Image Expression Room," *Proc. Intl' Conf. on Virtual Systems and Multimedia'97*, pp.178-186, Geneva, Switzerland, Sept. 1997.
3. T.Kanade et al., "A stereo machine for video-rate dense depth mapping and its new applications," *Proc. IEEE CVPR'96*, pp.196-202, San Francisco, June 1996.
4. M.Krueger, *Artificial Reality*, Addison-Wesley, 1983.
5. A.Lippman, "Movie-Maps: An application of the optical video disc to computer graphics," *SIGGRAPH'80*, 1980.
6. J.Park, N.Yagi, and K.Enami, "Image synthesis based on estimation of camera parameters from image sequence," *IEICE Trans. on Information and Systems*, vol.E77-D, no.9, pp.973-986, Sept. 1994.
7. J.Park and S.Inoue, "Toward occlusion-free depth estimation for video production," *Proc. Intl' Workshop on New Video Media Technology'97*, pp.131-136, Tokyo, Japan, Jan. 1997.
8. J.Park and S.Inoue, "Arbitrary view generation using multiple cameras," *Proc. IEEE ICIP'97*, vol.I, pp.149-153, Santa Barbara, USA, Oct. 1997.
9. E.Adelson, J.Wang, and S.Niyogi, "Mid-level vision: New directions in vision and video," *Proc. IEEE ICIP'94*, pp.21-25, Austin, USA, Nov. 1994.

Pop-Out Videos

Gianpaolo U. Carraro, John T. Edmark, J. Robert Ensor

Bell Laboratories
101 Crawfords Corner Road, Holmdel, New Jersey USA
paolo@bell-labs.com, edmark@bell-labs.com, jre@bell-labs.com

Abstract. This paper discusses a class of multimedia displays that we call *pop-out videos*. A pop-out video is a composition of multiple elementary displays. Some of these base elements are video streams, and some are three-dimensional graphic displays. The elementary displays of a pop-out video may be related in two ways. They may be contiguous portions of a single virtual world, forming what we call an *integrated video space*. Alternatively, they may be parts of distinct spaces, forming what we call a *complementary video space*. In both cases, the elementary displays are related to each other by coordinated event handling. In our on-going research, we are using pop-out videos to create multimedia virtual worlds and to orchestrate the presentation of data in multiple media. After a survey of related work, the paper outlines our initial implementations of pop-out videos and presents future plans.

1 Introduction

We are building *pop-out videos*. These are multimedia displays that combine video streams and three-dimensional graphic displays. The elementary displays of a pop-out video may be related in two ways. They may be contiguous portions of a single virtual world, forming what we call an *integrated video space*. Alternatively, they may be parts of distinct spaces, forming what we call a *complementary video space*. In both cases, the elementary displays are related to each other by coordinated event handling.

Fig. 1. Integrated Video Space   **Fig. 2.** Complementary Video Space

Figure 1 shows an integrated video space created by Peloton [1]—a sports simulator that creates virtual courses for bicycle rides. The central portion of this view is a video stream, which is displayed as a texture on a large rectangle—a two-dimensional video "screen." In the surrounding display, three-dimensional graphic elements represent the road and some roadside objects. The bicyclist avatars represent multiple simulation participants. As they explore this virtual world, users move through the three-dimensional synthetic terrain and view photo-realistic scenery.

Figure 2 illustrates an example of a complementary video space. In this case, the video display and the graphical display are not composed into a single virtual world. Rather, these displays are related only by their integrated responses to system events. This golf instruction program helps students associate the techniques of good golfers with the motions of simpler graphical figures. Students watch video clips showing golfers—who have exemplary technique—swing clubs to hit balls; they also watch three-dimensional humanoid figures demonstrate corresponding animations. By viewing both presentations, students learn to monitor the most important elements of successful club swings.

In our current research, we are creating new techniques to build pop-out videos and to orchestrate the presentation of data in multiple media. We are learning more about how to design and assemble collections of multimedia displays, and we are investigating ways to use them.

2 Background

A variety of applications integrate three-dimensional graphics with still images or video clips. Photographs are commonly used as textures and background elements in three-dimensional virtual worlds. In addition, image based modeling techniques, *e.g.*, [2] and [3], permit creation of three-dimensional models from two-dimensional photographs. However, these applications do not represent three-dimensional spaces with video, and they do not permit objects to move between graphical regions and video regions in response to user input/output events.

Virtual sets, *e.g.*, [4], [5], also combine video and three-dimensional graphics. In [6], live actors can move within computer-generated settings. Augmented reality systems, *e.g.*, [7], demonstrate another combination of these media; they lay computer-generated graphics over video inputs. The Interspace system [8], which supports multiparty conferences on the Internet, creates virtual spaces in which avatars have live video streams as "heads." [9] discusses virtual reality systems, containing video displays, in which the relative importance of model elements (objects) is specified and used as a quality-of-service control for video transmission. These examples represent steps towards integrated video spaces; however, they do not use video for the representation of spaces within three-dimensional graphic models. Television and Web documents can be combined with WebTV devices [10]. However, these devices do not create complementary video spaces because they do not provide any association between the television programming and the Web based materials.

The MPEG-4 standard proposal [11] is expected to allow specification of video graphical hybrid environments. Its video based objects might form an appropriate infrastructure for pop-out videos.

3 Integrated Video Spaces

An integrated video space represents some parts of a virtual world as three-dimensional objects and other parts of the same world as still images or video. Because these displays are parts of the same virtual world, we call them *regions* of the world. The size, shape, and position of each region is calibrated with its neighboring regions to create visual unity of the composite space. A common set of controls and integrated event handling mechanisms are associated with the single world. Objects can move from one part of an integrated video space to another. Hence, we must handle the movement of objects between graphical and video regions. We have developed two techniques to deal with these inter-regional object movements.

In the first technique, when an object moves from one region to another, the medium used to represent that object correspondingly changes. The new medium matches the one used to represent the other objects in the new region. For example, when an object goes from a three-dimensional region into a video-based one, it becomes a video element. We call this transform a *merge-in* because, in a sense, the object has "merged into" the video panel.

Figure 1 illustrates a world in which an avatar has moved from a graphical region into a video region and has become a video element. Figure 3 is a behind-the-scenes view of the same merge-in. On the far left, a semi-transparent avatar represents the red cyclist's "real" position in the virtual world. In conventional three-dimensional worlds, the video panel would occlude the yellow cyclist's view of the red cyclist's position. However, by performing the merge-in, Peloton allows the red cyclist to remain visible to the yellow cyclist. Using the red cyclist's real position, the animation system translates and scales the red cyclist's video panel for the yellow cyclist's view. Figures 5 shows a close-up from this point of view.

In our second technique, we permit objects to be designated as *traceable objects*. When a traceable object moves from a three-dimensional region to video panel, it does not become a video element. Instead, it is replaced in the three-dimensional foreground by a *trace object*. A trace object is an element of the foreground that represents an object "behind" the video panel. Figure 4 shows the same scene as Figure 3, but this time a trace object is used to maintain the red cyclist's visibility. The animation system translates, scales, and maintains orientation of the trace object

Fig. 3. Behind-the-Scenes View of a Merge-In

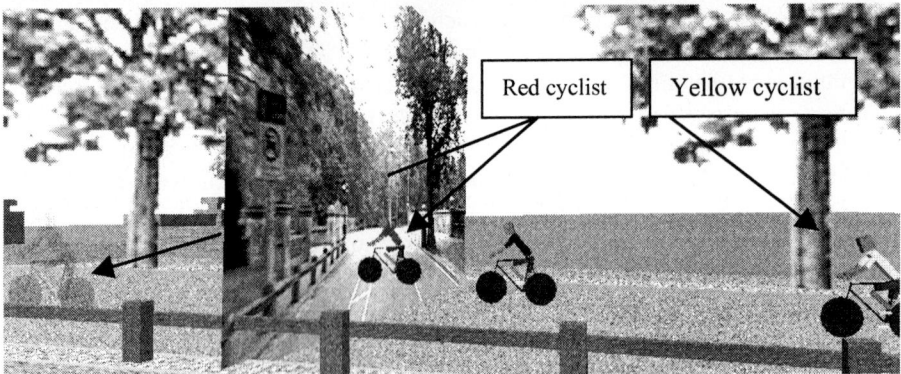

Fig. 4. Behind-the-Scenes View of a Trace

Fig. 5. Yellow's View of a Merge-In   **Fig. 6.** Yellow's View of a Trace

for the yellow cyclist's view, according to the red cyclist's real position. From the yellow cyclist's viewpoint, it is not possible to distinguish between the "real avatar" and the trace object. Figure 6 shows a close-up of the yellow cyclist's view of the scene.

4 Complementary Video Spaces

In this type of pop-out video, the video display does not integrate with other displays to form a single virtual world. Rather, the displays are related only through their coordinated response to the events that their common application handles. Without visual unity of a composite space, the common control interface and integrated event handling are created as distinct system components. Without regions for a common space, objects do not seamlessly move from one display to another. However, the elements represented in these regions are related through system actions.

In Figure 2, both regions display the same golfer but in different media. On the left-hand side, the golfer is represented as video, whereas on the right-hand side, it is represented as a three-dimensional humanoid. This configuration allows users to manipulate elements, *i.e.* the golfer, in one region and to see the effects in both regions. Multiple representations of data is not a new concept. What is new in complementary video spaces is the ability to associate manipulations in a graphical region to the ones in a video region (and vice-versa). For example, playing back the video stream of the golfer may trigger the animation of the humanoid. When the two regions respond "in synch," users experience the photo-realistic view of the video and also see the humanoid's swing from several viewpoints. Handling of events can also result in asynchronous responses.

To implement the environment described above, complementary video systems must provide users with a set of controls to perform the manipulations. Also, these systems must be able to "translate" the manipulations performed in one region to the corresponding ones in the other region.

5 Future Work and Conclusion

Pop-out videos provide apparent benefits in building virtual worlds as well as displaying information in multiple media. Shopping applications, similar to the golf program described above, could allow shoppers to pick objects from a video catalog or a commercial video and see them in other forms, or pick them from other regions and see them displayed in a video. Also, media melding techniques can be used within a multimedia virtual world to implement multimedia level-of-detail. For example, a surveillance application could display a region near the viewer (camera) in video, while displaying more distant areas through other media. Pop-out videos could enhance television programming by coupling video with information represented in other media. The closed caption (subtitle) concept of today's television allows text to be associated with video content. This concept can be extended to associate other information—displayed in other media—with video content. For example, hyper-textual Web documents and three-dimensional virtual worlds could be associated with video programming content. Various suppliers, including the producers of the original programming content or specialized providers, could supply these additional materials. In fact, several collections of additional material could be available for each program. Consumers could then select their preferred collections.

Pop-out videos can also be used to build distributed virtual worlds that react to performance constraints. Since region boundaries within a virtual world can vary dynamically, the relative media mix of a world can vary correspondingly. This variation provides an opportunity to tailor applications and their presentation of information to the needs and resources of the system user. For example, it could improve the performance of a distributed application executing on heterogeneous computers connected via the Internet. Application users with powerful machines but poor network connections could take advantage of their computing power by specifying that a virtual world be presented mainly as three-dimensional objects rendered locally. On the other hand, users with network computers—offering high-end network connections but less processing power—could specify that the scene be presented using minimal three-dimensional representation to view most of the scene as streamed video.

Although many issues still need to be resolved, these examples show that the integration of video in richer multimedia environments could open the doors of a very large set of interactive multimedia applications.

References

1. Carraro, G., Cortes, M., Edmark, J., and Ensor, J., "The Peloton Bicycling Simulator," Proc. VRML '98, Monterey, CA, 16-19 February, 1998.
2. Debevec, P., Taylor, C., and Malik, J., "Modeling and Rendering Architecture from Photographs: A hybrid geometry- and image-based approach," Proc. SIGGRAPH 96, 4-9 August, 1996, New Orleans, LA, pp. 11-20.
3. McMillan, L. and Bishop, G., "Plenoptic Modeling: An Image-Based Rendering System," Proc. SIGGRAPH 95, 6-11 August, 1995, Los Angeles, CA, pp. 39-46.
4. 3DK: The Virtual Studio. In GMD Web Site: http://viswiz.gmd.de/DML/vst/vst.html
5. Katkere, A., Moessi, S., Kuramura, D., Kelly, P., and Jain, R., "Towards Video-based Immersive Environments," Multimedia Systems, May 1997, pp. 69-85.
6. Thalmann, N., and Thalmann, D., "Animating Virtual Actors in Real Environments," Multimedia Systems, May 1997, pp. 113-125.
7. Feiner, S., Macintyre, B., and Seligmann, D., "Knowledge-Based Augmented Reality," Communications of the ACM, (36, 7), June 1993, pp. 53-62.
8. Interspace VR Browser. In NTT Software Corp. Web Site: http://www.ntts.com Interspace
9. Oh, S., Sugano, H., Fujikawa, K., Matsuura, T., Shimojo, S., Arikawa, M., and Miyahara, H., "A Dynamic QoS Adaptation Mechanism for Networked Virtual Reality," Proc. Fifth IFIP International Workshop on Quality of Service, New York, May 1997, pp. 397-400.
10. WebTV. In WebTV Site: http://www.webtv.net
11. MPEG Home Page. In http://drogo.cselt.stet.it/mpeg

Color Segmentation and Color Correction Using Lighting and White Balance Shifts

Philippe Gérard, Clifton Phillips, and Ramesh Jain

Visual Computing Lab. ECE building,
University of California, San Diego,
La Jolla CA 92037, USA

Abstract. A method was developed to segment an image foreground and background based on color content. This work presents an alternative to the standard blue-screen technique (weather man method) by exploiting the color shifts of light sources and filtering each camera lens and correcting white balances for each camera. we compressed the colors of the scene background into a chromaticity subspace to make the foreground-background segmentation easier to perform. The segmentation is singular decomposition (SVD) based.

Keywords: Color Segmentation, Blue Screen, 3D Shooting, Virtual Reality, Chroma-key.

1 Introduction

Applications demanding an automatic video stream segmentation are numerous. One of the most famous is the blue screen (weather man) method where a subject situated in front of a uniform blue wall or cycloid, is overlaid on an other image by an automatic chroma -key segmentation. In television productions, the blue screen is used in a studio environment and allows limited possible positions and orientations for the cameras. In virtual Reality applications such as the MPIV [1], one wants to segment a foreground subject from a background scene using the perspective of an arbitrarily positioned and orientated camera, building a 360 degrees blue screen is not usually feasible, as it would imply to paint an entire sphere in blue, position the subject inside and provide holes for each camera lens. Additionally, the blue screen method requires particular attention for shadows projected on the blue wall and the quality of the segmentation depends on the uniformity of the light spread on the background.

In our approach, the lighting of the background is more tolerant. This claim is justified because we do not have dark surfaces which generate noise. Our method is simple to realize in practice, and doesn't require caution on background lighting in terms of uniformity and shades of illumination. Another important improvement is that someone can wear blue clothes and still be segmented correctly. We can adapt the segmentation to the subject and the background scene instead of imposing constraints on the actors clothes and background colors. This provides new flexibility. We show that our method could be extended to a standard outdoor shooting with few constraints which could make it very useful.

This work provides three important benefits. It (1) provides another solution to the foreground-background segmentation problem by using local lighting conditions to force a separation of colors in the chromaticity color subspace; it (2) discusses the use of the white balance and exploits the relationship between white balance shift and the color tint; and (3) finally provides a solution for correcting a wrong camera white balance acquired in the data. Section 2 discusses the theory and development of the concepts used to support this work. Section 3 covers the color correction techniques. Section 4 discusses an SVD based segmentation and color clustering method. Section 5 describes the experiments we conducted and provides a discussion and conclusion of the results.

2 Theory and Concept Development

Understanding the results we present here requires a clear understanding of realizing the color shift through filtering and shifting of the camera white balance. In addition, the physics of the light sources, the appropriate filters, and their impact on the color compression in the chromaticity color sub-space must be understood. Finally all of the image data is acquired by a camera, therefore, the pit-falls of data acquisition using "off-the-shelf" and "broadcast quality" cameras should also be explored.

2.1 The Color Shift

Instead of shooting a subject in front of a specific colored background, we change the spectrum of the foreground light by applying a colored filter in front of the bulb. If we correct this shift only for the foreground and not for the background we "compress" the entire background in a region of the color space. There are two ways of doing this:

- Tuning the white balance of the camera(s) on the temperature of color of all the bulbs involved in the shooting (usually 3200 K for indoor lights, we used FAD 650W). Adding a filter on the lens of the camera, this filter is an opposite color of the one positioned on the foreground lights. We did two tests in using some Rosco filters :
  1. Test 1: Full blue (#3202 : boosts 3200 K to 5500K) on foreground lights and Roscosun85 (#3401:converts 5500K to 3200K) on the camera lens.
  2. Test2: Half blue (#3204K boosts 3200 K to 4100K) on foreground lights and Roscosun half CTO (#3408: Converts 5500K to 3800K) on the camera lens.

In these experiments, we used almost complementary filters , then because this completion is far from perfect the result of the correction will be a little bit tinted orange: a not desired shift that we could correct by the color correction method explained further.

– A second method for doing this, is to adjust the camera white balance to the light spread by the foreground sources (having the half blue or full blue filter on) . This method is usefull only for correcting small shifts.However, it gives some better results.

2.2 Light Sources

The filters were not the unique color shifts: Actually the white of equal energy doesn't exit, all the white lights we can see are in fact more or less tinted. An approximation of the spectrum of the white lights bulbs is given by the Planck's equation:

$$E(\lambda) = c_1 \lambda^{-5}(e^{c_2/\lambda T} - 1)^{-1} W.m^{-3} \qquad (1)$$

Where $c_1 = 3.7415.10\text{-}16 \ W.m^2$ and $c_2 = 1.4388.10\text{-}2 \ m.K$. T is the temperature of color of the source: the color of the source is usually described by the equivalent Planckian radiator. In our experiments, the bulbs had a temperature of color of 3200K(indoor lights). Applying some colored filters to a source is equivalent to a product of the light spectrum and the spectral transmission features of the filter.Figure 1 shows the spectrum of the light spread on the foreground. Several

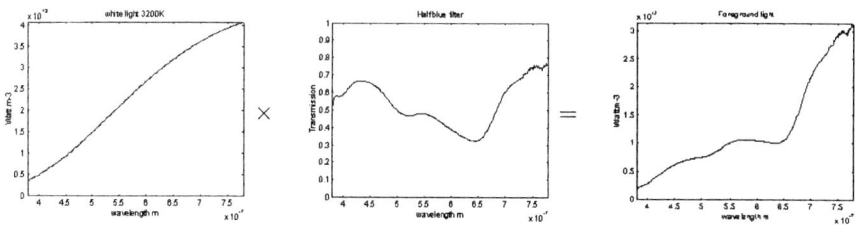

Fig. 1. Resulting light spectrum from a half blue filter added on a 3200K white light; (a)spectrum of the 3200K white light: f(λ); (b) transmission features of the half blue filter: g(λ); and (c) the resulting foreground light spectrum f(λ)g(λ).

spectra may create the same stimulus, this principle is called "metamerism". This phenomena is widely used in video to synthesize a specific color from only 3 rays of colored lights. For example consider the red, green and blue primaries. References [2][3][5][6][4] gives a good basis to start with.

Another representation of a light source passing through a filter would be a mixture of only one ray of a pure color and a white of equivalent energy. Here the tint is given by the wavelength of the ray, the saturation is given by the percentage of white added to this color, and the intensity is given by the total energy of this mixture. In order to obtain this new representation which is easier to interpret, we need to compute a product of convolution of the spectrum of a stimulus and the three curves of the sensitivity of a standard human vision system. The CIE has defined a set of three curves $(\bar{r}, \bar{g}, \bar{b})$ or $(\bar{x}, \bar{y}, \bar{z})$ [7][8][9] giving the sensitivity of a standard "eye" to a specific color. Thus, we obtain:

$$X = k \int_\infty R(\lambda)E(\lambda)\bar{x}(\lambda)d\lambda$$
$$Y = k \int_\infty R(\lambda)E(\lambda)\bar{y}(\lambda)d\lambda$$
$$Z = k \int_\infty R(\lambda)E(\lambda)\bar{z}(\lambda)d\lambda \qquad (2)$$
$$k = \frac{100}{\int_\lambda E(\lambda)\bar{y}(\lambda)d\lambda}$$

Where E is the illumination source, R is the spectral reflectance factor, and X,Y and Z, are the tristimulus values in the CIE representation. We can now represent the stimulus in the CIE chromaticity diagram (x,y). In the example below, we are studying how shift the light source, then we'll consider that on the entire visible spectrum.

$$x = \frac{X}{X+Y+Z}, y = \frac{Y}{X+Y+Z}, z = 1 - x - y \qquad (3)$$

The Figure 2 shows how to get the tint of a stimulus Wh, by computing the

Table 1. x,y coordinates in the CIE chromaticity subspace of the lights and filters

	Light 3200K	Light 3200K with a Half blue filter	Light 3200K with a Full blue filter
x	0.4234	0.3808	0.3387
y	0.3991	0.3806	0.3316

intersection of the line joining the white of equal energy (E) and the studied color (Wh) and the boundary of the CIE curves. For the purple colors, which do

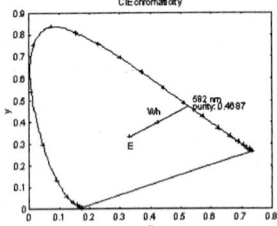

Purity of excitation: $P = \dfrac{\sqrt{(x_{wh} - x_{\scriptscriptstyle E})^2 + (y_{wh} - y_{\scriptscriptstyle E})^2}}{\sqrt{(x_b - x_{\scriptscriptstyle E})^2 + (y_b - y_{\scriptscriptstyle E})^2}}$

where:
x_{wh}, y_{wh} are the coordinates of the studied color.
x_b, y_b are the coordinates of the line E-Wh and the CIE boundary
$x_{\scriptscriptstyle E}, y_{\scriptscriptstyle E}$ are the coordinates of the Equienergy white E.

Fig. 2. Interpretation of a shifted white in the CIE diagram.

not correspond to a unique ray of light, we will use $-\lambda$ for describing the tint (this is actually the tint of the opposite color). Since the purity of excitation has some interesting geometric properties, we'll use it later for the color correction, but the colorimetric purity is more precise, this is the one will use here.

$$\rho = \frac{L_b}{L_b + L_e} = \frac{1 - \frac{x_{wh}}{y_{wh}}}{1 - \frac{x_b}{y_b}} \qquad (4)$$

Where L_e is the luminance of the white E and L_b the luminance of the pure color on the boundary of the CIE diagram. For adding two stimuli we know also that:

$$\begin{array}{lll} L_{wh} = L_b + L_e & \text{or} & Y_{wh} = Y_b + Y_e \\ X_{wh} = X_b + X_e & \text{and} & Z_{wh} = Z_b + Z_e \\ X = x\frac{Y}{y} & \text{and} & Z = z\frac{Y}{y} \end{array} \quad (5)$$

Then, knowing the x and y values for Wh, B and E, we can resolve a system of three equations for determining the luminance values and then the purity chromatic. One may choose $L_b = 1$, since we just need to compute the relative luminances.

Then, a stimulus may be represented as an addition of two stimuli: a part of achromatic light (E) and a part of a pure color light (B).

Since we are only considering the light source the reflection is 100% on the entire spectrum. , the resulting stimulus (Wh) is given by: (we will only do the proof for X, since Y and Z are similar)

$$X_{Wh} = (1 - \rho)X_E + \rho X_B \quad (6)$$

This interpretation replaces any colored stimulus by an addition of an equal energy white and a pure color ray. These relationships are very useful for correcting a color shift.

Our goal is to segment automatically a subject situated in the foreground of a scene. If we light the foreground with a blue light and the background with a 3200K light, the background requires lighting with a more "orange light" than the foreground. This effect will shift the color of the background toward the orange yellowish region of the chromaticity subspace. If we correct the foreground light at the camera the result will be a normal foreground while the background gets compressed into a selected region of the chromaticity subspace.

The first way of doing so is to tune the white balance of the camera on 3200K and filming through an orange filter complementary to the blue filter on the foreground lights. If the filters are really complementary, the foreground light is perceived white (3200K) and the entire background is shifted in orange, With full blue filters on the foreground lights and a full orange filter on the camera lens, the background is shifted of a full orange while the foreground appears correctly white balanced. In fact, in our experiments this correction is not perfect because the filters were not "exactly" complementary. There are no perfect complementary filters commercially available at this time. Next we present a way of correcting a shifted image after being segmented.

One might be interested in shifting the background by more than one full orange in order to perform a better segmentation based on color. It is possible to add some full orange filters on the background lights. In this case the background will be shifted twice of full orange which makes the background completely compressed in the orange subspace of the CIE representation.

Our method implies more power to lighten the foreground than in a blue screen method, for instance, If the light source is an equal energy light, and the filters applied on the light source and lens are respectively a full blue and a full orange filter, the camera will see only 10 to 30% of the energy of the light source. However ideals filters (spectrum of the correction flat for every λ) could make the camera see 50% of the source energy. We used another way for correcting the shift loosing less energy, using a white balance correction instead of a full orange filter on the lenses.

Some very interesting features are positioning this method as an alternative to the popular blue screen method. As the reader has probably noticed, we don't need to have a particular background. The best scenario would be to lighten the background with its most complementary color. This method doesn't demand a perfectly uniform light on a blue wall. Lightening it will be enough. Like in the chroma -key process, the black surfaces will be a difficult part to process because black is very sensitive to noise in color. In our post processing correction we remove the black under a threshold and replace them by interpolation using the neighbors of the removed area.

This method can also work for outdoor scenes. When photographers are usually using golden reflectors to simulate a sunset, they are in fact shifting the foreground with a light tinted differently that the background. A correction on the lens is done by the complementary filter to the reflector.

2.3 The Cameras

A stimulus is realized with three rays of light only, the values R,G and B are in fact a percentage of the primaries to mix to get a equivalent stimulus.

The camera is able to adjust its white balance in function of the tint of the light source. The following equations relate the R,G,B (video values) to the CIE tristimulus values X,Y and Z (it will be useful for the color correction process):

$$\begin{bmatrix} R \\ G \\ B \end{bmatrix} = \begin{bmatrix} K_r & 0 & 0 \\ 0 & K_g & 0 \\ 0 & 0 & K_b \end{bmatrix}^{-1} \begin{bmatrix} x_r & x_g & x_b \\ y_r & y_g & y_b \\ z_r & z_g & z_b \end{bmatrix}^{-1} \begin{bmatrix} X \\ Y \\ Z \end{bmatrix} \quad (7)$$

with:

$$\begin{bmatrix} K_r \\ K_g \\ K_b \end{bmatrix} = \frac{1}{y_w} \begin{bmatrix} x_r & x_g & x_b \\ y_r & y_g & y_b \\ z_r & z_g & z_b \end{bmatrix}^{-1} \begin{bmatrix} x_w \\ y_w \\ z_w \end{bmatrix} \quad (8)$$

where $x_r,y_r,z_r,x_g,y_g,z_g,x_b,y_b,z_b,x_w,y_w$ and z_w are respectively, the coordinates of the red, green and blue primaries in NTSC and of the white of reference.

The second possibility to correct the shift done by the blue filter on the foreground light, is to adjust the white balance on the new color obtained by the source + the filter. We choose to put the blue filter on the lights because the white at 3200K of the bulb is boosted to 4000K (half blue filter) and 5000K (full blue filter) which makes the white balance possible.

In this case , as expected, the only absorption of light is done by the blue filter. The result is better than the one we got in the former method. Here the foreground shift is properly corrected, and the background is then shifted in orange the same way. The limit of this method is the possibility for the camera to do the white balance. For instance, a camera is not able to correct a shift done by a orange filter on the 3200K light, but would be perfectly able to correct a shift done by an orange filter on HMI lights.

A mixture of the two methods might be worth to use.

3 Color Correction

We propose the following method to perform a correction in order to ameliorate an image, or in order to retrieve a color shift due to non-complementary filters in the first method. This color correction may also interest those who are concern by a video sequence acquired with a poor white balanced and want to retrieve a more acceptable result.

We will try to simulate the real stimuli, based on the data we acquired. The first step is to find the real white of the image we are analyzing. This may be given manually by indicating a white of reference, or automatically if one has shot a color bars, which is the case in our experiments. We used a 75% color bar chart with 100% white reference, in order to create a model for our camera for some particular shifts. We first shot the chart under the 3200K lights and tuned the white balance to get the best white as possible on the vector scope. This chart is then our reference for the visible spectrum. In further work we will probably design our own chart including more colors (a wheel of 300 calibrated colors). After shooting this chart once under the reference light, and a second time under the shifted light, we are able to create a robust model of the camera used and for a particular shift. Our current model is only using 6 colors for interpolating the entire spectrum, but the correction obtained is already quite interesting.

Using the representation of color extracted from the color bar, we first retrieve the correct tint of the stimuli. Next we correct the purity of the color obtained using our model. Some post processing are applied in order to treat the blacks differently.

3.1 White Retrieval

Here we describe how to correct a half orange shift. With the inverse matrix (7), we compute the position of the mean of the 100% white in CIE chromaticity diagram. The following discussion defines C as the white of reference.

$$WhHO = \begin{bmatrix} x = 0.3486 & y = 0.3517 \end{bmatrix}$$

An interesting way of correcting the shifted color bars is to find the stimulus complementary to the white we found here, and use this new value as the white appearing in equation (8).

We are looking for the stimulus which gives the white C when mixed with the white shifted above.

$$X_c = X_{co} + X_{ho}, \qquad Y_c = Y_{co} + Y_{ho}, \qquad Z_c = Z_{co} + Z_{ho}$$

Where indices c,co and ho correspond to the white C, stimulus complementary and the white shifted . We can choose arbitrarily $Y_c = 1$, because we are just interested by the relative luminance. Then, the equations above become:

$$\frac{x_c}{y_c} = \frac{x_{co}}{y_{co}} Y_{co} + \frac{x_{ho}}{y_{ho}} Y_{ho}, \qquad 1 = Y_{co} + Y_{ho}, \qquad \frac{z_c}{y_c} = \frac{z_{co}}{y_{co}} Y_{co} + \frac{z_{ho}}{y_{ho}} Y_{ho}$$

with $z_c = 1 - x_c - y_c$, $\qquad z_{ho} = 1 - x_{ho} - y_{ho}$, $\qquad z_{co} = 1 - x_{co} - y_{co}$

we find the three stimuli are on the same line having this following equation:

$y_{co} = ax_{co} + b$. $\qquad$ where $a = \frac{y_{ho} - y_c}{x_{ho} - x_c}$, $\qquad$ and $b = y_c - ax_c$

Now take the complementary stimulus to W_{ho} ,which has the same luminance: $Y_{co} = Y_{ho}$ (W_{co} and W_{ho} will be in the same luminance plane).
Then: $Y_c = 2Y_{ho}$, or $Y_{ho} = Y_{co} = \frac{1}{2} Y_c$. We get $x_{co} = 0.2787$ and $y_{co} = 0.2872$.

Now, we convert the RGB values to XYZ stimuli using the inverse matrix of equation (7) and using x_{co}, y_{co} and z_{co} as the white. Figure 3 compares the new stimuli, the reference color bars and the shifted color bars. We have represented

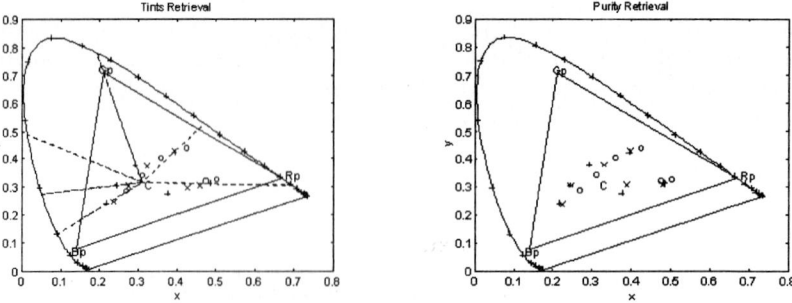

Fig. 3. (a)Representation of the retrieval of the tints of an half orange shifted color bars chart.(b)Result of the purity correction in the CIE diagram(+: represents the Reference color bars coordinates, O: the Half orange shifted color bars and X: the Corrected color bars

the tints of the reference color bars (dotted lines). Figure 3a shows that the green and magenta are a little bit different from what they should be , but the other tints are pretty correctly retrieved.

This result is not yet what we want. Even if the tints are almost correct, the purity of these colors are quite different of the reference color bars purity. The next step is to realize a filter of purity.

Figure 4a represents the purity filter, where the angles express the tints and the norm , the ratio $\frac{\rho_{ref}(\lambda)}{\rho_{ho}(\lambda)}$. $rho_{ref}(\lambda)$. We used only six colors to generate this function by interpolation. This function is related to the real sensitivity curves of our camera. This representation is quite the same as the Hue representation in the HIS color space. The result of color correction is presented in Figure 3b.

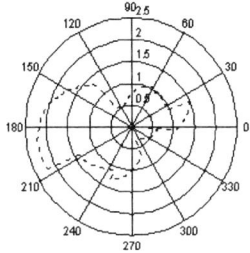 

Fig. 4. (a) Vector scope representation of the purity filter,(b) image to segment

4 Segmentation Using the SVD Method

We choose a sample from the background to apply a statistical method to segment the scene. Therefore if a new object appears in the foreground it is not necessary to change our scene background-based initialization. We classified the shifted colors using a SVD method of segmentation. A clustering method was used to group the shifted colors into sensible sets in the color space. The SVD was applied to each cluster and resulted in characterizing each grouped color with parameters of a 2-sigma ellipsoid. The ellipsoid is projected onto the chromaticity subspace.

4.1 Applying the SVD Segmentation

The singular value decomposition provides two benefits in this work[10]. First, we exploit the idea that the covariance of a color sample can be factored into $C = ULV^t$. Here, the matrix U represents a natural basis for the axes along the principal components. U^t is the linear transformation from the sampled basis to the natural basis of the principal components. Second, the variance along the principal components are given by the singular values in L. The variance is scaled by an arbitrary constant k^2. In this association k is related to the desired sigma value that characterizes the color sample.

4.2 Clustering

Early testing showed backgrounds that were widely spread across the chromaticity sub-space resulted in clusters that were too large. We applied a clustering method to deal with this issue. A clustering method such as the K-means algorithm [11] can be applied to the shifted colors. We used a modified version of the K-means algorithm. The entire background is first sampled. The singular value decomposition is applied to decompose the color sample covariance matrix into its principal components. Singular values provided by the SVD represent the variance for the principal components. We evaluate the variance against a threshold. If the maximum singular is higher than the selected threshold, the data is split along a hyper-plane that is orthogonal to the principal axis with the maximum variance. The process is re-iterated for each resulting cluster until each the singular values for each cluster are within the threshold constraints. We found the results are not appreciably different from one color space to another.

4.3 Segmenting a Clustered Color Sample

Consider extracting a sample set of m RGB points from a target, where the RGB color space is defined based on the NTSC receiver primary system definition. Each pixel sampled can be represented at a coordinate in RGB color space. The sampled mean for each set in RGB is determined as:

$$\hat{x} = \begin{bmatrix} \hat{r} & \hat{g} & \hat{b} \end{bmatrix}^t = \frac{1}{N} \begin{bmatrix} \sum_{i=1}^{m} r_i & \sum_{i=1}^{m} g_i & \sum_{i=1}^{m} b_i \end{bmatrix}^t \qquad (9)$$

where the entries of $\begin{bmatrix} \hat{r} & \hat{g} & \hat{b} \end{bmatrix}^t$ represents the means of each RGB component within the set of interest. First consider applying this technique to one set of sampled data, then the result shown can be extended to multiple sets where a sample has been partitioned into multiple sub-clusters. The variance can be used to establish a best ellipsoid in RGB space that contains the desired set of RGB pixels. Before any variance can be computed, it is necessary to carry out a transformation to a new basis centered about the sampled mean. The new basis is to be lined up with an estimate of the best principal axis of the sampled data. The transformation extracted from the SVD guarantees the estimated principal component axes are orthogonal. Therefore the statistics are de-coupled when estimated along the principal component axes.

Each RGB point consists of three values corresponding to the red, green, and blue components of color space. Let the set of n RGB points be formed into a matrix A, where A is $m \times n$, with $m = 3$, and $n \geq m$. Consider translating the RGB axis by $-\hat{x}$ such that the set of sampled points is transformed to a zero-mean set along its principal components by $B = U^t(A - \hat{x})$ where the transformation U is found from implementing the SVD.

Let C be the covariance matrix for all the sampled RGB data points represented as the columns of A. For each sampled set of data, the entries for the covariance matrix C are given as in (10).

$$C = \begin{bmatrix} C_{rr} & C_{gr} & C_{br} \\ C_{rg} & C_{gg} & C_{bg} \\ C_{rb} & C_{gb} & C_{bb} \end{bmatrix} \qquad (10)$$

where: $C_{rr} = \frac{1}{N}\sum_{i=1}^{N}(r_i - \hat{r})^2$, $C_{gg} = \frac{1}{N}\sum_{i=1}^{N}(g_i - \hat{g})^2$, $C_{bb} = \frac{1}{N}\sum_{i=1}^{N}(b_i - \hat{b})^2$.
and $C_{rg} = C_{gr} = \frac{1}{N}\sum i = 1^N (r_i g_i) - \hat{r}\hat{g}$ $\quad C_{rb} = C_{br} = \frac{1}{N}\sum i = 1^N (r_i b_i) - \hat{r}\hat{b}$
$C_{bg} = C_{gb} = \frac{1}{N}\sum i = 1^N (b_i g_i) - \hat{b}\hat{(g)}$.

It is interesting to note that U is the same, weather the SVD is performed on the data itself or the covariance matrix. The importance is that the columns of U span the space of A and are the desired orthogonal basis vectors corresponding to the principal values for the transformed ellipsoid. The data contained in A can be transformed to the zero-mean set $(A - \hat{x})$. The RGB column vectors in matrix A get transformed into the new range space B by (9) where B is $m \times n$, with $m = 3$, and $n \geq m$.

$$B = U^t(A - \hat{x}) \tag{11}$$

The matrix B contains the transformed vectors $\begin{bmatrix} \rho & \gamma & \beta \end{bmatrix}^t$. The sampled data is assumed to be normally distributed. The transformed data contained in B is aligned with the principal axes and the variance of the data can be found from (12).

$$\sigma_\rho^2 = \frac{\sum_{k=1}^{N}(\sigma_{\rho_k} - \hat{\sigma}_\rho)^2}{N-1} \quad \sigma_\gamma^2 = \frac{\sum_{k=1}^{N}(\sigma_{\gamma_k} - \hat{\sigma}_\gamma)^2}{N-1} \quad \sigma_\beta^2 = \frac{\sum_{k=1}^{N}(\sigma_{\beta_k} - \hat{\sigma}_\beta)^2}{N-1} \tag{12}$$

It is easy to show the result of equation (12) can be obtained directly by applying the SVD to the covariance matrix C instead of the data itself. As previously stated, the transformation U will be identical, however the singular values obtained from implementing this method on the matrix C are the variances σ_ρ^2, σ_γ^2, σ_β^2. These variances represent the eigenvalues of the covariance matrix C.

4.4 Establishing Sets of Probable Points

Each of the three values of the variance determined by applying the SVD represents the intersection of the one-sigma ellipsoid with either the semi-major or one of the semi-minor axes. An ellipsoid was selected as the bounding geometry because the location of its bounding surface is well understood when the data is normally distributed. Using these one-sigma values as characteristic parameters describing the boundary of a set of interest means that 63% of the sampled data falls within the set. Scaling the sigma values by two or three respectively results in 86% and 95% of the sampled data falling within the set. There is a trade-off with the selection of a scale value for the sigma value. One would like to hypothesize that any arbitrary pixel mapped into the established boundary from the transformation actually belongs to the set. For higher-scaled values of sigma there is a higher likelihood that a pixel classified in the set does not belong. There are four possible outcomes to the hypothesis test:
(1) A pixel identified as belonging to the set of interest belongs to the set. (2) A pixel identified as belonging to the set of interest does not belong to the set. (3) A pixel identified as not belonging to the set of interest does belong to the set. (4) A pixel identified as not belonging to the set of interest does not belong to the set.

The estimated variances should be scaled to maximize the probability of conditions one and four, and minimize the probabilities of conditions two and three. Let the parameter k be the scaled value for the each σ_i.

5. Fink, D.G: Handbook for Television Engineering, 3rd edition, McGraw-Hill, Academic,(1984).
6. James, T.H: Theory of the photographic process, 4th ed., Macmillan, New York, (1977).
7. Commission International de L'eclairage: Colorimetry, Publication **15**, Paris, (1971).
8. De Marsh, L.E: Colorimetric Standards in US Color Television, J.SMPTE **83** (1974) 1-5.
9. Judd D.B: The 1931 CIE Standard observer and coordinate system for colorimetry, J.Opt.Soc.Am. **23** (1933) 359-374.
10. Press W.H, Teukolosky W.T, Vetterling W.T, Flanery B.P: Numerical Recipes in C-The Art of Scientific Computing, 2nd ed., Cambridge University Press (1995).
11. Hartigan J.A: Clustering Algorithms, Wiley, (1975).

Designing Emergence
in Animated Artificial Life Worlds

Jeffrey Ventrella

There Studios

Jeffrey@Ventrella.com
http://www.ventrella.com

Abstract. A methodology is described for designing real-time animated artificial life worlds consisting of populations of physically-based articulated creatures which evolve locomotion anatomy and motion over time. In this scheme, increasing levels of emergent behavior are enabled by designing more autonomy into the simulation on progressively deeper levels. A set of simulations are discussed to illustrate how this methodology was developed, with the most recent simulation demonstrating the effects of mate choice on the evolution of anatomies and motions in swimming creatures.

1 Introduction

The art of animation as invented by the Disney animators has been called "The Illusion of Life." It seems that Computer Animation as a craft has never really caught up to the expressivity, humor, and lifelike motion possible with classic cel-based character animation. The animators at Pixar have been successful at adapting computer technology to the fine art of classic character animation technique. But as feature film animators refine this marriage of new and old technologies, a new form of animated character emerges, not in the film industry but from within various artificial life labs. Add to Disney's "Illusion of Life," the "Simulation of Life," and witness a new technology–one which is compatible with the goals of Virtual Reality–a future cyberspace in which characters are not just animated: they are autonomous, reactive agents as well.

This paper describes an approach to artificial life (alife) [9], stemming from animated art and a design process for creating it. It is an exploration of autonomously generated motion and form. The original impetus is not biological science, although biology has become an important aspect of the work. The angle on alife discussed in the paper may provide ideas and techniques that are useful in creation of populated virtual worlds for entertainment, education, and research.

I will discuss a family of simulations which were built upon each other, in which populations of artificial creatures evolve anatomy and motion over time. In these simulations, emergent behavior is enabled by progressively designing levels of autonomy into the model. The simulations are used to illustrate how this methodology was built, with the most recent simulation demonstrating the effects of mate selection on the evolution of anatomies and motions in swimming creatures.

Future enhancements will include wiring up an evolvable nervous system connected to various sensors and actuators, within which neural net-like structures might emerge, potentially enabling the creatures to evolve higher-level stimulus-response mechanisms and "states of mind," which emerge through direct contact with the environment.

Design Considerations. A main goal of alife projects is to construct models in which self-organization and adaptive behaviors can arise spontaneously, not by design, but through emergence. A duality is observed in the creation of real-time alife worlds: while the goal of an alife simulation is emergence, it is ultimately a designed artifact. Creating alife worlds, in this methodology, is a matter of *designing emergence*.

One must choose a level of abstraction, below which a number of assumptions are made about the ontology supporting the model. Above this level of modeling, emergent phenomena arise as a product of the design of the subsystem when the model is run. For instance, many alife simulations model populations of organisms whose spatial positions are represented by locations in a cellular grid, and whose physical means of locomotion (jumping from cell to cell) are not clearly specified. The emergent properties in question may not require a deeper level of simulation than this. However, a simulation in which an articulated body plan is integral to locomotion (as well as reproduction) requires a lower level of abstraction, and a deeper physical model becomes necessary. More design may be required to build the simulation foundations, however, it may allow for more complex emergent phenomena.

Towards the quest for more autonomy, the most recent simulation in the set which I will discuss consists of a population of many hundreds of swimming creatures which animate in real-time. The creatures come in a large variety of anatomies and motion styles. They are able to mate with each other, and choose who has the "sexiest" motions, enabling evolution of swimming locomotion and anatomy which is attractive (beauty of course being in the eye of the beholder). The best swimmers reproduce their genes (because they can swim to a mate), and the most "attractive" swimmers get chosen as mates. In this simulation, not only are the aesthetics of motion and form subject to the chaotic nature of genetic evolution, but the creatures themselves partake in the choice of what forms and motions emerge.

The methodology discussed in this paper includes the following key components:

- a morphological scheme with an embryology
- a motor control scheme
- a physics
- a nervous system
- genetic evolution
- computer graphics rendering

Each of these components are described throughout the sections below. They are not explained in great technical depth, but rather discussed as a general methodology, with some commentary.

1.1 Related Work

Early examples of using alife principles in computer animation include *Boids* [12], in which complex life-like behaviors emerge from many interacting agents. Badler [2] describes physically-based modeling techniques and virtual motor control systems inspired by real animals used to automate many of the subtle, hard-to-design nuances of animal motion. In task-level animation [22] and the space-time constraints paradigm [21] these techniques allow an animator to direct a character on a higher level.

The genetic algorithm [7, 6] has been used for the evolution of goal-directed motion in physically-based animated figures, including a technique for evolving stimulus-response mechanisms for locomotion [10]. Sims [14, 15] has developed impressive techniques for the evolution of morphology and locomotion using the genetic programming paradigm [8]. Also, a holistic model of fish locomotion with perception, learning, and group behaviors, which generates beautifully realistic animations, was developed by Terzopoulos, Tu, and Grzeszczuk [16].

1.2 Walkers

The first project in the series began an attempt to build a 3D stick figure which could stand up by way of internal forces bending various joints. The original goal was to model a human-like form, but this was too large a task at the time. To simplify the problem, the bipedal figure was reduced to the simplest anatomy possible which can represent bipedal locomotion: two jointed sticks, called "Walker," shown in Figure 1a.

Performance artists Laurie Anderson once described walking as a continual process of catching oneself while almost falling, by placing one foot out in the direction of the fall, stopping the fall, and then almost-falling again [1]. This notion inspired the idea to construct a 3D bipedal figure which has mass and responds to gravity and which is always on the verge of falling over and so must continually move its legs in order to keep from falling, to stay upright, and to walk.

Walker's "head" experiences a pull in the direction of its goal (an inaccurate model of the desire to be somewhere else, yet sufficient for this exploration). Walker can perceive how much its body is tilting. The amount of tilt is used to modulate the motions in its legs. As it's head is pulled towards its goal, its legs move in such a way as to keep it upright and afford locomotion. Internal forces cause the legs to rotate about the *head joint*, back and forth, in periodic fashion, using sine functions. Parameters in the sine functions for each leg, such as amplitudes, frequencies, and phases, are genetically determined, varying among a population of Walkers, and are allowed to evolve over time within the population. Responses to body tilt are also genetically determined.

At the start, the motions of most of the Walkers are awkward and useless, with much aimless kicking, and so most of the Walkers immediately fall as soon as they are animated, although some are slightly better at staying upright for longer. By using a simplified genetic algorithm which repeatedly reproduces the best Walkers in the population, with chance mutations, and killing off the rest, the population improves locomotion skill over time.

To demonstrate Walker's ability to react to a constantly changing situation, a virtual "leash" was attached to the head, which a user could gently pull around. Also, scenarios were constructed in which multiple Walkers had attractions and repulsions to each other, generating novel pursuit and evasion behaviors.

Walker is the first in a series of alife creatures in this system consisting of linked-body parts which are connected at their ends and which can rotate about each other. Figure 1b shows a creature from a later simulation of 2D creatures consisting of five interconnected segments, with four effective joints. As in the case of Walker, rotations about the joints are controlled by sine functions with evolvable parameters. Fitness in this scheme is based on distance traveled. Although creatures in this population are 2D, locomotion is possible, with evolved populations consisting of creatures ambulating either to the left or to the right.

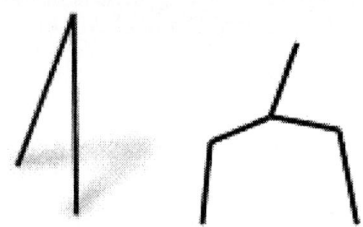

Fig 1. (a) Walker, (b) 2D walking figure.

2 A Morphology Scheme

It is one thing to link together a set of sticks in a predetermined topology and then allow the motions of the joints to evolve for the sake of locomotion. It is another thing entirely to allow morphology itself to evolve.

In the next incarnation of this alife methodology, a morphological scheme was designed which allowed the number of sticks, lengths, branching angles, and stick topology to vary. All of these factors are genetically determined. An important principle in this newer morphological scheme is that in this case, there are no implied heads, legs, arms, or torsos, as shown in Figure 3. Creatures are open-ended structures to which Darwinian evolution may impart differentiation and afford implicit function to the various parts.

Fig. 3. 3D creatures with variable morphology.

An extension of this scheme includes bodies with variable thickness among parts. Figure 4 shows a representative 3D creature from this set. These creatures are the most complex of all the morphological schemes, and can exhibit locomotion schemes and anatomies which exploit the effects of uneven distributions of mass among the body (consider for instance the way a giraffe uses the inertia of its neck when it runs). The figure in this illustration uses a tripod technique to stabilize itself. Creatures in this scheme tend to evolve 3 or 4-legged locomotion. Bipedal locomotion does not evolve: this is probably due to the fact that they have no sensors for balance, and thus no way of adjusting to tilt (as Walker did). A future enhancement will be to add 3D "vestibular" sensors, to enable bipedal locomotion.

Fig. 4. A 3D creature with variable thickness in parts.

2.1 Embryology

Each creature possesses a set of genes organized in a template (the genotype). Genotypes are represented as fixed-length strings of real numbers. Each gene is mapped to a real or integer value which controls some specific aspect of the construction of the body, the motion of body parts, or reactivity to environmental stimuli. Genotypes get expressed into phenotypes through this embryological scheme. The typical genotype for a creature includes genes for controlling the following set of phenotypic features:

number of parts
the topology (branching order) of parts
the angles at which parts branch off other parts
colors of parts
thicknesses of parts
lengths of parts
frequencies of sine wave motions for all parts
amplitudes of sine wave motions in each part
phases among sine wave motions in each part
amplitude modulators of each sine wave (reactivity)
phase modulators of each sine wave (reactivity)

The design of a genotype-phenotype mapping has been one of the most interesting components of the design process in building alife worlds in this scheme. It is not always trivial to reduce a variable body plan to an elegant, simple (and evolvable) representation. Dawkins [5] promotes the concept of a "constrained embryology," whereby global aspects of a form (such as bilateral symmetry or segmentation) can be represented with a small set of control parameters. A representation with a small set of genes which are able to express, through their interactions during embryology, a very large phenotypic space, is desirable, and makes for a more "evolvable" population.

2.2 Motor Control

The motor control scheme in this system is admittedly simplistic. Real animals do not move like clockwork, and do not move body parts in periodic fashion all their lives. However, as mentioned earlier, one must choose a level of abstraction. For the simulations designed thus far, this simplistic model of animal locomotion has been sufficient. Also, the addition of modulators to the periodic motions makes the motion less repetitive, and enables reactivity to the environment. A more reactive motor control scheme would be required if any behavior other than periodic locomotion is expected to evolve.

3 Physics

This alife system evolved from a simple animation technique whereby motion was made progressively more complex. The notion of a physics also became incorporated in progressive steps. In the figures modeled in this scheme, deeper levels of physical simulation were added as needed, as more complex body plans were designed.

In the present scheme, time is updated in discrete steps of unit 1 with each time step corresponding to one update of physical forces and one animation frame. A creature is modeled as a rigid body, yet which can bend its parts as in an articulated body. Torque between parts is not directly modeled in this scheme. The effects of moments of inertia and changing center of mass are modeled. A creature's body has position, orientation, linear velocity, and angular velocity. Position and orientation are updated at each time step by the body's linear and angular velocities. These are in turn affected by a number of different forces such as gravity, collisions of body part endpoints with the ground (for terrestrial creatures), forces from parts stroking perpendicular to their axes in a viscous fluid (for sea creatures), and in some cases, contact with user stimulus (a mouse cursor which pokes into the virtual space).

4 Nervous System

It is possible that brains are simply local inflammations of early evolutionary nervous systems, resulting from the need in early animals to have *state* and generate internal models in order to negotiate a complex environment. This is an alife-friendly interpretation of brains. The design methodology employed here is to wire up the creatures with connectivity and reactivity to the environment, and then to eventually plug in evolvable neural nets which complexify as a property of the wiring to the environment. Braitenberg's Vehicles [3] supply some inspiration for this bottom-up design approach.

The design philosophy used here does not consist of building a brain structure prior to understanding the nature of the organism's connectivity to the physical environment. If adaptive behavior and intelligence are emergent properties of life, then it is more sensible to design bodies first, and to later wire up a proto-nervous system in which brains (might) emerge. The "Physical Grounding Hypothesis" [4], states that to build a system that is intelligent it is necessary to have its representations grounded in the physical world.

In this system, there are not yet any brains to speak of. It includes a simple mental model which is (at this point) purely reactive: sensors in a creature detect aspects of the its relation to the environment, which can directly transition its state to another state, or which directly control actuators (real-time changes in the motions of body parts). For instance, while in "looking for mate state", a creature will react to certain visual stimuli, which can cause it to enter into a new state, such as "pursuing a mate". A future enhancement includes building an evolvable recurrent neural net which mediates the sensor-actuator pathways, and can grow internal structure and representation in the context of the creature's direct coupling with the dynamic environment.

5 Evolution

Models of Creationism are made implicit every time a craftsperson, animator, artist, or engineer designs a body of work and establishes a methodology for its creation. Darwinian models are different than Creationist models (though not absent of a creator). In Darwinian models, important innovation is relegated to the artifact. Invention happens after initial Design. Surprises often result. Genetic algorithms are Darwin Machines [11], designed to take advantage of lucky mutations. They are serendipity engines.

The earlier alife simulations discussed use a variation of the standard genetic algorithm: hundreds of creatures are initialized with random genes, then each is animated for a period of time to establish its fitness ranking (in most cases, determined by how far it has traveled from the position at which it started). After this initial fitness ranking, a cycle begins. For each step in the cycle, two statistically fit individuals are chosen from the population, mated, and used to create one offspring which inherits genes of both parents through crossover. The offspring undergoes embryology and then replaces the least fit individual in the population. The offspring is then animated to determine its fitness. The process continues in this way for a specified number of cycles. This technique guarantees that overall fitness never decreases in the population. The most fit creatures are never lost, and the least fit creatures are always culled [17]. Figure 5 shows 4 snapshots of a locomotion cycle showing a 3-legged anatomy and locomotion strategy, which evolved from one of these simulations.

Fig. 5. An evolved 3-legged locomotion strategy.

6 Sexual Swimmers

In the latest series of simulations, dimensionality was brought down from three to two, but the model was deepened by allowing reproduction to be spontaneous. To ground the simulation more in a physical representation, the concept of a "generation" was blurred. Instead of updating the entire population in discrete stages (a schedule determined by the "creator"), this system allowed reproduction to occur asynchronously and locally among creatures able to reach proximity to each other in a spatial domain. The notion of an explicit fitness function is thus removed [18].

Locomotion behavior evolves globally by way of local matings between creatures with higher (implicit) fitness than others in the local area. Figures 6a and b illustrate two swimming styles which emerged from this simulation.

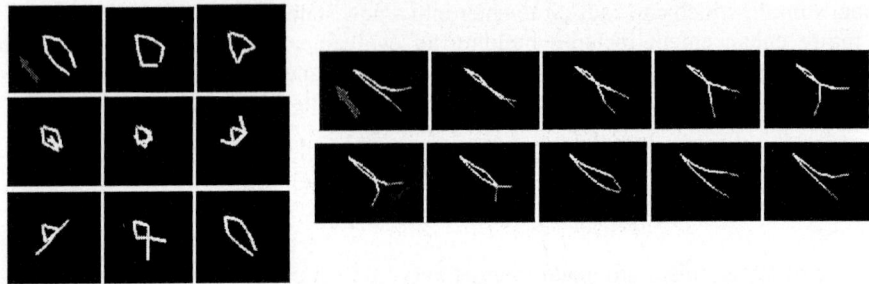

Fig. 6. Sequences of images of swimming strategies: (a) paddling-style, and (b) undulating-style, which emerged through evolution.

Turn That Body. In order to pursue a potential mate which is swimming around (possibly pursuing its own potential mate), a swimming creature has to be able to continually orient itself in the direction it wants to go. A reactive system was designed which allowed the creatures to detect how much it would need to turn its body while swimming (analogous the the "tilt" sensor in Walker, only now covering 180 degrees in a plane). Essentially, the creature senses the angle between the direction of its goal and its own orientation as the stimulus to which it reacts, as shown in Figure 7.

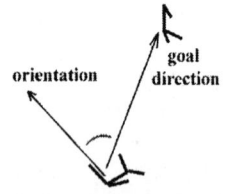

Fig 7. Turning stimulus

As opposed to Walker, which experiences a "magic pull" in the direction of its goal, these creatures must create their own means of propulsion, using friction with the surrounding fluid.

Since the number of possible morphologies and motion strategies in these creatures is vast, it would be inappropriate to top-down-design a turning mechanism. Since turning in a plane for a 2D articulated body can be accomplished by modulating the phases and amplitudes of certain part motions, it was decided that evolution should be the designer, since evolution is already the designer of morphology and periodic motion. Thus, modulator genes (shown in the list above) were implemented which can affect the amplitudes and phases in each part's motions in response to the stimulus.

A commercial product was derived from this simulation and called "Darwin Pond" [13]. It enables users to observe hundreds of creatures, comprised of 2D line segments, representing a large phenotypic space of anatomies and motions. They can be observed in the Pond with the aid of a virtual microscope, allowing panning across, zooming up close to groups of creatures, or zooming out to see the whole affair. One can create new creatures, kill them, move them around the Pond by dragging them, inquire their mental states, feed them, remove food, and tweak individual genes while seeing the animated results of genetic engineering in real-time. Figure 8 shows a screen shot of the basic Darwin Pond interface.

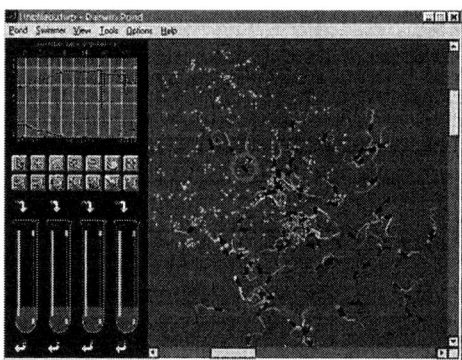

Fig. 8. *Darwin Pond* interface.

Physics and Genetics Are Linked. It is important to point out that in this simulation, genetic evolution is totally reliant on the physical model which animates the creatures. Not only does it take two to tango, but they have to be able to swim to each other as well. In this simulation, genotypes are housed in physically-based phenotypes, which, over evolutionary time, become more efficient at transporting their genotypes to other phenotypes, thereby enabling them to mate and reproduce their genes. This is the selfish gene at work. The emergence of locomotive skill becomes meaningful therefore in the context of the environment: it becomes physically grounded, and the fitness landscape becomes dynamic.

A variation on this simulation, called "Gene Pool" [20], was developed, and included a larger genotype-phenotype scheme, variable thickness in body parts, a deeper physics, and a conserved energy model. Figure 9 illustrates a collection of these 2D swimming creatures (before evolution has had any effect of body plan). They are called "swimbots".

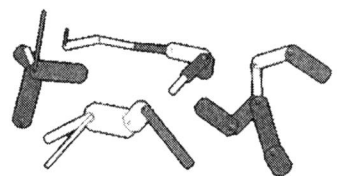

Fig. 9. Swimbot anatomies

What's Sex Got To Do With It? *Gene Pool* introduces mate choice in the process of reproduction. In this scheme, not only is the evolution of form and motion more physically grounded, and subject to the local conditions of the simulated world, but the aesthetic criteria which determine the "sexiest" motions also become a factor for reproduction.

What does "sexy" mean? Sexual selection in evolution is responsible for phenomena such as the magnificent peacock tail, and the elaborate colorful dances of many fish species, which sport curious body parts, adapted for mate attraction. Attraction-based features in many species may be so exaggerated and seemingly awkward that one would assume they decrease the overall fitness of the species, in which locomotion efficiency, foraging, and security are important. I arrived at an hypothesis: could mate preferences for arbitrary phenotypic features inhibit the evolution of energy-efficiency in a population of locomotive creatures? For instance, if the creatures in the population were attracted to slow-moving bodies, and only mated with the most stationary creatures in the population, would locomotion skill emerge? If so, what kind? What if they were all attracted to short, compact bodies? Would the body plan become reduced to a limbless form, incapable of articulated locomotion? If they were attracted to wild, erratic motion, would the resulting swimbots be burning off so much energy that they usually die before reproducing?

As an experiment, a simulation was built, including a variety of mate preference criteria determining which swimbots would be chosen [19]. In choosing a potential mate, a swimbot would take snapshots of each swimbot within its local view horizon, and then compare these snapshots and rank them by attractiveness. Criteria settings included: attraction to long bodies; attraction to lots of motion; attraction to bodies which are "splayed out," and attraction to massive bodies. The inverses of each of these phenotypic characteristics were also tested. As expected, in simulations in which length was considered attractive, populations with elongated bodies with few branching parts emerged. In these populations, locomotion was accomplished by a tiny paddle-like fin in the back of the body, or by gently undulating movements. Figure 10 illustrates a cluster of swimbots resulting from this simulation.

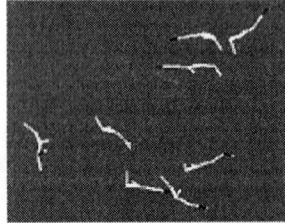

Fig. 10. Swimbots which evolved through mate preferences for *long* bodies.

Attraction to "splayed-out" bodies (in which the sum of the distances between the midpoints of each part is larger than average), resulted in creatures which spent a large part of their periodic swimming cycles in an "open" attitude, as shown in Figure 11. In this illustration, the creature is seen swimming to the lower right. Approximately one swim cycle is shown. Notice that the stroke recovery (the beginning and end of the sequence) demonstrates an exaggerated "opening up" of the body. It is likely that this behavior emerged because snapshots can be taken at any time by creatures looking for a mate, and so the more open a potential mate's body is, and the longer amount of time it is open, the more *attractive* on average it will be.

These experiments show how mate preference can affect the evolution of a body plan as well as locomotion style. The effects on energy-efficiency were non-trivial: locomotion strategies emerged which took advantage of attraction criteria yet were still efficient in terms of locomotion. As usual with many alife simulations, the phenotype space has unexpected regions which are readily exploited as the population adapts.

Fig. 11. Swimbots which evolved through mate preferences for *splayed* bodies.

6.1 Realtime Evolution

The alife worlds described here incorporate physical, genetic, and motor-control models which are spare and scaled down as much as possible to allow for computational speed and real-time animation, while still allowing enough emergent phenomena to make the experience interesting and informative. The effects of Darwinian evolution can be witnessed in less than a half-an hour (on an average Pentium computer). For educational and entertaining experiences, it is important that there be enough interaction, immersion, and discovery to keep a participant involved while the primordial soup brews. The average short-attention-span hardcore gamer may not appreciate the meditative pace at which an evolutionary alife system runs. But alife enthusiasts and artistically or scientifically oriented observers may find it just fine. For watching evolutionary phenomena, it sure beats waiting around a couple million years to watch interesting changes.

7 Computer Graphics Rendering

For the 3D stick figures, thick, dark 3D lines are drawn to represent the sticks. The interesting (and important) part comes in drawing a shadow, since this is largely the graphical element which gives the viewer a sense of the 3D geometry. The shadow is simply a "flattened-out" replica of all the lines (without the vertical component and translated to the ground plane) drawn with a thicker linewidth, and in a shade slightly darker than the ground color. Since no Z-buffering is used, the shadow is drawn first, followed by the sticks.

For the creatures with variable thickness in parts, a number of techniques have been used, many of them are graphics hacks meant to reduce polygon-count or to avoid expensive Z-buffering and lighting algorithms. Since these are specifically alife-oriented worlds, without any objects besides abstract articulated bodies, specific graphics techniques are used. At the point in which these creatures are imbedded in a more comprehensive virtual world, a more generalized renderer would be useful.

Rendering Behavior, Then Pixels. Part of the methodology is to take advantage of something that the eye-brain system is very good at: detecting movement generated by a living thing. It is important not to spend too much computational time on heavyweight texturemaps, lighting models, and cute cosmetics, when more computation can be spent on deep physics and animation speed (to show off the effects of subtle movements that have evolved). It is a purist philosophy: simply show what is there. No pasting 2D images of eyes and ears on the creatures. Instead, as the simulation itself deepens (for instance, when light sensors or vibration sensors are allowed to evolve on arbitrary parts of bodies, as evolution dictates) graphical elements visualizing these phenotypic features will be rendered. They may be recognizably eye and ear-like, or they may not.

8 Commentary: Why Are There No Humanoids Here?

The goal of Artificial Intelligence research is something magnificent, and something very human indeed. It appears as if the skills enabling one to play chess and use grammar are a very recent evolutionary trend, whereas climbing a tree is a much older skill, truly more complex, and in fact possibly an activity whose basic cognitive mechanisms are the primordial stuff of higher reasoning.

These simulations do not aim to model humans. But if that were the goal, it may be best to design a vestibular system and an environment in which vertical, bipedal locomotion *might* be advantageous. Best to design an evolvable neural system (and to allocate lots of computer memory!) and a highly complex, dynamic environment, whereby something brain-like *might* billow like a mushroom cloud as an internal echo of the external complexity. Best to design a simulation in which objects existing in the world *might* be exploited as tools and symbols, extended phenotypes, cultural memes. What might evolve then could be something more human-like than the wiggling worms shown in the illustrations of this paper. But in the meanwhile, there is no rush on my part to get to human levels with these simulations. And at any rate, imaginary animals can be very thought-provoking.

9 Conclusion

In this paper, I have described many of the techniques, concepts, and concerns involved in a methodology for creating animated artificial life worlds. This approach does not begin with a biological research agenda but rather an eye towards the creation of forms and motions which are lifelike and autonomous–a branch of character animation. The alife agenda of studying emergent behavior by way of the crafting of simulations has become incorporated into this animation methodology, and with it, some key themes from evolutionary biology, such as sexual selection. It is hoped that these concepts and techniques will be useful for further advances in animated artificial life, for education, entertainment, and research.

References

1. Anderson, L., *Oh, Superman* (record album)
2. Badler, N., Barsky, B., Zeltzer, D. Making Them Move. Morgan Kaufmann, 1991

3. Braitenberg, V., Vehicles: Experiments in Synthetic Psychology. MIT Press, Cambridge, Mass. 1984
4. Brooks, R., Elephants Don't Play Chess. Designing Autonomous Agents, (ed. Maes), MIT Press, 1990 page 3.
5. Dawkins, R.: The Evolution of Evolvability. Artificial Life Proceedings, Addison-Wesley 1989 pages 201-220.
6. Goldberg, D. Genetic Algorithms in Search, Optimization, & Machine Learning. Addison-Wesley, 1989
7. Holland, J. Adaptation in Natural and Artificial Systems. University of Michigan Press, Ann Arbor. 1975
8. Koza, J., Genetic Programming: on the Programming of Computers by Means of Natural Selection. MIT Press, 92
9. Langton, C., Artificial Life. Addison-Wesley, 1989
10. Ngo, T. and Marks, J. Spacetime Constraints Revisited. Computer Graphics . pp. 343-350. 1993
11. Penny, S. Darwin Machine (text published on internet) at:
    http://www-art.cfa.cmu.edu/www-penny/texts/Darwin_Machine_.html
12. Reynolds, C., Flocks, Herds, and Schools: A Distributed Behavioral Model. Computer Graphics, vol 21, number 4, July, 1987.
13. RSG (Rocket Science Games, Inc., producer) *Darwin Pond*, software product, designed by Jeffrey Ventrella, 1997. (contact: jeffrey@ventrella.com) or visit (http://www.ventrella.com).
14. Sims, K. Evolving Virtual Creatures. Computer Graphics. SIGGRAPH Proceedings pp. 15-22 1994.
15. Sims, K. Evolving 3D Morphology and Behavior by Competition. Artificial Life IV. MIT Press 1994
16. Terzopoulis, D., Tu, X., and Grzeszczuk, R. Artificial Fishes with Autonomous Locomotion, Perception, Behavior, and Learning in a Simulated Physical World. Artificial Life IV. MIT Press, 1994
17. Ventrella, J. Explorations in the Emergence of Morphology and Locomotion Behavior in Animated Figures. Artificial Life IV. MIT Press 1994
18. Ventrella, J. Sexual Swimmers (Emergent Morphology and Locomotion without a Fitness Function). From Animals to Animats. MIT Press 1996 pages 484-493
19. Ventrella, J., Attractiveness vs. Efficiency (How Mate Preference Affects Locomotion in the Evolution of Artificial Swimming Organisms, Artificial Life VI Proceedings, MIT Press, 1998
20. Ventrella, J., *Gene Pool* (Windows software application), at...
    http://www.ventrella.com, 1998
21. Witkin, A. and Kass, M. Spacetime Constraints. Computer Graphics. 22(4): 159-168 Aug. 1988
22. Zeltzer, David. Task Level Graphical Simulation: Abstraction, Representation, and Control. from Making Them Move. ed Badler. 1991

ALife Meets Web: Lessons Learned

Luigi Pagliarini[1], Ariel Dolan[2], Filippo Menczer[3], and Henrik Hautop Lund[4]

[1] The Danish National Centre for IT-Research
University of Aarhus, Ny Munkegade bldg. 540, 8000 Aarhus C., Denmark
[2] Institute of Psychology
National Research Council, 15 Viale Marx, 00137 Rome, Italy
[3] Computer Science & Engr. Dept.
Cognitive Science Dept., University of California, San Diego, La Jolla, CA 92093-0114 USA
[4] The Danish National Centre for IT-Research
University of Aarhus, Ny Munkegade bldg. 540, 8000 Aarhus C., Denmark
luigi@caio.irmkant.rm.cnr.it, aridolan@netvision.net.il, fil@cs.ucsd.edu, hhl@daimi.aau.dk

Abstract Artificial life might come to play important roles for the World Wide Web, both as a source of new algorithmic paradigms and as a source of inspiration for its future development. New Web searching and managing techniques, based on artificial life principles, have been elicited by the striking similarities between the Web and natural environments. New Web interface designs, based on artificial life techniques, have resulted in increased aesthetic appeal, smart animations, and clever interactive rules. In this paper we exemplify these observations by surveying a number of meeting points between artificial life and the Web. We touch on a few implementation issues and attempt to draw some lessons to be learned from these early experiences.

1 Introduction

In recent years, the Internet and its hypertextual and graphical World Wide Web subset have developed very rapidly. Even though new techniques — based on human-computer interaction, information retrieval, and network routing methodologies — have been applied to a range of Web problems, the emergence of suitable Web techniques has not been as rapid as the growth in size and complexity of the Web.

Can the field of artificial life (ALife) provide the growing Web community with useful inspiration? What new paradigms, methodologies, and algorithms does ALife offer? Is the Web a suitable artificial environment to foster new, useful artificial life forms? Should we bother to embark on the enterprise of populating the Web with intelligent, interactive, autonomous agents with life-like behaviors? These are important questions that deserve the attention of the ALife community. To stimulate this discussion, we start in this paper with a survey of some projects in which ALife has already, to variable degrees, met the Web.

We will focus on some Web-related issues where ALife, in our opinion, may come to play a positive role. These issues include aspects of distributed information search and management, such as scaling and user-adaptability (described in the Applications to Web Search and Management section); and aspects of Web interface design, such as aesthetic appeal, animation, and interactivity (surveyed in the Applications to Web Interface Design section). Throughout the paper, we discuss some lessons learned through these early experiences.

2 Applications to Web Search and Management

One of the central goals of ALife, in our opinion, is to apply algorithms inspired by natural systems to practical applications. The applications that best lend themselves to ALife approaches are those whose operating environments share important characteristics with natural environments. With the explosion of the Internet, it would have been difficult not to notice the striking similarities between this artificial environment and those in which real creatures evolve, adapt, strive, compete, collaborate, learn, grow, reproduce, and die. Like natural environments, the Web is very large; it is dynamic, with documents being added, removed, and moved all the time; it is heterogeneous — even considering text alone — with context-dependent languages, formats, and styles; it is noisy, with lots of irrelevant, outdated, or incorrect information; and it is distributed, so that actions have costs (for example the network latency associated with accessing a certain page).

Innumerable paradigms have been brought fourth to tame the Web into fitting some pattern familiar to users. Even the emerging field of autonomous software agents owes much of its success to the ready availability of virtually infinite information environments, and the difficulties encountered by users attempting to cope with such environments. The InfoSpiders project was born as an exploration of the possible matches between some of the features that make the Web a complex environment, and some of the mechanisms that allow ecologies of organisms to adapt to different — but at least equally complex — natural environments.

In particular, the large, dynamic, and distributed flavor of the Web leads to scaling problems when traditional information retrieval methods are employed to build search engines. Information often becomes stale before a search engine's database can be updated. The heterogeneous organization of information makes any single, global exploration strategy less than optimal — no matter how clever. What can nature teach us about ways to complement these methods with less traditional approaches? In nature, no single species is "optimal" with respect to the whole world; each is adapted to some niche in which members of that species have evolved. Populations of situated, mobile agents afford decisions based on local context, continuous adaptation, and robustness — in natural and artificial environments alike. Different subpopulations can specialize in dealing with the peculiar characteristics of the local environments they experience.

2.1 InfoSpiders

The aim of the InfoSpiders system is to apply and test several machine learning techniques, inspired by natural adaptation, for problems posed by searching and managing information on the Web. Different methods have been explored, extended, and integrated for this task. In the project, we experimented with versions of the genetic algorithm employing localized selection schemes, to overcome the problem of premature convergence and allow for distributed implementations; with different agent representations, to enable agents to internalize local textual features into their evolving behaviors; with reinforcement learning, to adapt individual strategies over short-term time and space scales, based on local context; and with relevance feedback, to permit the user to bias the search process, seamlessly and on-line, based on previous and current performance.

A detailed description of the implementation of the InfoSpiders system is out of the scope of this paper. Interested readers can find such details, as well as reports on preliminary experiments, elsewhere [14, 15, 16] or on-line [1]. Here we limit ourselves to outline the general ideas behind the model. The first step is to identify the crucial resource, the "food" of the artificial environment. For the task at hand, it is easy to equate resources with relevant information. Since relevance is subjective (actual relevance depends on the user, and must be estimated by agents), information must be transformed into a higher-entropy quantity; this single currency by which agents in a population survive, reproduce, and die is called "energy." Energy must be positively correlated with performance as defined by user and environment.

Agents asynchronously go through a simple cycle in which they receive input from the environment as well as internal state, perform some computation, and execute actions. Actions have an energy cost but may result in energy intake. Energy is used up and accumulated internally throughout an agent's life; its internal level automatically determines reproduction and death, events in which energy is conserved. Agents that perform the task better than average reproduce more and colonize the population. Indirect interaction among agents occurs without the need of expensive communication, via competition for the shared, finite environmental resources. Mutations and crossover afford the changes necessary for the evolution of dynamically adapted agents. This paradigm enforces density-dependent selection: the expected population size is determined by the carrying capacity of the environment. Associating high energy costs with expensive actions intrinsically enforces a balanced network load by limiting inefficient uses of bandwidth.

Collective Behavior Adaptation means for agents to concentrate in high energy areas of the Web, where many documents are relevant. Each agent's survival will be ensured by exchanging an adequate flow of information for energy. The situation is illustrated by the snapshots in Figure 1, illustrating a typical collective behavior of InfoSpiders in response to a query, and limited to a well defined chunk of the Web. After a while, blue agents have found what the user wanted;

they prosper and multiply in this relevant niche, while other agents continue to explore the world in search of alternatives.

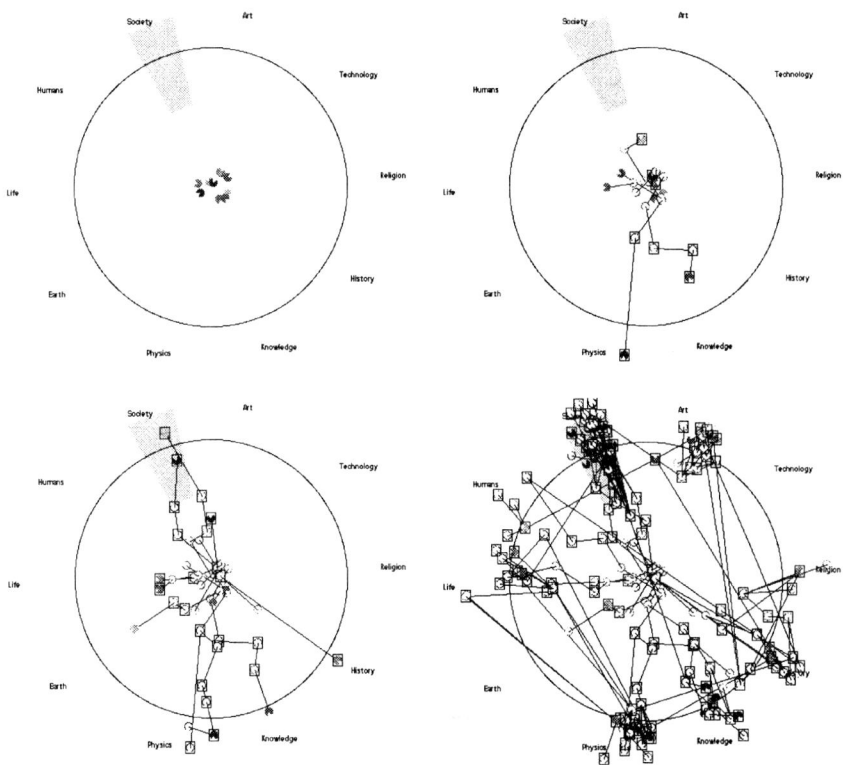

Figure 1. Snapshots of InfoSpiders searching the EB Web space for documents relevant to the query "Laws governing relations among sovereign states." The document's ontology is represented with more specific topics farther from the center of the circle, and actual articles outside of the circle. The relevant documents are represented by the yellow area, unbeknownst to the agents. A document is marked with a rectangle if it is estimated as relevant by the first agent visiting it. The color of an agent represents its lineage, so that all agents sharing a color descend from the same ancestor. (EB data is ©1997 Encyclopaedia Britannica, Inc. [2]; the visual representation is the author's.)

Search Efficiency One of the central results of the InfoSpiders project is to have shown that it is useful for information search algorithms to view the Web as a "natural" environment and characterize it in such terms. What are the environmental assets from a learning agent's perspective? Statistical features such as word frequencies are of course crucial dimensions. It has been argued that the "link topology" structure imposed by information providers upon the organization of documents is another important resource. Even in unstructured information environments, authors tend to cluster documents about related topics by letting them point to each other. This creates a landscape that agents can explore making use of correlation of relevance across links.

Preliminary results, based on theoretical analysis, simulations, and actual experiments on Web-based corpora, are very encouraging [14]. It has been shown that link topology can indeed be detected and exploited by distributed agents, outperforming exhaustive search by an order of magnitude. Moreover, the synergy between evolution, learning, and relevance feedback induces an additional, four-fold boost in performance [15].

3 Applications to Web Interface Design

Web Interface Design (WID) is drastically changing in its aspect and functionality. Yet it is unclear in what direction it is moving. There are at least three quality factors in WID: (a) clever interactive rules; (b) smart animation; and (c) aesthetic appeal.[1] Until recently, WID interactivity and smart animation, handmade or aided by artificial intelligence techniques, relied only on animators' or programmers' abilities; and the aesthetic appeal of a WID relied uniquely on graphic designers abilities. However, since users want to get out of this unexciting landscape, there is a demand for more appealing or artistic aesthetics, much smarter — if not life-like — animations, and more clever — if not human-like — interactions. ALife techniques appear among the earliest and most plausible candidates to address some of these needs. Indeed, in the remainder of this section we show some examples in which ALife helps us to fulfill these needs by providing for new ways to interact (a), by making animations richer and more "natural" (b), and by extending the human capabilities to build aesthetic artifacts (c).

3.1 Web Interactive Cellular Automata

WICA stands for "Web Interactive Cellular Automata." It is a Game of Life [13] (or any other) cellular automaton [20] that is controlled by free flowing text on an HTML page. The free flowing text is some active text that, when clicked, dynamically changes the state of the cellular automata. It was initially created to support Web-design and provide pleasing, changing and unpredictable animations for Web page logos. It was then extended to support dynamic computer art and other kinds of applications. Some examples of WICA can be seen on the WICA homepage [3]. Animation seems to be almost a requirement in the current fashion of Web pages; something must always move. If the page is "static," it becomes boring. Therefore we see a lot of animations on the net. Most of

---

[1] Here we will not take into account other important, but secondary factors, such as user-oriented interface personalization, interface legibility, multilevel functionality, etc.

them are GIF animations, and the others are usually simple Java animations. GIF animations are not very pleasing: monotonous, nagging, tiresome — sometime irritating! Java animations are just a little better. The endless repetition of exactly the same patterns is hardly inviting. WICA animations are different. Although they can be used for the same purpose as GIF animations (e.g., animated logos), they are far from monotonous. Their ALife flavor makes them always unpredictable, conveying a feeling of life.

A WICA-Based Homepage As an example, consider a WICA dynamic website logo shown in Figure 2. This usage of WICA was implemented in the homepage of Prof. Domenico Parisi of CNR [4]. Two CA's of different colors are superimposed on the page logo, and a new pattern is released into one of them each time another page is selected by clicking a hypertext link. Since the CA applet resides on a separate HTML frame, it is always visible, even when other frames are changed. Although the CA is played over the logo, the logo remains clear and is not hidden by it. The resulting animation is much more interesting, unpredictable, and "alive" than any animated GIF or pre-designed animation can be. We attribute this effect to the use of ALife techniques.

Figure2. The WICA dynamic website logo.

The specific WICA implementation was made so that the cellular automaton applet uses Conway's classic Game of Life rules. However, the CA world (implemented here as an arbitrary background picture) is shared by two parallel, independent, overlapping CA's. It is an interactive applet, where control is achieved through clicking on textual links rather than by the orthodox use of buttons and menus. The actual dimensions of the CA grid are arbitrary, but since WICA usually goes with a picture background, the size is dictated by the picture.

The CA algorithm implements three methods for making its calculations efficiently:[2]

1. While the current generation is displayed on the screen, the next generation is prepared on an off-screen buffer, and then replaces the current screen in a single step.
2. Only cells that changed their status are re-painted.

---
[2] The basic algorithm is due to Andreas Ehrencrona [5].

3. When calculating the number of live neighbors of each cell, knowledge from previous cell calculations is used: e.g., since the left column of the current cell is the middle column of the previous cell, the status of the left neighbors is known and need not be recalculated.

The dynamic character of WICA is based on two parallel, independent CAs playing simultaneously in the same world. The CA world is controlled by Javascript statements that activate a Java routine. When this routine is activated, a new pattern of cells is inserted into one of the CAs. The CA that receives the patterns is selected at random. Also selected at random are three parameters of the new pattern: the pattern itself, its color, and its location within the CA frame. The pattern itself is selected from a list of three interesting and well-known unstable patterns: the *R-Pentomino*, the *H-Heptomino* and the *Pi-Heptomino*. The color is selected at random from a list defined in the HTML file.

This implementation results in having exactly two colors (and two populations) at any given moment, but the colors may change giving the illusion of seeing new populations. It also gives a somewhat unexpected behavior, as one of the CA populations suddenly changes color and takes a new pattern.

Text Oriented Interactivity WICA animations can be integrated with a Text Oriented Interface (TOI) [17] so that they always renew themselves. JcaToi [6], shown in Figure 3, is such an extension of WICA and another example of value-added communication. JcaToi provides the user with an interactive Game of Life implementation that is controlled by free-flowing text. WICA was designed to react in parallel to regular HTML hypertext events, being a sort of by-product to regular Web page requests, and always producing the same (albeit unpredictable) behavior, namely adding a new CA pattern to the CA world. JcaToi, on the other hand, is designed to perform various predefined actions. In JcaToi, various hyperlinks mean different things and perform different dedicated actions. This is done by using a more diverse Java-Javascript interface, where multiple Java routines can be activated by the Javascript commands.

JcaToi makes use of three tools: HTML frames, Java, and Javascript. HTML frames are used for creating pages where one part of the page (the program or the picture) is static and constantly displayed in a predefined location, while the rest of the page can be scrolled or change content. This makes the size of the "user interface" practically unlimited. Java is used for the program itself, Javascript for manipulating the hypertext links, and the Java-Javascript interface is used to allow the text to control the program.

The text describes the CA applet that is displayed on the HTML page, and allows the browsing user to play and learn with it, by clicking on the appropriate words. The JcaToi application thus demonstrates that ALife techniques can add educational value to the Web, by making reading an interactive and "alive" process. For example, you can imagine an Artificial Life Interactive Handbook where, by using this technique, you can actually transform your reading into an active process. An example would be: if you do not know what a 'hidden unit' in a neural network is, you just click on the 'hidden unit' text and you see that the

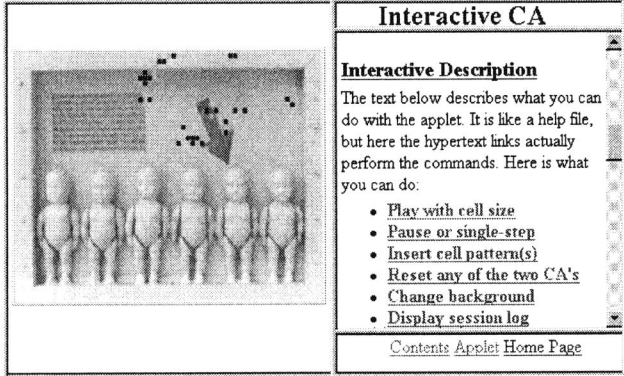

Figure3. The JcaToi website.

corresponding part of the neural network picture is flashing. That is what we mean by reading as an interactive process. Of course, this is the most static part of it. You can also think of 'introducing food' free flowing text into a running simulation, etc.

3.2 Flocking Web Creatures

Floys [7] are another example in which ALife issues cross over with Web interface issues. Floys (shown in Figure 4) belong to the flocking ALife creatures variety [19], sharing with them the social tendency to stick together, and the life-like emergent behavior which is based on a few simple, local rules. They differ from most other ALife flocking (boids-type) implementations by being territorial animats that defend their territory against intruders. In the WID system they are implemented as Java applets. The more advanced applets allow individual Floys to change traits and personality (iFloys and eFloys), and population of Floys to breed and evolve (eFloys). One can observe various applications of this technique. The boids-based algorithm has been used in the entertainment industry (e.g., in the "Jurassic Park" movie for animating a storm of prehistoric birds). For an example of its application to WID, see [8]. Animation realized with this kind of technique is more life-like, visually pleasing, and smarter than traditional Web animation techniques; it is also easy to realize — once one has learned to program the boids or simply use their applet.

Before further discussing Floys' implications for WID, let us go over a few details about their implementation. In general, the Floys behavior is governed by two rules:

- a rule specifying how to relate to one's own kind;
- a rule specifying how to relate to strangers.

Unlike most other flocking algorithms, a Floy does not relate to all members of its community, but only to its two closest neighbors. This idea was borrowed

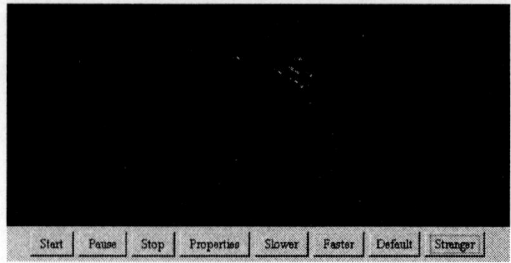

Figure4. The Floys website.

from Alex Vulliamy's Flies code [9], of which Floys is a descendant. Each Floy is "emotionally" attached to two other members (its neighbors) of the flock, and tries to stay close to them.[3] The Floy relates to the neighboring Floys by identifying whether they are of its own kind or strangers. It will chase a stranger away while in its own territory, or flee if chased by a stranger while outside of its own territory.

In the basic Floys applet, behavior parameters are common to the whole population. In iFloys, instead, each Floy can be assigned different traits. Among the parameters that can be assigned, we find acceleration, adhesion, collision distance and maximum speed. For example, an iFloy with higher acceleration and speed traits will tend to be faster, more abrupt, and will appear more nervous, spontaneous and individualistic; a Floy with higher adhesion value will tend to cling more to the community and will look like a conformist. When one iFloy is assigned high speed or acceleration traits, the whole group becomes a little confused and disorganized. An iFloy with slow and lazy traits will be left behind. Color codes for stranger vs. local Floys. Local iFloys have the aggressive behavior, while non-local iFloys have the flight behavior. When iFloys are transformed to the stranger color, they are attacked, even if they are the majority. However, when many strangers are present, the local iFloys appear confused and do not fight them effectively.

The most advanced of the three versions is the eFloys applet, which supports evolution. This setup allows manipulation of more than 30 different parameters. In addition, several pre-defined behavior styles can be assigned to the current population. The applet also supports the option of attaching a number graphically to each Floy in order to track individual Floys easily. Although applets do not support file access for security reasons, current status and results can al-

---

[3] An approximate neighbor detection algorithm is used for efficiency, which is of course a crucial aspect in Web design.

ways be displayed in a dedicated information screen. Where non-evolving Floys live eternally (or until their energy drops to zero), eFloys live one generation, and a generation ends when the stranger is finally killed. eFloys evolve sexually, where each eFloy is the descendent of two parents. The two parents are selected according to two fitness attributes, energy and safety. An eFloy can gain or lose these during its lifetime, and the more it has, the fitter it is. Energy is lost proportionally to speed, and safety is gained from proximity to neighbors. With this set-up, one can easily make experiments with populations of eFloys having predefined behaviors, or perform simulations of the evolutionary process tuning the relative weights of safety and energy in the fitness function.

3.3 Interactive Computer Art

Floys have exemplified how ALife models can be implemented to run across the Web. But do such systems afford anything useful from a WID point of view? A positive answer may be obtained by considering interactive computer art, where the user interacts with graphical objects rather than code. The Artificial Painter program [18, 21, 10] is one of several applications of ALife to computer graphic design. It is based on artificial neural networks and evolutionary algorithms. At the beginning of each evolutionary session it generates 16 random images which are a sort of "seed-images" for the painter to start its work. The user can select four of them as parents, which then produce sixteen new individuals constituting a new generation. The user can zoom out each of the images, carefully look at them, and observe changes, trends, and interactions in composition, color, texture, form, and perspective. The only parameter the user can control at each generation is mutation rate (which however can be assigned differently for each generation).

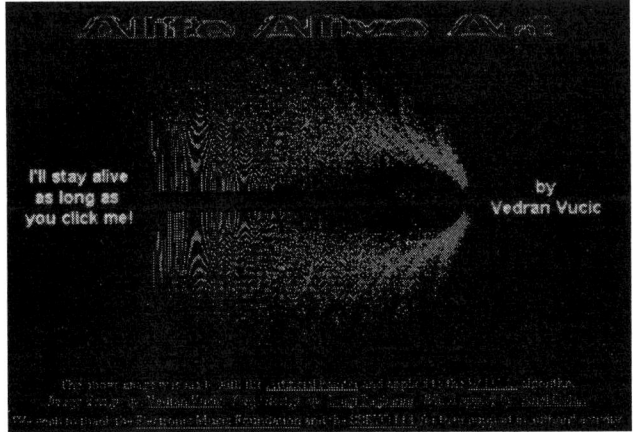

Figure5. The Alife Alive Art website.

Applications of this program can be seen in Vedran Vucic's homepage [11] and the Alife Alive Art site [12] shown in Figure 5. These sites demonstrate a couple of points. First, ALife techniques can be applied to graphic design and therefore to WID, as in the case of Vedran Vucic's site. Second, the user can interact with and influence a picture by controlling its ALife-based evolution. The Alife Alive Art site, derived from the Artificial Painter and Floys, allows the user to do so by interacting with the text that is attached to, and part of, the picture.

4 Conclusion

The projects surveyed in this paper offer a chance to highlight some of the meeting points between ALife and the Web. As we have been showing all along the paper, one can see the web as an enviroment where artificial creatures made up with ALife techniques can move. We also showed that one can imagine these creatures to be very different agents with very different function and properties.

Firstly, as shown by the InfoSpiders, the Web is a fertile ground to apply and explore ALife-inspired algorithms. As electronic information environments grow and become more complex, while the class of Web users extends from computer experts to elementary school students, the need for "soft" computing technologies can only become more stringent in our view. The more the Web looks like a natural, live environment, the more we must look at real, living systems for humbling inspiration.

This also seems to be the case for WID: we have found ALife techniques (inspired by living systems) to provide a number of suitable tools that might facilitate the design of pleasing Web interfaces. We have shown examples of uses of such techniques to achieve appealing aesthetic (as in the Alife Alive Art site and Vedran Vucic's homepage), smart animations (as in the WICA and Floys sites), and clever interactive rules (as in the JcaToi demonstration).

Finally, one can also view the Web as a shared testing ground for ALife models, as exemplified in the Floys system. The premise of the scientific method is the reproducibility of experiments. ALife techniques and simulators are often difficult to compare due to the fact that each defines a different class of environments. The Web provides ALife practitioners with a global laboratory in which they can examine their theories and do good science.

So, facing such problems as the synthesis of virtual worlds on the web it seems necessary to take into account those kind of approaches we have shown. The most important lesson learned is: think of the web as a natural enviroment where to place organisms and by doing that one quickly realizes that ALife techniques, at the moment, are the most fit ones for the realization of bio-like worlds.

References

[1] http://www.cs.ucsd.edu/~fil.
[2] http://www.eb.com.
[3] http://gracco.irmkant.rm.cnr.it/luigi/wica.
[4] http://gracco.irmkant.rm.cnr.it/domenico.
[5] http://www.student.nada.kth.se/~d95-aeh/lifeeng.html.
[6] http://www.aridolan.com/JcaToi.html.
[7] http://www.aridolan.com/JavaFloys.html.
[8] http://www.arch.su.edu.au/thorsten/alife/biomorph.html.
[9] http://www.vulliamy.demon.co.uk/alex.html.
[10] http://www.daimi.aau.dk/~hhl/ap.html.
[11] http://www.rex.opennet.org.
[12] http://gracco.irmkant.rm.cnr.it/luigi/vedran.
[13] M. Gardner. Mathematical games. *Scientific American*, 233:120–23, 1970.
[14] F. Menczer. ARACHNID: Adaptive Retrieval Agents Choosing Heuristic Neighborhoods for Information Discovery. In D. Fisher, editor, *Proceedings 14th International Conference on Machine Learning (ICML97)*. Morgan Kaufmann, 1997.
[15] F. Menczer and R. K. Belew. Adaptive Information Agents in Distributed Textual Environments. In *Proceedings 2nd International Conference on Autonomous Agents (Agents 98)*, 1998. To appear.
[16] F. Menczer, R. K. Belew, and W. Willuhn. Artificial Life Applied to Adaptive Information Agents. In *Working Notes of the AAAI Spring Symposium on Information Gathering from Distributed, Heterogeneous Environments*, 1995.
[17] L. Pagliarini and A. Dolan. Text Oriented Interactivity. Technical report, C.N.R., Rome, 1998. Submitted to Applied Artificial Intelligence (AAI) Journal Special Issue Animated Interface Agents: Making them Intelligent.
[18] L. Pagliarini, H. H. Lund, O. Miglino, and D. Parisi. Artificial Life: A New Way to Build Educational and Therapeutic Games. In C. Langton and K. Shimohara, editors, *Proceedings of Artificial Life V*, pages 152–156, Cambridge, MA, 1997. MIT Press.
[19] C. W. Reynolds. Flocks, Herds, and Schools: A Distributed Behavioral Model. *Computer Graphics*, 21(4):25–34, 1987.
[20] J. von Neumann. *The Theory of Self-Reproducing Automata*. University of Illinois Press, Urbane, 1966. A. W. Burks, ed.
[21] V. Vucic and H. H. Lund. Self-Evolving Arts — Organisms versus Fetishes. *Muhely - Hungarian Journal of Modern Art*, 104:69–79, 1997.

Information Flocking: Data Visualisation in Virtual Worlds Using Emergent Behaviours

Glenn Proctor and Chris Winter

Admin 2 PP5, BT Laboratories, Martlesham Heath, Ipswich, UK. IP5 3RE.
{glenn.proctor, chris.winter}@bt-sys.bt.co.uk

Abstract. A novel method of visualising data based upon the schooling behaviour of fish is described. The technique allows the user to see complex correlations between data items through the amount of time each fish spends near others. It is an example of a biologically inspired approach to data visualisation in virtual worlds, as well as being one of the first uses of VRML 2.0 and Java to create Artificial Life. We describe an initial application of the system, the visualisation of the interests of a group of users. We conclude that Information Flocking is a particularly powerful technique because it presents data in a colourful, dynamic form that allows people to easily identify patterns that would not otherwise be obvious.

1. Introduction

1.1 Flocking & Schooling

Birds flock, fish school, cattle herd. The natural world has many examples of species that organise themselves into groups for some reason, for example to reduce predation. It has been shown [1] that many predators are "tuned" to hunting individuals, and are confused by large numbers of animals organised into a flock or school. Although the evolutionary advantages in flocks had been well characterised no simple models reproducing such behaviours had been demonstrated.

Reynolds created computer simulations of such flocks by modelling a few simple rules [2], and christened individuals that undergo such flocking "boids". Animations based upon boid-like motion have appeared in a number of Hollywood films[1].

The *emergent behaviour* of the flock is the result of the interaction of a few simple rules. In Reynolds' simulation, these were:

---

[1] Examples: herds of dinosaurs in "Jurassic Park", flocks of bats in "Cliffhanger" and "Batman Returns" and the wildebeest stampede in "The Lion King".

- collision avoidance
- velocity matching (flying with the same speed and direction as the others)
- flock centring (trying to fly near the centroid of one's neighbours)

These rules are sufficient to reproduce natural behaviours, particularly if a predator is treated as an obstacle. However their simplicity allows the use of such self-organised behaviour to be extended to serve a more useful purpose: data visualisation. In Information Flocking, a fourth rule is added which modifies the motion of the individuals on the basis of some similarity measure. This measure can be derived from a set of data, with each individual boid associated with a single data item. The flocking motion then becomes a means of visualising the similarities between the individual data items.

A virtual world was created to display the flocking behaviour. Initially this consists of a school of fish swimming around in 3D, but it is easily extended to include such concepts as attractive and repellent objects (which might attract or repel specific items), and predators which might act as data filters.

The initial problem to which Information Flocking was applied is that of visualising the interests of a group of people. Previously, hierarchical clustering techniques [5] have been applied to such data sets. Neural network approaches have also been used [6]. In particular, Orwig and Chen [7] have used Kohonen neural nets [8] to produced graphical representations of such data. While these representations proved to be much faster and at least as powerful as subjective human classification, they are essentially static. Information flocking is dynamic in that the fish in the simulation can change their behaviour in response to changes in the underlying data set. The output is also dynamic (the fish "swim") which allows the human viewer to identify patterns more easily.

2. Methods

2.1 VRML

The prototype Information Flocking system was developed using VRML (Virtual Reality Modelling Language), version 2.0^2. This is a powerful, emerging technology that allows rapid development of graphical programs. Objects in a VRML "world" can be controlled by means of a Java script. This results in a system that can produce 3D, interactive graphical simulations that can be controlled using all the features of the Java programming language. VRML is also platform independent and allows easy creation of multi-user environments. A schematic of the system is given in Fig. 1.

---

[2] See the VRML Repository at http://www.sdsc.edu/vrml/ for more information on VRML.

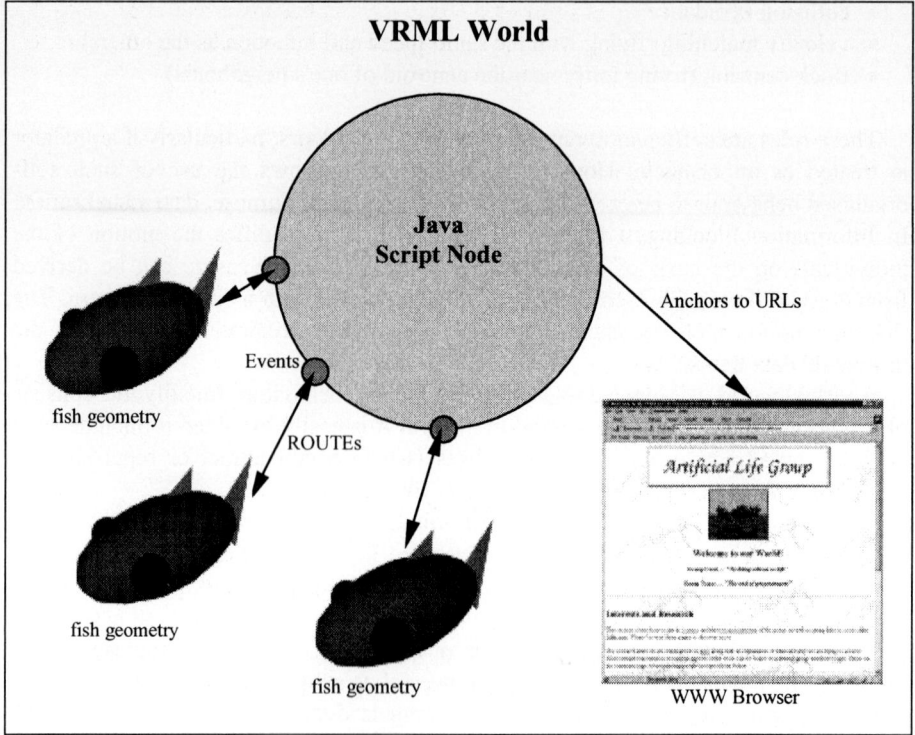

Fig. 1. Schematic of a VRML world. The world is organised hierarchically; different node types define geometry, appearance, camera views etc.. A Script node allows interfacing to a Java program. This controls the behaviour of the fish. Communication is event-driven, and events are connected by structures known as Routes. Objects (e.g. fish) can be "anchored" to URLs; thus when a fish is clicked upon, the relevant page can be opened in a normal web browser such as Netscape. A more detailed description of VRML can be found at the VRML Repository (see footnote on previous page).

2.2 Modelling Emergent Behaviour

The fish in the demonstration are initially positioned randomly. They then swim along a heading vector, which is the resultant of several component vectors, one for each of the behavioural rules. In the current system, these are:

- collision avoidance - avoid collisions with other fish if possible. The vector for this behaviour is calculated to take each individual away from its close neighbours.

- *velocity matching* - each individual tries to swim in the same direction and at the same speed as nearby fish, subject to a minimum and maximum speed.

- *origin homing* - try to swim towards the origin. This has the effect of keeping the fish on screen, and results in their swimming around in a simulated "bowl", rather than disappearing into infinity.

- *information flocking* - swim closer to fish that are similar, and further from fish that are different[3]. The vector for this is calculated as the weighted resultant of all the vectors between the current fish and its neighbours. The weights are obtained from the correlation matrix described in §2.3.

The result of these calculations is a vector representing the ideal heading for the fish in question. This ideal heading vector is averaged with the current heading to give the fish's actual new heading.

The calculation of the heading vector for a fish A is as follows:

$$\text{New heading} = w_{CA}\sum-(b_i - A) + w_{VM}\sum(C - A) + w_{OH}\sum(A - O) + w_{IF}\sum S_{ij}(b_i - A)$$

where:
$w_{CA}, w_{VM}, w_{OH}, w_{IF}$ = weighting applied to Collision Avoidance, Velocity Matching, Origin Homing and Information Flocking behaviours respectively
A, b_i, O = position vector of fish A, fish i and origin respectively
C = position vector of the centroid of fish A's neighbours (see below)
S_{ij} = similarity of fish A and fish i.

Notes:

1. The collision avoidance component of the heading vector is repulsive, while all the other components are attractive.

2. The similarity matrix is calculated at the start of the simulation, to maximise the speed. There is no reason that it could not be calculated on-the-fly from "live" data; this would result in the fish changing their behaviour dynamically to reflect the changes in the data.

3. At each time-step, two main calculations must be performed:

   i. The matrix of distances between the fish must be recalculated. This matrix is symmetric, so in order to optimise the speed of the simulation, only half of it is

---

[3] The weight, w_{IF}, applied to the Information Flocking behavioural component, determines the strength of inter-fish attraction. In the "interest" data set that is used for the current demonstration, w_{IF} lies between 0.0 and 1.0, so completely dissimilar fish have zero attraction. It would be feasible for w_{IF} to be in the range -1.0 to 1.0; this would result in a more marked separation. The "interest" data set was used as obtained by the authors, without modification.

calculated and then copied into the other half (since the distance between fish i and fish j is equal to the distance between fish j and fish i!) Distances are actually stored as their squares in order to avoid large numbers of calculations of computationally-intensive square roots.

ii. The near-neighbours of each fish must be recalculated. This is based on the distance matrix described above.

Each fish can sense its environment to a very limited extent. They can "see" for a fixed distance in a sphere around them. No attempt has been made to implement directional vision; the simple spherical model was considered sufficient for our purposes. The distance that the fish can "see" can be varied; in most of our investigations so far a distance approximately equal to four body lengths has been appropriate. This point is discussed in more detail below.

Each fish can be given a colour and a label, which appears when the mouse pointer is moved over it. URLs (Uniform Resource Locators) can be specified for each fish; when this is done, clicking on the fish will open the relevant web page in a browser such as Netscape.

It should be pointed out that the choice of the fish representation was an arbitrary decision based upon ease of construction and rendering. The behaviour of birds, bees or sheep could be modelled with very little modification. Other workers, notably Terzopoulos, Tu and Grzeszczuk have presented work that concentrates on the simulation of the behaviour of real fish [3].

2.3 Data Used

The data used for the Information Flocking needs to provide weights for all possible pairwise interactions between the fish. Thus, it needs to be in the form of a square, symmetric matrix. In the current application, this is in the form of a matrix of similarities between the interests of a group of Internet users [4], but any data in the correct format could be visualised using this technique.

The colours, labels and URLs of the fish are also read in from files. In the case of the 'interest' data, the labels represent the interests of the individuals, and the colour of each fish represents the primary interest of that person.

3. Results

An example screenshot is shown in Fig. 2.

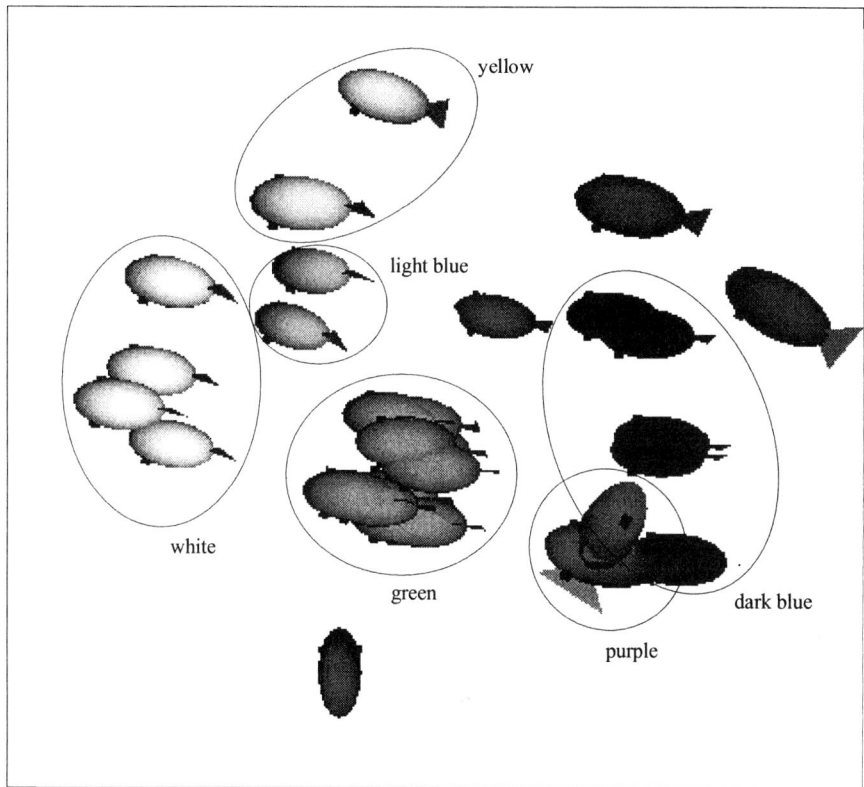

Fig. 2. Screenshot of the Information Flocking simulation. The labels represent the colours of the fish when seen on a colour monitor. Only the colours referred to in the text below are labelled. The ellipses in the figure serve only to delineate the colour groups; they do not appear in the actual simulation.

Watching the simulation for even a short period of time is very instructive. Several closely-related groups are immediately visible; the green, white and dark blue fish form small groups, indicating that the users in each of these groups have very similar interests. However, the individual groups also tend to form larger, more diffuse "supergroups"; for example the green, white, dark blue and purple fish all tend to move around in a large group, indicating a lower, but still significant, level of inter-group similarity.

Other small groups remain distinct from the main group. The light blue fish tend to exhibit markedly different behaviour, indicating that the users whom they represent have substantially different interests to the other users.

More subtle interactions can also be seen. The two yellow fish ostensibly represent people with the same primary interest, yet they do not swim close to each other. Upon further inspection, the two individuals turn out to be interested in different aspects of the same subject, which is the reason for the separation of the fish representing them.

4. Future Developments

Feedback on the prototype information flocking demonstrator described in this paper has been exceedingly positive; for this reason we are actively developing the system. Development is proceeding in three main areas:

1. Speed: currently the system runs at an acceptable frame rate (30 frames per second on a high-end PC with hardware 3D acceleration) for data sets represented by up to about 250 fish. Clearly this needs to be extended to handle data sets involving 1000 or more individuals (see note 2 below). Recent advances in VRML browsers, rendering engines and hardware graphics acceleration are also yielding considerable speed increases.

2. Data sets: we are investigating the properties of the system when applied to data sets other than the one initially used. Other correlation methods are also being tried.

3. Statistical investigations: through initial experiments with the current Information Flocking demonstrator, it appears that several factors can significantly affect the emergent behaviour. For example:

   - the weights applied to each of the component vectors in the calculation of the heading vector.

   - the distance within which the fish can detect each other

Preliminary results from some of these further developments are very illuminating. For instance, when a simulation with over 300 fish was set-up it was found that if the vision horizon was too long they formed a single, undifferentiated clump. If it was too short they never flocked but moved as individuals. There is clearly an optimal setting which leads to the formation of fluid groups, that keep partially breaking up and reforming. The suggestion here is that this phenomenon may be explained as a phase transition between a gaseous random state and a solid one, as the order parameter is changed. Clearly the system needs to be tuned into the phase transition zone to work best. Such phenomena are also seen in classical hierarchical clustering [5], and work is underway to reconcile these explanations.

As the exact values depend on all the parameter settings, and on the numbers of fish, their relative volume and that of the virtual space this could be difficult. We are now developing a system where the fish increase or decrease their horizon depending on their 'satisfaction' - the degree to which they have found similar fish near them. Early results suggests this leads to some particularly interesting phenomena akin to courtship behaviours.

5. Conclusions

This paper has described the concept of Information Flocking. It shows that ideas in artificial life, developed to mimic biology have much more powerful applications outside the arena of simulations.

The technique is powerful because it presents data in a form which is particularly suited to the human brain's evolved ability to process information. Human beings are very good at seeing patterns in colour and motion, and Information Flocking is a way of leveraging this ability. The dynamics of the system provide a much greater degree of understanding that the initial data would suggest.

Virtual worlds with virtual organisms could have a powerful impact on the way we use and visualise complex data systems. A number of demonstrators have now been built that show these concepts in action.

Acknowledgements

The authors would like to thank the following:
Barry Crabtree and Stuart Soltysiak for providing the initial data set on which this work was based.
Tim Regan at BT Labs, John DeCuir at Sony Pictures Imageworks and David Chamberlain at Silicon Graphics/Cosmo Software for VRML-related help.
Mark Shackleton, rest of the BT Artificial Life Group and Alan Steventon for many useful discussions.

References

1. Partridge, B.L., "The Structure and Function of Fish Schools", *Scientific American*, June 1983, 90-99.
2. Reynolds, C.W. "Flocks, Herds and Schools: A Distributed Behavioural Model", *Computer Graphics*, **21** (4), 1987.
3. Terzopoulos, D., Tu, X. & Grzeszczuk, R. "Artificial Fishes with Autonomous Locomotion, Perception, Behaviour, and Learning in a Simulated Physical World", *Proceedings of the Artificial Life IV Workshop*, MIT Press, 1994.
4. Crabtree, B. & Soltysiak, S. "Identifying and Tracking Changing Interests", IJCAL '97 Workshop on AI in Digital Libraries.

5. Salton, G., *Automatic Text Processing*, Reading, MA, Addison Wesley Publishing Company Inc, 1989.
6. Macleod, K.J. & Robertson, W., "A Neural Algorithm for document clustering", *Information Processing and Management*, **27** (4), 337-346, 1991.
7. Orwig, R.E., and Chen, H., "A Graphical, Self-Organizing Approach to Classifying Electronic Meeting Output*", Journal of the American Society for Information Science*, **48** (2) 157-170, 1997.
8. Kohonen, T., *Self-organisation and associative memory*, Springer-Verlag, 1989.

Nerve Garden: A Public Terrarium in Cyberspace

Bruce Damer, Karen Marcelo, and Frank Revi

Biota.Org, a Special Interest Group of the Contact Consortium

Contact Consortium,
P.O. Box 66866
Scotts Valley, CA 95067-6866 USA
Tel: +1 408-338-9400
E-mail:bdamer@ccon.org

Abstract. Nerve Garden is a biologically-inspired multi-user collaborative 3D virtual world available to a wide Internet audience. The project combines a number of methods and technologies, including L-systems, Java, cellular automata, and VRML. Nerve Garden is a work in progress designed to provide a compelling experience of a virtual terrarium which exhibits properties of growth, decay and cybernetics reminiscent of a simple ecosystem. The goals of the Nerve Garden project are to create an on-line "collaborative Artificial Life laboratory" which can be extended by a large number of users for purposes of education and research.

Introduction

During the summer of 1994, one of us (Damer) paid a visit to the Santa Fe Institute (SFI) for discussions with Chris Langton and his student team working on the Swarm simulation system [8]. Two fortuitous events coincided with that visit: SFI was installing the first World Wide Web browsers, and digital movies of Karl Sims' evolving "block creatures" [1, 7] were being viewed through the Web by amazed students (figure 1). It was postulated then that the combination of the emerging backbone of the Internet, a distributed simulation environment like Swarm and the compelling 3D visuals and underlying techniques of Sims' creatures could be combined to produce something very compelling: on-line virtual worlds in which thousands of users could collaboratively experiment with biological paradigms.

In the three years since the SFI visit, we founded an organization called the Contact Consortium [11]. This organization serves as a focal point for the development of on-line virtual worlds and hosts conferences and research and development projects. One of its special interest groups, called Biota.org, was chartered to develop virtual worlds using techniques from the natural world. Its first effort is Nerve Garden which came on-line in August of 1997 at the SIGGRAPH 97 conference [12].

Fig. 1. View of two of Karl Sims' original evolving creatures in a competition to control a block. Iterations of this exercise with mutations of creature's underlying genotypes yielding winning strategies created a large variety of forms. Above we see a two armed grasping strategy being bested by a single armed 'hockey stick' strategy. Courtesy K Sims. See [7] for the original MPEG movies of Sims' creatures.

Three hundred visitors to the Nerve Garden installation used L-systems and Java to germinate plants models into a shared VRML (Virtual Reality Modeling Language) world hosted on the Internet. Biota.org is now developing a subsequent version of Nerve Garden, which will embody more biological paradigms, and, we hope, create an environment capable of supporting education, research, and cross-pollination between traditional Artificial Life subject areas and other fields.

Nerve Garden I: Architecture and Experience

Nerve Garden I is a biologically-inspired shared state 3D virtual world available to a wide audience through standard Internet protocols running on all major hardware platforms. Nerve Garden was inspired by the original work on Artificial Life by Chris Langton [3], Tierra and other digital ecosystems by Tom Ray [2,3] and the evolving 3D virtual creatures of Karl Sims [1]. Nerve Garden sources its models and methods from the original work on L-systems by Aristide Lindenmayer, Przemyslaw Prusinkiewicz and Radomir Mech [5, 6] and the tools from Laurens Lapre [10].

Fig. 2. Lace Germinator Java client interface showing the mutator outputs on the left, the growth and naming interfaces at the bottom with a plant production visualized in the main window.

The first version, Nerve Garden I, was built as a client-server system written in the distributed Java language. The client program, called the Germinator (figure 2), allowed users to extrude 3D plant models generated from L-systems. The simple interface in the Java client provided an immediate 3D experience of various L-system plant and arthropod forms. Users employed a slider bar to extrude the models in real time and a mutator to randomize production rules in the L-systems and generate variants on the plant models. Figure 3 shows various plant extrusions produced by the Germinator, including models with fluorescences. After germinating several plants, the user would select one, name it and submit it into to a common VRML 2.0 scenegraph called the Seeder Garden.

Fig. 3. Plant models generated by the Germinator including flowering and vine like forms. Arthropods and other segmented or symmetrical forms could also be generated.

The object passed to the Seeder Garden contained the VRML export from the Germinator, the plant name and other data. The server-based Java application, called NerveServer, received this object and determined a free "plot" on an island model in a VRML scenegraph. Each island had a set number of plots and showed the user the plot his or her plant could be placed by moving an indicator sphere operated through the VRML external authoring interface (EAI). "Cybergardeners" would open a window into the Seeder Garden where they would then move the indicator sphere with their plant attached and place it into the scene. Please see an overview of the client-server architecture of Nerve Garden I in figure 4.

Various scenegraph viewpoints were made available to users, including a moving viewpoint on the back of an animated model of a flying insect endlessly touring the island. Users would often spot their plant as their bee or butterfly made a close approach over the island (figure 5). Over 10MB of sound, some of it also generated algorithmically, emanated from different objects on the island added to the immersion of the experience. For added effect, L-system based VRML lightening (with generated thunder) occasionally streaked across the sky above the Seeder Garden islands. The populated seeder island was projected on a large screen at the Siggraph hall which drew a large number of visitors to the installation.

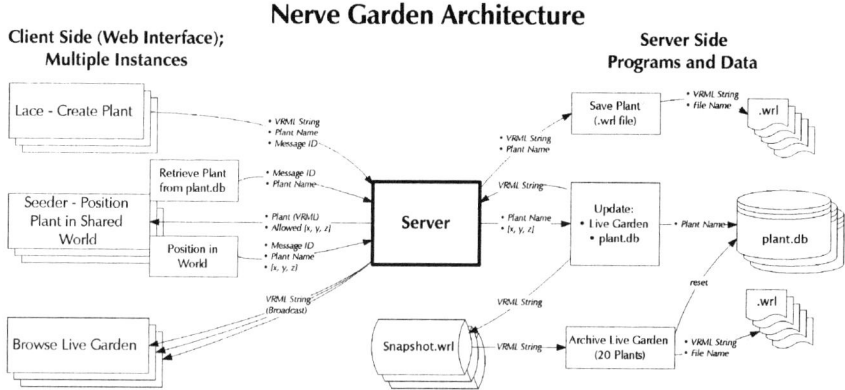

Fig. 4. Nerve Garden I architecture detailing the Java and VRML 2.0 based client-server components and their interaction.

NerveServer permitted multiple users to update and view the same island. In addition, users could navigate the same space using standard VRML plug-ins to Web browsers on Unix workstations from Silicon Graphics, PCs or Macintosh computers operating at various locations on the Internet. One problem was that the distributed L-system clients could easily generate scenes with several hundred thousand polygons, rendering them impossible to visit. We used 3D hardware acceleration, including an SGI Onyx II Infinite Reality system and a PC running a 3D Labs Permedia video acceleration card to permit a more complex environment to be experienced by users.

Fig. 5. Flight of the bumblebee above a Seeder Garden

In 1999 and beyond, a whole new generation of 3D chip sets on 32 and 64 bit platforms will enable highly complex 3D interactive environments. There is an interesting parallel here to Ray's work on Tierra [2,9], where the energy of the system was proportional to the power of the CPU serving the virtual machine inhabited by Tierran organisms. In many Artificial Life systems, it is not important to have a compelling 3D interface. The benefits to providing one for Nerve Garden are that it encouraged participation and experimentation from a wide non-technical group of users. The experience of Nerve Garden I is fully documented on the Web and several gardens generated during the SIGGRAPH 97 installation can be visited on-line with a VRML 2.0 equipped web browser [12].

What was Learned

As a complex set of parts including a Java client, simple object distribution system, a multi-user server, a rudimentary database and a shared, persistent VRML scenegraph, Nerve Garden functioned well under the pressures of a diverse range of users on multiple hardware platforms. Users were able to use the Germinator applet without our assistance to generate fairly complex, unique, and aesthetically pleasing models. Users were all familiar with the metaphor of gardens and many were eager to "visit their plant" again from their home computers. Placing their plants in the VRML Seeder Gardens was more challenging due to the difficulty of navigating in 3D using VRML browsers. Younger users tended to be much more adept at using the 3D environment.

In summary, while a successful user experience of a generative environment, Nerve Garden I lacked the sophistication of a "true -Life system" like Tierra [2,9] in that plant model objects did not reproduce or communicate between virtual machines containing other gardens. In addition, unlike an adaptive L-system space such as the one described by Mech and Prusinkiewicz [6] the plant models did not interact with their neighbors or the environment. Lastly, there was no concept of autonomous, self replicating objects within the environment. Nerve Garden II, now under development, will address some of these shortcomings, and, we hope, contribute a powerful tool for education and research in the ALife community.

The Next Steps: Nerve Garden II

The goals for Nerve Garden II are:
- to develop a simple functioning ecosystem within the VRML scenegraph to control polygon growth and evolve elements of the world through time;
- to integrate with a stronger database to permit garden cloning and inter-garden communication encouraging cross pollination between islands;

- to integrate a cellular automata engine which will support autonomous growth and replication of plant models and introduce a class of virtual herbivores ("polyvores") which prey on the plants' polygonal energy stores;
- to stream world geometry through the transmission of generative algorithms (such as the L-systems) rather than geometry, achieving great compression, efficient use of bandwidth and control of polygon explosion and scene evolution on the client side;

Much of the above depends on the availability of a comprehensive scenegraph and behavior control mechanism. In development over the past two years, Nerves is a simple but high performance general purpose cellular automata engine written as both a C++ and Java kernel [13]. Nerves is modeled on the biological processes seen in animal nervous systems, and plant and animal circulatory systems, which all could be reduced to token passing and storage mechanisms. Nerves and its associated language, NerveScript, allows users to define a large number of arbitrary pathways and collection pools supporting flows of arbitrary tokens, token storage, token correlation, and filtering. Nerves borrows many concepts from neural networks and directed graphs used in concert with genetic and generative algorithms as reported by Ray [3], Sims [1] and others.

Nerves components will underlie the Seeder Gardens providing functions analogous to a drip irrigation system, defining a finite and therefore regulatory resource from which the plant models must draw for continued growth. In addition, Nerves control paths will be generated as L-system models extrude, providing wiring connected to the geometry and proximity sensors in the model. This will permit interaction with the plant models. When pruning of plant geometry occurs or growth stimulus becomes scarce, the transformation of the plant models can be triggered. One step beyond this will be the introduction of autonomous entities into the gardens, which we term "polyvores", that will seek to convert the "energy" represented by the polygons in the plant models, into reproductive capacity. Polyvores will provide another source of regulation in this simple ecosystem. Gardens will maintain their interactive capacity, allowing users to enter, germinate plants, introduce polyvores, and prune plants or cull polyvores. Gardens will also run as automated systems, maintaining polygon complexity within boundaries that allow users to enter the environment.

Example of a NerveScript coding language

```
spinalTap.nrv:
DEF spinalCordSeg Bundle {
-spinalTapA-Swim-bodyMotion[4]-Complex;
-spinalTapB-Swim-bodyMotion[4]-Complex;
}
```

We expect to use Nerves to tie much of the above processes together. Like VRML, Nerves is described by a set of public domain APIs and a published language, NerveScript [13]. Figure 6 lists some typical NerveScript statements which describe a two chain neural pathway that might be used as a spinal chord of a simple swimming fish. DEF defines a reusable object `spinalCordSeg` consisting of input paths `spinalTapA` and `spinalTapB` which will only pass the token `Swim` into a four stage filter called `bodyMotion`. All generated tokens end up in `Complex`, another Nerve bundle, defined elsewhere.

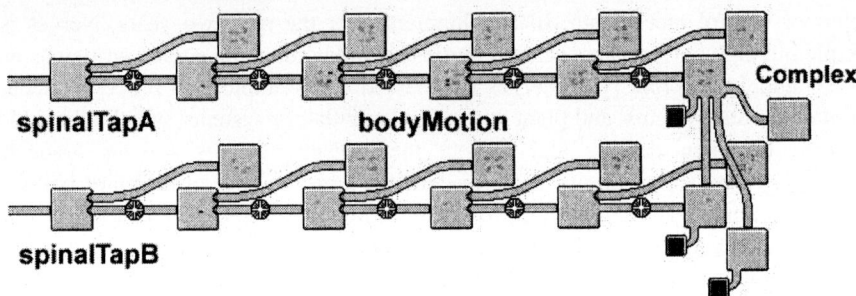

Fig. 6. Nerves visualizer running within the NerveScript development environment. In the VRML setting, the pathways *spinalTapA* and *spinalTapB* are fed by *eventOut* messages drawn out of the scenegraph while the Nerve bundles generate *eventIns* back to VRML using the EAI. *BodyMotion* are a series of stages where filters draw off message tokens to drive simulated musculature on the left and right hand side of the VRML model, simulating a swimming motion. Message tokens that reach *Complex*, a kind of simple brain, trigger events in the overall simulation, and exporting messages back into the external pool.

Figure 6 shows the visualization of the sample NerveScript code running in the NerveScript development environment. We are currently connecting Nerves to the VRML environment, where it will be possible to visualize the operation in 3D. Nerves is fully described at the web address referenced at the end of this paper.

Goals and Call for Participation

The goals of the Nerve Garden project are to create an on-line "collaborative A-Life laboratory" which can be extended by a large number of users for purposes of education and research. We plan to launch Nerve Garden II on the Internet and look forward to observing both the user experience and, we hope, the emergence of complex forms and interactions within some of the simple garden ecosystems. The Contact Consortium and its Biota.org special interest group would welcome additional collaborators on this project.

Acknowledgments

In addition to the extensive contributions made by the authors of this paper, we would like to thank the following sponsors: Intervista, Silicon Graphics/Cosmo Software, and 3D Labs. A special thanks goes to Przemyslaw Prusinkiewicz for inspiring this work in the first place and numerous other individuals who have worked on aspects of the project since 1995.

References

1. Sims, K., Evolving Virtual Creatures, Computer Graphics (Siggraph '94) Annual Conference Proceedings, July 1994, pp.43-50.
2. Ray, T. S. 1994a. Netlife - Creating a jungle on the Internet: Nonlocated online digital territories, incorporations and the matrix. Knowbotic Research 3/94.
3. Ray, T. S. 1994b. Neural Networks, Genetic Algorithms and Artificial Life: Adaptive Computation. In Proceedings of the 1994 ALife, Genetic Algorithm and Neural Networks Seminar, 1-14. Institute of Systems, Control and Information Engineers.
4. Langton, C. 1992. Life at the Edge of Chaos. Artificial Life II 41-91. Redwood City CA: Addison-Wesley.
5. Prusinkiewicz, P., and Lindenmayer, A., eds. 1990. The Algorithmic Beauty of Plants. New York: Springer Verlag.
6. Mech, R., and Prusinkiewicz, P. 1994. Visual Models of Plants Interacting with Their Environment. In Proceedings of SIGGRAPH 96 . In Computer Graphics Proceedings, 397-410. ACM Publications.

Online References

7. Karl Sims' creatures are viewable on Biota.org at: http://www.biota.org/conf97/ksims.html
8. The Swarm Simulation System is described at http://www.santafe.edu/projects/swarm/
9. Tom Ray's Tierra is fully described at http://www.hip.atr.co.jp/~ray/tierra/tierra.html
10. Laurens Lapre's L-parser L-system software tools and examples can be found at: http://www.xs4all.nl/~ljlapre/
11. Full background on the goals and projects of the Contact Consortium are at http://www.ccon.org and its special interest group, Biota.org are at http://www.biota.org
12. Nerve Garden I can be entered at http://www.biota.org/nervegarden/index.html with a suitable VRML 2.0 browser installed.
13. The Nerves home page, with language specification, examples and downloads is at: http://www.digitalspace.com/nerves/

A Two Dimensional Virtual World to Explain the Genetic Code Structure ?

Jean-Luc Tyran

Electricité de France - Direction des Etudes et Recherches
6, Quai Watier - BP49 - 78401 Chatou Cedex - France
Jean-Luc.Tyran@der.edfgdf.fr
jltyran@magic.fr

Abstract. In this study, we introduce a remarkable squared tiling of the plan whose characteristics meet in many points those of the genetic code: same number of structural levels (3), same number of elements at each level (4, 64 and 20), same relationships between the elements of the different levels. To conclude, we formulate one hypothesis to explain these results and consequently we propose new ways of research in Artificial Life, but also in structural molecular biology.

1 Introduction and Purpose

In Artificial Life studies, Mathematics and mathematical tools are important to explore and to experiment (by means of computer simulations) the behaviour and the fundamental structures of artificial living systems.

In real living systems studies, biological experiments are essential. In this domain, some recent experiments led by James Ferris (in collaboration with Leslie Orgel of the Salk Institute) show the importance of mineral surfaces[1] and – more precisely – the importance of geometrical constraints in the early stages of bio-molecular development (i.e. at the origin of life): mineral surfaces restrict the elementary molecular movements into a weak number of particular directions and consequently favorize the molecular polymerization (and polycondensation) processes on these surfaces [1].

Purpose: we propose to study, in a virtual mathematical plan, i.e. in a *two dimensional virtual world*, the consequences of geometrical constraints that have been observed in the real world (physico-chemical restriction of the directions of molecular movements).

---

[1] The hypothesis of the origin of life on mineral surfaces had remained, longtime, without determining clue. Now, the experimental works of James Ferris and al. bring some fundamental and decisive elements to satisfy to this hypothesis: *montmorillonite* surface for nucleotides polymerization (ImpA) and *illite* and *hydroxylapatite* surfaces for amino acids polymerization (glutamic and aspartic acids).

2 Simplest Tiling of the Ideal Mathematical Plan

2.1 Tiling by Squares Requires the Weakest Number of Tiled Directions

In the ideal mathematical plan, which is the equivalent representation of an elementary bio-molecule?

In response, we can choose an elementary piece of the plan surface: for example, a polygonal tile. To link these artificial bio-molecules (the linking of tiles is similar to a polymerization process), it is necessary to be able to pave the plan with the same (or identical) regular polygonal tiles.

Only three types of regular polygon can tiled the plan: equilateral triangle, square or regular hexagon (see Fig. 1). Among these possibilities, the simplest is the tiling by squares: it requires the weakest number of tiled directions and satisfies to the purpose of this study. Accordingly, we choose the tiling by squares.

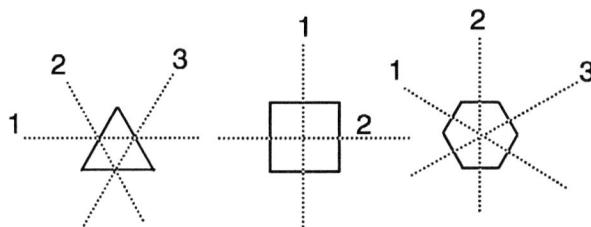

Fig. 1. The three tilings of the plan by identical polygons: equilateral triangles, squares or regular hexagons. The simplest is the tiling by squares: only two tiled directions are required in this case (three tiled directions are required in the other cases).

2.2 Simplest Tiling and Lowest Number of Squares

In biological world, *diversity* is everywhere. Life, into many different forms, is *diversity* in action. Also, we must introduce some minimal *diversity* in the tiling process. In this goal, we choose to tile the plan with the lowest number of all different squares. This choice corresponds to a *simple perfect squared square of lowest order* (see Fig. 2). It is the most economic tiling possible and its mathematical form is *uniqueness*. As a result of graph and combinatorial theories, this economic tiling has been found by A.J.W. Duijvestijn [2].

To obtain the *first generation square* (the most external and integrative square of length 112), we add *twenty different squares* to the first square or *germ* (the most inside and little square of length 2). And so on, all along the successive *generation squares*... It is a *russian doll* process: to obtain a new *generation square*, or new *integron*, we add 20 new squares to the former *generation square*, or former *integron*. The properties of these mathematical *integrons* are analogous to the properties of the *integrons* defined by F. Jacob for the living systems [3].

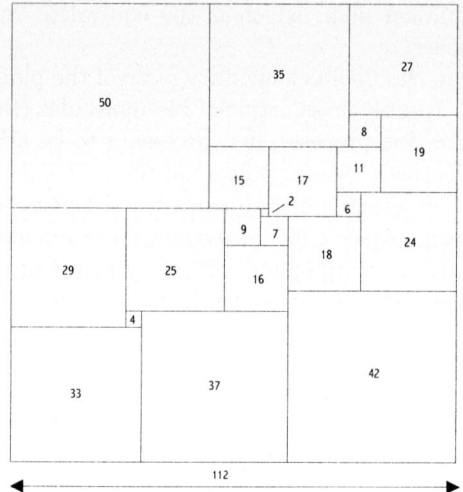

Fig. 2. An Artificial Life *integron*: the simplest tiling of a square by the lowest number of all different squares.

3 A Set of Analogies Between the Simplest Tiling of the Ideal Mathematical Plan and the Universal Genetic Code

The simplest tiling, or *integron*, showed Fig. 2, is an *asymmetrical* figure. This figure marks the four directions of the plan: Up (U), Down (D), Left (L) and Right (R): i.e. a *four* letters alphabet in relation to the four sides of the asymmetrical figure. It exists also a *twenty* letters alphabet: the set of the twenty new squares added at each new generation. Between these two alphabets (the *first* of *four* letters and the *last* of *twenty* letters), it exists an *intermediate* alphabet. The *sixty-four* letters of this intermediate alphabet are the sixty-four elementary segments of the simplest tiling.

With the same number of alphabets (3) and the same numbers of letters in these alphabets (4, 64 and 20), the structure of the universal genetic code (see Fig. 3) is *similar* to the structure of the simplest tiling. The *first* alphabet of the genetic code: the *four nucleotides* Uracil (U), Cytosine (C), Adenine (A) and Guanine (G). The *intermediate* alphabet: the *sixty-four codons*. And the *last* alphabet: the *twenty amino acids* (to make the proteins).

A Two Dimensional Virtual World to Explain the Genetic Code Structure ?   189

1st ↓	2d →	U	C	A	G	3d ↓
U		Phenylalanine Phenylalanine Leucine Leucine	Serine Serine Serine Serine	Tyrosine Tyrosine Stop Stop	Cysteine Cysteine Stop Tryptophan	U C A G
C		Leucine Leucine Leucine Leucine	Proline Proline Proline Proline	Histidine Histidine Glutamine Glutamine	Arginine Arginine Arginine Arginine	U C A G
A		Isoleucine Isoleucine Isoleucine Methionine	Threonine Threonine Threonine Threonine	Asparagine Asparagine Lysine Lysine	Serine Serine Arginine Arginine	U C A G
G		Valine Valine Valine Valine	Alanine Alanine Alanine Alanine	Aspartic acid Aspartic acid Glutamic acid Glutamic acid	Glycine Glycine Glycine Glycine	U C A G

Fig. 3. The universal genetic code for the translation of the 64 codons into the 20 amino acids. A codon is a mRNA word of three letters among four mRNA bases or nucleotides (U (Uracil), C (Cytosine), A (Adenine) and G (Guanine)): first (1st), second (2d) and third (3d) letters.

Now, we define a set of *"at least – at most"* rules, or **existence and association rules**, to specify the relationships between the 64 elementary segments and the 20 squares.

Each square (among the 20 squares) is bounded by β elementary peripheral segments: $4 \leq \beta \leq 7$ (see Fig. 2). **Existence or *"at least"* rule:** to exist, each square (by analogy, each amino acid), must depend on **one** of its β bounded segments (by analogy, of *one* codon). **Association or *"at most"* rule:** each square cannot depend on the totality of its β bounded segments. At the most, it depends on $(\beta - 1)$ bounded segments: it is the only one manner to establish some minimal *association links* within the unified simplest tiling structure.

By application of these rules, we have found the relationships showed Fig. 4. This figure exhibits some remarkable analogies with the genetic code. For example, the analogies that exist between the squares of length 35, 17 and 25 and the amino acids arginine, serine and leucine.

There are only three squares (35, 17 and 25) to have the highest value of β ($\beta_{max} = 7$). At the most, each of these three squares depends on 6 bounded segments $((\beta_{max} - 1) = 6)$. In the genetic code, this value (6) corresponds to the highest number of codons that code to one amino acid. And there are only three amino acids in this case: arginine, serine and leucine...

In the genetic code, arginine and serine are *adjacents* (i.e. in the same box of the AGX codons), and leucine is *alone*. In the simplest tiling, we have some similar relative positions: squares 35 and 17 are *adjacents* and the square 25 is *alone*...

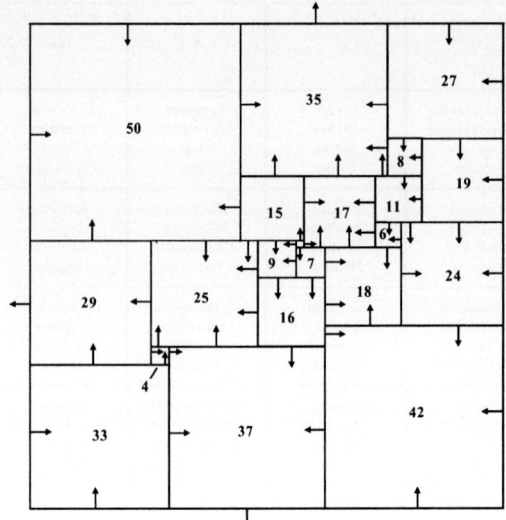

Fig. 4. Each arrow indicates a relationship between one particular bounded segment and one particular square. In the genetic code, it exists a similar relationship between one particular codon and one particular amino acid. The three outside arrows correspond to the three *Stop* codons.

4 Conclusions

4.1 How to Explain the Set of Analogies Between the Simplest Tiling of the Ideal Mathematical Plan and the Universal Genetic Code?

The results obtained and their precision lead to ask the question of a cause-to-effect relationship between the structure of the simplest tiling and of the genetic code.

How to explain the links between the mathematical elements of the 2D simplest tiling (bounded segments and squares of an unified mathematical form that is *independent* of all matter substrates) and the particular 3D molecular substrates of the genetic code (mRNA codons and amino acids)?

An answer can be found in a set of two dual graphs[2] that is the mathematical basis of the simplest tiling: a first Up–Down graph[3] links the horizontal opposite Up and Down sides of the Fig. 2, a second Left–Right graph links the vertical opposite Left and Right sides of the Fig. 2. The first graph has 11 vertices

---

[2] More precisely, two dual 3-connected planar graphs.
[3] Every horizontal line of the simplest tiling corresponds to a *vertice* of the Up–Down graph, and each square (between two successive horizontal lines) corresponds to an *edge*. Every vertical line of the simplest tiling corresponds to a *vertice* of the Left–Right graph.

and 22 edges. The second graph has 13 vertices and 22 edges. These graphs are isomorphic to convex polyhedra. Accordingly to the Euler formula[4]: the first polyhedron has 11 vertices and 13 faces[5] (10 triangles, one quadrilateral polygon, 2 pentagons); the second has 13 vertices and 11 faces[6] (4 triangles, 4 quadrilateral polygons, 2 pentagons and one hexagon).

In [4], it is suggested that the first genetic coding system can be started from specific interactions between two complementary 3D molecular substrates.

From an optimal space filling point–of–view (to favorize chemical interactions and to minimize energy), we think that the two unknown 3D molecular substrates have the same structures that the two previous dual polyhedra, and we propose to research the bio-molecules that could correspond (*new way of research*).

4.2 Some Propositions for New Ways in Artificial Life Research

The simplest tiling of this study, or *integron*, shows the emergence of an hierarchy of components (complexification process) and may be a potential source of new ideas (or open ways) in Artificial Life research:

- New rules for programming cellular automata... For instance, in a "particular" array (i.e. the *integron* of the Fig. 4 and its successive generations) with a rule that uses the *arrows* (to specify the authorized displacements) and works *differently* in each of the 20 squares of the Artificial Life *integron*...
- Which is the equivalent simplest tiling, or paving, of an other space? In other words, which is the equivalent genetic code of this other space? In spaces of dimension[7] ≥ 3 ? In non euclidean spaces? Life "as it could be"... Life is it an exclusive property of the euclidean space?
- Cross fertilization between the Artificial Life *integron* and the *arithmetical relator* language [5]. *Arithmetical relator* can express the world in structural levels (a quadratic form express the adaptation of the natural system to its environment). Artificial Life *integron* is also expressed by a quadratic form. The *integron* (see Fig. 4) presents a set of particular symetries: we think that the *arithmetical relator* – associated to the semisimple Lie algebra – can be an useful tool to study these symetries.

References

1. Ferris, J., Hill, A.R., Liu, R., Orgel, L.E.: Synthesis of long prebiotic oligomers on mineral surfaces. Nature **381** (1996) 59–61
2. Duijvestijn, A.J.W.: A simple perfect squared square of lowest order. Journal of combinatorial theory B **25** (1978) 240–243

---

[4] $V + F = E + 2$, where V is the number of vertices, F the number of faces and E the number of edges.
[5] Generally, non regular polygonal faces.
[6] Ibidem.
[7] The simplest paving of a cube, by all different cubes, is not possible.

3. Jacob, F.: La logique du vivant. Editions Gallimard (1970)
4. Trémolières, A.: Nucleotidic cofactors and the origin of the genetic code. Biochimie **62** (1980) 493–496
5. Moulin, T.: Imbrications de niveaux et esquisse d'un langage systémique associé à des relateurs arithmétiques. Revue Internationale de Systémique **5** (1991) 517–560

Acknowledgments

We thank Michel Gondran (EDF) for helpful discussions and encouragements, Antoine Trémolières (CNRS – Orsay) for technical interesting clues and the three anonymous reviewers for constructive comments on the manuscript.

Grounding Agents in EMud Artificial Worlds

Antony Robert, Fabrice Chantemargue, Michèle Courant

Institut d'Informatique, Université de Fribourg (IIUF),
Ch. du Musée 3, CH-1700 Fribourg, Switzerland,
`<firstname.lastname>@unifr.ch`

Abstract. This paper suggests that in the context of autonomous agents and generation of intelligent behavior for such agents, a more important focus should be held on the symbolic context that forms the basis of computer programs. Basically, software agents are symbolic entities living in a symbolic world and this has an effect on how one should think about designing frameworks for their evolution or learning. We will relate the problem of symbol grounding to that of sensory information available to agents. We will then introduce an experimental environment based on virtual worlds called EMuds, where both human and artificial agents can interact. Next, we show how it can be applied in the framework of multi-agent systems to address emergence based problems and report preliminary results. We then conclude with some ongoing and future work.

Keywords: autonomous agents, symbol grounding, virtual worlds.

1 Introduction

The development of virtual worlds provides new means to represent information stored or conveyed by computers. In recent years, much effort has been devoted to improving the overall sensory richness of such worlds to the benefit of human users. This has mainly been implemented through the development of better rendering algorithms, efficient graphical engines, the use of animation [1] or sound [12]. In parallel, toolkits aimed at providing facilities for virtual reality implementations (serial or distributed) have been provided to solve standardization issues (see for example [14]).

In contrast, work focusing on virtual worlds in themselves has led to new developments reaching the fields of artificial intelligence or artificial life, where virtual worlds serve as an environment for the agents under study. A typical integration of this type is found in [7] where a virtual reality toolkit, compatible with a language for the study of multi-agent systems, is available.

Our work enters this framework by studying agents living in a virtual world and stressing the importance of such a design for new artificial intelligence (AI). As environments, we use simple text based virtual worlds, inspired from multi-user games called Muds that have been described in [5]. This setup allows for a rich level of interaction between humans, artificial agents and the environment, providing a configuration well suited to test artificial agent behaviors as was shown in [17, 8].

2 Artificial Intelligence and the Grounding Problem

The field of artificial intelligence is torn between the classical top-down approaches and newer bottom-up methodologies. This gap originating in a form of the mind-body problem has led to important developments within each paradigm, while never allowing for a unification of methods.

2.1 State of the Art

In classical AI, cognition is considered as the capacity to form and manipulate internal representations or models of the world (the usual metaphor for mind in this paradigm is the computer, i.e. a symbol processing device) [9]. This leads to the use of rule-based systems applying transformations over symbols that have a signification within a representation of a problem domain. Such systems show impressive performance over specific tasks and provide a good framework for high level reasoning, but have a high sensitivity to internal failure of subcomponents, cannot be applied to new problems outside of their representation base and generally do not scale up from basic problems to more general ones. This has been subsumed under two general problems: the *frame problem* [21, 13], where classical systems fail to extend or adapt their internal representation, and the *symbol grounding problem* [11, 27], where classical systems fail to relate their symbolic representation to their sensory information.

On the other hand, the new AI methodologies take a more materialistic approach in believing we can "grow" minds from elementary interacting functionalities and define intelligence as an agent's capacity to interact with its environment [16]. Thus new AI is concerned with agents adapting their behaviors to use basic competences in an environment through learning or evolution. From the problem solving point of view, this leads to robust, adaptive, fault tolerant algorithms. The downside of these approaches being that they do not achieve optimal solutions even when such solutions exist, their internal working is usually difficult to understand and that if such systems proved their usefulness in solving basic robotic tasks in dynamic environments (such as obstacle avoidance), much work still has to be invested in order to tackle more complex tasks.

In conclusion, where classical AI fails to relate symbolic representations to sensory information (the grounding problem), new AI uses a "grounding hypothesis" to build systems from sensory information [2, 3], but fails to produce systems capable of reasoning (this should be called the *reverse grounding problem*). While new AI has the hope of seeing complex behaviors (comparable to those produced by reasoning) emerge from the interaction of simple functionalities, we believe that this bridging problem can be better addressed by starting off with perceptions of a higher level than that usually used. As we will show, this implies the use of simulations in symbolic virtual worlds as a starting point for the design of autonomous agents.

2.2 Embodiment

Traditionally, approaches to solving the grounding problem have accepted a bottom-up perspective to which we adhere, where it is supposed that if meaning is to become intrinsic to a computer program (as opposed to parasitic, linked to human interpretation), such a program will have to develop its understanding from sensory information. We call this the grounding hypothesis and what we question is the level at which this hypothesis is initially applied.

Most cognitive answers suggest using a representation, part of whose symbols are identified with sensory percepts based in the physical world, i.e. grounded symbols. New AI on the other hand uses the concept of embodiment [23] to consider agents linked to the physical world through sensory-motor input/output (in the robotic sense) without giving any abstract initial model of the world to their agent (see also [3]). This physical embodiment is then considered as the basis on which to try generating intelligent behavior. But this leads to diverging convictions about the concept of embodiment: when an agent is situated in an artificial environment, can it be an embodied agent, or does this concept of embodiment only apply to agents connected to the real world? There are two main reasons for this difference of opinion.

First, that a simulated environment eliminates the complexity found in the real world, limiting the amount of information that can be perceived by an agent. This apparent noise could be essential for acquiring the ability to distinguish between the relevant and the irrelevant information in the agent's environment, as well as learning to adapt and perform in a wide range of situations. To this objection, proponents of simulation state that there is no fundamental difference between perceptually grounding an agent in an artificial environment or in the real world and that the perturbations to the sensors due to the real world's richness of information or complexity can be considered random for all practical purposes and thus be replaced by pseudo-random signals superimposed on an agent's sensory input.

Second, that an agent evolved in an artificial environment might never be able to relate to the real world because it will be too tightly linked with its "tutorial" world to be able to generalize behaviors for real world operation. This objection arises from the idea that, following Maturana and Varela's enaction theory [23], the structural coupling induced by the embodiment of an agent in an environment defines its cognition, thus seemingly preventing the integration of such an agent in a new environment or the real-world. This debate remains open, although many authors now accept the idea of simulated embodiment. Actually, we believe that if an agent could be grounded in an artificial environment and allowed to evolve a sufficiently complex relationship with its environment, the coupling induced would allow such an agent to be introduced into new environments *through* its own environment without disrupting its functioning. This leads us to suggest that the embodiment of an agent in a virtual world is, in fact, essential for it to develop intelligent behavior and that the reason for this is linked with the type of sensory information a software agent can perceive.

2.3 Sensory Information

With the bottom-up approach to building agents, comes the feeling that such agents are naturally grounded and should thus have the basic attributes to develop cognitive processes, for they are from the sensory point of view as much part of the world as humans are. This has evidently not been shown to be true (to this day) and we believe one of the reasons can be found in asking a similar question as that posed by T. Nagel in his article "What is it like to be a bat?" [19]. Although we do not wish to delve into the existence of qualia, the question "What is it like to be a computer algorithm?" comes to mind and hints that whatever sensory apparatus an artificial agent is equipped with, his perceptions will remain purely symbolic in nature. This differs greatly with the perceptions available to living organisms in the physical world.

Although human beings are grounded in the physical world by their senses, allowing them to give meaning to abstract concepts, it should first be attempted to ground computer systems in their own symbolic world. We believe that meaning is strongly rooted in the type of sensory information available to an entity and there can be no equivalent of natural senses in a software agent. Thus, under the hypothesis that meaning can become intrinsic to a program, such a program will have to be able to give meaning to symbolic events in symbolic terms, before giving meaning to symbolically translated physical events. Our application will concentrate on making available a rich symbolic world where agents can perceive information of their own nature, that is, of a symbolic type and eventually access the physical world through the world they are grounded in. In that, our application provides a framework for simulated embodied agents.

3 EMuds

Based on the idea of adapting agents capable of symbolic level perceptions, we have developed an application providing virtual worlds in which agents can interact. The application takes inspiration from Internet games called Muds for the richness of actions they allow and we explain the principles on which a Mud functions, before describing the design of an EMud.

3.1 What Is a Mud?

The acronym MUD stands for Multi User Dungeon. Muds are Internet based computer games which were developed following the principles of role-playing games. In such games, the players take up the role of a character in an invented world, where they act in pursuit of a goal that has been set to them by the designer of the game's story line. The main interest of such games is to discover the worlds invented by the designer or other players and interact with the creatures that populate such worlds, usually with the aim of solving an enigma. Muds take this idea into the computer world by setting up an artificial environment (world) where players can connect via telnet sessions and direct the actions of a character within that environment. Through this character, the player can then live a virtual life in the environment, leading to human social interaction as described in [5], or simply explore the world and interact with computer-controlled creatures.

3.2 What Is an EMud?

EMud stands for Evolutionary MUD. An EMud is an instance of the EMud application, given a specific world setup. There can be many EMuds, since there is a limitless number of virtual worlds that can be given as an initialization for the application, each as a distinct experiment environment.

To give a description of the application structure, it is necessary to understand some basic terms used to speak of an EMud. As we have seen, an EMud has two components, one which is totally reconfigurable, its virtual world, the second, which is coded within the application, the rules for dynamic evolution of the virtual world. The virtual world is made of *loci* (places), *elements* (situated "things") and *exits* serving as links from one locus into another, allowing elements to move in the world and defining its topology. Elements come in many forms, typically they are *objects*, *creatures* (autonomous agents) or *player-characters* (human agents). Note that elements may additionally be loci in which case they are called *containers*. All of these elements and loci are described in an initialization file that must be provided by the user and that shall define the setting for the virtual world in which an experiment can take place. The way the world evolves is controlled by the application which defines a number of *skills* that elements can apply to the environment, these skills should be considered as reflecting the laws governing evolution in the virtual world. Every element has a set of skills that describe the actions he may undertake. To take an example, suppose the world is a house. In this house there are rooms, a library, a hallway, etc. these are the loci. The elements in the house would be a table, books, a suitcase (container), the cat (a creature), you (a player-character). The cat has the skills of moving past doorways (exits), eating and purring. You would have the skills of opening doors, picking up other elements and so on. This world would be described by an initialization file of the form seen in figure 1.

What remains to be defined is how the elements choose to apply their skills. The application incorporates a control system that can associate any control function to an element, provided that the function has an interface capable of interpreting messages sent by the environment to the element and capable of sending command messages to the element. Control algorithms must be programmed as plug-ins in the same way as a human player has to understand messages from the EMud when connecting to it via a telnet session.

3.3 EMud Agents

In an EMud, agents are the elements that possess skills, since they alone can transform the world by applying these skills. EMud agents should be considered as software agents [20]. Since the EMud allows any control mechanism to be used

```
BEGIN LOCUS Library
SIZE 200
CONTENTS Table, Book1, Book2, Cat, You
EXITS Hallway, Livingroom
END LOCUS Library

BEGIN ELEMENT Cat
SIZE 8
SKILLS look, move, purr, eat
CONTROL CatBehavior
END ELEMENT Cat

BEGIN CONTAINER You
SIZE 15
WHEIGHT ALLOWANCE 15
SKILLS look, move, get, drop, open, close
CONTENTS Book3, Glasses
CONTROL ByTelnet
END CONTAINER You
```

Fig. 1. a typical EMud initialization file

for an agent, different levels of autonomy can be achieved. Three fundamental levels can be distinguished [26]. From automatic agents, automaticity implying that the agent has access to its environment and can influence its own future existence through actions in that environment (a prerequisite for an agent to be autonomous [22]), on to operationally and behaviorally autonomous agents. Operational autonomy is seen as the ability for the agent to operate without human intervention and behavioral autonomy supposes the agent is capable of transforming its principles of operation. Such an agent must be able to express varied new behaviors as its needs or environment changes. The basic model of an autonomous agent is described by figure 2. In the preliminary token grouping experiment presented below, we are dealing with operationally autonomous agents, but apart from allowing human controlled agents to enter an EMud, in further experiments we will mainly be concerned with building behaviorally autonomous agents.

3.4 The EMud in Operation

From the terminology and description, it is clear that at the center of the application lies a coordinating entity that must handle the interaction between elements possessing skills and the world. In fact, due to the separation of the decision making algorithms and the environment, that is handled by a scheduler which scans the list of elements sequentially requesting a command from each

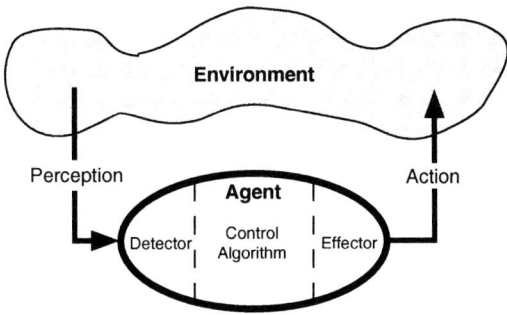

Fig. 2. an agent's architecture

of their control mechanisms. This command is then interpreted at the level of each element's skills and applied if possible. The world itself is independent of the type of control system, be it a human being or an algorithm of some kind, there is simply a link between an element and its control function in the control system, as can be seen on the figure 3.

3.5 Implementation Objectives

When implementing the application, we have held two main goals in mind; first, to maintain the independence between the virtual environment's kernel and the control algorithms for individuals or populations, second, to keep a large part of extensibility to the application, in view of a radically game oriented purpose. This reflects our interests of being able to study different control algorithms within the same environment and also, in a second phase, to be able to attract the large number of beta-testers available from the Internet when we start studying the effects of human interaction with computer adaptability (note that the beta version of the EMud is accessible via telnet to ufps5.unifr.ch on port 4000 when not under revision, send email to have a try). These two steps are part of a transition from the study of adaptation within a purely virtual dynamical world, to a world where some real world parameters have to be taken into account by the control systems.

4 EMuds as Experiment Environments

EMuds naturally provide environments for the classical animat experiments, such as the artificial ant problem [4] or Wilson's woods experiment [25], but due to the richness of functionality available for the description of a virtual world and agent's actions therein, they are more suited to approach multi-agent systems on a comparative level. Since agents are implemented as plug-in entities, driven by independent control algorithms, it is possible to carry out comparative

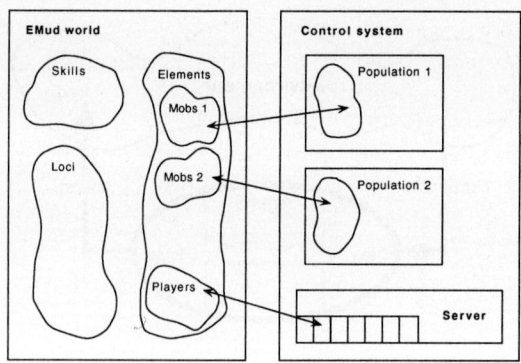

Fig. 3. EMud structure, "virtual world and control world"

experiments with interacting agents whose control algorithms are of a radically different nature. When used with populations of agents this possibility opens a new perspective for the study of cooperation and competition.

We further want to be able to confront artificial agents in their environment with real world influence and this can be done by using the game-like nature of the EMuds to build a virtual world rich enough to attract human players from the Internet. The disruption of regular patterns within an environment when human interaction appears should give indications of the robustness of the control algorithms used.

4.1 Preliminary Experiment

As an introductory experiment used to test the EMud application, we have implemented a regrouping agent world as in [6]. In this experiment, operationally autonomous agents are situated within a two-dimensional toroidal grid containing tokens. They can move in the four cardinal directions, picking up or dropping tokens along the way. From a very simple set of rules, regrouping or dispersing features can be observed to emerge in the environment. The control algorithm of the agent works as follows:

a) when an agent enters a empty cell, nothing happens and the agent moves on;
b) when an agent enters a non-empty cell while carrying a token, it drops the token and moves on;
c) when an agent enters a non-empty cell and does not have a token, it applies a probabilistic rule to decide whether it will pick up a token or not before moving on.

The probabilistic rule used in the decision to pick up a token is $P(\text{pick up}) = N^{-\alpha}$, where N is the number of tokens already in the cell and $0 \leq \alpha < 1$ a real value. We chose $\alpha = 0.3$ as it was experimentally seen to give good results. In the experiment, an agent can carry at most one token at any given time. When moving, the agent randomly selects one of the four available directions, with an equal chance to go in each direction. The only sensory information available to the agent here is the number of tokens in the cell he is standing in, and the presence or not of a token in his own inventory. One can see the speedup results of this experiment using one to fourteen agents in the world on figure 4 a). The results were generated using a five by five grid containing fifteen tokens. For

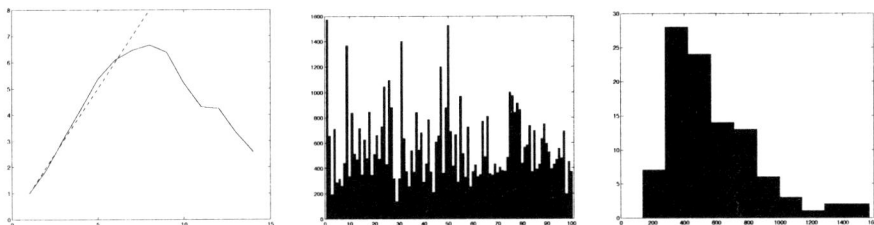

Fig. 4. a) speedup vs number of agents, b) & c) a typical experiment (5 agents)

each number of agents, a hundred experiments were run using different initial configurations, the results shown being an average over these hundred cases. As one can see, the problem can be solved with a linear to super-linear speedup using two to six agents. From then on, more agents tend to overcrowd the environment, disrupting the regrouping patterns exhibited when fewer agents are involved. To summarize, cooperation emerges in the multi-agent system when the number of agents ranges from two to eight. On figures 4 b) and c), we display the overall results of a hundred experiments using five agents. Figure 4 b) plots the number of iterations needed to achieve the task in each experiment. Figure 4 c) shows the distribution of experiments versus the number of iterations. The average number of steps used was 485, the maximum and minimum being 1571 and 137 respectively, underlining the fact that because of the autonomy of the agents, even though we know the goal will be reached, we cannot know how or when.

The origin of the regrouping problem lies in the study of cooperation within mobile robotic agents, where the functioning of a whole group depends on the individual competence of each robot as well as their interactions. Emergent properties of such a system were analyzed in [6], in view of porting the same behaviors to the Khepera mobile robot [18]. The advantage of such an approach in collective robotics is that it eliminates the need for a global positioning system or of a supervisor monitoring the stacks of tokens. The location of the stack containing all the tokens is a result of the agents interactions.

4.2 Further Experiments

We are currently implementing a more complicated environment where two types of behaviorally autonomous agents coexist, having different skills. In this experiment, agents have unsupervised learning capabilities and are rewarded for collecting tokens. One type of agent is allowed to pickup tokens, while the other can only steal them from agents already carrying some. From this setup, we expect to observe aggressive behavior emerging in the thieving agents, while the normal collecting agents will most likely develop a pick up and run strategy. The control algorithm for these agents will be made of a learning classifier system (LCS) [10, 24], giving them both symbolic condition-action rule mechanisms and learning through reinforcement and rule creation. The interaction of two learning classifier systems will give indication of how rule bases evolve when confronted with a dynamical environment.

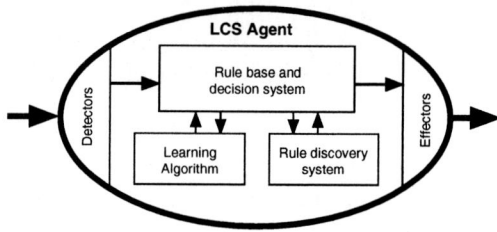

Fig. 5. the LCS model of an agent

As described in figure 5, the LCS agent architecture consists in a rule base, a reinforcement learning algorithm and a rule discovery system. Environment messages reach the detectors of the agent and are conveyed to the rule base where condition-matching is performed over the set of classifiers in the rule base. Matched classifiers then vy for their application by participating in an auction, the winner gaining the right to apply its action part. Consequences of actions are continually evaluated by the reinforcement learning algorithm which rewards or punishes the classifier or classifiers responsible for the last action. This reward strengthens (resp. weakens) the classifiers for the next time they take part in an auction. After a predetermined number of time steps, the rule discovery system generates new rules from the fittest old rules and replaces unfit ones in the rule base.

5 Conclusion

The innovative aspect of this work is to reconcile a symbolic approach with new AI by integrating characteristics of both top-down and bottom-up systems into a single system, namely an EMud, to compensate for the weakness of each system. On the one hand, top-down systems are non embodied systems, whose functioning is based on symbol manipulation. On the other hand, bottom-up systems are embodied systems, whose functioning is based on emergence. EMuds incorporate both embodiment and symbol manipulation features. The advantage of this hybrid system lies in its propensity to evolve reasoning agents and in the easy accessibility of the internal structure of the agent to the designer.

We have taken the view that physical grounding is not a necessary condition for an AI system to be grounded, rather, that symbolic grounding would be desirable as a first step along the way to building fully grounded systems. Under this assumption, systems able to give intrinsic meaning to the symbols they manipulate in their own symbolic universe will not be very far from giving meaning to objects outside their world (ie. in the physical world), and perceived through sensors. The agent's virtual world acting as a filter, through which the physical world is reached symbolically, in a symmetric way to that with which humans can reach into the abstract worlds through their high level cognitive functions based on physical processes.

We have then proceeded to build the EMud application, providing rich virtual worlds as environments for artificial agents to evolve in. Our main goal is now to begin full scale experiments taking advantage of the direct symbolic access to elements in these worlds, as well as including human controlled agents sharing the same environment. Of interest would also be to extend the EMud world possibilities by implementing a distributed version using a coordination language such as STL [15] of the EMud application, allowing agents to move between computers, reflecting symbolic ecological niches.

References

[1] J.F. Balaguer. *Virtual Studio: Un système d'animation en environnemen virtuel.* PhD thesis, EPF, DI-LIG, Lausanne, Switzerland, 1993. in french.
[2] R.A. Brooks. Intelligence without Reason. In *Proceedings of IJCAI-91*, Sydney, Australia, 1991.
[3] R.A. Brooks. Intelligence without Representation. *Artificial Intelligence, Special Volume: Foundations of Artificial Intelligence*, 47(1-3), 1991.
[4] R. Collins and D. Jefferson. Representations for artificial organisms. In J.-A. Meyer and S. W. Wilson, editors, *Proceedings of the First International Conference on Simulation of Adaptive Behavior*, volume From Animals to Animats, Cambrige, MA, 1991. MIT Press.
[5] Pavel Curtis. Mudding: Social Phenomena in Text-Based Virtual Realities. In *Proceedings of DIAC'92*, Berkeley, 1992.
[6] T. Dagaeff, F. Chantemargue, and B. Hirsbrunner. Emergence-based Cooperation in a Multi-Agent System. In *Proceedings of the Second European Conference on Cognitive Science (ECCS'97)*, pages 91–96, Manchester, U.K., April 9-11 1997.
[7] T. Duval, S. Morgan, P. Reignier, F. Harrouet, and J. Tisseau. ARéVi: une boîte à outils 3D pour des applications coopératives. *Calculateurs Parallèles*, 9(2), 1997.
[8] Leonard N. Foner. Entertaining agents: A sociological case study. In *Proceedings of Autonomous Agents '97*, 1997.
[9] S. Franklin. *Artificial Minds*. Bradford Books/MIT Press, Cambridge, MA, 1995.

[10] D. E. Goldberg. *Genetic Algorithms in Search, Optimistion and Machine Learning*. Addison-Wesley, Reading, Massachusetts, 1989.
[11] S. Harnad. The Symbol Grounding Problem. *Physica D*, 42, 1990.
[12] Jens Herder and Michael Cohen. Sound Spatialization Resource Management in Virtual Reality Environments. In *ASVA'97 - International Symposium on Simulation, Visualization and Auralization for Acoustic Research and Education*, pages 407–414, April 1997. Tokyo, Japan.
[13] J.H. Holland. Escaping brittleness: the possibilities of general purpose learning algorithms applied to parallel rule-based systems. In Michalski, Carbonell, and Mitchell, editors, *Machine learning, and artificial intelligence approach*, volume II. Morgan Kaufmann, Los Altos, CA, 1986.
[14] Hartman J. and Wernecke J. *The VRML 2.0 Handbook: Building Moving Worlds on the Web*. Addison-Wesley Publishing Company, 1996.
[15] O. Krone, F. Chantemargue, T. Dagaeff, M. Schumacher, and B. Hirsbrunner. Coordinating Autonomous Agents. In *ACM Symposium on Applied Computing (SAC'98). Special Track on Coordination, Languages and Applications*, Atlanta, Georgia, USA, February 27 - March 1 1998.
[16] H. Maturana and F.J. Varela. *Autopoiesis and Cognition: the realization of the living*. Reidel, Boston, MA, 1980.
[17] Michael Mauldin. Chatterbots, tinymuds and the turing test: Entering the loebner prize competition. In MIT Press, editor, *Proceedings of the Twelfth National Conference on Artificial Intelligence AAAI'94*, pages pp. 16–19, Cambrige, 1994.
[18] F. Mondada, E. Franzi, and P. Ienne. Mobile Robot Miniaturization: a Tool For Investigation in Control Algorithms. In *ISER'93*, Kyoto, October 1993.
[19] T. Nagel. What is it like to be a bat? *Philosophical Review*, 83:435–450, 1974.
[20] H.S. Nwana. Software Agents: an Overview. *Knowledge Engineering Review*, 11(3):205–244, 1996.
[21] Z.W. Pylyshyn. *The robot's dilemma, the Frame Problem in Artificial Intelligence*. Ablex, Norwood, NJ, 1988.
[22] L. Steels. When are robots intelligent autonomous agents? *Robotics and Autonomous systems*, 1995.
[23] F.J. Varela, E. Thompson, and E. Rosch. *The embodied mind: Cognitive science and human experience*. MIT Press, Cambridge, MA, 1991.
[24] S. W. Wilson. Classifier Fitness Based on Accuracy. *Evolutionary Computation*, 3(2), 1994.
[25] S.W. Wilson. Knowledge growth in an artificial animal. In *Proceedings of the first International conference on Genetic Algorithms and Their Applications*, pages 16–23, Hillsdale, NJ, 1985. Lawrence Erlbaum Associates.
[26] T. Ziemke. Adaptive Behavior in autonomous agents. *To appear in Autonomous Agents, Adaptive Behaviors and Distributed Simulations' journal*, 1997.
[27] T. Ziemke. Rethinking Grounding. In Austrian Society for Cognitive Science, editor, *Proceedings of New Trends in Cognitive Science - Does Representation need Reality*, Vienna, 1997.

Towards Virtual Experiment Laboratories: How Multi-Agent Simulations Can Cope with Multiple Scales of Analysis and Viewpoints

David Servat[1,2], Edith Perrier[1], Jean-Pierre Treuil[1], and Alexis Drogoul[2]

[1] Laboratoire d'Informatique Appliquée, Orstom
32, rue H. Varagnat, 93143 Bondy, France
[servat, perrier, treuil]@bondy.orstom.fr
[2] Laboratoire d'Informatique de l'Université de Paris 6
4, place Jussieu, 75252 Paris Cedex 05, France
[David.Servat, Alexis.Drogoul]@lip6.fr

Abstract. When studying complex phenomena, we face huge difficulties to conceive, understand, not to say handle the synthesis process which, from many interacting events, produces an emerging, recognizable, persistent and structurally stable, macroscopic event. Such a topical issue calls for specific tools, among which the development of multi-agent simulations has proved a promising approach. However, current multi-agent simulations provide no means of manipulating *as a whole* dynamically created groups of entities which emerge at different granularity levels. To our mind, giving full a sense to multi-agent simulations would consist though in making use of such potential groups, by granting them an existence of their own and specific behaviours, thus providing means of apprehending micro-macro links within simulations. We present here a conceptual reflexion on such an organization, in the light of our own experience in the development of the RIVAGE project at Orstom, which aims at simulating runoff and infiltration processes. We believe that the development of our methods in the field of physical processes will provide new ideas and tools useful for many multi-agent architectures and modelling purposes, so as to give shape to the concept of virtual experiment laboratories.
Keywords: multi-agent simulations, multiple level of abstractions and scales, emergent phenomena, micro-macro link.
This research is supported by a grant from the french Department of Higher Education and Research, and by Orstom.

1 Introduction

The context of our research is the application of multi-agent systems to the simulation of complex phenomena. Such an approach has aroused an increasing interest among the scientific community for the last few years. The simplicity of the multi-agent formalism is indeed appealing: building a computable representation of the studied reality by giving to each analysis entity of the studied domain an equivalent entity in the computer representation. The computer model results in a fairly good image of our own model of reality and as such is easier to apprehend than classic models. Moreover it enables the simulation of a wide range of systems which have so far fallen beyond the scope of classic models - e.g. ecosystem modelling, insects' societies as in MANTA (Drogoul et al 1993).

However, the design process proves much more difficult when studying complex situtations involving phenomena which proceed and interfere at different time and space scales, or situations in which the emergence of complex phenomena occurs. Current multi-agent simulations have so far provided but means of observing and *a posteriori* interpreting such emergence situations, and have not taken enough interest in the handling of multiple viewpoints within a simulation: for instance, when we naturely adopt both a reductionist and a holistic point of view on a phenomenon - if we wish to model the crowd of a demonstration, the procession may be considered as a multitude of individuals with their own behaviours and as some sort of a snake winding up the streets at an average speed. Such a capacity to gather many points of view and to give an ambivalent nature, collective set of individuals and individual with its own existence, to the observed reality is part of the intellectual gymnastics of the scientist, and as such enters in the specification of effective tools for conducting simulation experiments. To our mind it would give shape to the concept of virtual experiment laboratories mentionned in (Ferber 1995 p40-45) or (Treuil et al 1997).

In the RIVAGE project at Orstom (Perrier and Cambier 1996, Solignac 1996, Servat 1997), we try to apprehend the circulation of water in all the forms that hydrologists think worth considering - individual water entities, or waterballs, stagnating water zones, flowing water paths, etc. -, by giving them an agent representation. When considered at their own level, these forms do not obey the same behavioural laws and evolve according to different time and space scales. Their emergence during rainfall reveals a scale transfer: a pond results from the accumulation of interacting waterballs in the same area, its attributes - spatial extension, volume - come from the collective activity of these waterballs (in the same way as densities in statictical physics result from the collective activity of gaz particles); the attributes of a ravine, which results from the concentration on a given water path of a waterball train in constant renewal, can be seen as the synthesis of the historical records of all waterballs momentarily involved in the ravine.

The hydrologist's object of study thus seems to let itself organize in different entities which belong to different levels, recursively including one another. However, it is much more complex than that: several levels must be simultaneously considered to account for the reality of the ravine phenomenon - both global and individual. Indeed, some hydrologists would even call a ravine, the resulting erosion of the ground after rainfall, which shows how complex it is to give an exact definition of the phenomenon, and at the least rejects as simplistic the representation of a ravine as a mere train of waterballs.

We thus have to find a tangible equivalent to the scale transfer which will not only be observable *a posteriori* as in current multi-agent simulations, but explicit. We are convinced that such an issue may be tackleded by giving full a sense to the agent concept: allowing the dynamic creation of agents by agents themselves. Within the computer simulation, entities are locally and dynamically created by a group of agents which share for some time a structurally stable interaction and give shape to this interaction in the form of an agent of higher granularity. This interaction agent, or group agent, encapsulates both the knowledge of a physical law, either learnt or predefined - flow rate evolution in a ravine, spatial extension variation in a pond -, which is specific to its level, and the capacity to control the evolution of the lower granularity agents. Our approach is in keep with the natural reflex in computer science which consists in making the system's organization an object of the system itself.

We shall start our discussion with an overview of some examples of applications in the field of multi-agent simulations, which will show the generality of such questions. In the light of these examples and particularly of the RIVAGE project, we then present a conceptual reflexion on how to introduce groups in a multi-agent simulation. The implementation of a discrete version of the simulator enabled us to start an investigation on such matters (Servat 1997). In this contribution, we try to shed light on the following points: regrouping rules, group creation itself and control issue within the group agent and the group of agents.

2 The Need for Multi-Scale Viewpoints in Simulations

One should not consider the idea of an individual-based simulation as the apanage of the multi-agent approach. As a matter of fact, cellular automata have long before proposed such an approach. In the field of fluid mechanics, it has led to lattice gas models in which fluid praticles circulate through the cells of the automata network and undergo shocks between themselves, their trajectories thus deflected. Such models provide an alternative approach to the resolution of Navier-Stokes equations in order to apprehend the behaviour of a fluid in a space with any given bounding conditions. Numerous researches are led in this field, which meet promising success (Fredkin 1990, Toffoli and Margolus 1990). In these approaches, it is yet impossible to manipulate the emergent phenomena, and the experimentater is restricted to a passive observation: he can but record that phenomena occur, such as liquid or gas clusters' creation. Everything is considered at the lowest level of granularity, which does not coincide with the analysis level considered by the experimentater. At this point arises the essential problem of the observer's role in simulations (Balian 1995) and of the relevant scale of analysis (Perrier1990). In multi-agent simulations of pure physical process, the passage from a microscopic decription level to a macroscopic one becomes essential, due to the nature itself of the phenomena that we wish to model. The need for some intermediate level of agents which would handle the passage from a microscopic to a macroscopic level becomes crucial, as stressed in (Marcenac and Calderoni 1997) - a simulation of earth-quakes.

Such a lack is to be found in current multi-agent simulations as well. In MANTA (Drogoul et al 1993) for instance, simulations reveal the emergence of a division of work among ants: the artificial ants achieve in turn different tasks, such as taking care of the nest or searching for food, as if they were obeying to some sort of a fixed schema of existence and taking part in different social groups. Such emergent groups are essential objects of study for ethologists, which have gathered masses of information about them. However, such groups do not exist in the simulation and no proper means of intervening on them to conduct experiments are provided. The ethologist would like though to be able to introduce such social groups: the ants' nest would be considered, not only as a collectivity of individuals, but as an interaction between groups. Recursively, an agent could be created to incarnate the whole ants' nest, with its own characteristics: hunting area, consumed resources, laying cycles, etc. These abstract categories, such as the ant agent, the social group or the ants' nest agent are as many faces of one unique reality. According to the aims of the simulation, it will be, in turn, more convenient, as the ethologists do, to adopt such different points of view and to simultaneously manipulate them.

In a different domain, we may take a look at the TREMMA project, described in (Marcenac et al 1997), which aims at building a model of the learner in an Intelligent Tutorial System. In this project, the evolution of the learner's knowledge is simulated by the agregation of agents, representing some parts of the reasoning. This possibility of representing knowledge with multiple levels of granularity gives then an important gain to provide a relevant help to the learner.

In the case of the RIVAGE project, waterball agents move on a studied surface, with respect to gravity. Due to run-off, these waterballs agglutinate and give birth to pond and ravine agents. In the simulator (see figures 1, 2 and 3), the space is represented by a tridimensional network, where each cell is an agent and may receive a unique waterball. Rain is simulated by periodically introducing waterballs. At every cycle, balls move from one cell to the first free cell, among the lowest ones in a cubic neighbourhood of 26 cells. If there are several possible cells, one is randomly chosen. A cell, situated at the edge of the surface, evacuates its ball and the ball is removed from the simulation. The cells may take three inner states: state 0 if free, state 1 if occupied, state 2 if occupied by a ball which is trapped and may no longer move, due to the overcrowding of its neighbourhood. Cells update a history of their states, on the basis of which they proceed to regroupings and give birth to ravine and pond agents. These new agents take control over the regrouping cells, and in particular, they handle waterball flows themselves, via their outlets from groups to groups, without having balls moved from cells to cells. These group agents are given self-observation capacities which enable them to decide their own partial dissolution, when, in the case of a pond, a free neighbouring cell is found, or in the case of a ravine, the stock of waterballs received in one cycle decreases.

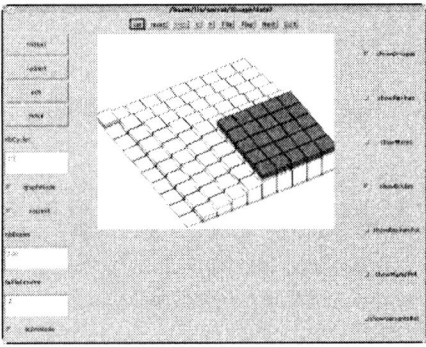

Fig. 1. Initial state. The user has set up a pond agent, shown in dark gray. The white cells represent the relief

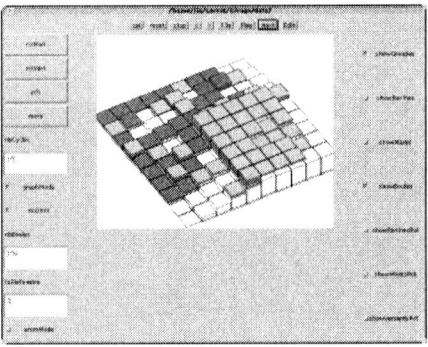

Fig. 2. The pond agent from Fig.1, obviously too extended, dissolves itself, freeing its cells, in light gray, and giving birth to the regrouping of cells in medium gray on the slope

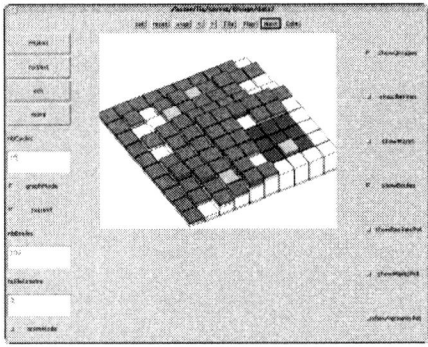

Fig. 3. Final state. The pond reappears in dark gray, with proper dimensions. The regrouping of cells in medium gray goes on, in one big ravine agent. A few free cells are also found, in light gray

3 Regrouping Rules

The regrouping of agents rests upon the recognition at some time of an interaction or a correlation between agents, see Fig.4, which, due to its persistency and characteristics, reveals a phenomenon, and as such, may potentially give birth to an agent which would incarnate the phenomenon: a set of waterballs confined in a space area and immobilized by their mutual congestion, premise of a pond or a puddle; a set of waterballs, taking close paths and forming a train of waterballs, premise of a ravine. This mutual recognition calls for memory capacities - for instance of the path followed, or of a state (moving or immobile) - and environmental perception capacities - agents close to one another in a given neighbourhood -, (Treuil et al 1997). Once the interaction reckonned, the creation of group itself may occur.

The implementation of a discrete simulator linked to the RIVAGE project has been an opportunity for us to start an investigation on the rules that would proceed for the regrouping of a set of agents. So far our investigation has led us to consider:

1. Similarities between inner states of agents: in the discrete version of the RIVAGE simulator, each cell may take different states - 0 if free, 1 if occupied by a waterball, and 2 if the ball that occupies it is trapped and may no longer leave the cell. A cell in state 2 observes its neighbourhood and, noticing that it is surrounded with cells in the same state, considers forming a pond agent. In general, the state of an agent may be a vector of attributes with various values - temperature, pressure -, or a task - food searching, taking care of the nest, etc.
2. Connecting relations or partnerships: our cells from the previous example are the nodes of a tridimensional graph, and have thus connecting relations among themselves, defined in a given topology. This neighbourhood is not necesseraly the set of cells they are directly connected to: for instance, we may imagine the modelling of a subway plan by a multi-agent system, in which agents representing stations reachable within a unique connexion would be considered in the same neighbourhood. Beyond that, we may also imagine partnership relations that link a producer agent with a consumer agent. In the case of agents that look for information on the web (Moukas 1996), we are often faced with such types of agents: a personal agent in charge of the user's requests, and a certain number of agents that actually look for information. Between such two types of agents exist relations of acquaintancies, more or less reinforced with respect to the success of their association - mutual confidence with respect to the user's satisfaction.

The communication between agents may be the support of the computing of similarities between neighbouring agents' states. Generally speaking, it is a computation of a distance, the definition of which depending of course on the objectives and the attributes to compare. Suppose that A and B are two agents and Ea, Eb their respective state vectors, we compute $|Ea - Eb| < \theta$, where θ represents a given vector of the minimum distance bellow which two agents are considered as close to each other.

Eventually, these criteria may have to be completed with some preconditions for creating groups, such as the number of agents involved in the regrouping, or owning an outlet for the creation of a ravine, so as to handle water transfers. Such preconditions are directly linked to the definition of groups. It seems for instance natural to consider that ponds are large clusters of waterballs.

Such a regrouping process may be considered as some sort of a dynamic local pattern recognition of emergent forms, or, as underlined by Treuil et al 1997, as a computation of correlations between agents, both spatially and functionally - a method used in the renormalization group in Physics. When brought to operation in the domain of social simulations, such recognition of emergence by the agents themselves could give the system the right level of complexity recquired to simulate human societies: "DAI simulations may have oversimplified important characteristics of specifically human societies, because the actors (agents) in these societies are capable of reasoning, and do so routinely, about the emergent properties of their own societies"(Gilbert 1995).

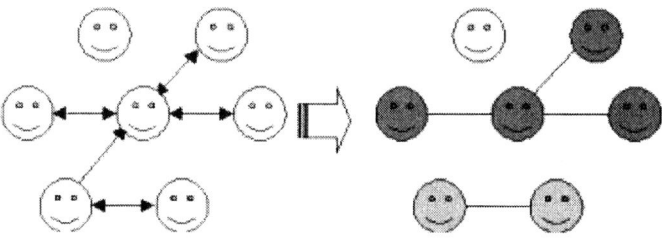

Fig. 4. Regrouping of individual agents

4 Adhesion to a Group

The bases of the regrouping of agents thus defined, we now have to think of the mechanisms which rule the creation of groups itself. Our cells have a capacity to agglutinate in clusters of cells which share some properties: as a matter of fact, it is a prestructuring of their environment. However, how do these prestructures become effective ones, or, in other words, how does the cluster give birth to the group?

First of all, we are faced with the problem of whether to predefine or not group types. We may actually imagine that agents could create one unique type of groups, completely general. However, the context of our applications and our objectives have led us not to do so and, on the contrary, to predefine some group types. Two main reasons account for our choice:

1. The predefinition of the group types that represent well-known objects of study for hydrologists, is a way to give them the opportunity to easily project

in the simulation their knowledge: attributes and behaviours of the group types. As a result they are provided with the extra opportunity to set up, at the beginning of a simulation, any pre-existing group, hypothetic though it may be, so as to conduct experiments: a well-observed ravine for instance, or an hypothetic pond, obviously spatially too extended, as shown in Fig.1. The simulation will then confirm or invalidate the existence of such groups. We may not simply introduce a group of waterballs in those cases, because the behaviour of the ravine for instance may be known at a global level - flow rate -, and we do not know how to build a set of waterballs that would account for it. We may only know, according to the volume, how many waterballs will do, not their individual positions and speeds.

2. Besides, even when we do not have information (or do not want to presuppose information) on the emergent groups, we do have yet a piece of information on the nature of the groups: waterballs create *water* agent group. As well as in Axelrod's experiments on dynamic alliance network between states (Axelrod 1995), considered from an internal point of view, alliance networks suffice to give shape to and represent emergent states (such as the United-States from the thirteen colonies), but from an external viewpoint, we need to have a new actor (agent) which is undoubtedly a state on its own (for example when a european state interacts with the United-States). We need to have a pond to enable water drawing from ponds by human action in a simulation.

Still we may want to obtain emergent group specification - that means without any predefinition of group types. It seems interesting, as we might be able to discover new group types that we do not know of and which give us means of describing some situations in a new way. However, we have not worked so far on such a pure emergence approach: undoubtedly this will mean accept rather difficult a challenge in the field of learning, which for now falls beyond the scope of our research.

At present, individual agents gather and create groups whose types are among those defined by the user, in other words, they adhere to a particular type of groups. Such an adhesion to a group may be considered as an election process among agents. They have gathered in some sort of constituencies and must give their opinion in favour of one group or the other. The predefined groups are the election's candidates as long as their preconditions are satisfied by the set of individual agents. Each one of them chooses one candidate, with respect to the nature of its interaction with the other agents. In the discrete version of the simulator, we have defined for each group, one typical individual agent that would adhere to it. Thus every agent compares itself to the typical pond agent or ravine agent and chooses the one which is closer to itself. The election proceeds in a first-past-the-post system, but we may imagine, keeping on with the same metaphor, different systems of voting so as to solve potential conflicts between several possible groups.

In order to incarnate such a deliberating assembly, it may be convenient to gather the involved agents in some pre-groups, in charge of the vote and the counting. Such pre-groups may moreover be a communication support between agents during the group's lifetime. Thus, we may imagine that the dissolution of groups be voted for or against by the set of agents that belong to the pre-group. Such pre-group notion is to be compared to that of abstract groups which do not have at the begining any behaviour.

5 Control Issue Within the Group Agent

We have to define the interaction rules, on the one hand between group agents that have been created and agents not yet involved in a group (macro-micro link), and, on the other hand among the agents that belong to the group and the group agent itself (micro-macro link). We must imagine a bubbling of free waterballs, ponds being created, and already existing ravines. How do we manage this set of agents from different granularity level, and how do we define the life cycle of the groups?

At issue is the control shared by individual agents and group agent and the destiny of the individual agents once regrouped. We may consider two visions:

1. The individual agents regroup but keep on existing as individuals. Thus they periodically participate in elections which decide of the group's destiny and the possible creation of new ones. For example, a pond exists but, periodically, the balls that belong to it, and other ones, still free, regroup and decide to create another pond, thus leading to the dissolution of the previous one, or to enlarge the existing pond, thus altering the pond's attributes.

   In this approach, the group agents do not have a complete autonomy, they are submitted to the decisions of the individual agents. Their behaviour is reduced to the computing of a certain number of macroscopic parameters - volume, spatial extension -, and to warning the user: hello, a pond has been created. The agents are but simple albeit exclusive observers of a given phenomenon.

2. The groups once created take control over individual agents and the group agent is given means of self-observation, through a polling mechanism among the agents that belong to itself. Thus a pond periodically observes its surroundings. Once aware that some of the balls may be evacuated, so it does and disolves itself to a certain extent - or even completely, if there is no ball left, as shown in Fig.2. The balls thus freed may agglutinate with other ones as usual, see Fig.3.

   In this approach, the group agents are themselves responsible for their lifes and deaths, in complete autonomy with the exterior. The agents are no longer just observers, they are as well actors of the phenomena they incarnate and control the agents of inferior granularity belonging to them.

For the reasons that we have evoked above - that a phenomenon may (must) be seen as an individual entity with own existence and as a collective set of individual entities, for instance when the pond dissolves itself -, this latter approach seems much more appropriate to our mind. It seems actually more elegant that each level have its own autonomy, as these different levels are submitted to different laws. Thus cells exchange balls one another, whereas ravines manage ball exchanges between two groups, via their outlets. This vision agrees with the hydrologist's who reasons in terms of flow rates. Moreover, such an encapsulation of levels with respect to increasing granularity gives true a sense, both in terms of optimization of computing and resources, and in terms of reality modelling, to the creation of groups. We are far from a model such as cellular automata in which the exchanges are always handled at the lowest granularity level.

Therefore, the agents belong to different granularity levels: individual, group level, etc. The exchanges between agents of the same level obey to the level's own rules: remember the transfer of balls above. The passage from one level to the other occurs while regrouping agents of the same level. The groups are provided with self-management capacities, in particular they can decide their partial or total dissolution with regard to their history, thus freeing the lower level agents that belonged to them. The individual agents that belong to groups have their behaviour altered, in the same way as a soldier marching in a troop must constantly adjust his walk with respect to the others. Thus a cell which belongs to a ravine keeps on receiving waterballs from its neighbouring cells, it no longer has a binary state (occupied or free). These balls increase the stock of the group ravine which from now on independently handles the flows from groups to groups. Balls are no longer transported from cells to cells within the ravine, but guided through the ravine's path, according to its flow-rate. The individual agents in a group become some sort of information relay unit, which the group agent periodically polls to manage itself autonomously.

6 Coexistence with Recursive Regroupings

It is natural to plan right from the start to give the user the opportunity to handle multiple level regroupings, see Fig.5. It actually enables to define the pertinent scale of analysis of phenomena and to simultaneously use several levels of analysis. The same mechanisms for the regrouping may be applied to all levels, providing that the criteria may somewhat be adapted. We may thus not speak of similarities or distances between agents of different kinds, such as ravines and ponds. We have to use new metaphors. We have already spoken about the notion of partnership, instead of the notion of neighbourhood. We should go further in this direction and define new types of rules: functional regroupings, social regroupings, etc. A ravine for instance may know the groups it interacts with - thanks to their outlets. On the bases of water transfers and flows, ravines may come to regroup within one large network which could handle the water flows on its own.

However further work is needed as far as the interactions between different granularity entities and between different types of groups are concerned. A possible way of research may consist in formalizing these interactions in the forms of rule systems. Can a pond merge directly with a ravine or dissolve itself ball after ball in the ravine? Is a waterball meeting a pond always absorbed by the pond?

All these questions have not been answered yet, and perhaps a reason for this is that we have led our investigations in a discrete domain on a tridimensionnal network of cells, fo which it is easy to test whether or not a cell is free, but which also hides the problems of interaction between entities and group borders.

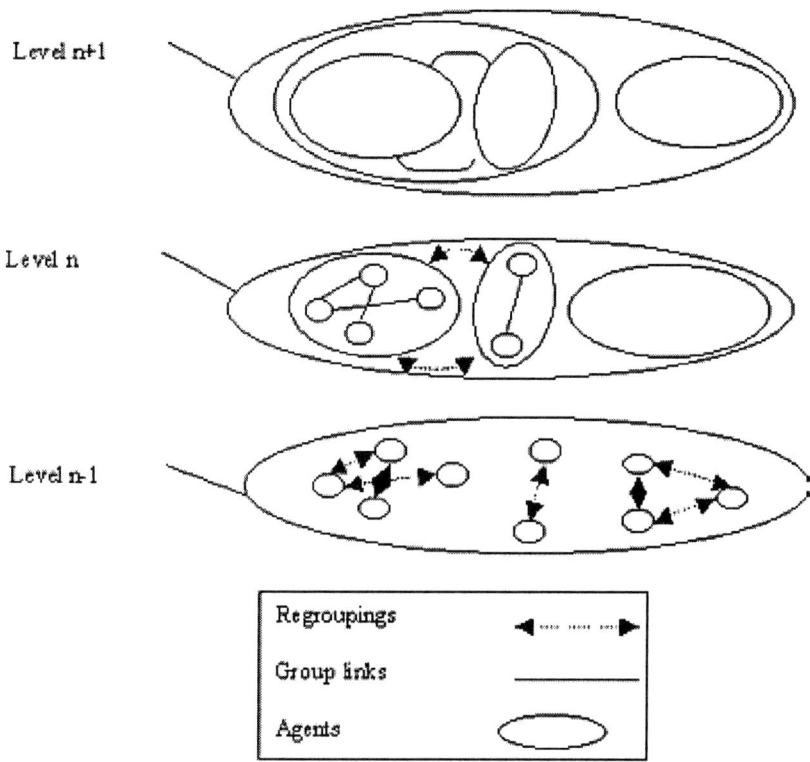

Fig. 5. Coexistence of several level of analysis during recursive regroupings

7 Conclusion

We have presented the state of our reflexion on how to introduce and make to coexist groups of agents with different granularities. Our vision rests upon notions that are at the heart of the multi-agent formalism - groups, inclusion of groups , etc - which enable us to build within simulations an image of reality which is more faithful to the hydrologist's.

However, in the light of our experimentations, our objective, simple as it may seem at first sight, turns out to be much more difficult when brought into operation and formalized in terms of agents, and leads us to wonder about the very definition of the phenomena we want to simulate. Even though they may be well-known and for long studied by the expert of the domain, we have experienced the necessity to build an operational typology of the analysis entities used in hydrology - or whatever the domain of application -, dedicated to their simulating within the multi-agent formalism. For instance, it has been so far rather difficult to give a proper definition, that is, an operational one, of what a ravine is, even if, basically, we may see it as a highly frequented water path which emerges due to run-off and that is responsible for some phenomena among which erosion, material transport, stream creation, etc. We need to work on the knowledge transfer of the domain, which is not quite surprising, as it is, if any, essential a process in the object oriented programming, from which the multi-agent approach inherits.

Besides, the use and implementation of a group recognition process among agents leads us to wonder about the very essence of the group. It is a set of entities showing some kind of unity with respect to objective parameters, correlations, but it is also a coherent, synchronized retroaction form the other group elements on the individuals themselves: in the same way as in a crowd or an orchestra. Specific architectures are needed, which go beyond the sole object modelling issues. In an object oriented system, the entities, their interactions and their organization are actually set up at design time, by the programmer. In multi-agent systems however, the organization, and even the interactions, are themselves objects within the system, and generally turn out to have higher a complexity level than the other objects of the system. In the case of such a simulator as in the RIVAGE project, the biggest part of the difficulty lies in such questions as the control within the group agent, the information distribution among agents, the organization of the recursive levels - in hierarchies or other models for instance -, the perception of time - relative to each entity, such as in Swarm (Swarm Team 1994). We have presented some of our views on these matters, but our work is still in progress and will undoubtedly bring new aspects into light that will give more precise a shape to our system.

Our goal is still a long way off, but already promising though, is a kind of new light shed on the agent concept itself. Such notions as groups, regroupings and recursive inclusions of groups, are at the heart of the multi-agent approach. They shape our vision of things and are thus to be found in the design of multi-agent systems that we conceive as models of this vision. However, the agent seems to have been so far reluctant to grow away from its elder, the object, its behaviour often reduced to a set of methods with a zest of asynchronism. With the underlying objective of integrating it among other agents which proceed in different time and space scales, the agent will have to provide the other with means of their creating itself. The ants' nest will not only be defined as an entity with its own attributes and behaviour - as in a classical approach - but indeed, as an entity which creation is let to the sole decision of the ant agents, these agents owning means of giving a material existence to the phenomena resulting from their collective activity, and furthermore, of coexisting with it. Its autonomy thus increased, the agent moves further away from the object, and the agent concept becomes even more meaningful.

References

Axelrod R.: A Model of Emergence of New Political Actors. Artificial Societies, Conte and Gilbert Eds., 1995.

Balian, R.: Le temps macroscopique. in *Le temps et sa flèche.* Editions Frontières. (1995) (in French).

Drogoul, A., Corbara B., Fresneau D.: MANTA : New Experimental Results on the Emergence of (Artificial) Ant Societies. Simulating Societies Symposium, Siena, C. Castelfranchi (Ed.), 1993.

Ferber J.: Les systèmes multi-agents : Vers une intelligence collective. InterEditions, 1995. (in French).

Fredkin E.: Digital Mechanics, an Informational Process Based on Reversible Universal Cellular Automata. Cellular Automata, Theory and Experiment, H. Gutowitz (Eds) MIT/North-Holland, p254-270, Amsterdam, 1990.

Gilbert N.: Emergence in Social Simulation. Artificial Societies, Conte and Gilbert Eds., 1995.

Marcenac P., Calderoni S.: Self-Organisation in Agent-Based Simulation. Proceedings of MAAMAW'97, Ronneby, Sweden, May 1997.

Marcenac P., Calderoni S., Courdier R., Leman S.: Construction expérimentale d'un modèle multi-agents. Proceedings of the 5th JFIADSMA, Hermès, 1997. (in French).

Moukas A.: Amalthea : Information Discovery and Filtering Using a Multi-Agent Evolving Ecosystem. Proceedings of the 1st International Conference and Exhibition on the Practical Application of Intelligent Agents and Multi-agent Technology, 1996.

Perrier E.: Modélisation du fonctionnement hydrique des sols. Passage de l'échelle microscopique l'échelle macroscopique. SEMINFOR IV Le transfert d'échelle, Orstom Editions, Brest, Septembre 1990. (in French)

Perrier E., Cambier Ch.: Une approche multi-agents pour simuler les interactions entre acteurs hétérogènes de l'infiltration et du ruissellement d'eau sur une surface de sol. Tendances nouvelles en modélisation pour l'environnement, Elsevier Ed., 1996. (in French).

Servat D.: Emergence et coexistence de groupes en multi-agents. Master Thesis at the University of Paris VI in Artificial Intelligence Pattern Recognition and their Applications, Paris, Septembre 1997. (in French).

Solignac Ch. Projet RIVAGE (Ruissellement et Infiltration Vu par des Agents). Master Thesis at the University of Paris VI in Artificial Intelligence Pattern Recognition and their Applications, Paris, Septembre 1996. (in French).

'94 Swarm Team: An Overview of the Swarm Simulation Systems. Santa Fe Institute, 1994.

Toffoli T., Margolus N.H.: Invertible Cellular Automata : a Review. Cellular Automata, Theory and Experiment, H. Gutowitz (Eds) MIT/North-Holland, p229-253, Amsterdam, 1990.

Treuil J-P., Perrier E., Cambier Ch.: Directions pour une approche multi-agents de la simulation de processus physiques. Proceedings of the 5th JFIADSMA, Hermès, 1997. (in French).

A Model for the Evolution of Environments

Claude Lattaud* & Cristina Cuenca**

* Laboratoire d'Intelligence Artificielle de Paris5 – LIAP5
UFR Mathématiques – Informatique
Université René Descartes
45, rue des Saints – Pères
75006 Paris
E – mail: latc@math-info.univ-paris5.fr

** Institut International du Multimedia
Pole Universitaire Leonard de Vinci
92916 La defense Cedex
E – mail : Cristina.CUENCA@DeVinci.fr

Abstract. In artificial world research, the environments as themselves are rarely studied. Both in multi – agents systems and artificial life domains, the dominant work turns around the active entities, the agents. The aim of this paper is to propose a theoretical approach of an environment model. It must allow to deal with the different existing environment types but also to add a creative touch by introducing the concepts of meta – environment and multi – environments. This model defines some evolutionary schemes for an environment, and the different ways of interaction between them.

Keywords: adaptive environments, environment model, environment interactions, multi – environments systems.

Introduction

John Holland quotes in one of its first papers, [1], « The study of adaptation involves the study of both the adaptive systems and its environment. In general terms, it is a study of how systems can generate procedures enabling them to adjust efficiently to their environments ». However, since 1962, most of the research work are focused mainly on the adaptive systems, rather than on their environment. This paper is a first step into the task of filling this gap, and proposes a theoretical study of an environment model.

Even if most of the works on adaptive systems integrate the idea of a dynamic environment, generally, it only has a weak level of dynamism and it doesn't really have a truly evolutionary process. That is why it seams important to consider the environment not as a dynamic support where agents populations, [2], or animats, [3], evolve, but as an entity by itself. This entity will be able to develop particular behavior models, but also a non – fixed structure. These environment behaviors should be able to evolve following the different interactions with its objects and agents.

Nowadays, most of the systems include an environment containing agents and objects. But, couldn't a system integrate more than one environment ? In such a case, it is necessary to define, from on side, the different interaction laws that can exist between the environments and, from the other, a meta – environment being able to manage this laws considering each environment as an agent.

The purpose of this paper is then to define an environment model which integrates all of these ideas. This model must allow to classify and to order the environments, giving by this way the possibility to determine transition and evolution stages between the different environment classes.

The task of the first part is to establish this classification in a hierarchical way. Then, the second part presents the concept of meta – environment and the different interaction types that a multi – environments system can have. The next part concerns the definition of a protocol for the environments evolution and finally, the last part shows an example of a multi – environments system using the model previously defined in this paper.

1. Environment Model

This model lays, from one part, on the definition of a taxonomy of environment classes, and, from the other, on the use of the characteristics and parameters of each of these classes. From an object classes point of view, and also for simplicity of use, the chosen hierarchy is a simple one, i. e. each object have one and only one father.

Taking into account the important use of some artificial life techniques such as genetic algorithms, [4], and classifier systems, [5], a genotypic description of the model classes is presented to conclude this part

1.1. Taxonomy and Classes Characteristics

This taxonomy defines five main classes. Two of them are abstract ones and the other three are concrete ones. The Fig. 1 shows this hierarchy.

The *abstract environment* class is the root class of the hierarchy. It has some parameters, which are common for all its sub – classes :
– *The environment size*, denoted S. This parameter determines if the environment is infinite or finite, and in this last case, S contains a positive integer value, which the unit depends on the environment type.
– *The set of the environment objects*, O. This set can be decomposed in some parts : the active objects set, i.e. the agents, the inactive objects set and the sub – environments.

– *The set of interaction laws* between the different environment elements, I. This laws concern the interactions between agents and objects, agents and agents, but also the interactions between the environment and its components.

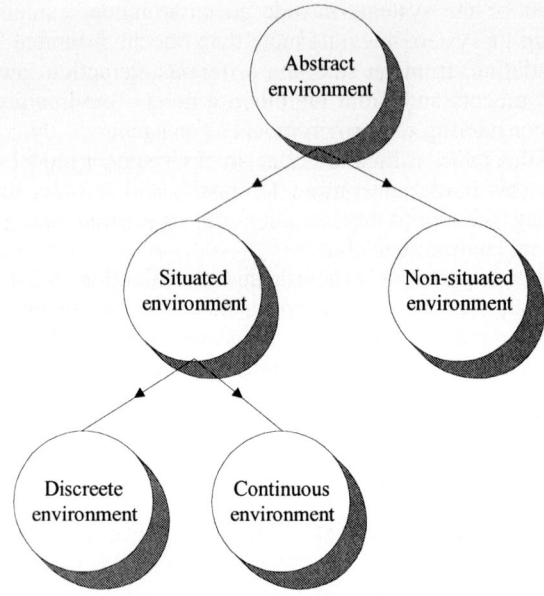

Fig. 1. : Environments taxonomy.

– *The set of evolution laws* of the environment, E. This set determines the rules followed by the environment to evolve in time, and also the transition functions which allow it to pass from one stage to another.

The quadruplet <S, O, I, E> defines then an abstract environment.

The *situated environment* class is generally used in the simulations concerning the multi – agents systems, and the different problems in artificial life. An environment is called *situated* if it is constructed from a space having a metric, and if its objects and agents have a position in relation to this space. The parameters of this environment type are :

– *The structure or architecture* of the environment, A. Different structure types exist, as a toroidal space, square, cylindrical or spherical.
– *The environment dimension*, D. The environment can have one, two, three or n dimensions.
– *The environment metric*, M. This metric defines the measure units and the scale to define the objects coordinates within.
– *The set of the space management properties*, P. This set is formed by some properties as the projection properties, from a dimension n to a dimension n-1, for

example, or even more, the rotation properties, useful for the visualization processes.

In this kind of environment, the agents may have some particular properties, related to their situated aspect, their coordinates, their movement coefficient - or their speed - representing their capacity to move.

A situated environment is then defined by the set <S,O,I,E,A,D,M,P>.

The *non – situated environment*, N, is the class that can be used to define an environment in a ruled – based system. An environment is called *non – situated* if the concepts of space and position into space don't exist in it. In this kind of environment, rules can be considered as the objects and meta – rules can be the agents. This class doesn't have any specific parameter, due to the fact that it is defined to be distinguished from the situated environment class.

The *discreet environment*, D, follows the principle enounced by Bergson, [6] : « The intelligence only represents clearly to itself the discontinues ». An environment is called *discreet* if is it cut up in a finite number of elementary parts, the cells, each one having a fixed number of neighbors. The parameters of this type of environment are :
- *The cells structure*, L. These may have different forms : square, hexagon, or triangle in a two – dimensional environment.
- *The integer environment metric*, Mi. The environment being cut up in elementary parts, the computation of coordinates and moves are done in the integer set, or in one of its sub – sets.

The *continuous environment* class, C, is the complementary class to class D. An environment is called *continuous* if, for every two points of it, there is at least one point between them. Even if, from a computing point of view, the idea of a strict continuity is impossible nowadays, a continuous environment can be built using a *real metric*, Mr, based on a real vectorial system. This kind of metric is the only parameter of this class.

1.2. Genotypic Approach

All the previous parameters can be coded to form a string, genome or chromosome. The elements of this genome, the genes, define then the different environment properties. Once this coding has been done, it is possible to apply a particular version of Genetic Algorithm (GA), used in artificial life area.

This kind of algorithm would be near to the BEA, Bacterial Evolution Algorithm, presented by Chisato Numaoka in [7]. In opposition to most of GAs, having a large number of strings, this one considers entities, the bacteroids, owning only one chromosome. The bacteroids behavior is then completely determined from this unique chromosome. The evolution phenomena is performed just when the bacteroid, weaken[1], inserts in its organism the chromosomes of its neighbors. It chooses a chromosome in this set and, eventually, makes a mutation on this new chromosome.

In the same way, environments following this approach have only one active string. This chromosome, which determines alone the environment *genotype*, defines

---

[1] The bacteroid have an energy level.

the environment itself, its *phenotypic* representation, and its behavior. The chromosome fitness is then defined according to some parameters like :
- The number of objects and agents in the environment.
- The agents efficiency, which can also be measured as a fitness.
- The utility of the environment laws.

However, as a difference with the bacteroid case, the environment keeps the old chromosomes in a kind of memory base. This memory is then used in the evolution process to eventually return to an older, but more adapted, state.

After the description of an isolated environment, a description of the possible relationships between different environments is presented in the next part.

2. Meta – Environment Notion

When the different elements of a system doesn't act and interact with the same time scales, it can be useful to decompose it in a set of sub – systems. Effectively, it is not always coherent to consider in the same way the events produced in a micro – second scale and others produced in a year scale. The temporal windows of the evolution are completely different and cannot be managed with the same rules.

At the environment level, this decomposition leads to the constitution of a multi – environments system. However, to take into account the different interactions that can be performed between the environments, it is necessary to establish the concept of meta – environment. This one doesn't act as a supervisor but as a service manager, giving its services to its sub – environments, avoiding them some tasks. And even more, this approach allows a modular development, creating a hierarchy of environments and sub – environments, managed by a unique meta – environment.

2.1. Characteristics

A meta – environment is a kind of specialized abstract environment, having the following properties :
- An infinite size.
- A set of objects, exclusively environments.
- A set of laws for the interaction between its sub – environments.
- A set of internal evolution rules.

2.2. Global and Local Meta – Environments

It is important to point out the fact that a parallel can be established between the environment / agent relation and the meta – environment / environment relation. In the second case, the environment acts as an agent in relation to its meta – environment.

Following this idea, an environment can contain other environments as components. In this case, the environment containing some sub – environments can

be considered also as a meta – environment. So, two types of meta – environment exist in this model :
- Global meta – environment : the root of the multi – environments system hierarchy. Its properties are those defined in the previous section.
- Local meta – environment : a node in the multi – environments system hierarchy. It is a component of another meta – environment, a global or a local one. It contains as a part of its objects set, a set of sub-environments, which can be considered as agents in relation to it.

2.3. Inter – Environments Interactions Types

A large number of interactions between environments can appear. This section describes some possible ones:
- *Environment dependence.* An environment is completely dependant from another and can only perform its own actions according to its master environment.
- *Transfer.* An environment can transfer either agents, or objects, or laws to another environment.
- *Communication.* An environment can establish a communication with another environment in order to ask for, or to offer, either some information or a transfer.
- *Union.* Two environments, both having almost identical elements, can join in order to form an unique environment, composed by the set of all the elements of both original environments[2].

The environment evolution can be caused, as in the next example, by its components, but also as a consequence of the evolution process of the other environments in its system. In this case, the environment evolution will be caused by a state change, controlled by its transition functions. Its corresponding meta – environment will detect this change and will inform the other environments. For example, if some environments share some resources, and one of them disappears, the meta – environment will transmit this information to the others to allow them to adapt to the new existing conditions.

The next part describes an example of an environment evolution caused by its agents.

3. Environment Evolution

In the evolution process, an environment can have different states. An environment has an *initial state* just after its creation, a set of *transitory states* during its life period and a *final state*, the one before its death. All this states are linked together by transition functions. This environment evolution concept is important for the meta – environment, who needs to know the situation of its sub – environments in order to make the necessary changes for all of them, but also to create a new one or to destroy an existing one.

---

[2] An environment could also have the possibility to be cut, to give two distinct environments.

3.1. Evolution Types

In the frame of the situated environments, these can be confronted to different kinds of evolution. This section presents the laws that allow them to evolve in different ways :
- *Structural evolution*, the environment deeply modifies its structure. For example, lets have E, a discreet situated environment. If E is a two dimensions environment, defined by a 15*15 grid then, after a structural evolution, E could increase the grid size to 16*16, or decrease it to 14*14. This type of evolution can also occur on the dimension parameter, so a two dimensions one can evolve to a three dimensions one.
- *Behavioral evolution*, the environment internal laws are modified. Considering the previous example environment, E, if it has some resources as a part of its objects set, an internal law can allow it to control the quantity of renewed resources at each step. A behavioral mutation will change this kind of criteria, increasing or decreasing it, in order to encourage or not the expansion of the agents feeding with this resource.
- *Component evolution*, the environment acquires or destroys types of objects that may compose it. In this way, the environment E, evolving by this principle, could define a new kind of resource, more appropriated to one type of agents.
- *Geographic evolution*, the environment creates or destroys some instances of its composing objects. In the environment E, after a geographic evolution, E would be able to create, on some cells[3], new objects, new resources or new obstacles. This evolution type, where instances of objects are created or destroyed, must be distinguished from the previous one, where types of objects are created or destroyed.

3.2. Evolution Example

This evolution example uses a two layers neurons network to determine the mutation of the environment genome. This kind of evolution fits to the interaction between the environment and its agents. Then, some specials environment interaction effectors, represented in the network by input neurons, are affected to each agent. At each gene of the environment genome fits also threshold functions, causing a gene mutation after their overall activation. These threshold functions are defined by the output neurons of the network. As shown in Fig. 2, each output neuron is connected to each input neuron.

When some agents activate the same environment interaction effector, the signals are transmitted to the corresponding output neuron. After that, if the function threshold is reached, a mutation of the corresponding gene will occur. This mutation may be interpreted as a demand of an environment modification from its agents. If a sufficient quantity of agents makes the demand, then, as a answer, the environment will adapt and transform itself, following the agents exigency.

---

[3] If the environment is discreete, or at a position in space if it is continuous.

It is necessary to make the right distinction of the output neurons, which represent the activate functions, and the genes of the environment genome. In the following example, the environment E is a discreet one, defined by a 10*10 cells grid. Then, a gene codes the environment size, however, two outputs neurons will be associated to this gene. The first one represents an increase of the environment size, if it is activated, while the second one represents a decrease of this value. Then, if a sufficiently important agents group demands to the environment, by the means of the neurons network, to increase its size, it could be able to undergo a mutation of its corresponding size gene. The environment will mutate then to a size of 11*11 cells.

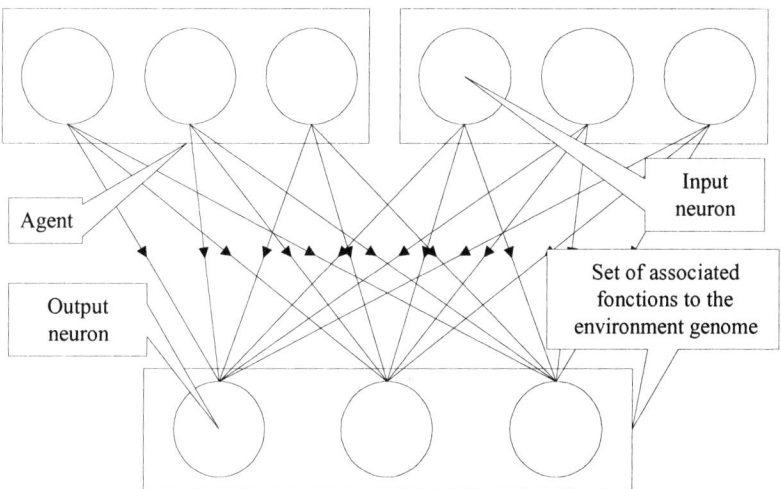

Fig. 2. : Two – layers neurons network.

4. Multi – Environments System Example

In [8], Nils Ferrand quotes some possible characteristics of a multi – agents system, applied to spatial planning : «
- Multiple scales : in space (from close neighborhood, to the nation or even continent), in time (from an instant for the perceived feelings of negotiators, to the centuries for the evolution of large scale ecosystems), and in organizations (from one – to – one interaction, to the transnational organizations) ;
- Multiple actors : except in some very local and specific situations (like a landowner planning some limited works on its own territory, with no visual or ecological impact), spatial planning implies many actors, with different interests, social and organizational position, spatial attachment, and personal qualities ;
- Multiple objectives : environmental, political, personal, economical, etc.

- Multiple modes : integrative (toward consensus through cooperation) or distributive (toward compromise through negotiation) ;
- Multiple criteria : ecology, economy, landscape, agriculture, laws and regulations, culture, society, ... »

The number of characteristics, non – exhaustive, denotes the difficulty of conceiving a complex multi – agents system using a unique environment and controlling a unique time unit. So, the necessity of building a multi – environments system appears, each of them having its own time and evolution criteria.

In a more precise example, which the aim is to simulate a ground area with its different components, the evolution time scales are very variable. If the simulation takes into account the underground level, the ground level and the atmosphere, it's clear that each of these elements and their internal elements doesn't evolve at the same speed. In this way, the life time of an ant is shorter than the anthill life time, which is shorter than the tree life time. However, the relationships between them are non – negligible and must lead to a co – evolution of each element. These distinctions induce then the creation of many environments having interactions properties to allow this co – evolution.

The

Fig. 3 shows an environment taxonomy allowing to model the anthill evolution, according to some possible sub – environments.

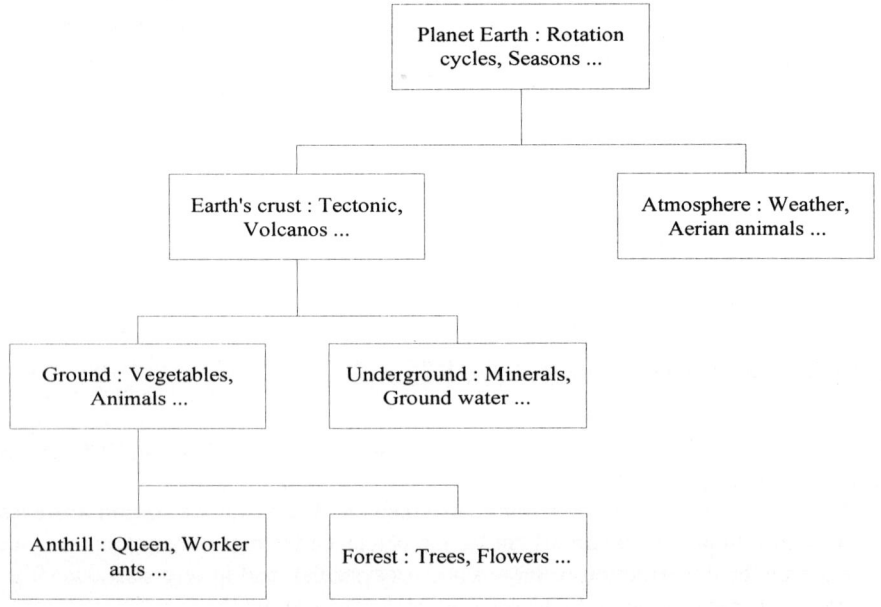

Fig. 3. : Example of multi – environments system.

Focusing only on the development of two sub – environments, one corresponding to the ground definition and its properties [9] and the other, modeling an anthill [10], the following characteristics are considered :

- Ground type (prairies, agricultural lands, forests, ...), water exchange (rain, evaporation, humidity level), carbon and nitrogen flow, temperature, plants decomposition (divided itself in some parts, following a chemical and physical protection index of the organic mater), plants production, ground textures (sand, clay, granite), ...
- Ants types (queens, workers, soldiers), cocoons and larvae with different states, ants cadavers, multiple ants nutrition forms, ...

Then, some interactions laws between these environments are indispensable to cause a co – evolution of the different components. This laws concerns :
- The substances transfers, an environment creates food for another environment agents, and these agents produce some rejects that allows the evolution of the first one.
- The geographic aspect, the anthill being an environment geographically placed at the ground level, as shown in the Fig. 3.

According to this decomposition principles it is possible to integrate, in a modular and progressive way, the other environment types to a developed system.

Conclusions

As it is shown in the example described in section 4, this environment model allows, from a practical point of view, to develop progressively a complex multi – agents system, defining and conceiving the sub – environments one by one. This model proposes different kinds of evolution for an environment. In this way, the agents evolution and the environment evolution leads to a co – evolving system.

In order to simulate artificial ecologies, the environment model described in this paper, can be combined to a food – web model, like this presented by Lindgren and Nordahl in [11]. These authors show different existing food links between many types of animals and vegetables, but they also put forward some special links : « Not only do plants and trees provide food for the herbivore, they also provide shelter from sun and wind, escape routes and places to hide from predators, and branches and twigs to make nests and squats from ». These types of interactions prove the difficulty to conceive a realistic model of a natural ecosystem, but the concepts brought in this paper should help to develop modular platforms.

Practically, the *componential model*, developed by Marc Lhuillier in [12], combined to this environment model would offer the possibility to construct multi – agents generic platforms. Those will tie together the notions of flexibility and dynamism of the componential model to the environmental evolution idea, described in this paper. In the future, a first platform of this kind will be developed, integrating the concepts of environmental evolution and meta – environment. Agents of this platform will be built with the macro – mutation concept, described in [13], allowing

It may be used for the rapid development (script programming) of applications using "real time" 3D visualization, with or without the immersion of human operators. These applications may be distributed for cooperative work. They can integrate universes inhabited by agents whose behavior is more or less complex.

In this article, we will mainly detail the behavior aspects of our platform. After indicating the particular constraints of virtual reality, we will present *ARéVi* in detail: its software architecture as well as the *oRis* multiagent language, the heart of the system. Then, we will present an example describing the system's possibilities. Finally, we will conclude on this platform evolution prospects.

2 Virtual Reality System Needs

The objective of a distributed virtual reality application is to allow a group of distant people to work together on a common project (for example interactive prototyping). In order to let the users concentrate on the problem they are trying to solve, the system they are using has to be as flexible as possible. Users don't have to adapt to the tool: the tool must be able to accept everything they need to do.

2.1 Modularity

The interactive prototyping notion involves at least the opportunity to add, remove or modify elements in the system. Thus, if we want the system to accept substantial changes in its structure, it must have a certain amount of flexibility.

The multiagent approach seems to be the most appropriate to carry out this goal. The system designer's attention is focused on the individual functioning of each of its components. These components have to be able to discern and act on their environment (system's other components). If we have a way to describe a component internal functioning as well as its interactions with its environment, this component will be able to take part in the general working of a system made of elements realized on the same way. There won't be any global controller and the system will be very modular. The general functioning will be the result of combined actions from each of the components and will change according to the user's intervention on each of them.

2.2 Immersion Through the Language

The main difference between simulation and virtual reality is that everything cannot be planned when launching a session. In fact, a person initiating a virtual world has previously planned to fill it up with various categories of entities, as well as the possible interactions with them. When connecting, a user has to discern it but does not have to be limited to this. He has to be given the opportunity to bring into the system his own entities, even if they were unknown to the designer. This entity supply has to be done without interrupting the system and reconfiguring everything. In the same way, to realize his work, a user may need to interact in the universe differently from the designer's plan. He must have as much freedom of action and interaction as possible. Whatever a virtual agent is able to do, a human operator has to be able to do it too, in order to be on the same level and to have the same freedom. The operator has to speak the agent's language: in this case, we can talk of immersion through the means of the language. It follows that this language has to be dynamic: it has to accept requests and modifications when executing.

2.3 Generics

The applications of virtual reality are numerous and involve activity fields very far from each other (for example: technical building ergonomics, insect population study, crowd movements, navigation in a reconstructed archeological site, computer-aided surgery, etc). It is important for the concerned system not to integrate restraints on the type of universe it can represent.

To sum up, integrating a generic and dynamic multiagent language in a virtual reality platform allows to obtain a tool which gives the users freedom concerning the kind of entities they wish to implement and on the interactions they wish to realize.

3 ARéVi

In this section, we present the *ARéVi* (in French, **A**telier de **R**éalité **Vi**rtuelle) platform. This platform is the result of our research work.

3.1 General Presentation

ARéVi lies in the *entity*, *scene* and *viewer* concepts. The entities are located agents with a 3D representation. This representation includes animations (succession of several representations) as well as levels of details (reduction of the facet number according to the distance from the camera). The entities may be derived (in the sense of object oriented programming) into cameras, lights or whatever the user wishes to.

To reduce the display costs, the entities are brought together in scenes: when in a particular scene, the only entities to be visualized are those which are part of it.

The entities in a scene are detected by a camera located in it (either provided by the user, or default created). The images shot by this camera are sent to a viewer (2D window) to be displayed.

All these notions are illustrated on Fig 1.

3.2 Software Architecture

The *ARéVi* kernel is a group of C++ classes. Figure 2 represents a part of the associated OMT model. The whole functionalities of the system, except for the

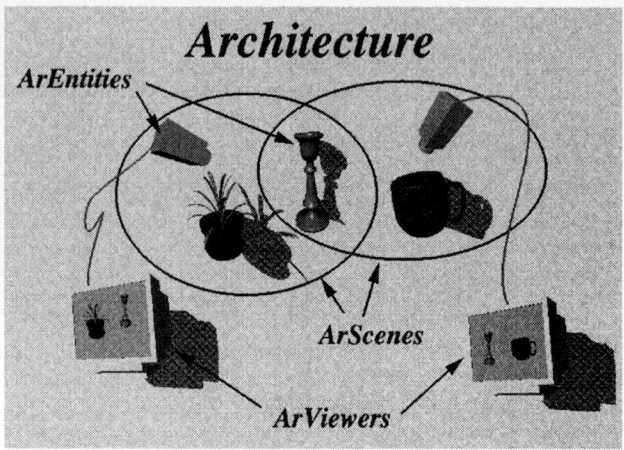

Fig. 1. *ARéVi* principle

display, are realized by classes (abstract or not). In particular, we have classes for the entity notion and its derivatives (`ArEntity, ArLight, ArCamera`), scene (`ArScene`) and viewer (`ArViewer`).The common derivation from the `Agent` class is explained in Sect 3.3.

An `ArEntity` has a geometry (`ArGeometry`) responsible for managing its position and cinematic.

The link with a particular rendering library is realized by derivation of the corresponding classes. For example, an `ArCamera` is derived into `ArXXCamera`, where `XX` represents one of the three libraries already supported: OpenInventor (SGI), Vision (Ilog), and OpenGL.

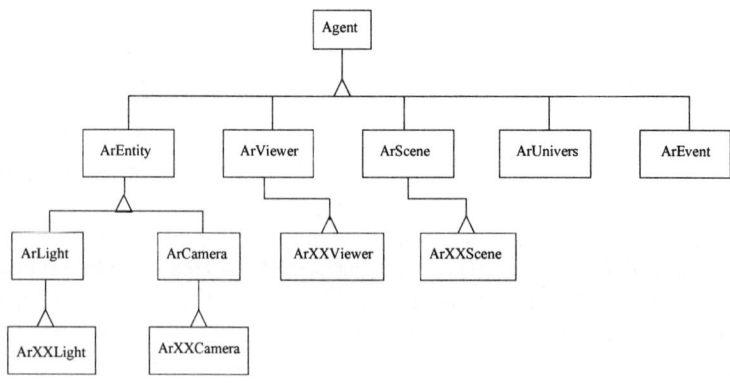

Fig. 2. Extract of the *ARéVi* kernel OMT diagram

3.3 oRis Language

As noted in Sect 2, the multiagent formalism, as well as the dynamic and generic characteristics of a language, are very interesting properties in a virtual reality system context.

Among the existing interpreted languages (for the dynamic aspects) we consider two categories:

1. Multiagent languages.
2. "General" languages (more precisely object oriented languages).

Multiagent Languages. Most of the existing multiagent systems are developed for a very particular application. However, more general systems exist too. We briefly describe two of them.

Starlogo [18] is a simulator and a language allowing a multiagent universe description. Each agent from this universe is equivalent to a Logo turtle whose behavior is easily specified by the user thanks to the language. These agents move in a 2D universe materialized by squares which can have a behavior similar to the turtle's (except for their ability to move). For example, this tool gives the possibility to simulate road traffic, termite colonies, and food collecting by ants, cell aggregation, prey/predator ecosystems. The aim of such a tool is to underline a different way of thinking the data processing problem (strongly parallel approach). Simulations with Starlogo implement hundreds or even thousands of agents.

The HOMAGE environment [17] makes it possible to describe multiagent systems, by implementing different languages adapted to each level of description. For decision making, the ALL language based on rules gives the ability to describe agents, whereas languages such as C++, CommonLisp and Java give the ability to describe the low level progress of each behavior elementary process. Communication between agents may be synchronous or asynchronous, but an agent cannot totally control another agent (for example destroy it). Unfortunately, known applications of this language only implement a small number of agents.

General Languages. In the rest of the paper, overdefinition means directly changing the code of an existing method.

General languages are opened enough to allow the representation of any universe. If the language includes object concepts, then, it is relatively simple to reach the agent level by re-programming a "scheduler". This scheduler is in charge of waking up in a cyclical way each object which then becomes an agent [7].

Some languages (particularly Java) have some interesting dynamic properties. At any time, it is possible without stopping the interpreter, to receive some code through the network and to execute it. This code may contain actions (method activations) as well as the definition of new classes or the overdefinition of methods of already existing classes. This dynamic aspect of the language would partly allow us to realize what we want to do: modify the entity's behavior or add new entities when executing. But the granularity of these actions is situated on the class level. For more freedom, we would like to have a granularity on the instance level. We want to be able to re-define a method not only on the class level, thus for all the instances at the same time, but also for a single instance. This single instance will, in a way, slightly become detached from its original class. For example, let's consider a virtual universe made up of a road, with cars racing on it. The cars may be instances from the same class provided by the creator of this universe. Another person connecting to the session may observe the evolution of the race and find it not really satisfactory. Then, he has the opportunity, without stopping the process, to choose one car, to suggest only for this car a new algorithm of driving and to observe the way this vehicle is acting compared to the others. If the new approach is considered to be better, the algorithm of piloting may then be changed from a status of methods for one instance to a status of methods of class so as to let all the instances benefit from it. Another example for the use of instance method overdefinition is given Sect 4.3.

Since the previously quoted languages do not totally fulfill our restraints, we have developed our own language: the *oRis* language [13].

oRis Main Characteristics. *oRis* is a multiagent language. It is object oriented (classes with attributes and methods, multiple inheritance). The syntax is close to C++. It is also an agent language: every object with a `void main(void)` method becomes an agent. This method is cyclically executed by the system scheduler and thus contains the entity behavior.

oRis is a dynamic language: it is able when executing to accept a new code, define a new class, change the method's code on the class level as well as on the instance level. It is also possible to add on the instance level the definition of a new method which does not exist in the original class.

oRis allows a deep coupling with C++: the programmer can specify a connection between an *oRis* class and a C++ class. The C++ object, which represents the *oRis* agent in the interpreter, is the object proposed by the user (deriving from the C++ Agent class, basis class for the *oRis* agents). The call of a native *oRis* method triggers the associated C++ method.

oRis is opened to other languages. We are already able to call Prolog predicates [22] or Fuzzy rules inside an *oRis* program to create reactive and cognitive agents.

oRis was successfully used in applications as varied as image processing [2], immunology [3], data processing networks [4] or insect populations [16].

Integration to ARéVi. Thanks to the *oRis* ↔ C++ coupling, *ARéVi* offers the user predefined *oRis* classes (native methods) which correspond to the previously presented C++ classes (Sect 3.2): `ArEntity`, `ArScene`, `ArViewer`, etc. Figure 3 represents the OMT diagram of the main predefined classes. This diagram is the exact reflection of the C++ classes (Fig 2).

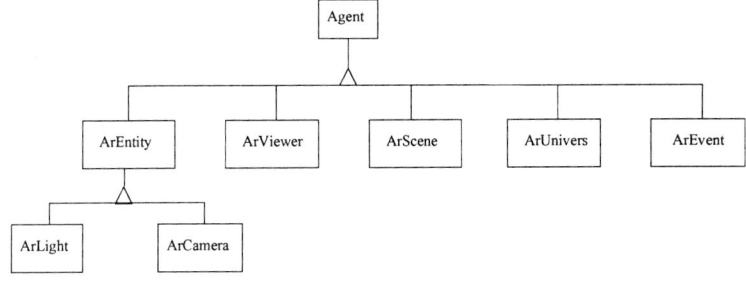

Fig. 3. OMT diagram of the *oRis* predefined classes for ARéVi

Nota: all the elements manipulated by *ARéVi* are agents: not only the "physical" `ArEntity` objects from the universe, but also the structures needed for the simulation setting. The main advantage of this approach is that it is easy, by derivation, to give them a behavior. For example, originally, the `ArScene` agent is only a list of agents which are visualized when watching the scene. With *oRis*, it is possible to create a `ProxyScene`, derived from an `ArScene`, providing a behavior through a `main()` method. For example, this behavior may be the automatic integration to the scene of any virtual object (any agent derived from `ArEntity`) entering the concerned zone. In the same way, an *ARéVi* viewer (`ArViewer`) has access to the frame rate. We can very easily create a viewer whose behavior is to reduce the generated image quality (wire, etc) if the rate becomes too low. We can then adapt the rendering level to the power of the graphic engine.

4 Examples

In this section, we illustrate the ARéVi multiagent and dynamic capacities. Firstly, we present the modeling of a simple mechanism. We continue with the presentation of a multiagent version of the Petri networks. Finally, we show a very simple way to couple both previous universes thanks to the overdefinition of methods of instance.

4.1 Trains of Gear Wheels

We wish to model a train of gear wheels. The problem here is not to realize a physical modeling (contact between the cogs) but a functional modeling: two gears in contact rotate in the opposite direction, the angular speed ratio being identical to the radius ratio.

The problem may be tackled on a general point of view: the train has four gears: gear 1 rotates clockwise, gear 2 anti-clockwise, etc.

It may be tackled on a local way: a gear E is an object (passive). It knows its successor and its predecessor in the mechanism. It can be called (call of methods) by its predecessor P. P indicates to E how much it has just rotated as well as its characteristics. Thus, E is supposed to deduce its own rotation and transmit it to its successor: the movement propagates step by step. Finally, we create an engine agent (it is the only agent of this example) whose behavior (`main` method) is to rotate. It only remains to "connect" the engine to the first gear to start the line. In the destructor code from the Gear class, we ask the killed gear to disconnect from its predecessor. Thus, when executing, if a gear is killed by the user, there will be no mistake induced (the previous gear no longer transmits movements) and the following gears will automatically stop, since nobody ask for them. We effectively get a system whose behavior is consistent with its real-life equivalent.

The previous example implements passive gears, which are objects but not agents. In order to get a more realistic universe, we can provide them with a behavior:

- Scrutinize the universe.
- When a gear E is detected close by (the addition of its radius and the E radius = the distance between the entities):
  - Connection to E

  $\Rightarrow$ Automatically start rotating if E was rotating.
- If we are connected to a gear and if the distance from it becomes too important:
  - Disconnection

  $\Rightarrow$ Automatically stop rotating.

Thus, now, by moving the gears, with an interface peripheral (mouse or else) we are able to modify the mechanism when this one is moving (see Fig 4).

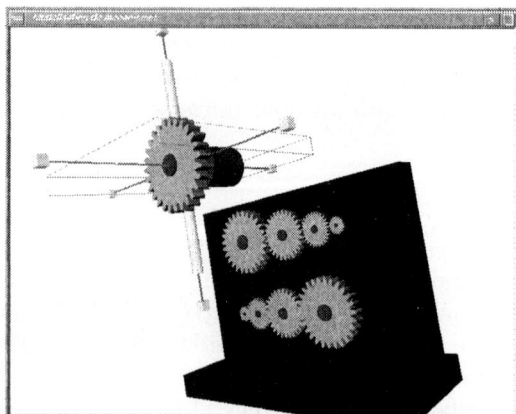

Fig. 4. Gears can be dynamically put in or taken off the mechanism

4.2 Petri Networks

The second universe example we present concerns the Petri networks. Usually, this kind of system does not have a graphic representation. However, we gave it one in order to visualize its behavior (see Fig 5). Nota: Several approaches

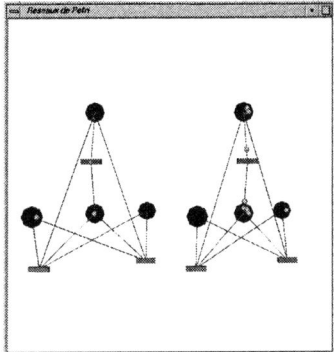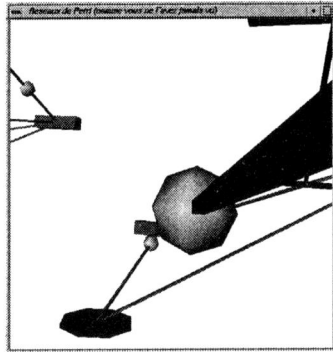

Fig. 5. Graphic representation of a Petri network

exist for the programming of Petri networks. When using *oRis*, we have selected an agent's approach: places, connections and marks are objects, transitions are agents. They decide themselves whenever they get activated citeHolvoet97a, [21].

4.3 Gears and Petri Network Coupling

Now, the next step consists in regrouping both previous examples in order for the Petri network to act as a controller for the gears which thus will act as an operative part.

Both universes were built separately. Therefore, they don't know each other. The coupling is realized in three steps:

1. Loading of the gears.
2. While the gears are functioning, loading of the Petri networks. Both universes coexist in memory and have their own display windows.
3. Triggering of the command on one of the network places: on a mark entrance, we start on the engine coupled to the gears. On an exit mark, we switch off this engine.

Point 3 is realized by dynamically entering (without stopping the system) the code on (Fig 6).

This code overdefines the addition and suppression methods of Place 2. The methods are not overdefined on the class level (thus for all the instances) but only on a particular instance level which then adopts a behavior slightly different from the others.

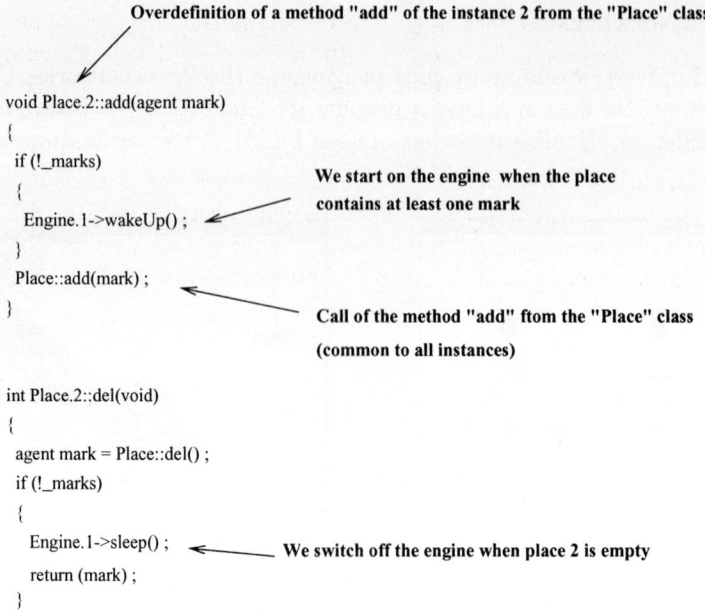

Fig. 6. Association of a behavior to a place of the Petri network

Nota: during the overdefinition of an instance method, it is always possible to call a method of class (for example, call of `Place::add()` in `Place.2::add()`). This very simply allows to add another action to the default behavior proposed by the class.

5 Conclusion and Perspectives

The *ARéVi* platform, built around the *oRis* language, is a developing platform for virtual reality applications. It has been successfully used in several industrial projects (ergonomics study of technical buildings, sea deeps 3D visualization, 3D interactive representation of a district, prototyping of a manufacturing system [8]). The existence of a dynamic multiagent language in the system makes it possible for us to:

- create modular universes; the modularity is realized by the absence of general controller and thus by the use of elementary "bricks" with their own goals: the agents,
- interact freely in these universes; the dynamic characteristics of the *oRis* language allow us, as users, to act on the lowest level on the entities (everything an agent is able to do, a user is able to do it too), then realizing an immersion through the language.

The previous version of the platform did not include the *oRis* language but allowed the creation of a universe distributed through the network [10]. We now work on a distributed version of *ARéVi / oRis* allowing the repartition of agents and so of universes through the network. The low level communications are made thanks to Java and support the different modes (Unicast, Broadcast, Multicast). In our project, the choice of this language is penalizing when talking about performances (-20%), but it offers some very interesting development facilities in terms of simplicity (multithread programming supported by this language), safety (pre-existing group of safe communication classes), HCI (JavaBeans), integration of multimedia processing (Java Media Players), high level network extension (servlets, RMI, aglets), interoperability (CORBA) and connection to the databases (JDBC).

References

[1] Balaguer J.F. *Virtual Studio : Un système d'animation en environnement virtuel*. PhD thesis, EPFL DI–LIG, 1993.

[2] P. Ballet, V. Rodin, and J. Tisseau. Edge Detection using a Multiagent System. In *SCIA'97, IAPR Scandinavian Conference on Image Analysis*, pages 621–629, Lappeenranta (Finlande), June 1997.

[3] P. Ballet, J. Tisseau, and F. Harrouet. A Multiagent System to Model an Human Secondary Immune Response. In *IEEE Transactions on Systems, Man, and Cybernetics*, Orlando (USA), October 1997.

[4] F. Bourdon. The Interactional Semantics of Knowledge. In *International Joint Conference on Artificial Intelligence, Poster Session*, page 15, Nagoya (Japan), August 1997.

[5] Brutzman D.P. *A Virtual World For an Autonomous Underwater Vehicle*. PhD thesis, Naval Postgraduate School, Monterey, California, 1994.

[6] Carlsson C. and Hagsang O. DIVE – a Platform For Multi–user Virtual Environnement. *Computer and Graphics*, pages 663–669, 1993.

[7] M. Carroll. Active Objects Made Easy. *Software, Practice and Experience*, 28(1):1–21, January 1998.

[8] Chevaillier P., Tisseau J., Harrouet F., and Querrec R. Prototyping Manufacturing Systems. Contribution of Virtual Reality, Agents and Petri Nets. In *INCOM'98*, Nancy et Metz (France), June 1998.

[9] Codella C.F, Jalili R., Koved L. , and Lewis J.B. A Toolkit for Developing Multi-User, Distributed Virtual Environnements. In *IEEE Virtual Reality Annual International Symposium*, 1993.

[10] T. Duval, S. Morvan, P. Reignier, F. Harrouet, and J. Tisseau. ARéVi : une boîte à outils 3D pour des applications coopératives. *Calculateurs Parallèles*, 9(2):239–250, 1997.

[11] Gobbetti E. *Virtuality Builder II, vers une architecture pour l'interaction avec des mondes synthétiques*. PhD thesis, EPFL DI–LIG, 1993.

[12] Green M., Shaw C., and White L. Minimal Reality Toolkit, version 1.3. Technical report, Department of Computing Science, University of Alberta, 1993.

[13] F. Harrouet, R. Cozien, P. Reignier, and J. Tisseau. oRis, un langage pour simulations multi-agents. In *Journées Francophones de l'Intelligence Artificielle Distribuée et des Systèmes Multi-Agents*, La Colle-sur-Loup, April 1997.

[14] Hartman J. and Wernecke J. *The VRML 2.0 Handbook : Building Moving Worlds on the Web*. Addison-Wesley Publishing Company, 1996.

[15] Macedonia M.R. *A Network Software Architecture For Large Scale Virtual Environnements*. PhD thesis, Naval Postgraduate School, Monterey, California, 1995.

[16] M. Martin. Application d'un simulateur multi-agents à la modélisation de populations d'invertébrés en milieu bocager. Master's thesis, Ecole Nationale Supérieure Agronomique de Rennes, September 1997.

[17] A. Poggi and G. Adorni. A Multi-language Environment to Develop Multi-agents Applications. In *ECAI*, pages 325–340, Budapest (Hungary), August 1996.

[18] M. Resnick. StarLogo : An Environment for Decentralized Modeling and Decentralized Thinking. In *CHI*, pages 11–12, April 96.

[19] Roohlf J. and Helman J. IRIS Performer : A High Performance Multiprocessing Toolkit for Real–Time 3D Graphics. In *ACM SIGGRAPH*, pages 381–393, 1994.

[20] Strauss P.S. and Carey R. An Object-Oriented 3D Graphics Toolkit. In *ACM SIGGRAPH*, pages 341–347, 1992.

[21] Tisseau J., Chevaillier P., Harrouet F., and Nédélec A. Des procédures aux agents. Application en *oRis*. Technical Report LI2TCH98RPI01, ENIB, Laboratoire d'Informatique Industrielle, February 1998.

[22] Jan Wielemaker. SWI-Prolog 2.9. ftp://swi.psy.uva.nl/pub/SWI-Prolog, 1997.

[23] Zeleznik R.C., Conner D.B., Wlocka M.M., Aliaga D.G., Wang N.T., Hubbard P.M., Knepp B., Kaufman H., Hugues J.F., and van Dam A. An Object-Oriented Framework for the Integration of Interactive Animation Techniques. In *ACM SIGGRAPH*, pages 105–112, 1991.

Investigating the Complex with Virtual Soccer

Itsuki Noda and Ian Frank

Complex Games Lab
Electrotechnical Laboratory
Umezono 1-1-4, Tsukuba
Ibaraki, Japan 305
{noda,ianf}@etl.go.jp

Abstract. We describe Soccer Server, a network-based simulator of soccer that provides a virtual world enabling researchers to investigate the complex system of soccer play. We identify why soccer is such a suitable domain for the creation of this kind of virtual world, and assess how well Soccer Server performs its task. Soccer Server was used in August 1997 to stage the simulation league of the first Robotic Soccer World Cup (RoboCup), held in Nagoya, Japan. This contest attracted 29 software soccer teams, designed by researchers from ten different countries. In 1998, an updated version of Soccer Server will be used to stage the second RoboCup in France, coinciding with the real World Cup of football.

1 Introduction

The rules of soccer, or association football, were formulated in 1863 in the UK by the Football Association, and the game has since become one of the most widely played in the world. The popularity of the game is illustrated by the following passage:

> Contrary to popular belief, the world's greatest sporting event in terms of prolonged, worldwide interest is not the Olympic Games. Rather, it is the World Cup of football, which, like the Olympics, is held just once every four years and is played out over a period of two weeks or more. The United States hosted this global spectacle in 1994—and what a spectacle it turned out to be. The championship game between Brazil and Italy was witnessed live by a crowd of over 100,000 people in the Rose Bowl in Pasadena, California, and by a crowd of at least a billion on television the world over.

We quote this description in our introduction not simply because it illustrates the popularity of soccer, or because the publication of this paper coincides with France-98, the successor to the American World Cup. Rather, we are just as interested in the source of the excerpt — not a sports book or newspaper, but the opening paragraph of the opening chapter of a book on science: *Would-be Worlds*, by John Casti [Casti 97a].

Casti's purpose in describing the football World Cup is to introduce the notion of *complex systems*. Football is an excellent example in this context because it is not possible to understand the game by analysing just individual players. Rather, it is the interactions in the game, both between the players themselves and between the players and the environment, that determine the outcome. This is the essence of complex systems: they resist analysis by decomposition.

We share Casti's belief that the arrival of cheap, powerful widespread computing capability over the past decade or so has provided us with a tool for studying complex systems as complete entities. Casti himself suggests that such computer simulations (virtual worlds, would-be-worlds) "play the role of laboratories for complex systems", which, in contrast to more conventional science laboratories "allow us to explore information instead of matter" [Casti 97b]. It is to provide this kind of laboratory for research on complex systems that we have developed a simulation of the game of soccer. This system, Soccer Server, enables a soccer match to be played between two teams of player-programs, and has already been used to stage a 29-team contest at the First Robotic Soccer World Cup (RoboCup), in Nagoya, Japan. In this paper, we describe Soccer Server, identifying in particular why soccer is such a suitable choice as a simulation domain. We also take care to evaluate the success of Soccer Server, demonstrating that the properties of *fidelity*, *simplicity*, *clarity*, *bias-free*, and *tractability* are effective measures for assessing this kind of simulation.

2 Soccer as a Domain for Modelling

There were many reasons behind the choice of soccer for our simulator. Initially, of course, there was the appeal that soccer is fun and easily understood by large numbers of people. More important than this, however, was the significant challenge offered by trying to formalise and understand the domain.

2.1 Soccer as a Complex System

To illustrate the difficulty of the soccer domain, let us return to the discussion of complex systems that we started in the Introduction, and to Casti's book, *Would-be Worlds*. In discussing how a theory of the complex might be formalised, Casti introduces a number of characteristics he describes as the "key components" of complex, adaptive systems. Briefly, these are (1) a medium-sized number of agents, that (2) are intelligent and adaptive, and (3) only have local information.

It should not be too hard to convince the reader that the game of soccer is a very good fit for these properties. Soccer has 22 agents. This falls comfortably between Casti's examples of systems with large numbers of agents (galaxies, which have enough agents to be treated statistically), and small numbers of agents (conflicts between two superpowers). The agents in soccer are also intelligent and adaptive, with the players on each team striving to perform well together, and to out-manœuvre the opponents. Finally, the information in soccer is clearly limited, as the players can only see in the direction they are facing,

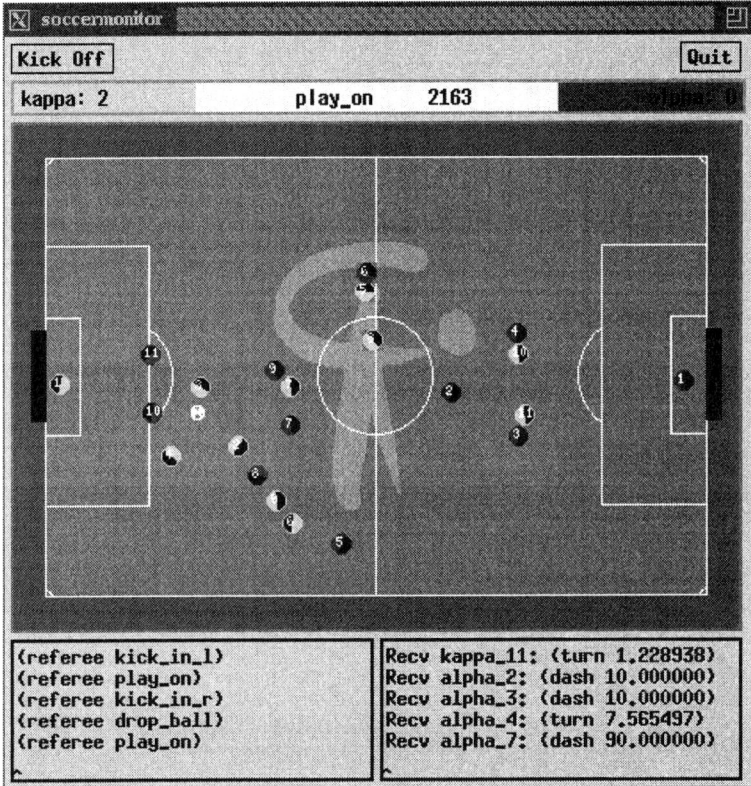

Fig. 1. Window image of Soccer Server

and verbal communication is hampered both by distance and by the importance of concealing intentions from the opponents.

Thus, understanding soccer is a significant challenge: it has the characteristics of a complex system, for which, as Casti emphasises, "there exists no decent mathematical theory" [Casti 97b]. However, as well as being a good example of a complex system, another important factor also influenced our choice of soccer: the feasibility of constructing a simulation. We examine this question below.

2.2 The Nature of Play

One of the foremost tasks in the design of a simulation is the creation of a *model* of the domain in question; it is the implementation of the rules and principles of the model that produces the simulation. In this respect, we found that soccer was a very amenable domain, simply by virtue of being a game.

An excellent study of the nature of play is given by Huizinga [Huizinga 50]. Although primarily interested in the significance of play as a cultural phenomenon, some of the main characteristics of play identified by Huizinga are relevant to our theme here. For instance, the first properties of play identified by Huizinga are that it is voluntary (or, as Huizinga says, "Play to order is no longer play"), and that play is not "ordinary" or "real" life. These properties already suggest some kind of modelling process. Huizinga then notes that "all play is limited in locality and duration" — another feature that makes play a promising candidate for convenient simulation.

Further general properties identified by Huizinga are that "all play has binding rules" and that "play can be repeated and transmitted". The presence of rules means that part of the work of modelling is already done. Indeed, in implementing Soccer Server, we took the simple approach of basing our model primarily on just the rules of the game. The remainder of the Soccer Server model was then formulated to allow maximum scope for the investigation of how the rules of soccer can actually be followed in the best way; that is, how to create a team that can play well. Huizinga's final property of repeatability and transmittability then indicates how our model can be used as an ideal testbed for allowing researchers to investigate and discuss the properties of the domain.

2.3 The Type of Model Represented by Soccer Server

As we suggested above, Soccer Server models the rules of the game of soccer in a way that allows the system to be used as a testbed for research on the nature of the domain. The intention is that different soccer player-control algorithms can be tested against each other to discover which are stronger. Thus, Soccer Server can be viewed as a predictive model of the relative strengths of these algorithms. We agree with [Casti 97a, Page 25] that "the first and foremost test that a model must pass is that it must provide convincing answers to the questions we put to it". Note, though, that the questions we want to answer with Soccer Server are not just which algorithms perform better, but also *why* the better algorithms are superior. This is a consequence of viewing the system as a testbed for research; the ultimate goal is to advance the theory of complex systems.

We should also note that although this paper concentrates on the virtual world created by Soccer Server, the RoboCup tournaments themselves also include competitions for teams of real robots. In our view, this link is very important, since there are many results that show that real-world experiments can produce results that could not be expected from simulation alone (*e.g.*, see [Thompson 97], [Brooks 86]). With this caveat said, then, let us move on to take a detailed look at our implementation of a model of soccer.

3 Soccer Server Itself

Soccer Server enables a soccer match to be played between two teams of player-programs (possibly implemented in different programming systems). A match using Soccer Server is controlled using a form of client-server communication. Soccer Server provides a virtual soccer field (such as the one we presented in Figure 1) and simulates the movements of players and a ball. A client program

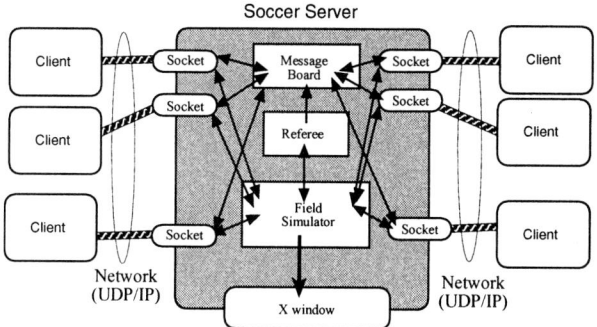

Fig. 2. Overview of Soccer Server

can provide the 'brain' of a player by connecting to the Soccer Server via a computer network (using a UDP/IP socket) and specifying actions for that player to carry out. In return, the client receives information from the player's sensors.

Figure 2 gives an overview of how the Soccer Server communicates with clients. The three main modules in the Soccer Server itself are:

1. **A field simulator module.** This creates the basic virtual world of the soccer field, and calculates the movements of objects, checking for collisions.
2. **A referee module.** This ensures that the rules of the game are followed.
3. **A message-board module.** This manages the communication between the client programs.

Below, we give an overview of each of these modules. A more detailed description of the Soccer Server can be found in [Noda *et al* 98]. Also, a large collection of related material, including sources and full manuals, is maintained at the Soccer Server home page: http://ci.etl.go.jp/~noda/soccer/server.

3.1 Simulator Module: The Basic Virtual World

The soccer field and all objects on it are 2-dimensional. This means that, unlike in real football, the ball cannot be kicked in the air and the players cannot make use of skills such as heading or volleying. The size of the field, measured in the notional internal equivalent of metres, is 105m × 68m. On the field, there are objects that move (the players and the ball) and objects that are stationary (flags, lines and goals). The stationary objects serve as landmarks that clients can make use of to determine their player's position, orientation or speed and direction of movement. Clients are not given information on the absolute positions of their own players, but only on the relative location of other objects. Thus, the fixed objects are important reference points for the client programs' calculations.

All communication between the server and each client is in the form of ASCII strings. Therefore, clients can be realized in any programming environment on any architecture that has the facilities of UDP/IP sockets and string manipulation. The protocol of the communication consists of:

- **Control commands**: Messages sent from a client to the server to control the client's player. The basic commands are `turn`, `dash` and `kick`. Communication is conducted through the `say` command, and a privileged goalie client can also attempt to `catch` the ball. The `sense_body` command provides feedback on client status such as stamina and speed, and `change_view` selects a trade-off between quality of visual data and frequency of update.
- **Sensor information**: Messages sent from the server to a client describing the current state of the game from the viewpoint of the client's player. There are two types of information, visual (`see`) and auditory (`hear`) information.

Soccer Server is a discrete simulation of continuous time. Thus, both the control commands and the sensor information are processed within a framework of 'simulator steps'. The length of the cycle between the processing steps for the control commands is 100ms, whereas the length of the step cycle for the sensor information is determined by the most recent `change_view` command issued by a client (we discuss the timing of these steps in more detail in §4). Note that all players have identical abilities (strength and accuracy of kicking, stamina, sensing) so that the entire difference in performance of teams derives from the effective use of the control commands and sensor information, and especially from the ability to produce collaborative behaviour between multiple clients.

As a final feature, when invoked with the `-coach` option, the server provides an extra socket for a privileged client (called a coach client) that has the ability to direct all aspects of the game. The coach client can move all objects, direct the referee module to make decisions, and announce messages to all clients. This facility is extremely useful for tuning and debugging client programs, which usually involves repeated testing of the behaviors of the clients in many situations. An extension being considered for further versions of Soccer Server is a modified version of the `-coach` option that allows teams to include a twelfth client that has a global view of the game and can conduct sideline coaching during play by shouting strategic or tactical advice to players.

3.2 Referee Module: Playing by the Rules

The referee module monitors the game and, as in real soccer, regulates the flow of play by making a number of decisions based on the rules of the game (announcing goals, throw-ins, corner kicks, and goal kicks, and time-keeping). In the first RoboCup tournament, the referee made no decisions about fouls. The new version of Soccer Server, however, introduces an offside rule, adding to the possible judgments of the referee. Remaining fouls, like 'obstruction', are difficult to judge automatically as they concern players' intentions. The server therefore also includes an interface allowing a human user to instruct the referee to award a free kick. Since such decisions about fair play actually call for significant understanding of the game, future versions of Soccer Server may include a dedicated socket for referee clients, thus encouraging research on automatic refereeing.

3.3 Message Board Module: Communication Protocol

The message board module is responsible for managing the communication between the players. A basic principle of Soccer Server is that each client should control just one player, and that communication between individual clients should only be carried out via the say and hear protocols introduced in §3.1.

When a say command is issued, the message is broadcast to *all* clients immediately as auditory information. In early versions of Soccer Server, teams could use this communication to sidestep the local nature of information in the game by, for example, having each player broadcast his own location and interpretation of the game at each time step. Another possible strategy was to use one client in a team (*e.g.*, a 'captain') to direct and inform all the others. In the current Soccer Server, however, not all the other clients are guaranteed to hear all the broadcast information, since there is a maximum range of communication of 50m, and any player can only hear one message from each team during each two simulation cycles. Also, the length of the message itself is restricted. Thus, effective and efficient use of the say command is encouraged, imparting information only when it is useful and timely.

Note that the server can connect with up to 22 clients, but that to facilitate testing it is possible for a single program to control multiple players (by establishing multiple socket connections). In a competitive situation such as RoboCup, such programs are only permitted on the understanding that the control of each player is separated logically. In practice, it is also not technically difficult to cheat the server and establish inter-client communication outside the server, so the 'one-client one-player' rule is effectively a gentlemans' agreement.

3.4 Uncertainty

In order to reflect the nature of the real world, the server introduces various types of uncertainty into the simulation, as follows:

- Noise added to the movement of objects. The amount of this noise increases with the speed of the object.
- Noise added to command parameters. Small random numbers are added to the parameters of commands sent from clients.
- Limited command execution. The server executes only one command for each player in each simulation cycle. Each client program can get feedback on how many commands its player has executed via use of the sense_body command (*successful* execution must of course be monitored by the clients themselves; for instance, a dash has no effect if a player's path is blocked).
- Inexact sensing. The further an object, the less reliable the information returned about it from the server.

The presence of these uncertainties re-enforces the importance of robust behavior, and of the reactive monitoring of the outcomes of a player's actions.

4 Assessing the Soccer Server

How can we meaningfully assess the Soccer Server? In §2.3 we suggested that the main test of a good model is whether it provides answers to the questions we ask of it. Thus, since we constructed Soccer Server to enable the investigation of soccer, we could simply examine the quality of the conclusions learned about agent behaviour in the domain. However, a more fundamental review is also possible. For instance, [Casti 97a, Page 175-176] summarises several properties that can be used to assess models and simulations:

- **Fidelity**. The model's ability to represent reality to the degree necessary to answer the questions for which the model was constructed;
- **Simplicity**. The level of completeness of the model, in terms of how "small" the model is in things like number of variables, complexity of interconnections among sub-systems, and number of *ad hoc* hypotheses assumed;
- **Clarity**. The ease with which one can understand the model and the predictions/explanations it offers for real-world phenomena.
- **Bias-free**. The degree to which the model is free of prejudices of the modeler having nothing to do with the purported focus or purpose of the model.
- **Tractability**. The level of computing resources needed to obtain the predictions and/or explanations offered by the model.

Note that these qualities are more subtle than simply assessing whether a model faithfully captures all aspects of the phenomenon it represents. Let us examine the results of evaluating Soccer Server against each of the criteria.

4.1 Fidelity

One of the most important considerations during the development of Soccer Server was the level of abstraction for representing the client commands and the sensor information. One possibility was a low-level, physical description, for example allowing power values for drive motors to be specified. However, it was felt that such a representation would concentrate users' attention too much on the actual control of a players' actions, relegating true investigation of the multi-agent nature of team-play to the level of a secondary objective. Further, it is difficult to design a low-level description that is not implicitly based on a specific notion of robot hardware; for example, control of speed by drive motors is biased towards a physical implementation that uses wheels. On the other hand, a more abstract representation, maybe using tactical commands such as `pass-ball-to` and `block-shoot-course`, would produce a game in which the real-world nature of soccer becomes obscured, and in which the development of soccer techniques not yet realised by human players becomes problematic. Thus, our representation — using basic control commands such as `turn`, `dash`, and `kick` — is a compromise. To make good use of the available commands, clients will need to tackle both the problems of control in an incomplete information, dynamic environment and also the best way to combine the efforts of multiple players. Thus, we believe that Soccer Server achieves our goal of providing a simple test-bench with significant real-world properties.

The choice of abstraction level is also relevant to a further question that often occupied us during the design of Soccer Server: whether the simulator should be designed to model human soccer play or robot soccer play. This question has many facets, but in general the solution adopted in the Soccer Server is to be faithful to human soccer whenever possible. The justifications for this include the reasoning that real-world soccer is more immediately understood (and more attractive) to the casual observer, and that robot technology can change, whereas the nature of human soccer players is largely constant. Also, the closer the simulation to real-world soccer the more likely that knowledge acquisition from human expertise (*e.g.*, see [Frank 97]) will be directly applicable.

Of course there are differences between real soccer and the model represented by the server, most notably the 2-dimensional nature of the simulation. Also, the simulation parameters are tuned to make the server as useful as possible for the evaluation of competing client systems, rather than to directly reflect reality (for example, the width of the goals is 14.64m, double the size of ordinary goals, because scoring is more difficult when the ball cannot be kicked in the air). This question of whether human soccer is being directly simulated is also important in the context of the overall RoboCup challenge, which we discuss further below.

4.2 Simplicity

The ultimate goal of RoboCup, as described in [Kitano *et al* 97a], is "to develop a robot soccer team that can beat the Brazil world-cup team". Since this goal is well beyond current technologies, the RoboCup initiative defines a series of well-directed subgoals that are achievable in the short and mid-term. Implementing clients for Soccer Server is one of these challenges. The objective of RoboCup is that, as the level of sophistication of existing technology improves, the simplicity of the simulation should be altered appropriately.

One of the primary concerns about simplicity is the timing of the simulation cycles that govern the processing of commands and sensor information. The sensor information received by clients is rich, but the actions are simple. This is an argument for making the time between information updates longer than the time between action execution (*i.e.*, having an action processing cycle that is shorter than the information sensing cycle). If the information sensing cycle becomes too long, the ability to react to the opponents' actions becomes hampered. On the other hand, if the information sensing cycle becomes too short, the benefits of attempting to learn and predict the opponents' actions are diminished. The current lengths of these time steps are a compromise intended to strike a balance between these two conflicting goals.

4.3 Clarity

A large number of researchers have already used Soccer Server (we have already mentioned that the first RoboCup contest featured 29 teams from ten different countries). This is evidence that the workings of Soccer Server can be easily understood. In considering the 'clarity' of the system, though, we also have to take into account the ease with which one can understand the lessons learned through the course of such research. So, we are interested in questions like, "What results have emerged out of the teams produced by the first RoboCup contests?" To some extent, the answer to this type of question is dependent on the efforts of the Soccer Server users themselves. However, the RoboCup initiative requires all the teams entering any tournament to write a paper describing their approach. These papers show that in the original contests, the programs that performed well were simple hard-coded systems with little learning ability. For example, at the Pre-RoboCup'96 tournament held in Japan in November 1996, the winning team was the Ogalets, which essentially relied on constraining each player to stay within a small, pre-determined area of the pitch and to choose between a small number of hard-coded passing directions when they could reach the ball. In the RoboCup-97 tournament held in August 1997, on the other hand, the winning teams were more sophisticated. The winners, from Humboldt University, used case-based reasoning and agent-oriented programming, the runners-up used reinforcement learning, and the third place team used an explicit model of teamwork, based on joint intentions.

As well as demonstrating the clarity of Soccer Server, it should be pointed out that sometimes the users of the system can show almost the opposite: that the system was not actually fully understood by the designers themselves. This happens when bugs are found in the simulation that can be exploited to the advantage of the client programs. One example of such a bug was an error in the implementation of stamina. Generally, the stamina of a player decreases when the player issues `dash` commands, thus limiting the player's ability to make further movements. However, it was found by some users that by using *negative* parameters in this command, a player's stamina could be increased!

A further flaw was found with the version of Soccer Server used for the RoboCup-97 contest, in which a problem with the handling of simulation cycles sometimes allowed players to kick the ball three times in very quick succession, thus imparting three times the normal 'maximum' speed. However, it is in the spirit of the RoboCup contest that such bugs are reported to the designers, so that all users are working from an even footing. This spirit is also an illustration of the bias-free nature of Soccer Server.

4.4 Bias-Free

Although developed solely at the Electrotechnical Laboratory, Soccer Server has benefited substantially from the opinions and suggestions of many users. In particular, there is a mailing list dedicated to discussing RoboCup, on which a consensus is usually reached before modifying the model represented by the simulation (this mailing list averaged over 200 messages per month between Dec 1997 and March 1998). To give a feel for the speed of change of the simulator, here is a partial list of some of the features changed since RoboCup-97: the introduction of the `sense_body` command, the ability to *see* the direction that other players are facing, the introduction of off-sides, the introduction of a goalie, and a re-modelling of the implementation of stamina. All these changes are designed to increase properties such as the similarity of the simulation to the human game, the importance of modelling the opponents' play, or the importance of modelling the teamwork being produced by a client's own team-mates.

Further evidence of the bias-free nature of Soccer Server is the presence of a public library of code (the RoboCup Simulation Code Archive, located at http://www.isi.edu/soar/galk/RoboCup/Libs/). Researchers can use this code to help reduce the development time of RoboCup clients. Some code is specific to particular situations, whereas some is general enough to provide infrastructure for complete agents (the code for the winning clients from RoboCup-97 is available). In particular, the archives contain the 'libsclient' library, a collection of low-level functions intended to abstract away many details of tasks such as maintaining sockets, parsing the information from the server, and sending commands to the server.

4.5 Tractability

Soccer Server has to simulate a game of soccer and communicate with each client program in real time. The system can run on a PC or a workstation with only modest memory and processor resources (although typically a user will also require at least one further computer to run the teams of clients). A more problematic limitation on Soccer Server in practice is the capacity of the network connecting the system to the clients. A large load on the network can lead to collisions that prevent client commands reaching Soccer Server or information being returned. Indeed, some teams at RoboCup-97 found it necessary to re-calibrate their software to the particular conditions found at the tournament site. However, it is difficult to predict the exact effects of changes in network conditions, so client programs with some flexibility in their interpretation of the state of play are encouraged. In general, this may not be an adverse property of the system; the need to understand adaptation and to cope with only local information were two of the prime qualities of complex systems identified in §2.1.

5 Conclusions: Towards a Theory of the Complex

We have discussed how the game of soccer is a good example of a complex system, well-suited to the task of modelling. We also described and assessed our implementation of Soccer Server, clarifying the nature of the model it represents.

Let us close by noting that the challenges represented by the domain of soccer have recently led to it being proposed as a new standard problem for AI research [Kitano *et al* 97b]. Of course, the notion of a standard problem has long been a driving force for engineering research. Historically, for example, the acceptance of the 'Turing Test' [Turing 50] focused attention on the mimicking of human behavior as a test of machine intelligence. More recently, chess has received significant attention, generating important advances in the theory of search algorithms and search control, as well as motivating cognitive studies into the ways that humans approach the same problems (*e.g.*, see [Levinson *et al* 91]).

Soccer (in particular contrast to chess) is a dynamic, real-time, multi-agent, system with incomplete information. We see Soccer Server as a virtual world that provides a tool for investigating such complex domains. It does this by providing a predictive model of the strengths of software algorithms for controlling agents in these environments. In the words of [Casti 97b], Soccer Server is a "would-be-world" that "has the capacity of serving as a laboratory within which to test the hypotheses about the phenomena it represents". It is our hope that, for complex systems such as soccer, the efforts of researchers using the laboratory of Soccer Server will rectify the situation where "at present, there seems to be no known mathematical structures within which we can comfortably accommodate a description" [Casti 97a, Page 214].

References

[Brooks 86] R. A. Brooks. A robust layered control system for a mobile robot. *Journal of Robotics and Automation*, RA-2(1), 1986.

[Casti 97a] John L. Casti. *Would-be Worlds: how simulation is changing the frontiers of science.* John Wiley and Sons, Inc, 1997.

[Casti 97b] John L. Casti. Would-be worlds: toward a theory of complex systems. *Artificial Life and Robotics*, 1(1):11–13, 1997.

[Frank 97] I. Frank. Football in recent Times: What we can learn from the newspapers. In *First Intl. Workshop on Robocup in conjunction with RoboCup-97 at IJCAI-97*, pages 75–82, Nagoya, Japan, 1997.

[Huizinga 50] Johan Huizinga. *Homo ludens: a study of the play element in culture.* Beacon Press, 1950. ISBN 0–8070–4681–7.

[Kitano *et al* 97a] H. Kitano, M. Asada, Y. Kuniyoshi, I. Noda, E. Osawa, and H. Matsubara. RoboCup: A challenge problem for AI. *AI Magazine*, pages 73–85, Spring 1997.

[Kitano *et al* 97b] H. Kitano, M. Tambe, P. Stone, M. Veloso, S. Coradeschi, E. Osawa, H. Matsubara, I. Noda, and M. Asada. The RoboCup synthetic agent challenge 97. In *Proceedings of IJCAI-97*, pages 24–29, Nagoya, Japan, 1997.

[Levinson *et al* 91] R. Levinson, F. Hsu, J. Schaeffer, T. Marsland, and D. Wilkins. Panel: The role of chess in artificial intelligence research. In *Proceedings of the 12th IJCAI*, pages 547–552, Sydney, Austr alia, 1991.

[Noda *et al* 98] I. Noda, H. Matsubara, K. Hiraki, and I. Frank. Soccer Server: a tool for research on multi-agent systems. *Applied Artificial Intelligence.* To appear.

[Thompson 97] A. Thompson. An evolved circuit, intrinsic in silicon, entwined with physics. In T. Higuchi *et al*, editors, *Proceedings of ICES '96 — The First International Conference on Evolvable Systems: from biology to hardware*, pages 385–400. Springer-Verlag, Berlin, 1997.

[Turing 50] A.M. Turing. Computing machinery and intelligence. *Mind*, 59:433–460, 1950.

Webots: Symbiosis Between Virtual and Real Mobile Robots

Olivier Michel

Microprocessor and Interface Lab,
Swiss Federal Institute of Technology,
Lausanne, Switzerland
Tel: ++41 21 693 52 64
Fax: ++41 21 693 52 63
Olivier.Michel@epfl.ch,
http://diwww.epfl.ch/lami/team/michel

Abstract. This paper presents Webots: a realistic mobile robot simulator allowing a straightforward transfer to real robots. The simulator currently support the Khepera mobile robot and a number of extension turrets. Both real and simulated robots can be programmed in C language using the same Khepera API, making the source code of a robot controller compatible between the simulator and the real robot. Sensor modelling for 1D and 2D cameras as well as visualisation and environment modelling are based upon the OpenGL 3D rendering library. A file format based on an extension of VRML97, used to model the environments and the robots, allows virtual robots to move autonomously on the Internet and enter the real world. Current applications include robot vision, artificial life games, robot learning, etc.

1 Introduction

Autonomous robotics represents a very wide research area including control, machine learning, evolutionary computing, artificial life, vision, man-machine interface, mechanical design, etc. In order to investigate this area, researchers often make use of real robots as well as software tools for simulating and monitoring these real devices. This paper presents a new generation of mobile robots simulators, open to the real world and to the Internet. The Webots software is a first attempt to investigate this promising research area, by proposing realistic sensor simulations and standard definition language for virtual and real robots.

2 Real Mobile Robots

Mobile robot locomotion is achieved by equipping robots with wheels or legs. Most of wheeled robots rely on two independent motor wheels. The linear speed of the robot is given the average speed of each wheel and the angular speed results from the difference of speed between both wheels. Other wheeled robots have a gear wheel controlled by an actuator defining the orientation of the robot and a couple of wheels connected to a single motor defining the speed of the robot. Legged robots usually have between two and eight legs. Two-legged robots are often humanoids. Most four-legged robots try to acquire the appearance and dynamics of mammalians[2] while six legged robots try to imitate insect gaits (like the alternate tripod gait). Legged robots are much more difficult to design and control than wheeled robots, but they are more promising since they can handle complex environments (stairs, rough terrain) where their wheeled counterparts feel quite uncomfortable.

The Khepera mini-robot[9] is a 5 cm diameter mobile robot distributed by K-Team S.A. It is widely used for research and education purposes. It has its own 68331 micro-controller and memory, two independent motor wheels and eight infra-red sensors. It is possible to control the robot by cross-compiling and downloading any user program written in C with the Khepera API (Application Program Interface). This API provides access to the sensors and actuators of the robot and is compatible with the Webots simulator. That is, the same C source code can be compiled either for the real robot or the simulator without changing a line of code. Alternately, it is possible to control the robot with a remote computer connected to the robot through a serial link. The motor wheels of the robot can take different, positive or negative, speed values, so that the robot can move forward, backwards, turn right or left and spin round. The infra-red sensors are used to detect obstacles around the robots. They can also be used to measure the level of ambient light.

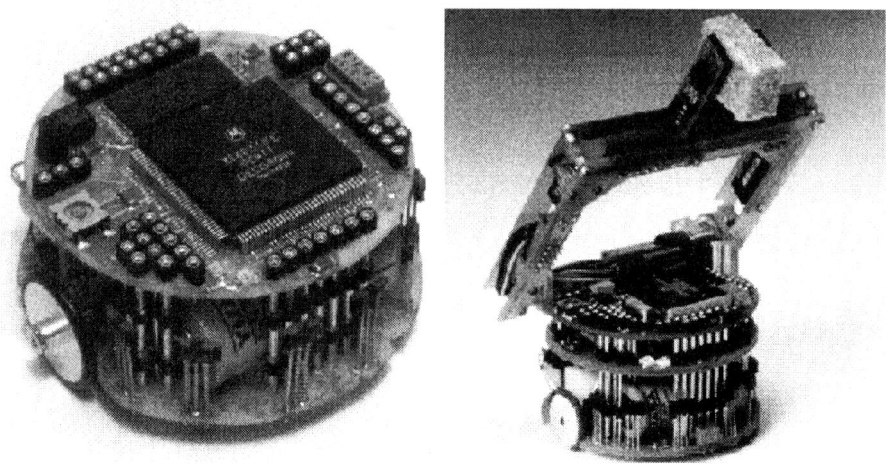

Fig. 1. Left: a basic Khepera mini-robot. Right: a Khepera equipped with a gripper turret.

The Khepera robot is expandable: a number of extension turrets is available and provides the robot with new sensors and actuators. Linear and colour matrix vision turrets allow the robot to perceive better its environment while a gripper turret allows the robot to grasp objects and move them around (see figure 2).

3 Mobile Robot Simulation

3.1 Simulation Software

More and more researchers use mobile robots simulations to save money and development time. Indeed, such simulators can be used to design the mechanical structure of robots as well as to develop intelligent controllers driving the robots. Simulators are especially appreciated when using computer expensive algorithms for learning or evolution of intelligent controllers. They should be considered as prototyping tools. In fact, despite that it has been demonstrated that training or evolving robots in the real environment is possible, the number of trials needed to test the system discourage the use of physical robots during the training period.

3.2 Realism Versus Symbolism

The first robot (or autonomous agent) simulators were designed to observe overall behaviours (learning, evolution, multi-agent dynamics). Hence, they didn't need to model realistic sensors and motors. The environment model was also very simple, often made up of a grid. Objects were lying on this grid and the robots could jump from one grid square to another. These simulators are said to be symbolic because sensors return symbolic values like "I see an apple in the above square". Hence, such simulation could hardly be transferred to real world with robots equipped with real sensors and actuators.

The increase of computer power, especially in 3D capabilities, allows for more and more precise models leading to more and more realistic simulations. Realistic simulators are usually specific to robotics devices. Some mobile robot companies (like Nomadic Inc.) developed realistic mobile robot simulation and monitoring software for their family of mobile robots. However, such simulations do not handle vision sensors.

3.3 Khepera Simulator

Khepera Simulator [5] is a simulation software specific to the Khepera robot. It relies on a 2D environment modelling. The infra-red sensors are modelled so that they can handle both light measurement and obstacle detection. The user can write C programs to control the robot. The simulator is able to drive real robots connected through the serial port of the computer. At any time, it is possible to switch between the simulation and the real robot by clicking on a user interface button. Then, the robot controller gets inputs from and send outputs to the real robot. The robot controller can display any text or graphic information in a specific window area, so that the observer can understand what is going on with the robot. Multi-robot simulations are supported. This simulator was made available for free on the Internet in 1995. Since this date, more than 1200 people downloaded it and many of them are using it for research and education purposes.

4 Webots

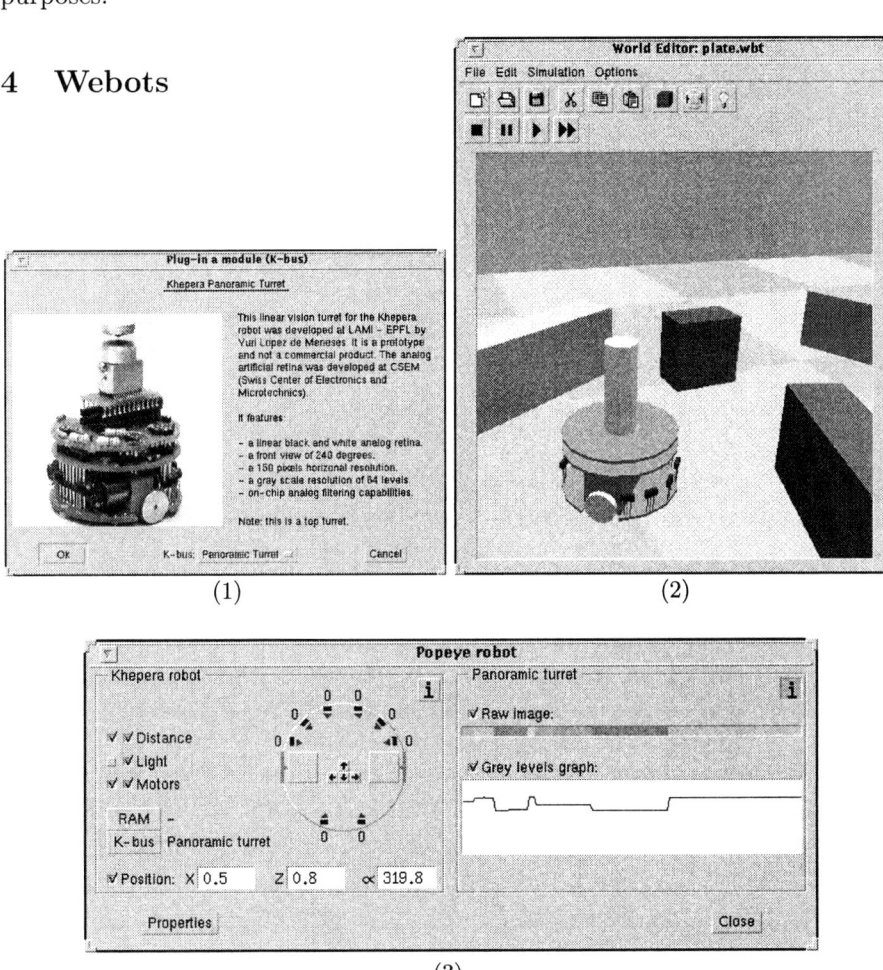

Fig. 2. Panoramic vision module (1), 3D scene editor (2) and robot control (3)

4.1 Virtual Robots in a Network of Virtual Environments

Webots is an ambitious project in autonomous agent simulation. Our preliminary goal was to improve Khepera Simulator by adding vision sensors modelled with a realistic 3D rendering engine (see figure 4) and by opening the simulator to any robotics architecture (wheeled robots, legged robots and robot arms). The capabilities to use compatible source codes between real robots and simulated robots raised new interesting perspectives: since simulated robots are defined by a geometrical structure, a controller and possibly a data memory, such robots are be able to move from one virtual environment to another through the Internet. Hence, we may consider a network of virtual environments populated by virtual robots. All these environments would be connected together by virtual gates that robots could enter to move to distant virtual environments running on remote computers. In order to propose ideas for a standardised protocol allowing virtual robots to move on the Internet, the Webots definition language was designed as an extension of VRML97 (Virtual Reality Modelling Language). The concept of scaling up simulations to the level of the whole Internet is similar to the Tierra project[11].

4.2 Virtual Robots Entering the Real World

A symbiosis between virtual and real robots is made possible with reality gates. In a virtual environment, a reality gate allows the virtual robot to enter the real world: If a virtual robot enters such a gate, its controller and data memory are downloaded onto a real robot so that the "saoul" of the simulated robot can enter the body of a real robot and continue to run. This is made possible with the Khepera API that ensures a source code compatibility between virtual and real robots. However, a cross-compilation stage is mandatory to produce an executable file running on the real robot. Of course a way back to the simulation should be defined in the real world. It can be a sort of garage: when the robot enters, it stops and its controller and data memory are sent back to the host computer running the simulated world. These connections between the real world, simulations and the Internet are close to the concepts developed in telerobotics systems and could become a theoretical basis for new applications in teleoperation and surveillance[7].

4.3 Realistic Sensor Modelling

In order to achieve a fluent transfer to the real world, sensor modelling is an important issue. The problem of the validity of simulation is particularly relevant for methodologies that use machine learning techniques to develop control systems for autonomous robots. Many techniques may be used to achieve realistic sensor modelling: An accurate model of a particular robot-environment dynamics can be built by sampling the real world through the sensors and the actuators of the robot [8,3]. Webots uses this sampling principle to model the response of the infra-red sensors of the Khepera (see figure 3). The performance gap between the obtained behaviours in simulated and real environments may be significantly reduced by introducing a "conservative" form of noise in the simulations. If a decrease in performance is observed when the system is transferred to the real environment, successful and robust results can be obtained by continuing the adaptive process in the real environment for a few more iterations.

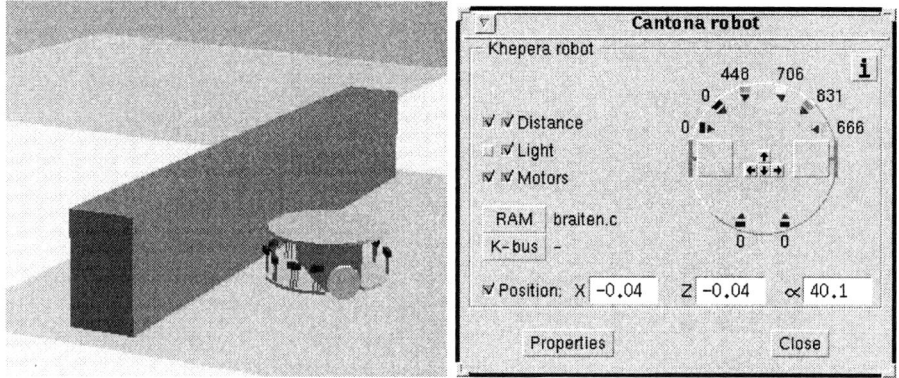

Fig. 3. Infra-red sensors modelling for obstacle detection.

4.4 Robot Metabolism

The concept of robot metabolism[6] is useful to evaluate the behaviour of a situated robot in a straightforward way. It could be considered as a kind of fitness function. The robot is given an initial amount of energy, corresponding to food or electrical power supply. When the robot moves, uses its sensors and actuators making its energy level slowly decrease (normal consumption). Then, if the robot performs a bad action, for example, bumps into a wall, it looses an big amount of energy (punishment). But if it performs good actions, i.e., finding and connecting to a recharge station, it earns a big amount of energy (reward). However, good and bad actions are pre-defined. Hence, the designers of the virtual (and real) environments have to build their scenarios upon this, i.e., make the recharge station up and ready only when the robot has fulfilled an arbitrary task in the environment, or create a device that spanks the robot (bump) when it behaves wrong. When the energy level of a robot reaches zero, the robot dies: its controller program stops and its data memory is erased. Then, it is up to the designer of the environment to remove this "dead body" (or download a new controller and memory inside). This way, it is expected that a selection process will make bad robots automatically disappear while good robots will survive.

5 Current Applications

5.1 Vision

Synthetic Vision[10,12] for camera sensor modelling rely on powerful 3D engines, like OpenGL. In Webots, an image is obtained via OpenGL rendering taking into account the field of view, lighting conditions, materials, etc. Then, this image is processed to add optical distortions and eventually some random noise. A model of a 240 degrees panoramic camera (see figure 4) was developed using two rendered images, each one covering 120 degrees. This is because OpenGL rendering engine doesn't support fields of view greater than 180 degrees. Some mathematical transforms are necessary to paste one image next to the other, in order to map images properly. The camera is linear, that is, the resulting image has one pixel height. Since it is a device providing up to 64 grey levels, a standard PAL colour transform has been applied to get grey levels from a colour image. Robotics experiments using both a real robot and the Webots simulator demonstrate the possible transfer of control algorithms [4]. A standard 2D colour camera model (with 60 degree field of view) is also available in Webots.

5.2 Artificial Life Games and Robot Football

Robot games, and especially football tournaments, turn out to be very stimulating events for the mobile robotics research community. Indeed, the various tasks a mobile robot has to address in order to play football are very interesting from the point of view of the autonomous agents theory: Competitors must take care of design principles of autonomous agents, multi-agent collaboration, strategy acquisition, machine learning, real-time reasoning, robotics, and sensor-fusion. The number of robot football tournaments being held recently is quite impressive:

- Autonomous Robot Football Tournament (Brighton - UK, July 1997, London - UK, July 1998).
  http://www.dcs.qmw.ac.uk/research/ai/robot/football/
  FirstARFT.html and SecondARFT.html
- Coupe E=M6 de robotique (La Ferté-Bernard - France, May 1998).
  http://www.ifitep.cicrp.jussieu.fr/coupe98.html
- Danish Championship in Robot Football (Aarhus - Denmark, December 1997). http://www.daimi.aau.dk/ hhl/robotDME.html
- Festival International des Sciences et Technologies (Paris - France, July 1998)
  http://www.planet.fr/techno/festival/festival98/
  Robot_Footballeur.html
- MiRoSoT (Taejon - Korea, July 1996, Taejon Korea, June 1997, Paris - France, July 1998). http://www.fira.net, http://www.mirosot.org
- Morges Expo (Morges - Switzerland, 1998)
- Munich Technical University Tournament (Munich - Germany, July 1997).
  http://wwwsiegert.informatik.tu-muenchen.de/lehre/prakt/
  khepera/bericht/bericht.html

- RoboCup (Nagoya - Japan, August 1997, Paris - France, July 1998).
  http://www.robocup.org

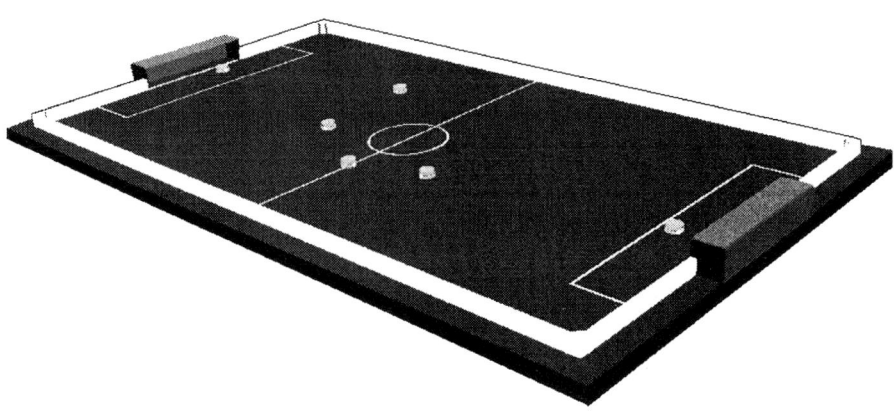

Fig. 4. RoboCup soccer field: 2 x 5 Khepera robots playing soccer (modelled by E. Ornella)

Some of these tournaments include real world leagues as well as simulation leagues with official robotics simulators. But, usually these softwares are not realistic. They often rely on noise-free symbolic data that would be almost impossible to get from real robots with real sensors. Hence the transfer from simulations to real robot is not considered. Moreover, none of these simulators models vision sensors, which appears to be a very strong limitation for football game-playing. Some researchers already started to use Webots to prepare for robot football tournaments and other multi-agent games. E. Ornella from Padova University (Italy) developed a soccer field for the RoboCup tournament (see figure 5.2) and is developing intelligent controllers using 2D colour vision sensors available in Webots.

6 Learning, Evolution, and Multi-Agent

Research in robot learning often makes use of computer expensive algorithms. Evolutionary algorithms, as well as learning systems such as neural networks usually require large amounts of computational power which is not always available on real robots. Moreover, co-evolution of robots has proved to lead to interesting results [1]. Unfortunately, when involving more than two robots, such experiments can hardly be done on real robots. Simulations are very well suited for such research frameworks. The Khepera Simulator software is often used to speed up learning or evolutionary processes. The Webots software offers new sensors (vision) and new supervising capabilities to facilitate complex power-consuming experiments with evolution, learning and multi-agent.

Moreover, with the possibility to create interconnected virtual environment via virtual gates, it becomes feasible to set-up evolutionary experiments with populations of virtual (and real) robots roaming the whole Internet. This is might be a nice way to achieve a very high computational power by distributing experiments on several machines all over the world, and let them run only when the CPU resources are not used, that is during the night. Moreover, if virtual robots are aware of the CPU load on their local host computer and if the fact of being slow is a bad thing (i.e., from the natural selection point of view), they could decide on their own to move to another computer with more CPU resources available[11]. This way, we could imagine that computers on the dark side of the earth would be crawling with virtual robots, moving slowly, from computers to computers, to remain in the dark side and hence benefit of a large computer horsepower.

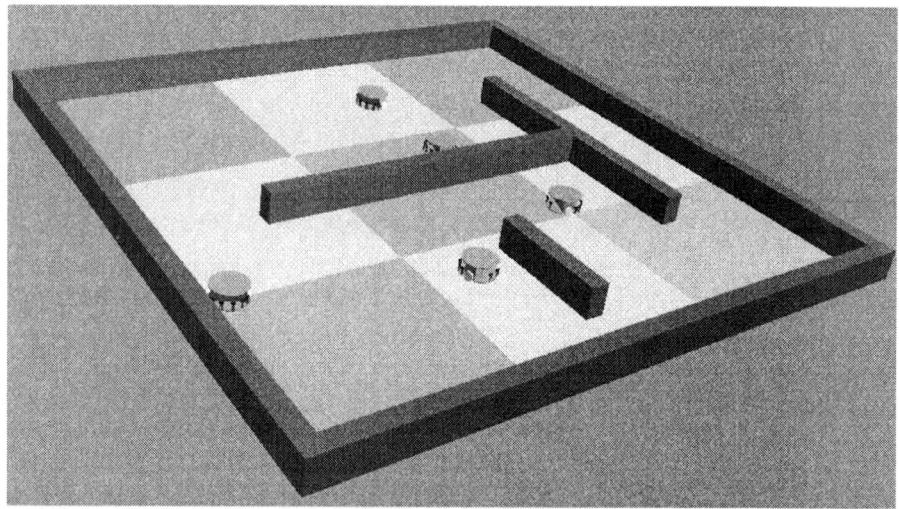

Fig. 5. Multi-robot simulations

7 Conclusion and Perspectives

The Webots simulator has great potentialities of development, especially if an artificial metabolism is considered. It might lead to the emergence of a kind of bio-reserve for virtual robots distributed in sub-networks of interconnected virtual environments. Robots evolving in these virtual spaces could enter the real world, accomplish some missions and go back to the Internet bringing back some information gathered in the real world. Internet users could interact with these "living" robots. They could have their own pet-robots and teach them to do many things (games, surveillance, teleoperation). Actually, the perspectives of development of such a technology are unpredictable, but we believe the Webots will on one hand contribute to the development of artificial life in the sense that it will provide a powerful tool for investigations and confrontations of results, and on the other hand it will add a new dimension to the Internet by connecting real robots to a network of virtual worlds.

References

1. Floreano, D. and Nolfi, S.: Adaptive Behavior in Competitive Co-Evolutionary Robotics. In P. Husbands and I. Harvey, *Proceedings of the 4th European Conference on Artificial Life*, Cambridge, MA: MIT Press, (1997).
2. Fujita, M. and Kageyama, K.: An Open Architecture for Robot Entertainment. In *Proceedings of the First International Conference on Autonomous Agents*, Marina Del Rey, California, USA (1997) 435-442.
3. Jakobi, N.: Half-baked, Ad-hoc and Noisy: Minimal Simulations for Evolutionary Robotics. In *Advances in Artificial Life: Proc. 4th European Conference on Artificial Life*, Phil Husbands and Inman Harvey (eds.) MIT press (1997).
4. Lopez de Meneses Y.: Vision Sensors on the Webots Simulator. Submitted to VW'98.
5. Michel, O.: Khepera Simulator Package version 2.0. Freeware mobile robot simulator dedicated to the Khepera robot. Downloadable from the World Wide Web at http://diwww.epfl.ch/lami/team/michel/khep-sim/ (1996).
6. Michel, O.: An artificial life approach for the synthesis of autonomous agents. In J.-M. Alliot, E. Lutton, E. Ronald, M. Schoenauer, and D. Snyers, editors, *Artificial Evolution*, volume 1063 of LNCS, Springer Verlag, (1996) 220-231.
7. Michel, O., Saucy, P. and Mondada, F.: "KhepOnTheWeb": an Experimental Demonstrator in Telerobotics and Virtual Reality. In *Proceedings of the International onference on Virtual Systems and Multimedia (VSMM'97)*. IEEE Computer Society Press (1997) 90-98.
8. Miglino O., Lund H.H. and Nolfi S.: Evolving Mobile Robots in Simulated and Real Environments, *Artificial Life*, (2), 4, (1995) pp.417-434.
9. Mondada, F., Franzi, E. and Ienne, P.: Mobile robot miniaturisation: A tool for investigation in control algorithms. In: Yoshikawa, T. and Miyazaki, F., eds., *Third International Symposium on Experimental Robotics 1993*, Kyoto, Japan (1994).
10. Noser, H. and Thalmann, D.: Synthetic vision and audition for digital actors. In *Proceedings Eurographics*, Maastricht, The Netherlands (1995) 325-336.
11. Ray, T.S.: An evolutionary approach to synthetic biology: Zen and the art of creating life. In C.G. Langton, editor, *Artificial Life, an overview*, MIT Press (1995) 178-209.
12. Terzopoulos D., Tu, X. and Grzeszczuk, R.: Artificial fisheds: Autonomous locomotion, perception, behavior, and learning in a simulated physical world. In *Artificial Life*, (1), 4, December (1994) 327-351.

apply a lowpass, a bandpass or a highpass filter on the image. An odd-impulse-response filter can also be applied, producing the derivative of the image. The filter output can be accessed by a microprocessor thanks to the internal A/D converter present on the retina. In this way, a 64-gray-level image can be used by the robot for any further processing.

The EDI retina has been mounted on a Khepera turret known as Panoramic turret, together with the necessary ancillary devices and bias circuits. The turret has been included as a plug-in module in the Webots simulator. The following section discusses the simulation of the Panoramic turret and the EDI retina.

Figure1. The Khepera Panoramic turret incorporates an EDI artificial, linear retina.

3 The Panoramic Turret on the Webots Simulator

The simulation of the EDI retina follows its functional blocks, which comprise the optics, the photodetectors, the filters and the digital conversion. Each block will be briefly discussed in the subsections that follow. A final subsection will cover the software interface and its compatibility with the real retina.

3.1 Optics

The first step of the simulation is to calculate the incident light intensity on each photodetector. We will consider the pixel values of the OpenGL rendering engine as the light intensity falling on the pixel surface. The real EDI retina has a spheric mirror and a lens that focus the image on the photosensors, which lie on the chip as seen in figure 2. Ideally, the incident light that reaches the silicon surface should be the same as the incident light that hits a ring on the spheric mirror. Taking this hypothesis, we will try to obtain the incident light on this ring.

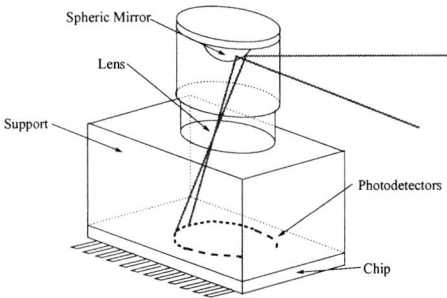

Figure2. The optics of the EDI retina

The OpenGL rendering engine produces the image of the scene as it would be seen by a flat screen camera. However, the EDI retina is spherical, as it sees an image on 240 degrees in azimuth and 11 degrees in elevation. To solve this problem, the 240-degree view is obtained from two 120-degree (azimuth) by 11 degrees (elevation) projections on a flat surface, each one projecting on a 75 x 7 pixel array, as shown in figure 3.

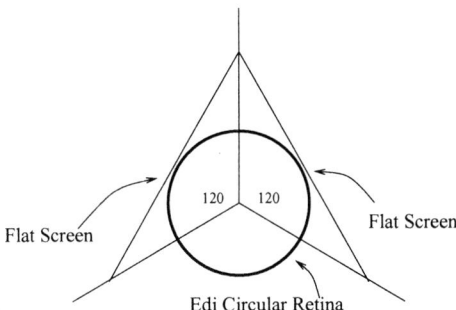

Figure3. Decomposition of a 240-degrees, cylindrical view into 2 flat views.

Next, both arrays are warped by using the transformations as it can be inferred from figure 4. The flat-screen coordinates x,y are transformed into the cylindrical coordinates ϕ and θ as a function of the focal distance f, which is equal to the radius of the cylinder:

$$x = f \cdot \tan(\theta) \implies \theta = \arctan\left(\frac{x}{f}\right)$$

$$y = \sqrt{x^2 + f^2} \cdot \tan(\phi) = f \cdot \tan(\phi) \cdot \sqrt{1 + \tan^2(\theta)} \implies \phi = \arctan\left(\frac{y}{\sqrt{x^2+f^2}}\right)$$

Eventually the vertical pixels are averaged to obtain two 75 x 1 pixel vectors, and the two vectors are concatenated to produce a 150 pixel vector.

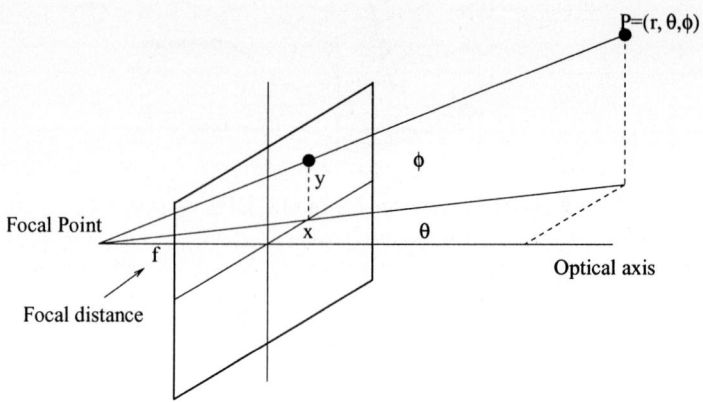

Figure4. Projection of a world in spherical coordinates on to a flat screen

3.2 Photodetectors and Normalization Circuit

The image obtained in the previous subsection is considered as a measure of the incident light intensity on each of the 150 photodetectors. The RGB image is converted to gray scale by using the RGB to Y (luminance) transformation of the PAL TV standard. This transformation gives a certain weight to each color channel. A better modelization could be achieved if the spectral response of the photodetectors were used to generate the luminance. The luminance thus generated is considered as the photocurrent on each photodiode. Next, a normalization circuit divides each pixel's photocurrent by the average current of the whole array. This affords to obtain an illumination-invariant image, that is, an image that will not be perturbed by changes in the global illumination settings of the scene. The normalized current is stored in the model's `analog[ ]` array.

3.3 Filtering Layer

The filtering layer simulates the filtering capabilities of the artificial retina. These are implemented with VLSI resistive diffusion networks [11] that can be combined to enhance the image and to extract some characteristic features from it. A simple resistive diffusion network has a spatial-lowpass characteristic that can be used to reduce noise in the image and detect uniform regions. Other filters are generated by combining such networks. For instance, the highpass or edge-enhancing filter is obtained by subtracting from the original image its lowpass version. The odd impulse-response filter is generated by subtracting the output from two unidirectional diffusion networks. It produces the derivative of the input image, and it can be used to detect sharp edges in the scene.

1-D resistive diffusion networks behave as low-pass filters of exponential impulse response in the spatial and spatial-frequency domains:

$$h(n) = e^{\frac{-|n|}{\lambda}} \overset{\mathcal{F}}{\Longleftrightarrow} H(\omega) = \frac{\lambda}{\pi} \cdot \frac{1}{1+(\lambda \cdot \omega)^2}$$

Resistive diffusion networks are parallel, locally-connected systems, that perform computations on a real-time basis. This makes it difficult to recreate on a single processor. However, since the system is made out of resistors, that is, linear devices, it can be shown that the output is the convolution of the input signal with a kernel or impulse response of the forms that can be seen in figure 5.

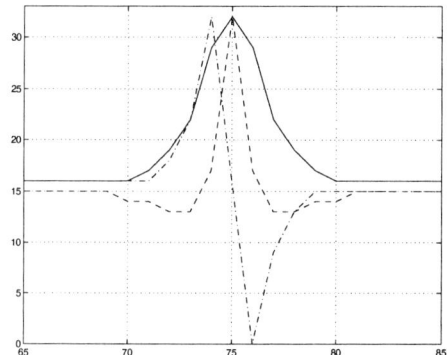

Figure5. Impulse responses of the lowpass (-), highpass (--) and odd (-.) filters.

The result of convolving the `analog[ ]` array with the resistive network impulse response is stored in the `filtered[ ]` array.

3.4 Digital Conversion

The EDI retina has a 6-bit successive-approximation A/D converter, that digitizes the output current from the resistive grid into 64 gray levels. Since the analog filters can produce negative values, the higher bit is used as a sign bit. The conversion, defined by the formula $digital[] = 31.5 \cdot (1 + \frac{filtered[\,]}{I_{bda}})$ depends on the variable I_{bda}, which represents a bias current on the EDI chip. In the simulator this variable has been set to a value that makes the output barely saturate when there is a single maximally iluminated photodetector.

3.5 Software Interface: The Khepera API

The benefits of such a sensor-based simulator would be lost if the algorithms developed on a Webots simulated robot cannot be easily applied on a real robot. To that end, we have developed a common interface for the real and simulated Panoramic turret and Khepera robot, in the form of an Application Program Interface: the Khepera API [5]. Such a common interface allows the user to use the same C source code, without having to change a single comma, on both platforms. Two different libraries, one for the real robot and one for the virtual one are provided with the Webots simulator.

The Khepera API contains several functions to access the Panoramic turret. Some functions allow the user to enable or disable a given filter and other functions are used to read the output of the desired filter. The configuration functions allow the user to set the filter spatial cutoff-frequency, the gray-scale resolution and the region of interest.

4 Experiments: A Robot Regatta

To analyze the validity of the Webots simulator and the Panoramic turret, we have run on simulation a control algorithm that was already tried on the real Khepera. To do so, first we had to rewrite the old code using Khepera API and test it on the real robot. Then we applied the resulting C code to the Webots simulator, and observed whether the same behavior was obtained.

The algorithm combined two different behaviors, obtaining a new, emergent behavior. The first behavior is based on Braitenberg's obstacle avoidance behavior [1], using the 8 IR sensors of the Khepera robot. The IR proximity-sensor values control the motor command through a feed-forward neural network as it can be seen in figure 6. Two bias neurons ensure a forward motion of the robot in the absence of any IR-sensor stimuli. The second behavior is light seeking by using the Panoramic turret. The odd impulse-response filter is used to obtain a derivative of the image, from which the light-intensity local maxima are detected. The robot steers towards the maximum (i.e. light source) that is closer to the center pixel by commanding the motors with a signal proportional to the pixel distance between the light and the center pixel. This motor command is added to the IR network output, producing a smooth transition from obstacle avoidance behavior to light following behavior.

The real and simulated robots are placed on a square arena on which 3 light sources or "buoys" are set forming a triangle (figure 7). The light buoys lie at the height of the retina and are therefore always visible, except if hidden by another buoy. The Khepera will move towards the buoy that lies ahead, and once it reaches it, the IR sensors make it turn away from the light. However, the retina still tries to steer the robot towards the buoy and the combination of

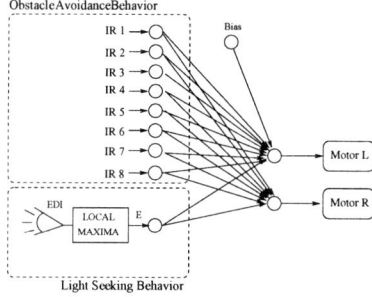

Figure6. The neural network used in the regatta experiment

both commands makes the robot turn around the buoy until it sees a new buoy lying ahead. It will thus move from buoy to buoy as in a regatta. In case there is only one light buoy on the arena, the robot will steer towards it and then turn endlessly around it.

 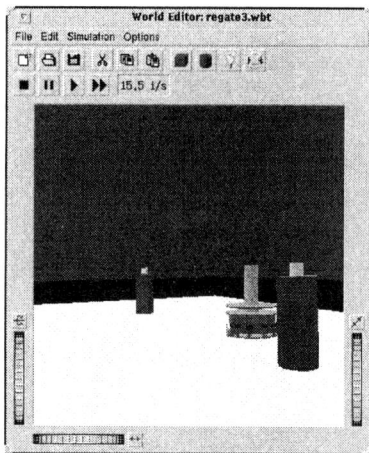

Figure7. The real (a) and simulated (b) Khepera regatta.

The control algorithm does not contain a description of the steps to be taken when a buoy is encountered, nor a definition of what a buoy is. It is a simple combination of two simple behaviors, obstacle avoidance and light-seeking, and yet we can observe the emergence of a new, unforeseen behavior that makes the robot navigate from buoy to buoy. The emergence of this new behavior depends on the balance between the algorithm parameters, i.e. the network weights.

In the simulated part of the experiment, the light buoys are simulated as cylinders with a bright object on top of them (figure 7b). The same C source-code program is downloaded on the simulated Khepera, and the same behavior can be observed: the Khepera moves from buoy to buoy without running into them and turns around the light buoy when there is only one on the arena.

The Panoramic turret simulation is validated by the fact that not a single parameter (i.e. the IR-network weights and the angle-to-speed constant of the light-seeking behavior) of the real controller had to be changed. However, a simulated behavior closer to the real one is obtained if the IR-network gain is doubled. This occurs because the real buoys are covered with IR-reflecting film to allow the robot to sense them form a higher distance, since the cylindric shape and the material from which the buoys are made produce a small IR cross-section. The fact that a realistic behavior is obtained when reflecting against a flat surface seems to support this hypothesis. Since IR-reflecting coatings are not simulated in the Webots simulator, the IR sensor sensitivity or the IR network gain have to be doubled to allow the simulated robot to detect the buoys at the same distance as in the real experiment. This evidence indicates that the Webots simulator models realistically the IR-sensor responses.

5 Conclusion

The paper describes the modelling of a vision sensor within the frame of the Webots mobile-robotics simulator. Great care has been given to model the physical processes underlying the sensor to obtain a realistic sensor reading. The sensor presented in this paper is a very particular one, since the EDI artificial retina is a linear, panoramic (i.e. spheric) sensor with signal processing capabilities. However, the same principles can be applied to simulate other vision sensors and standard cameras. The Khepera's commercially available K213 vision turret is currently being developed in the Webots simulator along the same line.

Our second concern in developing the simulated retina and turret was software compatibility. We see simulators as a tool for the time-consuming development of complex algorithms and for sharing data and results among different research teams. In both cases it is highly desirable to be able to test the algorithm on a real robot, and to easily do so, the code should be compatible. For the Webots simulator, an application program interface (API) has been defined, allowing to interface the real and simulated Khepera robot and its turrets with the same C source code.

A simple experiment has been used to validate the simulated EDI and the Webots simulator. A demonstration program that had previously been run on a real Khepera robot has been tested on the Webots simulator. We were able to reproduce the same behavior without having to change a single parameter of the robot controller. A more thorough validation would require evolving the same behavior on a real and a simulated robot.

The Webots simulator and the Panoramic turret are currently being used in a landmark-navigation experiment. The simulator is used to partially train the robot and eventually the evolved controller will be transferred to the real Khepera for a final, shorter learning stage. The success of such experiment will further prove the adequacy of the simulator.

Acknowledgements

We wish to thank Eric Fragnière and Olivier Landolt for the helpful discussions on analog VLSI circuits.

References

[1] Valentino Braitenberg. *Vehicles: Experiments in Synthetic Psychology*. MIT Press, Cambridge, MA, 1984.//
[2] L.M. Gambardella and C. Versino. Robot Motion Planning Integrating Planning Strategies and Learning Methods. In *Proceedings of 2nd International Conference on AI Planning Systems*, 1994.
[3] M. Mataric. Designing and Understanding Adaptive Group Behavior. *Adaptive Behavior*, 4(1):51–80, 1995.
[4] O. Michel. Webots, an Open Mobile-robots Simulator for Research and Education. http://www.cyberbotics.com/.
[5] Olivier Michel. *Khepera API Reference Manual*. LAMI-EPFL, Lausanne, Switzerland, 1998.
[6] J.R. Millán. Reinforcement Learning of Goal-directed Obstacle-avoiding Reaction Strategies in an Autonomous Mobile Robot. *Robotics and Autonomous Systems*, (15):275–299, 1995.
[7] F. Mondada, E. Franzi, and P. Ienne. Mobile Robot Miniaturization: A Tool for Investigation in Control Algorithms. In T. Yoshikawa and F. Miyazaki, editors, *Proceedings of the Third International Symposium on Experimental Robotics 1993*, pages 501–513. Springer Verlag, 1994.
[8] Nomadic Technologies, Inc. *Nomad User's Manual*, 1996.
[9] P. Toombs. *Reinforcement Learning of Visually Guided Spatial Goal Directed Movement*. PhD thesis, Psychology Department, University of Stirling., 1997.
[10] C. Versino and L.M. Gambardella. Ibots. Learning Real Team Solutions. In *Proceedings of the 1996 Workshop on Learning, Interaction and Organizations in Multiagent Environments*, 1996.
[11] E. Vittoz. Pseudo-resistive Networks and Their Applications to Analog Computation. In *Proceedings of 6th Conference on Microelectronics for Neural Networks and Fuzzy Systems*, Dresden, Germany, September 1997.

Grounding Virtual Worlds in Reality

Guillaume Hutzler, Bernard Gortais, Alexis Drogoul

LIP6 - OASIS/MIRIAD, Case 169, UPMC, 4, Place Jussieu, 75252 Paris Cedex 05 France
{Guillaume, Bernard, Alexis}.{Hutzler, Gortais, Drogoul}@lip6.fr

Abstract

We suggest in this article a new paradigm for the representation of data, which is best suited for the real-time visualization and sonorisation of complex systems, real or simulated. The basic idea lies in the use of the garden metaphor to represent the dynamic evolution of interacting and organizing entities. In this proposal, multiagent systems are used to map between given complex systems and their *garden-like* representation, which we call *Data Gardens (DG)*. Once a satisfying mapping has been chosen, the evolution of these *Data Gardens* is then driven by the real-time arrival of data from the system to represent and by the endogenous reaction of the multiagent system, immersing the user within a visual and sonorous atmosphere from which he can gain an intuitive understanding of the system, without even focusing his attention on it. This can be applied to give life to virtual worlds by grounding them in reality using real world data.

1 Introduction

Let's imagine a virtual garden whose visual and sonorous aspects continuously change to reflect the passing of time and the evolution of weather conditions in a distant place. Looking at it or simply listening to its musical rhythm will make you feel just as if you where there, looking at your garden through the window. *'It's raining cats and dogs. Better stay home!'* Connected to real meteorological data, it really functions as a virtual window, opened on a distant reality. This is what the computer-art project called *The Garden of Chances* (*GoC* to make it short) [11] is all about. Beyond its artistic interest, we believe it to have very important implications for the representation of complex systems by means of visual and sonorous metaphors.

Keeping a close watch on meteorological data in order to secure airplanes landings, monitoring the physical condition of a patient during surgical operations, observing Stock Market fluctuations so as to determine the best options to chose, are three examples of situations where decisions are subjected to the real-time understanding of complex systems, respectively physical, biological, and social or economical. Those representation and interpretation issues are transposable for artificial complex systems such as multiagent systems, for which adequate real-time representation may provide insight into the inner mechanisms of the system at the agent level, or *topsight* [10] over the functioning of the system as a whole. Visualization in Scientific Computing (ViSC) has proven very efficient to represent huge sets of data, by the use of statistical techniques to synthesize and class data in a hierarchical way, and extract relevant attributes from those sets, before presenting them to the user (Fig. 1). But it has not been so successful when dealing with distributed and dynamic systems since it is based, among other things, on a delayed treatment of the data.

The basic proposal is to consider any complex system one wish to represent as a metaphorical garden, the evolution of which reflects in real-time the evolution of the system. In this paradigm, the measures made on the system are not only stored, waiting for a further statistical processing, but they are also immediately transmitted to a *Data Garden*, a virtual ecosystem with the same global dynamics as the system to represent but with a stronger visual and sonorous appeal (Fig. 1). Indeed, the garden metaphor has the interesting property to be both very complex in its functioning, and still completely familiar to anybody, enabling a very fast and intuitive perception. Moreover, it doesn't require a sustained attention, since it relies for the most part on peripheral perception mechanisms, following the same principles as those that make us perceive weather conditions effortlessly. Finally, the *Data Garden* paradigm doesn't reduce the complexity of the system to represent but transform this complexity to integrate it into a meaningful environment, creating a visual and sonorous ambient atmosphere from which to gain a continuous understanding of the studied system.

In section 2, we present the concepts of scientific visualization and we explain why they fail to satisfy the needs of complex systems representation. By contrast, we present in section 3 *The Garden of Chances*, an artistic project which succeeds in mapping numerical meteorological data in an abstract, yet meaningful, representation of the weather. We finally extend the principles developed with this project in section 4, explaining the characteristics that *Data Gardens* should share in order to prove meaningful for complex systems representation, before concluding.

2 Scientific vs. Artistic Visualization and Complex Systems

Scientific visualization on the one hand is based on quantitative information display [22], visually in most cases but also using different modalities [4]. Fig. 1 shows the classical iteration cycle of scientific visualization whereby experiments are undertaken, during which data are collected. Only afterwards are the data analyzed and visualized, which allows to draw conclusions about the experiment and design complementary experiments. The cycle then iterates. This is well fitted for a great number of applications but doesn't qualify for the representation of complex, dynamic and distributed phenomena. Painting on the other hand, considered as a system of colored graphical elements is inherently distributed and based on the organization of those elements. According to Kandinsky, "analysis reveals that there is a construction principle which is used by nature as well as by art: the different parts become alive in the whole. Put differently, the construction is indeed an organization" [15]. Furthermore, painters try, and sometimes succeed, in transmitting complex perceptive and emotional experiences to their spectators. They so establish what J. Wagensberg [23] calls a "communication of unintelligible complexities", complexities that language and numbers cannot express since they cannot be formalized.

We're now going to analyze in further details the reasons why scientific visualization concepts appear inadequate to us for the representation of dynamic and complex data. It appears in the classical taxonomy that a processing of the data is necessary in order to extract from huge sets of data, a restricted number of attributes that best synthesize the nature of the data. To this purpose, a great number of statistical techniques and data analysis are available that we won't detail here [3]. The results are then presented using a number of standard representations such as histograms, pie or time charts and so on. New presentation models [19] are also developed that make the visualization easier by focusing on some specific aspects of the data depending on the context. An alternative to this general scheme is when the phenomenon has physical reality and may be visualized directly or using appropriate color scales. Physical numerical simulations make a large use of this techniques, and medical visualization is a rapidly expanding domain that also exploits the same principles.

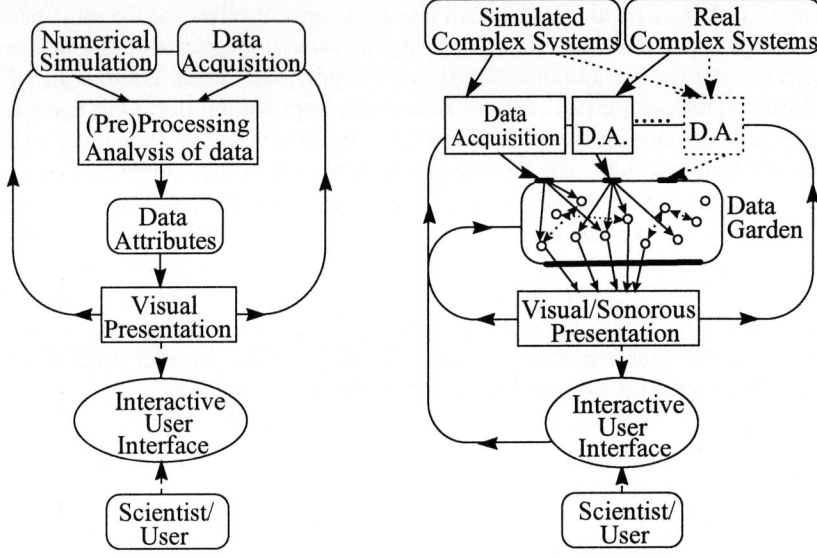

Fig. 1. Classical (partial view from [6]) vs. Data Gardens' visualization taxonomy

We propose to handle, with artistic visualization, phenomena which are both distributed and with spatial and temporal dynamicity. Our hypothesis, based on the analysis of scientific visualization techniques, is that such complex systems cannot be well represented using purely quantitative and objective means. This may be explained by the fact that we have an almost qualitative and subjective experience of such complex phenomena as meteorology, biological ecosystems, social groups, etc. Most of the knowledge that we have about those systems is derived from our everyday-life perceptions, which give us an intuitive grasp about such systems but which we don't know how to transcribe into numbers.

3 The Garden of Chances

We have explored with the computer-art *The Garden of Chances* an artistic alternative that is useful in making qualitative aspects visually or sonorously sensible in the representation of complex systems. Furthermore, the distributed aspect of complex systems is integrated as the basis of the functioning of the project and we think it qualifies as the first step in the representation of complex systems by means of colored and sonorous metaphors.

3.1 The Artistic Paradigm

The philosophy underlying this artistic work is to let the automatic generation of images be directed by a real time incoming of real world data. This has led to the development of a first computer artwork called *Quel temps fait-il au Caplan? (What's the weather like in Caplan?)*. In this project, weather data coming in hourly from *MétéoFrance* stations were used to suggest the climatic atmosphere of a given spot (actually a small place in Britain) by means of color variations inside an almost fixed abstract image. To put it naively, rather warm tints were used when the temperature was high, dark tints when clouds appeared to be numerous, etc. In addition to meteorological parameters, the system also took astronomical ones (season and time of the day) into account, which eventually allowed very subtle variations. When functioning continuously all year long, the animation makes the computer screen become a kind of virtual window, giving access to a very strange world, both real and poetic.

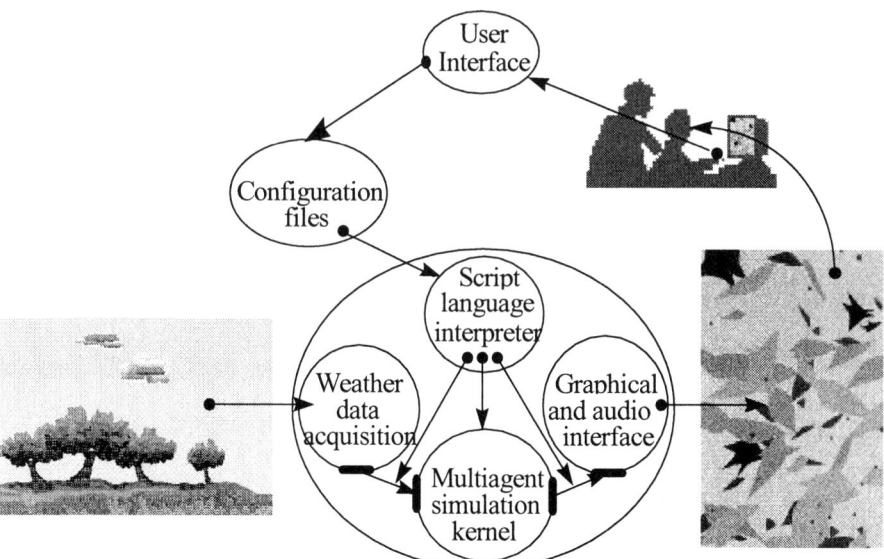

Fig. 2. The *Garden of Chances*

The *GoC* (Fig. 2) is basically designed with the same principles, namely using real data for the creation of mixed worlds, imaginary landscapes anchored in real world. In addition to colors modulations, the weather data are used to give life to a set of two-dimensional shapes, so as to create a metaphorical representation of a real garden. Thus, each graphical creature is able to grow up like a plant, benefiting from the presence of light and rain, competing against similar or other hostile shapes, reproducing and dying like any living creature. By so doing, the goal is definitely not to produce accurate simulations of natural ecosystems nor realistic pictures of vegetation. The focus is rather put on enabling the artist to experiment with lots of different abstract worlds until he obtains some imaginary ecosystem fitting his aesthetic sensitivity. The graphical space doesn't have the passiveness of coordinate systems anymore; we rather consider it as an active principle giving birth to worlds, as the raw material from which everything is created.

3.2 The Multiagent System

In agreement with artistic requirements, the system has been implemented as a programmable platform, allowing the artist to undertake a true artistic research. Capitalizing on our experience with biological simulation systems [7], we designed it as a genuine vegetal simulation platform, supplying growth, reproduction, and interaction mechanisms similar to those observed in plants. Indeed, we believe the difference between metaphorical and simulated ecosystems only resides in the perspective adopted during the experimentation process.

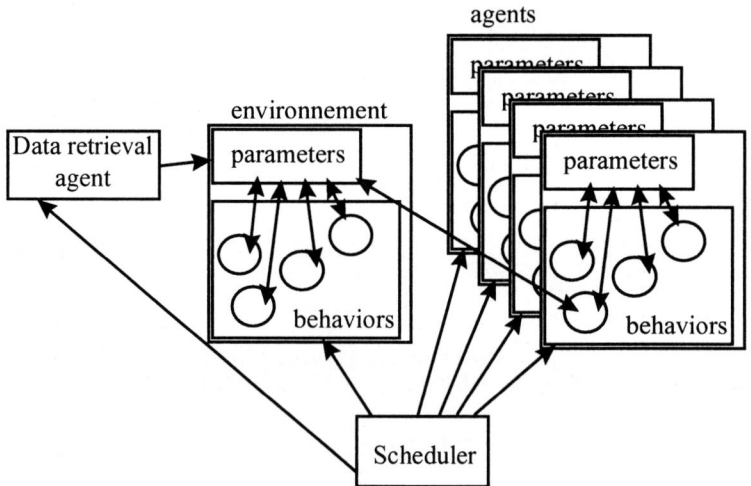

Fig. 3. The multi-agent simulation system

The core of the platform is a multiagent simulation system (see Fig. 3), representing plants as very simple *reactive agents* evolving in a simulated *environment*. Both the agents and the environment are characterized by sets of *parameters* that define their characteristics at any given time. The activity of the agents is defined as a number of *behaviors* which are programmable using a little scripting language. Those behaviors are handled by a *scheduler* which activates them whenever needed, either periodically (each n simulation cycles) or upon reception of some particular *events* (those are related most of the time to changes in one or several parameters). Finally, agents will be represented on the screen by colored shapes, which won't have necessarily something to do with plants but may be freely designed by the artist. A given still image will thus be close to his painting work, while the dynamics of the whole system will more closely rely on the artificial side of the project, i.e. the simulation of natural processes of vegetal growth.

3.3 Agents and Environment

Parameters constitute the basis for the representation of both agents and the environment. Actually, six types of parameters have been defined in order to describe the simulated world and the incoming data flow.

Agents are characterized by reserved, internal and external parameters as shown in Fig. 4. Reserved parameters are common for all agents whereas internal and external parameters may be defined specifically for each agent. Reserved parameters include information about age, speed, color, size, etc. Internal parameters describe the resources of the agent (water, glucose, etc. with the vegetal metaphor, or any other quantifiable resource). By contrast, external parameters represent any substance or information that the agent may propagate around him (chemical substances that plants release in the soil or the atmosphere, signals, etc.).

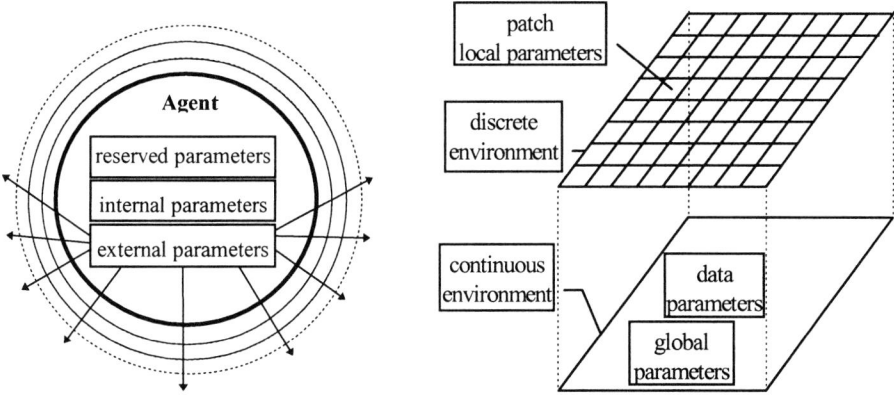

Fig. 4. Agent's parameters   **Fig. 5.** Environment's parameters

The environment is characterized by local and global parameters as shown in Fig. 5. Local parameters correspond to variables whose value and evolution can be defined in a local way, i.e. for each square of the grid covering the environment (substances present in the soil, water or mineral materials for example). On the contrary, global parameters represent variables which have a nearly uniform action on the whole and we presented with *The Garden of Chances* the outline of a possible alternative. So what are the basic features that *Data Gardens* should integrate in order to fulfill the requirement of adequately representing complex systems, that is providing the user with a global understanding of the functioning of the system. And how could this be achieved ?

- As a first thing, *DG* should rely on a *dynamic* representation, necessary get a perceptive sensation of a system's dynamics and to easily detect discontinuities. This representation should be both *visual* and *sonorous*, vision being best fitted to the perception of spatial dynamics through a parallel treatment of information while audition is more adapted to the perception of temporal dynamics through sequential treatment of information. The aim is to limit the use of high-level cognitive processes, trying to take advantage of the "peripheral", rather than active, perception capabilities of the user (many experiments in augmented reality, like in the MIT MediaLab's Ambient Room [12], rely on this approach).

The graphical and sonorous aspects of *The Garden of Chances* have been designed so that the user can interpret the painting in the same way he could interpret his daily environment for extracting critical information. Animation on the other hand is an essential part of the *GoC*, and it carries out two different kinds of information via two different dynamics: a slow, homogeneous dynamics, intended to reorganize the whole environment during a long period of time, is used to represent the seasons. Within this dynamics, a few punctual and rapid animation of some agents or sets of agents are used to represent important short-term fluctuations of the data values.

- When representing complex systems, complexity shouldn't be reduced a priori with synthetic indices and means, but should be directly integrated in the representation system. Therefore, *Data Gardens* should be based on a *multiagent modeling* (accurate or metaphoric) of the system to represent. But because complex data are generally just too complex to represent directly, distributed principles for *organizing* and *synthesizing* the represented data must be integrated, that decrease the perceptual load of the user without significantly altering the meaning of the data.

In *Data Gardens*, incoming data influence both the activity and the evolution of the agents. The synthesis is then realized at two levels : in the individual evolution of each agent, and in the mutual interactions they engage in. The development of an agent, which is graphically translated by a modification of its shape or color, can be the consequence of the variations of different data, like the evolution of a plant within an ecosystem.

- The representation must be *metaphorical*, that is, use cognitive categories aimed at being easily interpreted and managed by the user. This is a way of decreasing the complexity, mapping abstract data into a meaningful representation from which one can get instantaneous understanding.

In that respect, one of the most interesting aspects of *Data Gardens* is the "garden" or "ecosystem" metaphor, already developed in the *GoC*. Analyzed at the light of the first two points we developed, the garden metaphor has the interesting property to have natural significance to anybody, while being very complex in its functioning. This functioning relies on the interactions of three types of complex systems: physical (the weather), biological (vegetal and animal) and social (social animals such as ants). This results in various audio-visual dynamics which look very familiar, from the slow evolution of vegetal landscapes to the fast interactions of animal life, and continuously changing meteorological ambiances.

- The representation should be *programmable*, at a user's level. The user must be able to express subjective choices about the representation, either to make it more significant with regards to data visualization, or to make it more aesthetically pleasing. Perception is a mostly individual and subjective feature of human cognitive functioning. The representation should therefore fit the user's own subjective conceptions of how the data are best visualized. Moreover, different types of representation of the same data may reveal different aspects of this data.

In the *GoC*, the whole simulation system is programmable allowing the user to filter the input data, define the behaviors of the agents to make them react to the data, and choose their graphical representation. In the process, the user will need to be guided by the system, which should propose sets of dynamics and graphical vocabularies. Our collaboration with a painter in the *GoC* project has proven very useful for that particular matter, and we intend to cooperate more closely with various artists in order to define basic instances of *Data Gardens*.

- The representation should be *interactive* to allow dynamic exploration and perturbation of the multiagent system. Once a general framework has been found efficient, it must be made possible for the user to refine the representation acting as a kind of gardener by adding, removing, moving, changing agents on the fly. The user should also be able to visualize the system from different points of view. If the default functioning of *Data Gardens* exploits peripheral perception, the user may also choose to focus his attention on a specific part of the representation, getting then more detailed information about this part. Finally, the user should be integrated as a particular agent of the system, with extended capabilities, that would enable him to experiment the reactions of the system when perturbed.

In the *GoC*, the basis for these interactions is set. The user can make agents reproduce, die or move, and one can view or change the parameters of agents or of the environment. When associating specific behaviors to a "perturbing agent" and when moving it around with the mouse, one can also visualize how the system may spontaneously reorganize.

- The system should finally be *evolutive*, taking into account the interactions of the user in order to learn something of his tastes and evolve accordingly. The reason is that a given user will most of the time be unable to express how he would like the data to be represented in the formalism of the system. But if he can't formalize it, he can point out aspects of the representation that he finds pleasing or some others that he dislikes, just as in the gardener metaphor. This last point is mostly prospective for now, since nothing like it exists in the *GoC* yet.

As a result, *Data Gardens* should be designed as "meaning operators" between the flow of data and the user, who is supposed to identify and follow, in the evolution of the system, that of the outside world. However, it must be clear that they are not intended to replace the existing environments used to track and trace data (histograms, textual presentation, curves, etc.), which are still the only way to know the precise value of a variable. They are to be viewed as complementary tools that allow an instantaneous and natural perception of complex situations and propose a global perspective on them. *The Garden of Chances* is the first of such systems we built and it should now be studied in a systematic way, and with an experimental perspective, in order to develop operational design and evaluation methodologies.

5 Conclusion

We propose with *Data Gardens* hybrid environments that graphically represent information gathered in the real world for users likely to take decisions in this real world. The goal is to let a complex and dynamic system of numeric data become visually intelligible without catching the whole attention of the user. We explained how the application of DAI concepts, along with real-time visualization, allows to compensate for some of the deficiencies of more classical approaches. In particular, it enables to handle dependent data without a priori reducing the complexity of the data but only as the result of a dynamic hierarchisation and synthesis of the different pieces of the data through the organization of a multiagent system. Furthermore, the representation is evolutive and adaptive, because of its dedicated endogenous evolutionary mechanisms, and also because of the user's actions. We presented with *The Garden of Chances*, both the artistic work that initiated the reflection on *Data Gardens*, and the first concrete application of this paradigm. But it is obvious that *Data Gardens* are not limited to given data nor graphical representation types, each application domain requiring however that the representation be adapted to specific cultures and representation habits. Further work will put the focus on systematizing this adaptation process, through the constitution of libraries proposing various dynamics, based on previous works in DAI, and various graphical and sonorous schemes, based on a collaboration with artists. The aim is ultimately to be able to interpret complex and interacting systems of data, almost as naturally as one can perceive meteorological subtle variations, which could be of fundamental importance for the interpretation of multiagent systems themselves.

'Mmm. Looks like rain has stopped. Would be perfect for a walk but it's getting cold outside and the wind has turned east. Better stay home!'

References

1. Boden M. A., "Agents and Creativity", in Communications of the ACM, Vol. 37, No. 7, pp. 117-121, July 1994,
2. Bruning J. L. and Kintz B. L., *Computational handbook of statistics*, Glenview, IL: Scott, Foresman and Company, 1968.
3. Bonabeau G. and Theraulaz E. eds., *L'intelligence Collective*, Hermès, Paris, 1996.
4. Coutaz J., "L'art de communiquer à plusieurs voies", Spécial La Recherche "L'ordinateur au doigt et à l'oeil", n°285, mars 1996, pp. 66-73.
5. Deneubourg J.-L. and Theraulaz G., Beckers R., "Swarm-Made Architectures", in Towards a Practice of Autonomous Systems, MIT Press, Cambridge, pp. 123-133, 1992.
6. Domik G., "The Role of Visualization in Understanding Data", Lecture Notes on Computer Science 555, "New Trends and Results in Computer Science", pp. 91-107, Springer Verlag, 1991.
7. Drogoul A., "De la simulation multi-agents à la résolution collective de problèmes", Thèse de l'Université Paris VI, Novembre 1993.
8. Ferber J., *Les systèmes Multi-agents*, Interéditions, Paris, 1995.
9. Gebhardt N., "The Alchemy of Ambience", Proceedings of the 5th International Symposium on Electronic Art, Helsinki, 1994.
10. Gelernter D., *Mirror Worlds*, Oxford University Press, Oxford, 1992.
11. Hutzler G., Gortais B., Drogoul A., "The Garden of Chances : an Integrated Approach to Abstract Art and Reactive DAI", 4th European Conference en Artificial Life, Husbands P. and Harvey I. eds., pp. 566-573, MIT Press, 1997.
12. Ishii H. and Ullmer B., "Tangible Bits: Towards Seamless Interfaces between People, Bits and Atoms", Proceedings of CHI '97, ACM, Atlanta, 1997.
13. Ishizaki S., "Multiagent Model of Dynamic Design - Visualization as an Emergent Behavior of Active Design Agents", Proceedings of Conference on Human Factors in Computing Systems (CHI '96), ACM, Vancouver, 1997.
14. Kandinsky W., Du spirituel dans l'art et dans la peinture en particulier, Gallimard, Paris, 1989.
15. Kandinsky W., *Point et ligne sur plan - Contribution à l'analyse des éléments de la peinture*, Gallimard, Paris, 1991.
16. Klee P., *Théorie de l'art moderne*, Denoël, Paris, 1985.
17. Larkin J. H. et Simon H. A., "Why a Diagram is (Sometimes) Worth Ten Thousands Words", Cognitive Science, 11, pp. 65-69, 1987.
18. Penny S., "The Darwin Machine: Artificial Life and Art", Proceedings of the 5th International Symposium on Electronic Art, Helsinki, 1994.
19. Rao R., "Quand l'information parle à nos yeux", Spécial La Recherche "L'ordinateur au doigt et à l'oeil", n°285, mars 1996, pp. 66-73.
20. Resnick M., "Overcoming the Centralized Mindset: Towards an Understanding of Emergent Phenomena", in Constructionism, Harel I. and Papert S. eds., pp. 205-214, Ablex, Norwood, 1991.
21. Risan L. ""Why are there so few biologists here?" - Artificial Life as a theoretical biology of artistry", Proceedings of the Fourth European Conference on Artificial Life, Husbands P. and Harvey I. eds., pp. 28-35, MIT Press, 1997.
22. Tufte E. R., *The Visual Display of Quantitative Information*, Graphics Press, Cheshire CN, 1983.
23. Wagensberg J., *L'âme de la méduse*, Seuil, Paris, 1985.
24. Wright R., "Art and Science in Chaos: Contesting Readings of Scientific Visualization", Proceedings of the 5th International Symposium on Electronic Art, Helsinki, 1994.

Growing Virtual Communities in 3D Meeting Spaces

Frédéric Kaplan[1,2], Angus McIntyre[1], Chisato Numaoka[1], and Silvère Tajan[3]

[1] Sony CSL Paris, 6 rue Amyot, 75005 Paris, France
[2] LIP6 - OASIS - UPMC - 4, place Jussieu F-75252 Paris
[3] Consultant - 100bis rue Bobillot, 75013 Paris, France
{kaplan,angus,chisato}@csl.sony.fr, tajan@captage.com

Abstract. Most existing 3D virtual worlds are based on a "meeting-space" model, conceived as an extension of textual chat systems. An attractive 3D interface is assumed to be sufficient to encourage the emergence of a community. We look at some alternative models of virtual communities, and explore the issue of promoting community formation in a 3D meeting space. We identify some essential or desirable features needed for community formation – Identity, Expression, Building, Persistence and Focus of Interest. For each, we discuss how the requirements are met in existing text-based and 3D environments, and then show how they might be met in future 3D virtual world systems.

1 Introduction

The history of the Internet is one of adaptation. Tools and technologies conceived for serious purposes - electronic mail, Usenet, the World Wide Web - have been swiftly seized upon by ordinary users and used to exchange personal information or information related to personal interests. As much as a carrier of scientific information, the Internet is a channel for social interactions.

This new understanding of the Internet as a social medium constitutes a basic assumption for many developers of browsers for 3D virtual worlds. Environments such as Blaxxun Interactive's Community, Cryo's Deuxième Monde, OnLive! Technologies' Traveller, and Sony's Community Place are all based on a similar model – a more or less realistic visual world in which people meet to socialise. While the browsers also lend themselves to other uses, the showcase applications are typically based on this idea of virtual worlds as social spaces; homes for virtual communities that will emerge and exist in the context of the virtual world.

We intend to explore two main issues. First, we propose a basic classification of some different types of Internet-based communities. This will lead us to ask some basic questions about the ways that 3D virtual world systems are used and whether those uses really represent the most appropriate ones for such systems.

The second section of the paper will suggest some requirements for systems designed to support virtual communities. We will look at the way these requirements are met in existing 3D virtual world systems, at features of earlier systems that might be adapted for use in 3D virtual worlds, and at unique features of 3D virtual worlds that could be exploited to capitalise on the strengths of the medium.

2 Communities on the Internet

The success of the Internet in fostering virtual communities in a world in which real communities are becoming increasingly fragmented and unstable has not gone unnoticed. As Bob Rockwell of Blaxxun puts it:

> "... community is ... being seen as the long-sought 'killer app' that will turn the Internet ... into a profitable resource." [11]

The desire to create (and exploit) 'community' appears to underlie many of today's 3D virtual world systems. The common characteristics of such systems can be briefly stated as follows: the 3D world is designed as a virtual meeting place, reminiscent in some important ways of our own world. Users connect, interact, and a community emerges. The promotion of 3D virtual world systems for this use appears to be motivated by the assumption that the 'familiarity' of the world – with its physical spaces and embodied avatars – will make it more accessible and intimate than more abstract environments.

There are a number of assumptions here that seem to require further examination; one important one is that we can hope to make the virtual world enough like the real world that familiarity factors will work in our favour (and that the overhead of the simulation won't work against us by making the tool too slow or awkward to use). Another is that interaction in an arbitrary context is, by itself, sufficient to create community, something which is not necessarily the case.

More subtle is the assumption that this is the only or the most appropriate model for community formation, and the best model for the application of 3D virtual world technologies. In the remainder of this section we will examine some alternative models (shown schematically in Figure 1) and discuss their implications for 3D virtual worlds.

2.1 Shared Interest Communities

A common type of Internet community is based on the exchange of information about a shared topic of common interest. Such a community often already exists in a potential form. The worldwide population of Jimi Hendrix fans, for instance, is a potential net community. The Internet provides a way for the members to communicate and for the community itself - with its roles, conventions and communication patterns - to come into being.

Communities of this kind are likely to be multi-modal, by which we mean that they employ a variety of different communication channels. Favoured 'core modes' include mailing lists, Usenet newsgroups and topic-specific Internet Relay Chat (IRC) channels. As the community becomes established, members exploit other channels to extend the activity of the community. The community

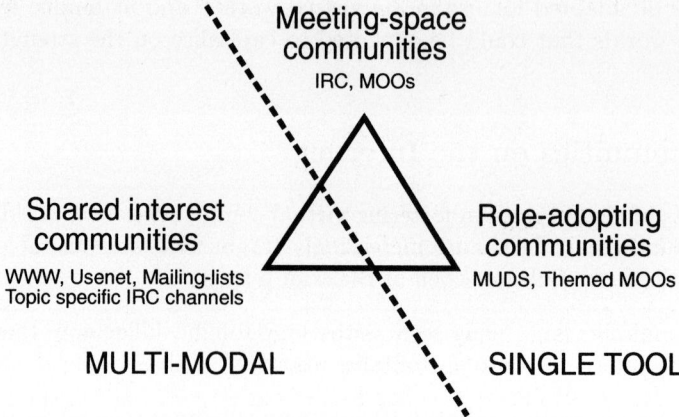

Fig. 1. Community types

based around the network game Quake, for example, has its own Websites, IRC channels, and Usenet newsgroups. Members of a graphics software mailing list, KPTList, show off their work on their Websites and exchange techniques using ICQ (an IRC equivalent). Even users of community-focused chat systems may use alternative channels; MOO (Multi-User Dimension, Object-Oriented) users exchange private email and users of several virtual world systems use Web rings to provide access to their worlds and related materials. In a sense, multi-modal shared interest communities are perhaps the final state of any Internet community; any successful community will, ultimately, tend towards this type.

In passing, it is worth asking whether 3D virtual worlds might not have a role to play as an 'extra mode' in multi-modal communities. 3D worlds are typically presented as a main channel for interaction in a community. They might equally well act as a supplementary channel much as Web sites are today. This possibility is, at present, relatively little explored or supported.

2.2 Role-Adopting Communities

A second kind of community might be termed a 'role-adopting' community. Such communities are typically based (at least initially) around a single mode of interaction and a strong 'theme' which typically takes the form of a story or imaginary context. Participants assume roles appropriate to the context and take care to 'act in character'. This is a kind of 'shared activity' community but with the difference that the shared activity is embedded in the medium of interaction. Users are not using a channel (email) to talk about a common interest (Jimi Hendrix) which exists independently of that channel; they are engaging in an interaction whose form is determined by the channel. In this category we include both online adventure games (i.e. MUDs) and non-gaming environments (i.e. themed social worlds); the characteristic features are the importance of a strongly-defined context and of adopting and maintaining a distinctive role or character.

2.3 Meeting-Space Communities

Historically, role-adopting communities have often evolved towards a third kind of environment in which the context or theme is largely stripped away. In such 'meeting space' communities there are no defined topics of conversation, and the environment (if any) serves a primarily decorative purpose (although the conventions of the community may make it impolite to ignore the context too blatantly: see [4]). For such a community to emerge and flourish, there must be a large number of regular repeat visitors, who engage in extended interactions. With no specific shared interest to draw in and retain participants, the social interactions themselves need to act as the 'glue' that binds the community together. Communities of this kind are commonly seen in MOOs, IRC and similar chat systems. They are also the primary model for 3D virtual world systems.

The fact that so many 3D virtual world systems appear to be aiming to support this kind of community is interesting. On the face of it, one of the greatest strengths of a 3D virtual world system is its ability to create a rich environment, yet the 'meeting space' model largely ignores the environment. Building a community 'in vacuo' is a much more challenging task than creating one in the context of a shared activity or interest. Moreover, because social interactions are fundamental to community formation, tools used must make interactions as fluid and expressive as possible. The machinery needed to render a 3D world is computationally expensive, resulting in sluggish performance on all but the most powerful hardware while the chat window in which the interaction takes place is typically shrunk to a minimum. By contrast, an IRC or MUD client can run on almost any machine and there is nothing to take away screen space from the text window in which the interaction occurs.

These observations raise the following questions: is the 'meeting place' model of community necessarily the most appropriate one for exploiting the potential of 3D virtual worlds? If we adopt this model, what can the 3D world contribute in terms of improved interaction quality which can justify the extra cost of the client? Are there other techniques we could also use to promote community-building in our virtual worlds?

In the next section, we will try to look at ways in which we might make 3D virtual world environments more effective in promoting community. We propose five requirements that we see as essential or desirable for community formation. For each of these, we offer a justification and then examine how the requirement is met in existing systems, both 3D and 'traditional'. We then suggest how future 3D systems might meet the requirement, drawing on both 3D-specific and more general techniques.

3 Promoting Community in 'Meeting Spaces'

Community formation is a complex business. Many of the factors that lead to the formation of a successful community are intangible and cannot easily be engineered. Such factors include the occurrence of formative events (see [7]) and the commitment or dynamism of individual members ([9] speaks of 'keystone players'). Whether a community flourishes or stagnates will depend on the type of interactions that take place within it.

There are, however, some factors that may be amenable to control. [12] presents a useful list of requirements, focusing chiefly on the computational features of the supporting environment. Here we present our own list of rather more abstract requirements, although there will often be a degree of overlap.

Briefly, we believe that community formation requires that the environment has some, if not all, of the following properties: users must have the means to create a distinctive identity, the means to use non-verbal forms of expression, and the means to build spaces and objects. The world itself should be evolving and persistent, and ideally there should also be a common activity or focus of interest. These requirements are summarized schematically in Figure 2.

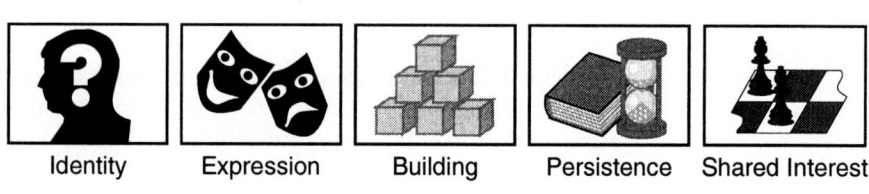

Identity Expression Building Persistence Shared Interest

Fig. 2. Five requirements for community formation

3.1 Identity

One of the first features that we see as necessary for the formation of community is a mechanism for members to create and maintain an identity (not necessarily the same as their real-world identity, but nonetheless distinctive and recognisable). [11] argues that identity is fundamental to establishing the relationships necessary to conducting business and regulating group behaviour. An inability to present ourselves as individuals will directly impact our ability to form social relations.

Identity is multi-faceted. Who we are is defined by our relations with others, by what we say and do and by the way we present ourselves, and by the things that we own and control. Our relations with others are typically defined in ways that are independent of the environment. The environment may contribute critically, however, in the facilities it provides for users to present themselves. It is this issue we will consider here.

Identity in Other Channels A striking feature of many environments supporting virtual communities are the limited means they offer for conveying identity. In electronic mail, Usenet or Internet Relay Chat (IRC), participants are judged almost exclusively on what they write. A premium is placed on qualities such as wit, articulacy, originality, and familiarity with shared conventions. Beyond their writing, users can convey identity only through their 'handle' (IRC) or mail address (mail or news, not always under the user's control) and use of signatures (mail or news). Surprisingly, some of the most coherent and colourful communities seem to emerge in precisely such limited environments. Restrictions may even encourage creativity and assertion of identity.

Richer facilities are offered by augmented text-based environments such as MUDs, where users may provide descriptions of themselves, ostensibly physical but often used to convey something about the owner's actual or desired personality (see [6]). Someone who describes themselves as *"Short, fair-haired, slightly chubby, wearing jeans and a denim jacket."* is communicating something rather different from someone who describes themselves as *"A nervous-looking three-legged centaur wearing two Cecil the Seasick Sea-Serpent puppets on its hands."*

Graphical environments offer different possibilities. In 2D visual environments such as Palace, users can select graphics to represent themselves much as MUD users select textual descriptions. While a picture is not necessarily worth a thousand words, the use of graphics to convey character (and, as we shall see later, mood) can be quite subtle and expressive.

Identity in 3D Virtual Worlds Users in 3D virtual worlds are represented by avatars, graphical representations of their virtual persona. These avatars are typically picked from a set of customisable stock types. Unfortunately, the range of avatars available is often very limited and the customisation possibilities may be too restricted to communicate anything meaningful about the owner. In many existing 3D environments the limitations of the available avatars hinder the establishment of any real identity.

Improving Identity in 3D Virtual Worlds To try to make avatars more 'identifiable', there are two possible approaches. One is to borrow from text-based virtual worlds by attaching inspectable textual descriptions to avatars. Attached descriptions can include additional meta-information; several 3D systems support 'hypercards', virtual business cards which can carry names (real or imaginary), mail addresses and Website URLs.

At the other end of the scale are techniques which make use of the unique properties of visual 3D worlds. One possibility is to map the user's real-world likeness to their avatar, as either a still or a moving image (e.g. [3]). While this might appear to resolve the issue of identity in the most direct way possible, it is unclear how popular it is likely to be in practice; the blending of the real and the virtual can sometimes damage the illusion and many users may prefer to present an abstract imagined identity rather than their real-life appearance.

An alternative might be to use avatar body language which is under indirect rather than direct control of the user. Use of a smiley in text could prompt the avatar to grin momentarily. Users could set parameters to indicate their general state of mind, and the world would respond by animating the avatar continously in such a way as to suggest the appropriate mood – boredom, apprehension, anxiety, etc. (see [10]). It remains to be seen how effective such systems will be in conveying mood in real interactions, but if we intend to exploit the features of the 3D world to the maximum this looks like a useful direction to explore.

3.3 Building

For a community to form, users should have some kind of involvement in the world that they occupy. In channels that support an explicit 'world' (3D virtual worlds, MUDS and MOOs, rather than IRC or email), there seems to be an instinctive desire for users to contribute to the world in some way. Building not only gives the user a personal stake in the world, but it can also enrich the world for other users (consider the case mentioned in [9] of a user who introduced fish and fishing poles to the Pueblo educational MOO).

Building is also an activity that helps to form identity and encourage interactions. A 'virtual home' can reveal as much about us as an avatar description (see the description of Dr Jest's room in [7]). Creation of a useful or interesting object gives the creator status ([2]), while exchange of desirable objects or technical information may form the basis of interactions with other users.

Building has other roles. Objects that are built serve as a tangible reminder of the history or the conventions of the community. The creation of verbs to encapsulate running jokes in MOOs is a good example of this. Built objects may also serve as the focus for interactions and in particular for the kind of ritualised verbal slapstick characteristic of MOOs.

Building in Other Channels Building is not a feature of email, news or IRC. Some MUDs and MOOs, however, permit users to add new objects to the world, ranging from furniture to simple automata to spaces which other users can enter and explore. Objects are typically part of a full object-oriented system which allows new objects to inherit (or override) behaviours from their parent objects. Some programming skill is required to define interesting behaviours, but the implementation languages are generally simple enough that new objects can be added to the world without too much difficulty.

Building in 3D Virtual Worlds The nature of 3D virtual worlds means that building is likely to be more complex than in textual worlds. Among the 3D virtual world systems that do allow some kind of building are Cryo's Deuxième Monde and Circle of Fire's AlphaWorld. Deuxi'eme Monde provides each user with a customisable 'home', but the possibilities appear relatively constrained and the emphasis is on selection and configuration rather than building. In many ways, this parallels the issue of avatar choice discussed above. AlphaWorld is rather more interesting; users may create objects based on pre-built components (Renderware RWX objects) and assign them properties – visibility, solidity – and behaviours – reactions to clicks, collisions etc.

Improving Building in 3D Virtual Worlds The power and flexibility of MOOs arises largely from the fact that the system is built around an object-oriented model, which encourages code-sharing and re-use. A similar model will probably be necessary in the case of 3D virtual worlds if the world is to be easy to extend and maintain. This may require considerable changes to the underlying architecture of the server and even to the representation language used for the world (see [1]).

Appropriate authoring tools will also be required. It might be desirable to integrate the tools with the browser so as to allow the user to work directly with objects in the world rather than going through a build-test-edit cycle.

Allowing the user to build and add arbitrary objects using the full expressive power of VRML and Java (or a similarly complex implementation language) poses a large number of significant technical problems, particularly where efficiency and stability is concerned. In the present state of technology, it would be all too easy for a user to build objects that either consumed huge quantities of client and server resources or caused runtime errors on the client. Nevertheless, it seems reasonable to suggest that this is the direction in which 3D virtual worlds may ultimately move.

3.4 Persistence

Allowing building leads necessarily to consideration of issues of persistence. Clearly, if users expend effort in constructing objects, they will expect the objects to be there the next time they connect. Object-building implies the need for a persistent storage mechanism to record all changes made in the world.

There can be other aspects to persistence as well. Social interactions constitute a kind of persistence – the social group acts as a 'memory' for past events, individual identities, shared conventions and so forth. This is not something that can easily be engineered and is, in fact, directly related to the growth of community. As a community grows, it becomes persistent.

Persistence can also be interpreted in another way. Paradoxically, a persistent world is one that evolves over time. A world which is identical each time we connect to it lacks any real 'existence'; it seems to exist 'outside time', and this frozen quality can detract seriously from the appeal of the world.

Persistence in Other Channels MUDs and MOOs which support building implement object persistence by regular backups of the database. By copying objects to backing storage, it is possible to ensure that crashes or server reboots will not destroy created objects.

MUDs and MOOs also provide a kind of support for social persistence in the shape of news systems. Issues of the day and contributions from members of the community may be recorded in a readable form that constitutes, in a certain sense, a kind of recent history of the community.

Persistence in 3D Virtual Worlds For obvious reasons, only those worlds that support making changes to the world have persistent features, and only for a relatively limited set of properties. As far as we are aware, no current 3D world supports the kind of far-reaching and pervasive persistent model seen in MOOs. Explicit support for social persistence (i.e. news systems) is typically provided externally if at all, in the form of Web pages (the Deuxième Monde, for example, has an extensive Web-based news service).

Improving Persistence in 3D Virtual Worlds A fully object-oriented world model will require persistence mechanisms similar to those found in MOOs. While the implementation of such database systems is well-understood, it remains to be seen how easily it can be adapted to the needs of 3D worlds.

Issues of social and contextual persistence are less technically challenging, but may require a new approach to the provision of 3D worlds. In particular, the act of world-building may need to be seen not so much as a one-off engineering activity but as a process of continuous creation. The world builders need to provide their world with an evolving context in order to enhance the user's perception of being *in* a world which is consistent and enduring. This may involve not so much adding new features to the world as exploiting the visual representation to convey the idea of passage of time – day and night, seasons, even decay; in short, anything that will help to give the impression of a living and changing world rather than a mere model.

3.5 Shared Purpose and Activity

Our last requirement returns us to our earlier discussion of different community types. It is in some senses a desired rather than a required characteristic, so we shall not analyse it in as much depth as the others. The example of MOOs and IRC show that communities can emerge and thrive without any shared activity other than that of talking to others. Nevertheless, observation suggests that users are likely to be more tolerant of the limitations of a tool if they have a valid external reason for using it. If we want people to use our 3D virtual worlds instead of the simpler, swifter channel of IRC, we need to look for applications in which the use of a 3D virtual world provides an added value, rather than merely an encumbrance.

Finding suitable applications is a wide-open research area. One possibility would be to move away from the 'meeting space' model towards the 'role-adopting' model, and use the power of the 3D world to create a compelling context for interactions (Sony Pictures have made an interesting step in this direction by using the Sony Community Place system to create movie tie-in worlds in which users play roles based on the film). Other applications might include virtual improvisational theatre, collaborative work using visual elements or multimedia 'jam sessions'.

4 Conclusion

Current uses of 3D virtual worlds are typically based on a 'meeting space' model of community. This is not the easiest model to exploit the capabilities of 3D worlds. To encourage community growth in this context we must find ways to promote social interactions and involvement in the world. To do so, we will need to draw on both existing mechanisms and advanced 3D-specific technologies to try to make our virtual environment more natural and compelling.

We should also keep in mind that successful communities of all kinds tend to evolve into shared interest communities that make use of a variety of different communication channels. When designing browsers for 3D virtual worlds, it may be useful to take this into account and plan for their use as part of a collection of tools rather than a unique channel for interaction.

There is no Golden Rule for community building. Nevertheless, a useful rule of thumb for implementors may be to review each new functionality proposed in terms of the five requirements we have identified in this article - identity, expression, building, persistence and shared interest - and consider how it might contribute to each of them.

References

[1] Curtis A. Beeson. An object-oriented approach to vrml development. In *Proceedings of VRML '97*, 1997.
[2] Amy Bruckman. Identity workshop: Emergent social and psychological phenomena in text-based virtual reality. Technical report, MIT Media Laboratory, 1992.
[3] Pierre-Emmanuel Chaut, Ali Sadeghin, Agnès Saulnier, and Marie-Luce Viaud. Création et animation de clones. In IMAGINA [8].
[4] Lynn Cherny. The modal complexity of speech events in a social mud. *Electronic Journal of Communication*, 5(4), 1995.
[5] Lynn Cherny. 'objectifying' the body in the discourse of an object-oriented mud. In C. Stivale, editor, *Cyberspaces: Pedagogy and Performance on the Electronic Frontier*. 1995.
[6] Pavel Curtis. Mudding: Social phenomena in text-based virtual realities. Technical report, Xerox PARC, 1993.
[7] Julian Dibbell. A rape in cyberspace, or how an evil clown, a haitian trickster spirit, two wizards, and a cast of dozens turned a database into a society. *The Village Voice*, 1993.
[8] *IMAGINA '97*, Monaco, 1997. INA.
[9] Vicki L. O'Day, Daniel G. Bobrow, Billie Hughes, Kimberly Bobrow, Vijay Saraswat, Jo Talazus, Jim Walters, and Cynde Welbes. Community designers. In *Proceedings of the Participatory Design Conference*, 1996.
[10] Ken Perlin. Improv: A system for scripting interactive actors in virtual worlds. In *SIGGRAPH 1996 Conference Proceedings*, Reading, MA, USA, 1996. Addison-Wesley.
[11] Bob Rockwell. From chat to civilisation: the evolution of online communities. In IMAGINA [8].
[12] Vijay Saraswat. Design requirements for network spaces. Technical report, AT&T Research, 1996.
[13] Neal Stephenson. *Snow Crash*. Bantam Spectra, 1993.

A Mixed 2D/3D Interface for Music Spatialization

François Pachet[1], Olivier Delerue[1]

[1] SONY CSL Paris, 6, rue Amyot, 75005 Paris, France
Email: pachet{delerue}@csl.sony.fr

Abstract. We propose a system for controlling in real time the localisation of sound sources. The system, called MidiSpace, is a real time spatializer of Midi music. We raise the issue of which interface is the most adapted for using MidiSpace. Two interfaces are proposed: a 2D interface for controlling the position of sound sources with a global view of the musical setup, and a 3D/VRML interface for moving the listener's avatar. We report on the design of these interfaces and their respective advantages, and conclude on the need for a mixed interface for spatialization.

Active Listening

We believe that listening environments of the future can be greatly enhanced by integrating relevant models of musical perception into musical listening devices, provided we can develop appropriate software technology to exploit them. This is the basis of the research conducted on "Active listening" at Sony Computer Science Laboratory, Paris. Active Listening refers to the idea that listeners can be given some degree of control on the music they listen to, that give the possibility of proposing different musical perceptions on a piece of music, by opposition to traditional listening, in which the musical media is played passively by some neutral device. The objective is both to increase the musical comfort of listeners, and, when possible, to provide listeners with smoother paths to new music (music they do not know, or do not like). These control parameters create implicitly control spaces in which musical pieces can be listened to in various ways. Active listening is thus related to the notion of *Open Form* in composition [8] but differs by two aspects: 1) we seek to create listening environments for *existing* music repertoires, rather than creating environments for composition or free musical exploration (such as *PatchWork* [11], *OpenMusic* [2], or *CommonMusic* [18]), and 2) we aim at creating environments in which the variations always preserve the original semantics of the music, at least when this semantics can be defined precisely.

The first parameter which comes to mind when thinking about user control on music is the spatialization of sound sources. In this paper we study the implications of giving users the possibility to change dynamically the mixing of sound sources. In te next section, we review previous approaches in computer-controlled sound spatialization, and then propose a basic environment for controlling music spatialization, called MidiSpace. We then describe a simple 2D interface for controlling sound sources, and then describe a VRML interface which gives users a more realistic view on the music heard. We compare the two approaches and argue in favor of a mixed solution integrating both interfaces. The last section describes the overall design and implementation of the resulting system.

Music Spatialization

Music spatialization has long been an intensive object of study in computer music research. Most of the work so far has concentrated in building software systems that simulate acoustic environments for existing sound signals. These works are based on results in psychoacoustics that allow to model the perception of sound sources by the human hear using a limited number of perceptive parameters [4]. These models have led to techniques allowing to recreate impression of sound localization using a limited number of loudspeakers. These techniques typically exploit differences of amplitude in sound channels, delays between sound channels to account for interaural distances, and sound filtering techniques such as reverberation to recreate impressions of distance and of spatial volume.

For instance, The *Spatialisateur IRCAM* [10] is a virtual acoustic processor that allows to define the sound scene as a set of perceptive factors such as azimuth, elevation and orientation angles of sound sources relatively to the listener. This processor can adapt itself to any sound reproduction configuration, such as headphones, pairs of loudspeakers, or collections of loudspeaker. Other commercial systems with similar features have recently been introduced on the market, such as Roland *RSS*, the *Spatializer* (Spatializer Audio Labs) which allows to produce a stereo 3D signal from an 8-track input signal controlled by joysticks, or Q-Sound labs's *Q-Sound*, which builds extended stereophonic image using similar techniques. This tendency to propose integrated technology to produce 3D sound is further reflected, for instance, by Microsoft's DirectX API now integrating 3D audio.

These sound spatialization techniques and systems are mostly used for building various virtual reality environments, such as the Cave [5] or *CyberStage* [6], [8]. Recently, sound spatialization has also been included in limited ways in various 3D environments such as *Community Place*'s implementation of VRML [12], ET++ [1], or proprietary, low-cost infrastructures [3].

Based on these works, we are interested in exploiting spatialization capabilities for building richer listening environments. In this paper, we concentrate on the interface issue, i.e. how to give average listeners the possibility of exploiting sound source spatialization in a natural, easy way. We will first describe our basic spatialization system *MidiSpace*, which precisely allows user to control in real time the spatialization of sound sources. Then we describe two interfaces for MidiSpace, and compare their respective advantages.

The Basic MidiSpace System

MidiSpace is a system that gives listeners control on music spatialization. We first outline the characteristics of midi-based spatialization before describing the system.

Midi-Based Spatialization

MidiSpace is a real time player of Midi files which allows users to control in real time the localization of sound sources through a graphical interface (extensions to audio are not discussed in this paper). MidiSpace takes as input arbitrary Midi files [9]. The basic idea in MidiSpace is to represent graphically sound sources in a virtual space, as well as an avatar that represents the listener itself. Through an appropriate editor, the user may either move its avatar around, or move the instruments themselves. The relative position of sound sources and the listener's avatar determine the overall mixing of the music, according to simple geometrical rules illustrated in Fig. 1. The real time mixing of sound sources is realized by sending Midi volume and panoramic messages.

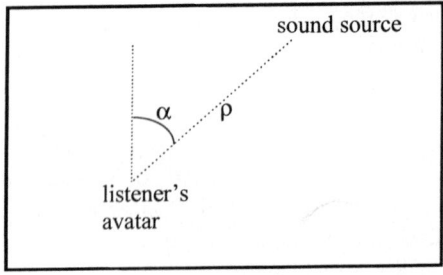

Fig. 1. Volume of sound_source$_i$ = f(distance(graphical-object$_i$, listener_avatar)). f is a function mapping distance to Midi volume (from 0 to 127). Stereo position of sound source i = g(angle(graphical_Object$_i$, listener_avatar)), where angle is computed relatively to the vertical segment crossing the listener's avatar, and g is a function mapping angles to Midi panoramic positions (0 to 127).

It is important to understand here the role of Midi in this project. On the one hand, there are strong limitations of using Midi for spatialization *per se*. In particular, using Midi panoramic and volume control changes messages for spatializing sounds does not allow to reach the same level of realism than when using other techniques (delays between channels, digital signal processing techniques, etc.), since we exploit only difference in amplitude in sound channels to create spatialization effects. However, this limitation is not important in our context for two reasons : 1) this Midi-based technique still allows to achieve a reasonable impression of sound spatialization which is enough to validate our ideas in user interface and control, and 2) more sophisticated techniques for spatialization can be added in MidiSpace, independently of its architecture.

We will now describe the interfaces for MidiSpace: first, a 2D interface, which provides a global view on the musical setting, and allows to move sound sources around. Then we describe a VRML interface and discuss its relevance for music listening. We conclude on the interest of a mixed approach.

The 2D Interface of MidiSpace

In the 2D interface of MidiSpace, each sound source is represented by a graphical object, as well as the listener's avatar (see Fig. 2.). The user may basically play a midi file (with usual tape recorder-like controls), and move objects around. When an object is moved, the spatializer is called with the new position of the object, and the mixing of sound sources is recomputed accordingly. Other features allow to mute sound sources, or select them as "solo".

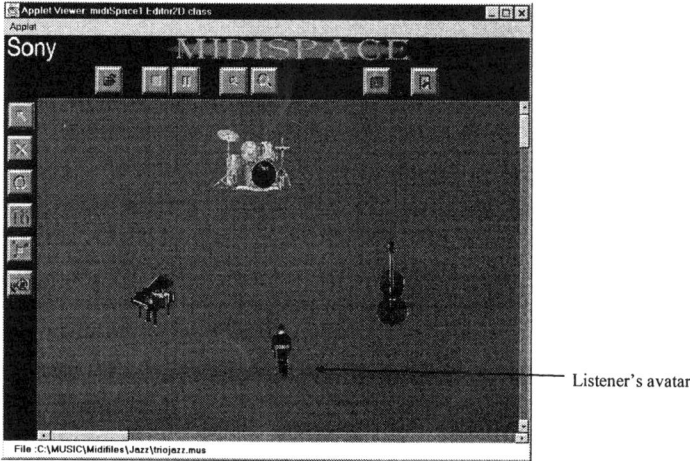

Fig. 2. The 2D Interface of MidiSpace. Here, a tune by Bill Evans (Jazz trio) is being performed

In an initial version, we allowed *both* sound sources and the avatar to be moved. However this was confusing for users. Indeed, moving sound sources amounts to changing the intrinsic mixing of the piece. For instance, moving the piano away will changes the relationship between the piano sound and the rhythmic part. Moving the avatar simply amounts to changing the mixing in global way, but respects the relationships between the sound sources. The effect is quite different since in the second case the structure of the music is modified.

The interface provides a global view on the musical setup, which is very convenient to edit the musical setting. However, there is no impression of musical immersion in the musical piece : the interface is basically a means for editing the piece, not to explore it.

The VRML Interface for Navigating in MidiSpace

Second, we have experimented with interfaces for navigating in the musical space. Several works addressed the issue of navigating in virtual worlds with spatialized sounds. The most spectacular are probably the Cave system [5] or CyberStage [8], in which the user is immersed in a fully-equipped room with surrounding images and sound. Although the resulting systems are usually very realistic, their cost and availability are still prohibitive.

Instead, we chose to experiment with affordable, wide-spread technology. A 3D version of MidiSpace in VRML has been built (see Fig. 3.), in which the VRML code is automatically generated from the 2D interface and the Midi parser. The idea is to create a VRML world in which the user may freely navigate using the standard VRML commands, while listening to the musical piece. Each instrument is represented by a VRML object, and the spatialization is computed from the user current viewpoint. In this interface, the only thing the user can do is move around using standard commands; sound sources cannot be moved.

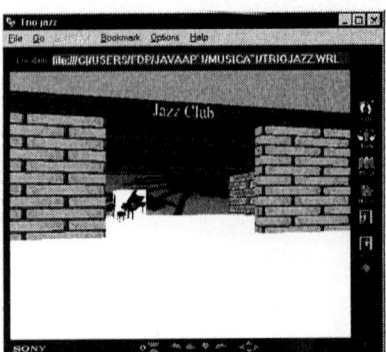 

Fig. 3. MidiSpace/VRML on the Jazz trio, corresponding to the 2D Interface of Fig. 2. On the left, before entering, on the right, inside the club.

Although the result is more exciting and stimulating for users than the 2D interface, it is not yet fully satisfying because the interface gives too little information on the overall configuration of instruments, which is a crucial parameter for spatialization. When the user gets close to an instrument, she loses the sense of her position in the musical set up (e.g. the jazz club, see Fig. 3.). Of course, this problem is a general problem with VRML interfaces, and is not specific to MidiSpace, but in the context of a listening environment, it is particularly important to provide a visualisation which is consistent with the music being played. This consistency is difficult to achieve with a 3D virtual interface on a simple screen.

The Mixed Interface

Based on experiments with users on the two interfaces, we concluded on the interest of combining them for obtaining an optimal satisfaction on user control. The 2D interface is used for *editing* purposes, i.e. moving sound sources. Moving the avatar is not possible in this interface. The VRML interface is used for *exploration*, in a passive mode, to visualize the musical setting in 3D, and move the avatar around. Moving objects is not possible.

The communication between the two interfaces is realized through the VRML/Java communication scheme, and ensures that when the avatar is moved in the VRML interface, the graphical object of the 2D interface is moved accordingly. The overall architecture of MidiSpace is illustrated in Fig. 4.

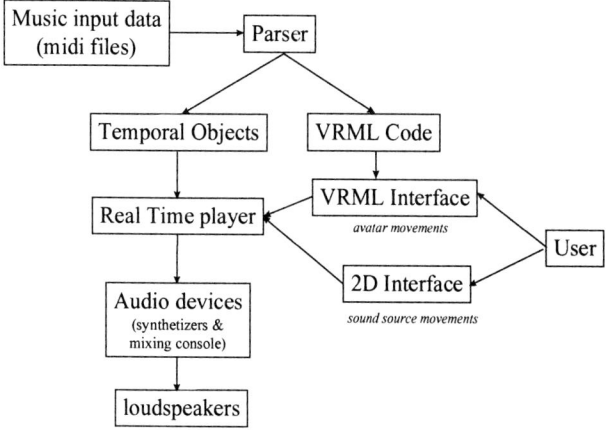

Fig. 4. The architecture of MidiSpace User Interaction.

Implementation

The implementation of the MidiSpace Spatializer consists in 1) translating Midi information into a set of objects within a temporal framework, 2) scheduling these temporal objects using a real time scheduler, 3) the interfaces.

The Parser

The Parser task is to transform the information contained in the Midi file into a unified temporal structure. The temporal framework we use is described in [18], an object-oriented, interval-based representation of temporal objects. In this framework, each temporal object is represented by a class, which inherits the basic functionalities from a root superclass *TemporalObject*.

One main issue the Parser must address comes from the way Midi files are organized according to the General Midi specifications. Mixing is realized by sending volume and panoramic Midi messages. These messages are global for a given Midi channel. One must therefore ensure that each instrument appears on a distinct Midi channel. In practice, this is not always the case, since Midi tracks can contain events on different channels. The first task is to sort the events and create logical melodies for each instrument. This is realized by analysing program change messages, which assign Midi channels to instruments, thereby segmenting the musical structure. The second task is to create higher level musical structures from the basic musical objects (i.e. notes). The Midi information is organized into notes, grouped in melodies. Each melody contains only the notes for a single instrument. The total piece is represented as a collection of melodies. A dispatch algorithm ensures that, at a given time, only one instrument is playing on a given Midi channel.

Scheduling Temporal Objects

The scheduling of MidiSpace objects uses *MidiShare* [14], a real time Midi operating system, with a Java API. *MidiShare* provides the basic functionality to schedule asynchronously, in real time, Midi events, from Java programs, with 1 millisecond accuracy. More details on the scheduling are given in [7].

MidiSpace Interfaces

The 2D interface uses the standard Java *awt* library, and follows a straightforward object-oriented interface design. The VRML interface is generated automatically from the Parser. More precisely, the Parser generates a file, which contains basically 1) the information on the global setup, 2) description of individual sound sources, corresponding to the various sound tracks identified, and 3) routing expressions to a spatializer object, which is defined as a Java script, using the VRML/Java communication scheme [12]. An excerpt of the VRML code is shown in Fig. 5.

```
WorldInfo {title "Trio jazz"}

# Various global settings
NavigationInfo {speed 2   type   [ "WALK" ]}
# The viewpoint from which the spatialization is computed
DEF USERVIEWPOINT Viewpoint {position -13 0 45}

# The definition of the musical setting (here, a Jazz Club)
...
```

```
# the Label
Transform {
  translation -2 4.7 21
  children [
    Shape {
      appearance Appearance {
        material Material {
          diffuseColor 1 1 1}}
      geometry Text {
        string "Jazz Club"}}]}


# The sound sources, as identified by the Parser in
General Midi
DEF PIANO Transform {
  children [
    Shape {
      appearance Appearance {
        texture ImageTexture {
          url      "piano.jpg"
          repeatS FALSE
          repeatT FALSE}
        textureTransform TextureTransform {}
      }
      geometry Box {
        size 3 3 3}}]}
DEF DRUMS Transform { ...}
DEF BASS Transform {...}


# The Java script for handling movements and
spatialization
DEF MY_SCRIPT Script {
 url "MusicScript.class"
 field            SFString             midiFileName
"http://intweb.csl.sony.fr/~demo/trio.mid"
 field SFNode channel10 USE DRUMS
 field SFNode channel2 USE BASS
 field SFNode channel3 USE PIANO
 eventIn   SFVec3f     posChanged
 eventIn   SFRotation orientation
```

```
      eventOut  SFRotation   keepRight
      eventOut  SFVec3f      keepPosition}

" The routing of VRML messages to the Java script
ROUTE        DETECTOR.position_changed                       TO
MY_SCRIPT.posChanged
ROUTE    MY_SCRIPT.keepPosition                              TO
USERVIEWPOINT.set_position
ROUTE            DETECTOR.orientation_changed                TO
MY_SCRIPT.orientation
ROUTE    MY_SCRIPT.keepRight                                 TO
USERVIEWPOINT.set_orientation
```

Fig. 5. The generated VRML code for describing the musical setting from a given midi file

Conclusion, Future Works

The MidiSpace system shows that it is possible to give some degree of freedom to users in sound spatialization, through an intuitive graphical interface. We argue that a unique interface is not appropriate for both moving sound sources and avatars, while giving users a realistic feeling of immersion. In the case of spatialization, although they appear at first to be similar user actions, moving sound sources and moving the avatar bear significantly different semantics, and we concluded that allowing these two operations in the same interface is confusing. We propose an approach combining a standard 2D interface, appropriate for moving sound sources and editing the setup, and a VRML interface appropriate for moving avatars and exploring the musical piece. The prototype built so far validates our approach, and more systematic testing with users is in progress.

Future work remains to be done in three main directions. First we are currently adding a *constraint-based* mechanism for maintaining consistency in sound source positions [15]. This mechanism allows users to navigate in a restricted space, which will always ensure that some mixing properties of the music are satisfied. Second, an audio version of MidiSpace is in progress, to 1) enlarge the repertoire of available music material to virtually all recorded music, and 2) improve the quality of the spatialization, using more advanced techniques such as the ones sketched in the introduction of this paper. Finally, an *annotation* format is currently being designed to represent information on the content of musical piece, to enrich the interaction. These annotations typically represent information on the structure of the piece, its harmonic characteristics, and other kinds of temporal information [17]. These extensions are in progress, and remain compatible with our choice for user interface design proposed here.

References

1. Ackermann P., *Developing object-oriented multimedia software*, Dpunkt, Heidelberg, 1996.
2. Assayag G., Agon C., Fineberg, J., Hanappe P., "An Object Oriented Visual Environment For Musical Composition", Proceedings of the International Computer Music Conference, pp. 364-367, Thessaloniki, 1997.
3. Burgess D.A., "Techniques for low-cost spatial audio", ACM Fifth Annual Symposium on User Interface Software and Technology (UIST '92), Monterey, November 1992.
4. Chowning, J. (1971), "The simulation of moving sound sources", *JAES*, vol. 19, n. 1, p. 2-6.
5. Cruz-Neira, C., Leight, J., Papka, M., Barnes, C., Cohen, S.M., Das, S., Engelmann, R., Hudson, R., Roy, T., Siegel, L., Vasilakis, C., DeFanti, T.A., Sandin, D.J., "Scientists in Wonderland: A Report on Visualization Applications in the CAVE Virtual Reality Environment", Proc. IEEE Symposium on Research Frontiers in VR, pp. 59-66, 1993.
6. Dai P., Eckel G., Göbel M., Hasenbrink F., Lalioti V., Lechner U., Strassner J., Tramberend H., Wesche G., "Virtual Spaces: VR Projection System Technologies and Applications", Tutorial Notes, Eurographics '97, Budapest 1997, 75 pages.
7. Delerue O., Pachet F., "MidiSpace, un spatialisateur Midi temps réel", Cinquièmes Journées d'Informatique Musicale, Toulon, 1998.
8. Eckel G., "Exploring Musical Space by Means of Virtual Architecture", Proceedings of the 8th International Symposium on Electronic Art, School of the Art Institute of Chicago, 1997.
9. IMA, "MIDI musical instrument digital interface specification 1.0", Los Angeles, International MIDI Association, 1983.
10. Jot J.-M., Warusfel O. "A Real-Time Spatial Sound Processor for Music and Virtual Reality Applications", Proceedings of International Computer Music Conference, September 1995.
11. Laurson M., Duthen J., "PatchWork, a graphical language in PreForm", Proceedings of the International Computer Music Conference, San Francisco, 172-175, 1989.
12. Lea R., Matsuda K., Myashita K., Java for 3D and VRML worlds, New Riders Publishing, 1996.
13. Meyer L., *Emotions and meaning in music*, University of Chicago Press, 1956.
14. Orlarey Y., Lequay H. "MidiShare: a real time multi-tasks software module for Midi applications", Proceedings of the ICMC, 1989, ICMA, San Francisco.
15. Pachet, F. Delerue, O. A Temporal Constraint-Based Music Spatialization system, submitted to ACM MultiMedia 98, 1998.
16. Pachet F., Ramalho G., Carrive J. "Representing temporal musical objects and reasoning in the MusES system", *Journal of New Music Research*, vol. 25, n. 3, pp. 252-275, 1996.
17. Pachet, F. Delerue, O. "Annotations for Real Time Music Spatialization", International Workshop on knowledge Representation for interactive Multimedia Systems, KRIMS-II workshop, Trento, Italy, 1998.
18. Taube H., "Common Music: A Music Composition Language in Common Lisp and CLOS", *Computer Music Journal*, vol. 15, n° 2, 21-32, 1991.

Organizing Information in 3D

Claudia Cavallar and Daniel Dögl

virtual real-estate, Breitegasse 3/2, A-1070 Vienna, Austria
tel.: +43-1-526 29 67 fax: +43-1-526 29 67-11
cc@dc.co.at, dani@dc.co.at
http://www.dc.co.at/index.html

Abstract. This paper deals with various aspects of organization in 3D-space. Section 2 of this paper is derived from our experiences during the making of "A Scientific Universe", a VRML based 3D-environment for the Austrian Academy of Sciences. In this section we discuss different approaches we used to organize data in 3D. In section 3 we included some thoughts on future directions, derived from our experiences with a project that we are currently working on, known under the working title of "NAMEisBUNT". The goal of this project is to develop a toolbox, that enables users to retrieve information from the world wide web and to display the results in three dimensions. A spatial mapping generated by the query, enables the user to interactively evaluate the nature of the results in 3D, to retrieve the most promising items and to create his/her own archive of retrieved information.

1 Introduction

Originally devised as part of an exhibition called "schafft:wissen" (lit.: produce knowledge; a pun on Wissenschaft, science, in german), "A Scientific Universe" grew into a project of its own, when the exhibition was canceled and only the virtual part remained. The project is a Netscape based VRML application. The different parts, some 100 VRML models, the sound and accompanying text (spoken or as HTML) are connected and organized using Java. The goal of the project was to make the work of Austrian scientists and research teams accessible and understandable to a broader audience. The sheer mass of material and the heterogeneous content that had to fit into the environment called for organizational structures that would allow the user to retrieve the information and to understand the connections between the topics. On the other hand we were confronted with the problem of organizing the various presentations. We decided to solve both problems through 3D-structures.

2 Organizational Structures in 3D-Space

In this paper we distinguish 3 different approaches to organizing objects and information in three-dimensional space. These approaches were conditioned by the nature of the data that had to be visualized (i.e. geographical, conceptual, architectural etc.) and by the necessity to maintain a coherent navigation functionality and interface language throughout all parts of the environment.

2.1 Abstract Structures

This approach might be useful when mapping some aspect of the content (e.g. categories, such as branches of science) on a spatial arrangement of objects. [1] In this case it was used to illustrate the overall organization. Given the heterogeneous content, we thought it best to confront the user with a unified, simple structure, where he could retrieve information and get an idea on how the topics were connected.

"Smarties". In the entry level each topic is represented by an object, a so-called "smartie". They are all the same size and are labeled with a text string according to their content. When no item has been selected, all the "smarties", share the same color: a neutral gray. The color changes to a bright yellow when a "smartie" has been selected and to red when the user reemerges from the topic (analogous to a visited link, the "smartie" becomes a visited "smartie"). In this way the user can keep track of his position and his movements. The shape of the "smarties" was conditioned by the tasks they had to perform: In the overview it was important to have an object that would be very simple, in order to work in close up as well as from a distance. We chose to give the object a distinct orientation, i.e. one direction was more prominent than the others, since the orientation of the "smarties" provided the visual clue to which was the main plane. The entry level can be easily expanded or modified by adding or subtracting "smarties" in order to accommodate new topics or changes in content.

Spatial Arrangement. Since all the topics displayed in the overview are given equal importance, and there is no particular order in which they have to be explored, we decided to focus on the relationship between the topics. Thus all "smarties" are loosely grouped by category, e.g. all "smarties" containing worlds that deal with biology are arranged in a cluster. Most topics, e.g. high-energy physics dealt with a number of different concepts and approaches, and had to be split into sub-worlds. Clicking on yellow, i.e. selected "smarties", that contain sub-topics, displays a substructure made from pale yellow "smarties" connected by threads, explaining the connection between the sub-topics (See also: Fig. 1). The introduction of expandable substructures also helped to avoid cluttering the entry level with too many objects. [2] The user can choose the "smarties" by pointing and clicking at them: The selected topic becomes the center of the world, prominently placed in the middle of the screen. All the other "smarties" are now grouped around this point, thus "smarties" placed nearer to the central one contain topics related to it, while those farther away obviously deal with issues that are only remotely connected or are not related at all. The user can orbit around this new center by using the arrows at the edges of the 3D-frame (See also: Fig. 1). Spatial sound was used to enhance the orientation.

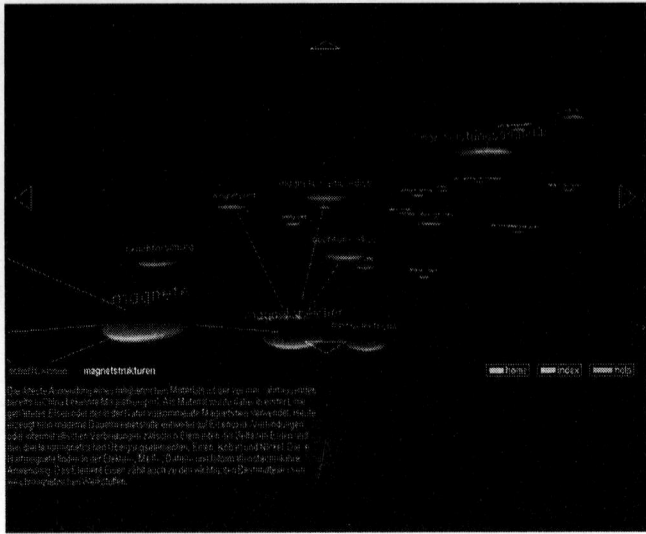

Fig. 1. The entry level of the environment, showing *labeled smarties, substructures* and *arrows for navigation*.

Conclusion. The setup described in the previous sections works well for explaining the relations between the topics: it effectively conveys a sense of the spatial arrangement of the objects, and therefore about their relation to each other. It turned out to be great fun for people who just wanted to explore the environment, without looking for anything in particular, and it helped people keep track of visited/unexplored areas. On the other hand it turned out to be rather cumbersome for people looking for specific topics: organizing the "smarties" spatially and labeling them is not enough for easy retrieval. This effect was worsened by the fact that it was rather hard to find a suitable size ratio between object and text: either the text would appear much too large when the object was close or it would be barely readable when viewed from a distance that allowed all objects to be seen. Several approaches can be thought of:

Scaling the size of the text according to the viewpoint changes in a scene. This option was dropped since the effect was rather bewildering.

Scaling the size of the text according to the viewpoint changes in a scene. This option was dropped since the effect was rather disorientating.

Replacing the entry level structure with a superstructure, where each "smartie" replaces a group of "smarties" from the original configuration. This solution was discarded since it would take the user one more – repetitive – step to reach the models.

Replacing the "smarties" with icons, would still require labeling, since they allow for a broad range of interpretation.

2.2 Organizational Structures Resembling the Real World.

Many topics are easier to grasp when the user is confronted with a representation of the real thing, not just a description or illustration. For "A Scientific Universe" this was true for topics that dealt with spatial arrangements of some kind, e.g. archaeological sites, a geographical area, the solar system or topics that involved processes, e.g. experiments in quantum physics or production steps during molecular beam epitaxy. Organizing the necessary information for these topics through models in 3D-space just came natural and worked fairly well.

Models as Organizational Structures. In some cases most of the information to be communicated is inherent in an object, such as a building or a machine. The example we discuss here dealt with the excavations of the "Hanghaus 2" in Ephesus, a project by the Austrian Archeological Institute and the Austrian Academy of Sciences. The model represents a partial reconstruction of the ruins of a Roman apartment.

Fig. 2. The model of the Roman apartment in Ephesus, showing the *labels* used for navigation and information retrieval.

Navigation. While it was easy to connect the information to the objects, it was not so easy to communicate to the visitor which objects to use. This problem was not confined to the Ephesus model: the idea was to make the objects stand out clearly, while on the other hand avoiding that the marked objects would interfere with the atmosphere and overall impression of the model. More generally speaking it was important to find a navigation and retrieval method that could be adapted to the various situations and also to the entry level. We experimented with painting clickable objects a particular color, an approach that soon proved to have many drawbacks: small objects were not distinguishable enough, unfamiliar objects, such as parts of machines or devices needed additional information on their purpose. Usually the coloring also affected the aesthetics of the model. Another approach consisted in not marking the objects and relying on the cursor to change from an arrow to the symbol of a hand. This proved rather tedious, since, even with the simplest objects it involved frustrating trials. We finally settled for white labels designating clickable objects and dark or black labels that served as explanatory notes only. Labeling helped explain an object and therefore helped the visitor decide, whether she/he wanted to know more about it. Words allocated in the lower right corner of the VRML frame served as links to concepts and related topics, not attached to an object. To explore the house the user clicks on the various labels marking places of interest: by doing so he/she moves through the rooms and is presented with background information. The sequence of labels also regulates the order in which the model can be explored.

2.3 Merging Both Systems

For some topics it seemed a good idea to combine "realistic" models with an abstract structure. We used the "smarties", since the user was already familiar with them from the entry level and recognized them as extraneous elements placed in the model for orientation and information retrieval.

The "Smarties" as Markers. The CERN accelerator might serve as an example where "smarties" were used to mark distinctive locations in a model. Since the accelerator was represented schematically, the "smarties" could be used as markers that called for attention while it was sufficiently clear that they did not correspond to "real" objects.

Fig. 3. The CERN accelerator, showing *"smarties" used as markers*

The "Smarties" as Carriers of Content. Abstract concepts that are not easily visualized, might be easier to understand by using 3D-structures for organizing information. For this contribution, part of the high-energy physics section, it seemed best to use an abstract representation of the events taking place in the first moments after the universe started to exist. Again the "smarties" were employed as markers, this time on a time-scale. As soon as they are clicked, they spill their content, illustrating the particles and forces existing at the various stages of development.

Fig. 4. The Big Bang model, showing *"smarties" used as carriers of content*

3 Future Directions

3.1 Towards a New Information Architecture

The process of mapping existing content in 3D-space gives access to connections and aspects that had previously been neglected or were just not visible. The patterns recognizable in spatial arrangement of things allow the user to instinctively grasp connections and subsequently focus on the most interesting or promising spots.

3.2 Conclusion

We tried to individuate some areas we consider important for future development.

Data Driven Structures. The organizational structures we employed in "A Scientific Universe" were mostly custom tailored for the task at hand. The mapping of the content onto 3D-structures was not automated, i.e. each part had to be manually positioned, labeled and endowed with a specific functionality. For some tasks, e.g. the situations described in section 2.2 and 2.3, this approach works well, and it is hard to think of a substitute method. For abstract structures, as described in section 2.1, a more data driven approach, e.g. the automatization of the content mapping according to a predefined set of rules, allows for the design of more flexible environments. In "NameIsBunt" the query is submitted by choosing concepts from a 3D-representation of the underlying ontology, while the retrieved documents are displayed as objects in a spatial system.

Improved Navigation and Orientation might be achieved through design elements, such as by introducing landmarks for better orientation, or by adding a grid, to better evaluate distances [3], or by offering preferential views, such as overviews or plans, that let the user check his/her position in space, and the overall arrangement of the objects. In this context levels of representation, that allow the user to switch from very detailed views to overviews of the environment, are an important issue [4].

Alternative Ways for Representing Information, i.e. switching between 2D and 3D representations of the content according to different necessities. [5], [6] On the other hand the environment might appear different according to an user's access status or his/her preferences, e.g. the user may customize an environment or be denied access to view certain parts of it.

Allowing for a Wider Range of Interactions i.e. giving the user the possibility to rearrange the environment, or to create a personal environment. The user might also be given the capability to change the appearance of the objects, leave traces in the environment, post messages, communicate with other users etc.

References

1. Young, P.: Three Dimensional Information Visualisation. Computer Science Technical Report, No. 12 (1996)
   http://www.dur.ac.uk/ dcs3py/pages/work/documents/lit-survey/IV-Survey/
2. Chalmers, M.: Design Perspectives in Visualising Complex Information (1995)
   http://www.ubs.com/info/ubilab/projects/hci/e_viz.html
3. Young, P.: op. cit. (1996)
4. Chalmers, M.: op. cit. (1995)
5. Benford, S. et. al.: Experience of using 3D graphics in database visualisation (1994)
   ftp://ftp.comp.lancs.ac.uk/pub/vds/
6. Boyle, J., Leishman, S., Fothergill, J. and Grey, P.: Development of a Visual Query Language (1993)
   http://www.biochem.abdn.ac.uk/ john/vlq/vlq.html

Human Centered Virtual Interactive Image World for Image Retrieval

Haruo Kimoto

NTT Information and Communication Systems Labs.
309A, 1-1, Hikari-Oka, Yokosuka-Shi, Kanagawa 239-0847, JAPAN
Phone +81 468 59 3387, Fax +81 468 55 1152
kimoto@dq.isl.ntt.co.jp

Abstract. In this paper, the implementation of a virtual world which is used for image retrieval is described. This virtual world is called Moving-VW, which consists of a large number of images to be retrieved. At this stage, Moving-VW has 400 images of flowers, brush paintings and Japanese fine arts. Moving-VW shows images to human, and changes its configuration during the interactions with human who wishes to explore and find images in the world. When showing the world, the center of the world is always a key image which is selected by human, so this is a human centered world. The world has directions such as color directions, and reconfigure itself as the center of the world changes. The world can show images to human by animation, and offers a good image indexing tool. We are making such a world to realize the world which responds to our own mind in the process of the interaction for searching something. Here, in this paper, the process of searching images is described as one of the applications of exploring the virtual world. The most original idea here is that the world changes its configuration in accordance with the every interactions with human so that he could find what he wants quickly, and moreover, he would encounter with something which he does not know in advance. It is the very characteristics of a virtual world in a computer memory to change its configuration easily.

Keywords:

Image retrieval, 3DCG, Visualization, Interactive search, Human Interaction, Human centered world, Artificial direction, Directional display of information, Kaleidoscope, Reconfigulation of world, Animated world, Relative Indexing.

1 Introduction

We are making a virtual world which changes its configuration during the interactions with human who wishes to explore the world and get something from the world. The reason why we are making such a world is to realize the world which responds to our own mind in the process of the interaction for searching something in a way that a human can find what he wants quickly and easily. Here, in this paper, the process of searching images is described as one of the applications of exploring the virtual world. The most original idea in this paper is that the world changes its configuration in accordance with the every interactions with a human so that he could find what he wants quickly, and moreover, he would encounter with something which he does not know in advance. It is the very characteristics of the virtual worlds in a computer memory to change its configuration easily. In the real world, we have only one world at one time, but we can have as many virtual worlds as we wish, which reflect our human mind shown in the process of the interactions with the world. We are now making this virtual world and we call this world as Moving-VW.

In the following sections, Moving-VW will be described. In section 2, an image retrieval system which is a test bed of Moving-VW will be introduced. In section 3, we explain that Moving-VW is a human centered world. In section 4, direction in Moving-VW will be explained. In section 5, reconfiguration of Moving-VW by human interaction will be discussed. In section 6, animation of Moving-VW will be shown. In section 7, how relative position in Moving-VW will be used to index images will be explained.

2 Image Retrieval as an Application of Moving-VW

We adopted image retrieval as an application of Moving-VW. When Moving-VW is applied to image retrieval, it is natural to think that Moving-VW is a kind of museum that has many digitized paintings and the placement of these paintings could be changed easily by computer programming. The scheme of image retrieval in this paper is that the retrieval is made by similarity matching between images, so the user always give a key image for search. The system returns the search result in a similarity order to the key image. The similarity order can be made by any feature of the images. In case RGB color system is applied to represent images, the degree of Red constituent and/or the degree of Green constituent and/or the degree of Blue constituent can be used for calculation of the similarity. In case HSI color system is applied, hue and/or the degree of saturation and/or the degree of intensity can be used for calculation of the similarity. Even keyword could be used for the calculation of the similarity, if keywords are indexed to images. Keyword similarity can be calculated and was already used in the field of document retrieval, such as newspaper retrieval, patent retrieval and so on. There are several works in the field of document retrieval which shows the retrieval results in a two dimensions space [1], [2] [3], [4], or in a three dimensions space [5], [6]. There are few works which shows the retrieval result of images in a three dimensions space.

3 Human Centered World

Moving-VW is a human centered world both in a physical sense and in a logical sense. Physically, the search key is always located at the center of Moving-VW.

Logically, the retrieval result using any feature of images is shown in the similarity order from the key image. So, the key image, which is selected by the user, is always at the center of Moving-VW. Figure 1 shows a search key located at the center of Moving-VW.

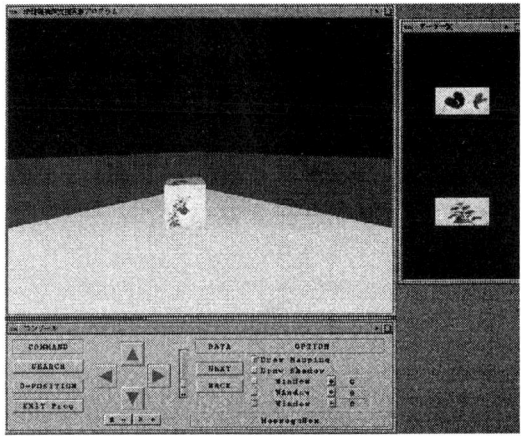

Fig. 1. Search key at the center of Moving-VW.

4 Direction in the World

When we were lost in a jungle, which direction should we take? Looking for an certain image in a large number of images is the same situation of being lost in a jungle. Surely, we will take the directions from which a ray comes, directions ¿from which warm wind comes or good smell comes. So, there are always directions to take. Moving-VW shows directions for the user. The directions which we have already implemented in the Moving-VW system are such as the degree of constituent of red, green, blue, hue, saturation and intensity. Of course, there are many other directions which we can think of. They are single keyword direction, cluster direction, concept direction and so on. The implementation and evaluation of the effect of these directions are next research theme for us. Figure 2 shows the result of image retrieval shown in a directional way in the image world. In Figure 2, planes of bottom, middle-left and middle-right are I-H Plain, S-I Plain, H-S Plain of HIS color system, and the images are located in the similarity order to the key image which is located in the middle-center plain.

5 World Reconfiguration by Human Interaction

The user can select a new search key image from the previous search result, i.e. from the previous virtual world. And then, the next search will be made

Fig. 2. The result of image retrieval shown in a directional way.

using this search key. As a result, the new search result will be displayed , in other words, the new world was created and is shown now on the display with the directions. Figure 3 shows the selection of a new search key for the next retrieval. The image at the left-bottom whose frame was emphasized is the selected new search key. This new search key was located at the center of the world at the same time.

This process is what we call reconfiguration of the world by human interaction. The selected new search key is located at the center of the world, and the new search result was displayed. Making a retrieval in such a way repeatedly, the recursive search can be made infinitely, and during this recursive search, the user could find the virtual world which he likes best and find the best fit image for him. Besides, he could encounter the unknown world which he likes. The user can travel the virtual worlds time by time, that is, as if he were looking into a kaleidoscope like a child who is excited to find a new world.

6 Animated World

When the world has a large number of images, it is difficult to display all of the images on a screen at one time. For such a case, the images are animated in turn so that the user can see them well. Figure 4 shows the animation of images for showing the retrieval result to the user. During the animation, the user can select the image which he likes by clicking the image on the screen.

On the Internet, usually, the user must make a search and look for what he wants over the large list of search result. Here, the new search interface, that is, searching in the animated windows was introduced. The effect of this method is the elimination of the search access from the user to the system, and the demerit is the increase of the time to get a result. The evaluation of the use of animated window is now in progress.

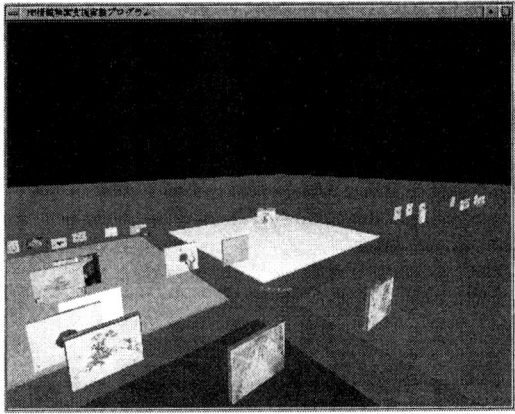

Fig. 3. Selection of the next search key.

Figure 5 shows the total views in the whole process of the search. The image world is at the left-top of the figure, the animated images is at the right-top and the final images which the user has got are at the center and at the right-bottom of the figure.

7 Relative Indexing of Images in the Image World

In the field of information retrieval, documents, such as newspaper articles, technical papers and books, are indexed by keywords or n-gram of characters. Controlled term indexing using thesaurus is one of the well established way of indexing. Other indexing methods are free term indexing and n-gram indexing. Categorization of documents and facet indexing are also used for indexing documents.

On the other hand, in the field of image retrieval, images are retrieved by contents such as color or objects which the images have in themselves. Colors and objects are physical features of images. It is difficult to recognize objects in images by computers. If keywords which represent the concepts of images were indexed, it must be useful for retrieving images.

We propose a method of indexing images by keywords. We call this method as relative indexing. This method assumes that there are some images which are already indexed by keywords. As is shown in Figure 6, the images which are already indexed are located at some corners of a sphere, and an image which is going to be indexed is located at the center of the sphere in the beginning. The user can move the to-be indexed image near to the images which, he thinks, are near to the to-be indexed image in some sense such as that the theme of the images are close or most of the contents of the images are same. Then, the to-be indexed image gets the same keywords from the nearby images with weights in

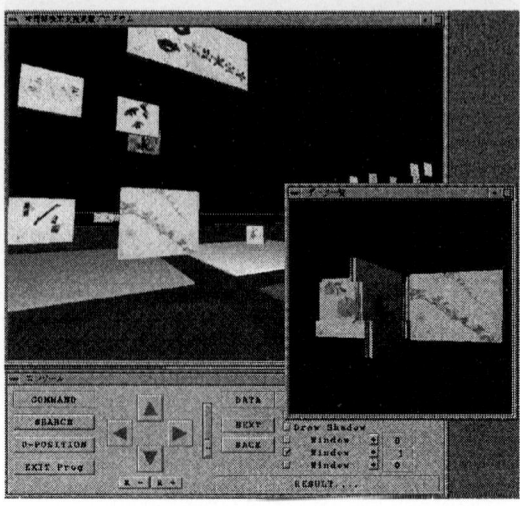

Fig. 4. Animation of images.

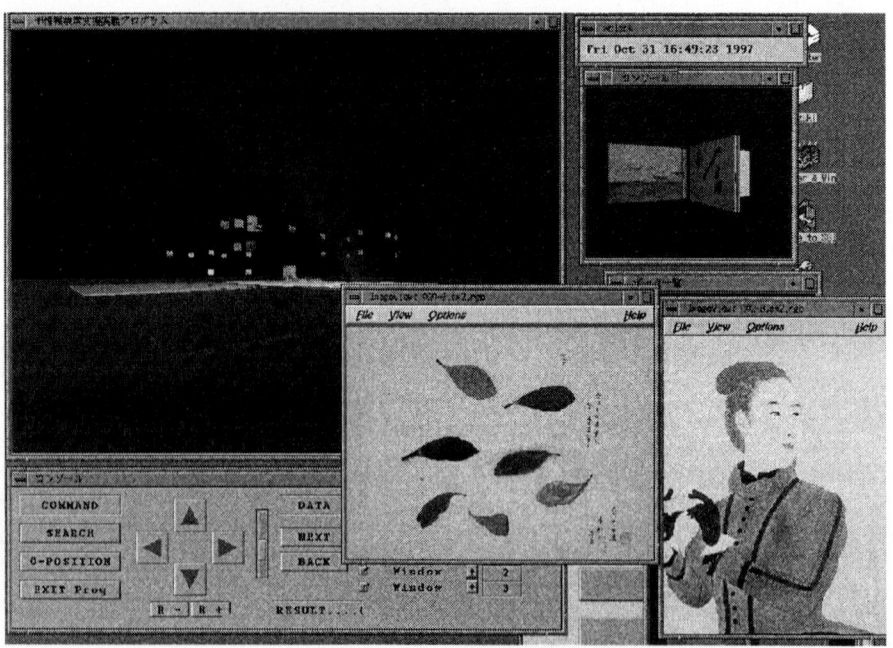

Fig. 5. Total views of Moving-VW.

proportion to distances from nearby images. These keywords and their weights can be changed manually for completion.

We implemented the relative indexing and evaluated by an experiment. We compared the keywords indexed by the relative indexing and the keywords indexed manually. The result of the experiment shows that 70in the manual indexing and in the relative indexing. There is an experimental result which shows that among the keywords which were indexed to a same image by different two persons, 70is nearly same as the manual indexing.

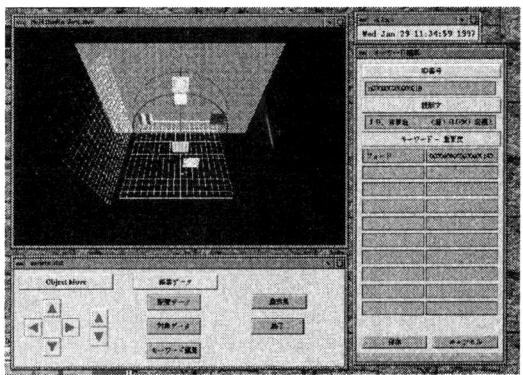

Fig. 6. Relative indexing in the image world.

8 Summary and Future Works

Moving-VW was described. Moving-VW is a human centered world, whose content is a collection of images, such as flowers, brush paintings and Japanese fine arts. The world has directions in it and reconfigures itself as the center of the world is changed by human. So, the world corresponds to human. The world can animate images in order to give a good view of the images. And also, in order to index images, it offers a tool which visualizes relative relations of images. This indexing method is called the relative indexing.

Moving-VW has just implemented, and is being evaluated now. Some experiments show that the relative indexing is as precise as manual indexing.

Our future works will be, animating of the whole world, giving rays to the world, creating a view points which gives human a new perspectives of the world and superimposing of the outlines of the objects in images on the display for giving integrated views.

References

1. X. Lin: A self-organizing semantic map for information retrieval, in Proceedings of the annual international ACM SIGIR conference on research and development in information retrieval, pages 262-269, 1991.
2. C. Williamson and B. Shneiderman: The dynamic HomeFinder: Evaluating dynamic queries in a real-estate information exploration system, in Proceedings of the annual international ACM SIGIR conference on research and development in information retrieval, pages 338-346, 1992.
3. C. Plaisant: Dynamic queries and visual information seeking interfaces, in Proceedings of the international symposium "Info-Tech '94", pages 26-32, 1994.
4. H. Kimoto: The interactive multi-directional information displaying system, in Proceedings of FADIVA3, an international workshop sponsored and organized by the Esprit working group 8422 "FADIVA", Gubbio, Italy, pages47-55, 1996.
5. M. Hemmje, C. Kunkel, A. Willett: LyberWorld - a visualization user interface supporting fulltext retrieval, in Proceedings of the annual international ACM SIGIR conference on research and development in information retrieval, pages 249-259, 1994.
6. R. Rao, J.O. Pedersen, M.A. Hearst, J.D. Mackinlay, S.K. Card, L. Masinter, P. Halvorsen and G.G. Robertson: Rich interaction in the digital library, Communications of the ACM, Vol.38, No.4, pages29-39, 1995.

Virtual Great Barrier Reef: A Theoretical Approach Towards an Evolving, Interactive VR Environment Using a Distributed DOME and CAVE System

Scot Thrane Refsland[1], Takeo Ojika[1], Tom Defanti[2], Andy Johnson[2], Jason Leigh[2], Carl Loeffler[3], and Xiaoyuan Tu[4]

[1]Virtual System Laboratory, Gifu University, 1-1 Yanagido, Gifu, 501 JAPAN
[2]Electronic Visualization Laboratory, University of Illinois at Chicago,
[3] Simation, P.O. Box 1984, Cranberry PA 16066,
[4]Intel Corporation, 2200 Mission College Blvd., RN6-35, Santa Clara, CA 95052

Abstract. The Australian Great Barrier Reef is a natural wonder of our world and a registered UNESCO World Heritage site hosting 1.5 million visitor-days in 1994/95. Tourism is currently the main commercial use and is estimated to generate over $1 billion annually.[1] With the coming 2000 Olympics in Australia, tourism increases will substantially present a major conservation and preservation problem to the reef. This paper proposes a solution to this problem through establishing a virtual reality installation that is interactive and evolving, enabling many visitors to discover the reef through high quality immersive entertainment. This paper considers the technical implications required for a system based in Complexity: a distributed DOME and CAVE architectural system; a mixed reality environment; artificial life; multi-user interactivity; and hardware interfaces.

1 Introduction

"Well, life emerged in the oceans," he adds, "so there you are at the edge [diving off the continental shelf], alive and appreciating that enormous fluid nursery. And that's why the 'edge of chaos' carries for me a very similar feeling: because I believe life also originated at the edge of chaos. So here we are at the edge, alive and appreciating the fact that physics itself should yield up such a nursery..."
   - Chris Langton, artificial life pioneer, commenting on Complexity.[1]

---

[1] Waldrop, M. Mitchell, 1992 Complexity, The Emerging Science at the Edge of Order and Chaos, page 231. Simon & Schuster, 1992.

1.1 A Cinematic Narrative Virtual Walkthrough

Jack, Jill and Tanaka have entered the Virtual Barrier Reef Exhibition, where "Nintendo" meets classroom. Before going into the environment, they have to choose from several different experiential options: Jack picks the "Marine Biologist," Jill picks the "Dolphin" and Tanaka the "Snorkeler."

Fig. 1. Overview of the Virtual Great Barrier Reef installation consisting of a 15 meter diameter DOME, Interactive WALLs, 3 CAVE systems and a motion simulator.

When they put on their equipment mainly consisting of 3D shutter glasses, audio communication and other interactive devices, they enter the Dive Vehicle (motion simulator) that takes them on a small "journey" to the reef. The Immersion hatch opens and they exit into the main DOME [Fig. 1] finding themselves immersed in 20 meters (60 feet) of water. The main DOME [2] (15 m diameter x 15m high, 360° x 180°), enables them to see fish and other species swim about in 3D. They see a mix of autonomous fish, avatars and avatar guides that assist, guide and role-play. They hear soundscapes of the reef. They can also see 3 CAVEs [3]. They were told that the installation was directly linked to the real reef to affect the climatic conditions within the installation. The installation's environment was persistent, evolving and adapting just like the real reef.

Jack finds a school of fish that holds his interest, and points to it using the "laser and" pointer on top of his Dive Panel. The panel displays the information about the fish, life habits, predators, eating, mating habits, etc. Then, a big grouper swims to him (guide avatar) and engages him in a conversation about the reef. A dolphin joins in and he finds out its Jill, and they are able to communicate together through the group communication channel with their headsets.

Tanaka finds an autonomous fish guide and several descriptor icons floating nearby. He selects the Japanese version. He inserts his smart card in the nearby stand, then experiments with the inter-related lives of the species inhabiting that community by moving the various avatars around with a Fish data Glove. At one point a mythical aboriginal character swims by and heads for one of the CAVEs. At the warning beep on each of their timers, Jill and Tanaka to return to the visitor's center. Jack extends his visit by buying more air directly through his smart card and Dive Panel. Once in the visitors' center, Jill and Tanaka insert their smart cards to get a color print out of their activities during their visit.

1.2 The Complex Architecture

The system is a large distributed network based upon proven, stable DOME and CAVE technologies. Similar reference models in which this project is based upon can be found in the past projects of NICE [4] and ROBOTIX: MARS MISSION [5].

The NICE project is a collaborative CAVE-based environment where 6 to 8 year old children, represented as avatars, collaboratively tend a persistent virtual garden. This highly graphical, immersive virtual space has primarily been designed for use in the CAVE, a multi-person, room-sized virtual reality system. As the CAVE supports multiple simultaneous physical users, a number of children can participate in the learning activities at the same time.

Interactive DOME projects including the Carnegie Science Center's "ROBOTIX: MARS MISSION, was the first example of Interactive Virtual Reality Cinema. Each audience member had a three button mouse device that allowed them to make group decisions on story and piloting spacecraft. The graphics were rendered in real-time, called from an extensive database of Mars's terrain from NASA. The partial dome sat 35 people, and was 200 degrees wide and 60 degrees high. The system used a SGI ONYX, with 4 R10000 processors, Infinite Reality Engine, Audio Serial Option board, and display boards. The polling system, custom built, fed into a PC which talked to the SGI. Majority vote ruled. The dome display used 3 state of the art Electrohome RGB projectors. Most important, only one graphic pipeline was used, and split into three views using custom built software and edge blending. The overlap on edges was 25%, and it appeared seamless and no distortion. Performance, 30-90+ fps, no lag. Audio was 3-D spatialized, custom built software, with floor shakers. It ran for 9 months, no glitches. Effective, there were some people who *thought* they went to Mars.

1.3 Methodology of Application

Whilst the true objective of this installation is to install a strong sense of conservation and preservation to the future visitors of the Great Barrier Reef, it seeks to apply it through a Constructionist [6] and "Immersive role-play" educative model steeped heavy in "Nintendo" style interaction of total consciousness submersion. Thus, our methodology objectives are simple – give the visitor an experience that they constructed for themselves, immerse them in wonder and inspiration, give them a reason to care, in their minds really take them there, and finally, afterwards give them something material they can use to prove and remember their experience.

2 Distributed DOME and CAVE Architectural System

2.1 The DOME Zone

The DOME zone is constructed of CG and real-time/pre-captured video which is projected onto the scrim of the DOME together in layers to assist with overall processing quality of CG and simulations. The background is a mix of live or pre-recorded scenes in the reef, and the CG fish are projected bright enough over the top of it to create the mixed illusion. Of course there will have to be certain areas, such as coral and other big blocks of CG that have to be animated, but these aren't that computationally intensive as they update on a slightly slower level.

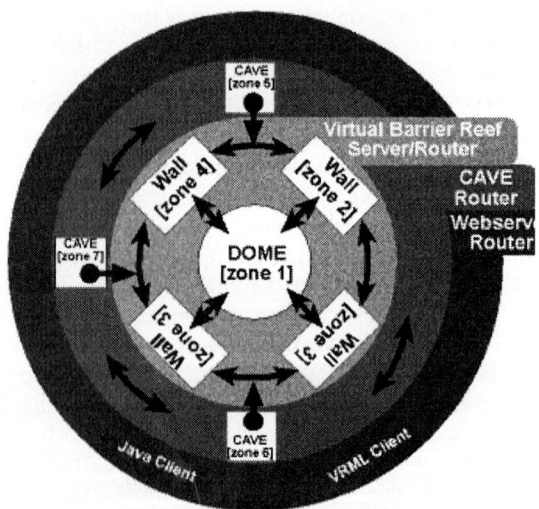

Fig. 2. Distributed Relationship of the DOME, CAVES, WALLs and the Internet.

2.2 Multiplexing and Mixed Topologies

Since the DOME is the central "Hub" [Fig. 2] of the environment physically, and holds the most connectivity to all other zones, we will use it as the focus to consider the many facets of multiplexing within the environment and the various other network topologies and protocols that connect to it.

2.3 The WALL Zones (4 WALLs)

The walls will be the most computational expensive of all the zones in the environment as most of the direct interactivity will happen around them. Walls are interactive in that they might have species that will react when visitors walk by them. Example would be an alife moray eel might come out to feed, and when a visitor walks up to it quickly, a sensing device gives it spatial reaction information. Spot projectors and smaller independent computer systems are displaying various small interactive displays, while the meta environment was separate and being processed by the SGI system.

2.4 CAVE Zones: (3 CAVEs)

CAVEs are separate zones or environments that are story related. They can host indigenous or mythical stories related to the reef and its inhabitants. Here the visitors can have a more immersive, intimate experience with the denizens of the reef, as the sea creatures swim and interact with the visitors within the 3 meter cube of each CAVE.

The CAVEs use the standard network topologies and protocols being developed as part of the CAVERN network [7] to deal with the multiple information flows maintaining the virtual environments.

Each of the CAVEs, WALLs, and the DOME making up the environment will be connected via a high-speed network, allowing information such as avatar data, virtual world state / meta data and persistent evolutional data to pass between them. This will allow avatars in the CAVEs to swim over onto the WALLS or the DOME, and allow museum guides in the guise of reef inhabitants to interact with the visitors. This will also allow remotely located CAVE users in the United States, Europe, and Asia to join into the collaboration. Similar connectivity has been used in the NICE environment [8] to link multiple CAVE sites in the United States to Europe and Japan.

3 Mixed Reality Environment

The environment of this project uses video, lighting, and sound techniques to establish an environment that convinces the user that they are indeed immersed in the Great Barrier Reef.

Video: Video will be used in strategic places includes some parts of the walls and the floor. The main imaging of the floor is video, with spot CG projections to provide a better illusion of immersion and non-repetition.

Sound: immersive and 3D in its localization, the sound system provides authentic sounds from autonomous life and "extra spatial" depth sounds.

3.1 Real-Time Connectivity to the Reef

Climatic Interference: The virtual model is connected real-time to a section of the real reef so that it can automatically adjust the virtual model. Temperature, current, air pressure and other climatic conditions on the reef will cause several actions in the virtual environment, such as temperature of the room, flow of the virtual debris, virtual water currents, etc.

3.2 Complex and Evolving Environment

This environment is considered to be a "living entity", possessing an authentic as possible simulation to the real reef.

For simulating simple fluid flow, we consider techniques similar to the ones used by Wejchert and Haumann Wejchert 91 [9] [Fig. 3] for animating aerodynamics.

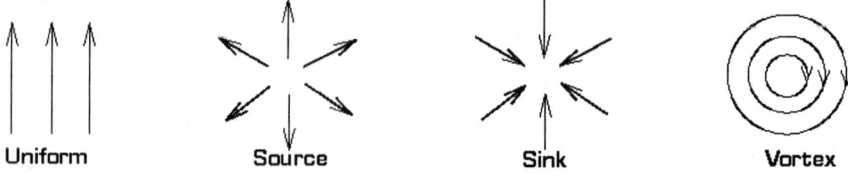

Fig. 3. The flow primitives (reproduced from the paper by Wejchert and Haumann)

Assuming inviscid and irrotational fluid, we can construct a model of a non-turbulent flow field with low computational cost using a set of *flow primitives*. These include *uniform flow* where the fluid velocity follow straight lines; *source flow*--a point from which fluid moves out from all directions; *sink flow* which is opposite to the source flow; and *vortex flow* where fluid moves around in concentric circles. This process is also directly linked with the real reef current flow that is constantly supplying real-time information. Both of the processes integrated together enable lower computation requirements and increase the authenticity of the virtual environment.

Much of the seaweed, plankton, coral and other movable plant/marine life are simulated and respond dynamically to water currents and movements of other life in a realistic manner. In this case it is proposed to use a system which builds the plants in a mass-spring chain assembly. In order to obtain computational efficiency, we do not calculate the forces acting on the geometric surface of each plant leaf, rather, we approximate the hydrodynamic force at each mass point.

4 Artificial Life

The artificial life treatment in this project is an exciting and innovative one. As mentioned earlier, one of the educative goals in this project is to enable people to "think like a fish" so they can experience first hand through the "eyes of a fish" what it's like to live on the reef.

To achieve this, we have developed two types of models for Alife. The first model is a totally autonomous animal that behaves according to the events in the environment. It has a life span, is integrated into the ecological system, and possesses authentic behaviors of its real life counterpart.

The second model is a similar model, only that the "brain and motor skills" are detached and placed into the control of a visitor using a dataglove to direct the fish. The innovation here is that even though a visitor is controlling the "will and motor" of the artificial fish, it still has behavior and characteristic traits that will not allow you to act outside of the character set for that fish.

4.1 Artificial Animals for Life-Like Interactive Virtual Reef Creatures

What's the key to bringing you a captivating experience as a tourist of the virtual Great Barrier Reef? Whether you are merely observing the schools of sardines, playful dolphins and vicious sharks, or you are living the aquatic life by playing the role of one of the virtual reef dwellers (want to be a dolphin, parrot fish or maybe a reef shark? Sure you can), realism is the password to the ultimate immersive experience. Here we are not just talking about visual authenticity in the appearance of the digital sea creatures, but also in their physical environment, and most importantly, in the way they move, perceive and behave. In an interactive environment like ours, behavioral realism, especially, autonomy of the virtual creatures is indispensable.

How are we to achieve such integrated realism? Our answer is to build Artificial Life (or Alife) models of the aquatic animals. The properties and internal control mechanisms of these artificial animals should be qualitatively similar to those of their natural counterparts. Specifically, we construct animal-like autonomy into traditional graphical models by integrating control structures for locomotion, perception and action. As a result, the artificial fishes and mammals have 'eyes' and other sensors to actively perceive their dynamic environments; they have 'brains' to interpret their perception and govern their actions. Just like real animals, they autonomously make decisions about what to do and how to do in everyday aquatic life, be it dramatic or mundane. This approach has been successfully demonstrated by the lifelike virtual undersea world developed in [10, 11].

We tackle the complexity of the artificial life model by decomposing it into three sub-models:
- *A graphical display model* that uses geometry and texture to capture the form and appearance of any specific species of sea animal.
- *A bio-mechanical model* that captures the physical and anatomical structure of the animal's body, including its muscle actuators, and simulates its deformation and dynamics.
- *A brain model* that is responsible for motor, perception and behavior control of the animal.

As an example of such an artificial life model, [Fig.4] shows a functional overview of the artificial fish that was implemented in [10, 11]. As the figure illustrates, the body of the fish harbors its brain. The brain itself consists of three control centers: the motor center, the perception center, and the behavior center. These centers are part of the motor, perception, and behavior control systems of the artificial fish. The function of each of these systems will be previewed next.

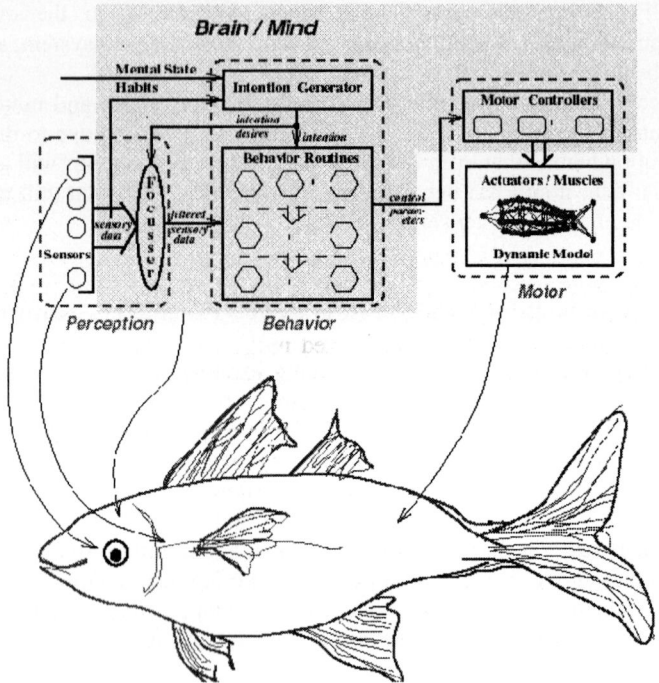

Fig. 4. Diagram of an autonomous and avatar model fish

4.2 Motor System

The motor system comprises the dynamic model of the sea creature, the actuators, and a set of motor controllers (MCs) which constitutes the motor control center in the artificial animal's brain. Since our goal is to animate an animal realistically and at reasonable computational cost, we seek to design a mechanical model that represents a good compromise between anatomical consistency, hence realism, and computational efficiency. The dynamic fish model [12, 13] represents a good example. It is important to realize that adequate model fidelity allows us to build motor controllers by gleaning information from bio-mechanical literature of the animal [14, 15] Motor controllers are parameterized procedures, each of which is dedicated to carrying out a specific motor function, such as ``swim forward'', ``turn left'' or ``ascend''. They translate natural control parameters such as the forward speed, angle of the turn or angle of ascent into detailed muscle or fin/leg actions. Abstracting locomotion control into parameterized procedures enables behavior control to operate on the level of motor skills, rather than that of tedious individual muscle/limb movements. The repertoire of motor skills forms the foundation of the artificial animal's functionality.

Given that our application is in interactive VR systems, locomotion control and simulation must be executed at interactive speed. Physics-based dynamic models of animals offer physical realism but require numerical integration. This can be expensive when the models are complex.

There are various ways to speed things up. One way is to have multiple models of increasing complexity for each species of animal. For example, the simplest model will just be a particle with mass, velocity and acceleration (which still exhibits basic physical properties and hence can automatically react to external forces, such as water current, in a realistic manner). The speed-up can then be achieved by way of 'motion culling', where when the animal is not visible or is far away, only the simplest model is used and the full mechanical model is used only when the animal is near by. This method, however, is view-dependent and can be tricky when the number of users is large. Another way is to use bio-mechanical models whenever possible (when they are simple enough to run the simulation at real time) and with more complex animals, we can build pre-processed, parameterized motion libraries (which can be played back in real time), like what is used by most of today's games. These (canned) motion libraries can be built from off-line simulations of elaborate bio-mechanical models of the animal or from motion-captured data. One thing to keep in mind is that, no matter what the underlying locomotion model is, its interface to the behavior system should be kept comparable as parameterized procedures of motor skills.

4.3 Perception System

Perception modeling is concerned with:
1. Simulating the physical and optical abilities and limitations of the animal's perception.
2. Interpreting sensory data by simulating the results of perceptual information processing within the brain of the animal.

When modeling perception for the purposes of interactive entertainment, our first task is to model the perceptual capabilities of the animal. Many animals employ eyes as their primary sense organ and perceptual information is extracted from retinal images. In a VR system, such "retinal" images correspond to the 2D projection of the 3D virtual world rendered from the point of view of the artificial animal's "eyes". However, many animals do not rely on vision as their primary perceptual mode, in which case vision models alone may not be able to appropriately capture the animal's perceptual abilities.

It is equally important to model the limitations of natural perception. Animal sensory organs cannot provide unlimited information about their habitats. Most animals cannot detect objects that are beyond a certain distance away and they usually can detect moving objects much better than static objects [14]. If these properties are not adequately modeled, unrealistic behaviors may result.

Moreover, at any moment in time, an animal receives a relatively large amount of sensory information to which its brain cannot attend all at once. Hence there must be some mechanism for deciding what particular information to attend to at any particular time. This process is often referred to as attention. The focus of attention is determined based upon the animal's behavioral needs and is a crucial part of perception that directly connects perception to behavior.

Unfortunately, it is not at all well understood how to model animal sensory organs, let alone the information processing in the brain that mediate an animal's perception of its world. Fortunately, for our purposes, an artificial animal in its virtual world can readily glean whatever sensory information is necessary to support life-like behavior by directly interrogating the world model and/or exploiting the graphics-rendering pipeline. In this way, our perception model synthesizes the results of perception in as simple, direct and efficient a manner as possible.

The perception system relies on a set of on-board virtual sensors to provide sensory information about the dynamic environment, including eyes that can produce time-varying retinal images of the environment. The brain's perception control center includes a perceptual attention mechanism which allows the artificial animal to train its sensors at the world in a task-specific way, hence filtering out sensory information superfluous to its current behavioral needs. For example, the artificial animal attends to sensory information about nearby food sources when foraging.

4.4 Behavior System

The behavior system of the artificial animal mediates between its perception system and its motor system. An *intention generator*, the animal's cognitive faculty, harnesses the dynamics of the perception-action cycle and controls action selection in the artificial animal. The animator establishes the innate character of the animal through a set of *habit parameters* that determine whether or not it likes darkness or whether it is a male or female, etc. Unlike the static habits of the animal, its mental state is dynamic and is modeled in the behavior system by several *mental state* variables. Each mental state variable represents a distinct desire. For example, the desire to drink or the desire to eat. In order to model an artificial animal's mental state, it is important to make certain that the modeled desires resemble the three fundamental properties of natural desires: (a) they should be time varying; (b) they should depend on either internal urge or external stimuli or both; (c) they should be satisfiable. The intention generator combines the habits and mental state with the incoming stream of sensory information to generate dynamic goals for the animal, such as to chase and feed on prey. It ensures that goals have some persistence by exploiting a single-item memory. The intention generator also controls the perceptual attention mechanism to filter out sensory information unnecessary to accomplishing the goal in hand. For example, if the intention is to eat food, then the artificial animal attends to sensory information related to nearby food sources. Moreover, at any given moment in time, there is only one intention or one active behavior in the artificial animal's behavior system. This hypothesis is commonly made by ethologists when analyzing the behavior of fishes, birds and four-legged animals of or below intermediate complexity (e.g. dogs, cats) [15, 16]. At every simulation time step, the intention generator activates behavior routines that input the filtered sensory information and compute the appropriate motor control parameters to carry the animal one step closer to fulfilling the current intention. The intention generator Primitive behavior routines, such as obstacle avoidance, and more sophisticated motivational behavior routines, such as mating, are the building blocks of the behavioral repertoire of the artificial animal.

5 Interfaces

Because it is our past experience that all technology much be bulletproof and withstand the rigorous demands of an unrelenting public, this equipment is designed along the lines of actual DIVE equipment which is very durable and rugged, big and easy to use.

5.1 Tracking/Sensing

A number of tracking options are available, his environment will consider the use of mix from magnetic [17], to un-encumbered technology such as camera based systems [18]. Sensing the bulk of visitors is done with infrared and video. Specific occupant tracking is done either with localized gloves cabled to the specific site location, or through wireless. Shutter glasses should be independent and able to sense any WALL or CAVE. Artificial Life use sensing to establish the location of visitors within the environment and can respond to them as a normal fish would respond.

5.2 Weight Belt with Dive Panel

This equipment enables visitors to interact with the environment and gain statistical information about the life species in the installation. The weight belt holds the battery pack and wireless communications, tracking and wand/pointer hardware, and a smart/memory card slot for recording individual data and experiences. Attached to it is a "Dive Panel" which is a pointing wand, and small LCD monitor to display information about the species that are under investigation, and other climatic information. Through this, the visitor is able to access the knowledge base stored on the memory card and other data being generated real-time.

5.3 Enhanced Shutterglasses

Shutter glasses are connected to a timer so that when the visitor's use all their "air", they shut down and are inoperable. This makes the environment very difficult to see and forces the visitor to exit the installation. Some of the more sophisticated models for avatars and "Marine Biologists" have audio communications built in.

5.4 Taking Home a Bit of the Virtual Reef

Something else that we think is really important from NICE is giving people some kind of artifact from the experience. Since VR is such a rare experience, and you really can't take anything physical away from the virtual space, it helps people when they try to describe what they did to other people, and enhance the experience and memory of the event.

Each participant in the virtual reef environment gets a smart/memory card to record a "narrative" of everything they did, characters they talked to, actions they performed.

The narrative structure captures these interactions in the form of simple sentences such as: "Mary (disguised as a dolphin) stops by to see Murray the Moray eel to find out what he eats. Mary and Murray have dinner together."

The story sequence goes through a simple parser, which replaces some of the words with their iconic representations and stores the transcript onto their Memory card. This gives the story a "picturebook" style that the visitor can print out and keep to remember the various aquatic life they met that day.

5.5 Smart/Memory Cards

We are currently investigating the use of Smart/Memory Cards to perform functions like: tracking and recording the user's actions, supplying a knowledge database, and providing financial calculations for visitation fees.

6 Interactivity

6.1 Visitor Interactivity

Avatar: There are many species in which a visitor can explore, from fish and other animals. Avatars can be as simple as the ones found at the localized exhibits for tourists to try out, to the sophisticated ones like dolphins and sharks. Avatars ultimately come under the domain of the simulated eco-cycle, so anything could happen: the visitor's avatar could be eaten at any time, and eventually will go through the entire life cycle of the reef.

Snorkeler: This level is simple roaming and exploring the environment with minimal hardware, such as shutter-glasses to immerse them in 3D. The smart card enables them to utilize the local interactive stands available throughout the environment.

Marine Biologist: This level of interaction is highly independent and is able to program their own interactivity levels for simulation, planning, studying, etc. The equipment this visitor has is the most advanced versions of the standard models.

6.2 Artificial Life Interactivity

The artificial life in the environment is just as interactive towards visitors as visitors are to them. They can and will interact with visitors in many different behaviors, from being friendly, territorial, viscous, funny, etc. Fast movement will scatter fish. In this way, true interactivity is two-way, creating a complex environment.

6.3 Staff Interactivity

Guides: These are sophisticated avatars that can interact with anyone in the environment. These people can be in the environment or hidden from view. They have audio and visual communication devices to drive avatars such as Mermaids, large fish, human animations or indigenous characters. This level of interactivity can be used for guided tours, assistants, observers and other special requirements. At this level, the guide is able to leave discovery objects which visitors can touch and find out more information.

7 Conclusion and Future Works

This system has been designed using existing and known solutions of virtual reality, networking, evolutionary theory and artificial life, and yet, the innovation lies within the organization of each application into complexity. It has been designed with the forethought of being able to use the physical architecture as a generic shell to enable other stories besides the reef to be told, and the application able to be used in other systems, including retrofitted Planetariums.

Acknowledgements

The Gifu Research and Development Foundation and The International Society on Virtual Systems and MultiMedia, Gifu Japan
The virtual reality research, collaborations, and outreach programs at the Electronic Visualization Laboratory (EVL) at the University of Illinois at Chicago are made possible through major funding from the National Science Foundation (NSF), the Defense Advanced Research Projects Agency, and the US Department of Energy; specifically NSF awards CDA-9303433, CDA-9512272, NCR-9712283, CDA-9720351, and the NSF ASC Partnerships for Advanced Computational Infrastructure (PACI) program. EVL also wishes to acknowledge Silicon Graphics, Inc. and Advanced Network and Services for their support. The CAVE and ImmersaDesk are trademarks of the Board of Trustees of the University of Illinois.

References

1. McPhail, I. The Changing Environment of Managing Use in the Great Barrier Reef World Heritage Area Presented at the ABARE Outlook '96 Conference, Melbourne, February 1996. Great Barrier Reef Marine Authority
2. Goto Virtuarium DOME system.
3. Cruz-Neira, C., Sandin, D.J., and DeFanti, T.A. "Surround-Screen Projection-Based Virtual Reality: The Design and Implementation of the CAVE." In Proceedings of

SIGGRAPH '93 Computer Graphics Conference, ACM SIGGRAPH, August 1993, pp. 135-142.
4. Leigh, J., DeFanti, T., Johnson, A., Brown, M., Sandin, D., "Global Tele-Immersion: Better than Being There,." In the proceedings of 7th International Conference on Artificial Reality and Tele-Existence. Tokyo, Japan, Dec 3-5, 1997, pp. 10-17.
5. Carnegie Science Center, "ROBOTIX: MARS MISSION",
6. Piaget, J. To Understand is to Invent: The Future of Education. Grossman, New York, 1973.
7. Leigh, J., Johnson, A., DeFanti, T., "Issues in the Design of a Flexible Distributed Architecture for Supporting Persistence and Interoperability in Collaborative Virtual Environments,." In the proceedings of Supercomputing '97 San Jose, California, Nov 15-21, 1997.
8. Johnson, A., Leigh, J., Costigan, C., "Multiway Tele-Immersion at Supercomputing '97." To appear in IEEE Computer Graphics and Applications, July 1998.
9. Wejchert, J. and Haumann, D. Animation aerodynamics. ACM Computer Graphics, SIGGRAPH'91, 25(4): pp.19-22. 1991.
10. Tu, X. 1996. Ph.D Thesis, Department of Computer Science, University of Toronto.
11. Tu, X. and Terzopoulos, D. Artificial fishes: Physics, locomotion, perception, behavior. In ACM Computer Graphics, Annual Conference Series, Proceedings SIGGRAPH'94, pages 43-50, Orlando, FL. ACM Computer Graphics. 1994
12. Blake, R. Fish Locomotion. Cambridge University Press, Cambridge, England. 1983.
13. Alexander, R.. Exploring Bio-mechanics. Scientific American Library, New York. 1992.
14. Tansley, K. Vision in Vertebrates. Chapman and Hall, London, England. 1965.
15. Tinbergen, N. The Study of Instinct. Clarendon Press, Oxford, England. 1951.
16. Manning, A. An Introduction to Animal Behavior. Addison-Wesley Publications, Massachusetts, 3rd edition. 1979.
17. Semwal, S., Hightower, R. Stansfield, S., Closed form and Geometric Algorithms for Real-Time Control of an Avatar, Proceedings of IEEE, VRAIS96, pp. 177-184 (1996).
18. Krueger, M., Artificial Reality II. Addison Wesley Publishing Company, Reading, MA pp. 1-277 (1991).

The Development of an Intelligent Haulage Truck Simulator for Improving the Safety of Operation in Surface Mines

Mr. Matthew Williams, Dr. Damian Schofield, and Prof. Bryan Denby.

AIMS Research Unit, School of Chemical, Environmental and Mining Engineering,
University of Nottingham, UK.
enxmw@unix.ccc.nottingham.ac.uk

Abstract. Surface mines are in operation world-wide, the vast majority employ large haul trucks for the transfer of material both to the outside world and around the site. The sheer size of these trucks and the operating conditions means there is a high level of risk. Allied to this, the commercial nature of the operation means that down time is extremely costly and driver training expensive. The AIMS Research Unit has developed a PC based system to improve driver training which is currently being developed into a commercial application.

Scenarios are created by importing site specific data through industrial CAD systems, road systems are then added through an editor to create good replicas of the environment facing drivers on a day to day basis. The world is further enhanced by allowing the user to specify a number of intelligent objects including haulage trucks, excavators with load points and various static objects.

Once scenarios have been created training is carried out on a full screen real time simulation which allows trainees to drive or be driven by computer through the world. At any given point the trainee is able to stop the simulation and identify potential hazards, their associated risk, and take possible corrective action.

Keywords: Driving Simulators, Safety Training, Virtual Reality, Hazard Awareness, Surface Mining.

AIMS Unit

The AIMS Research Unit at the University of Nottingham has been involved in the fields of computer graphics and virtual reality for a number of years and has identified a number of potential applications for the engineering industry. In particular it now appears that the technologies have developed sufficiently and costs reduced to levels that mean even the smallest companies can seriously consider them.

The AIMS Unit uses a range of commercial packages and programming languages to create new computer based applications. Development takes place on both PC and Silicon Graphics platforms. However the unit has found that systems developed using PC technology are more easily ported to the industry due to reduced costs, the existing user base and the familiarity of PC technology [1].

Background

There are many surface mines in operation throughout the world, all of these require the safe transfer of material around the site. In many cases this is achieved by haulage trucks, these large vehicles, often the size of a small house, have many associated safety issues.

Their huge size together with the difficult environmental conditions introduces handling and visibility problems. There is a high level of risk associated with each truck, as the consequences of an accident can be extremely severe. Strict operational rules are enforced to minimise the potential for disaster, whilst these have been successful in reducing accidents, by 1995 industrial trucks were still the second leading cause of fatalities in the private sector behind only highway vehicle fatalities [2]. Indeed the OHSA found on average 107 fatalities and 38,330 injuries occurred annually in the workplace, furthermore it found present training standards to be ineffective in reducing the number of accidents involving powered industrial trucks.

At the moment only trained operators can drive these trucks, periodic evaluation of each truck drivers performance is also required. Competency will depend on the ability of the vehicle operator to acquire, retain, and use the knowledge, skills and abilities that are necessary.

Financially, haulage trucks are the largest cost item in the operating costs of a surface mine in some cases accounting for an estimated 50% of operating costs [3]. The large initial cost of these trucks also makes driver training expensive.

Attitudes towards industrial safety have advanced significantly in recent years and the mining industry has not been an exception to this. The introduction of new legislation in the UK [4] has changed the emphasis of industrial law from prescriptive legislation into new management systems.

Large mineral organisations are now continually looking for ways to improve their safety performance and techniques, which may help to reduce accident statistics, need to be investigated. The capacity to remember safety information from a three dimensional world is far greater than the ability to translate information from a printed page into a 'real' three-dimensional environment [5].

AIMS Unit Truck Simulator

System Details

The system has been designed to run on a PC platform, prospective users identified this as particularly important due to the wide availability and low cost of the platform. The system used for training operates as a full screen application and provides both visual and 3D audio output. Trainees are able to interact with the system in a number of ways including through a custom built steering wheel and pedals.

The system is split into two modules, the first is an editor allowing the trainer to configure and save a number of different scenarios, the second runs as a full screen simulation during training sessions. Both parts have been programmed in Visual C++ and DirectX is used as the graphics and sound API, this allows access to acceleration across a wide range of hardware.

System performance varies according to the size of environment, however advances in graphical accelerators mean that high frame rates have been maintained despite using large pit meshes. The system has a high level of graphical detail, this is quite important during the process of training as it is often the ability to spot visual details that ultimately leads to safe operation.

World Modelling

As mining progresses from phase to phase, haul road networks and truck routes must adapt as the landform changes. To create more relevant training scenarios, it was important that the trainer should be able to accurately recreate the work place and conditions. This ranges from road layouts, truck movements and loading points through to lighting and fogging conditions to simulate different weather conditions.

The application we have developed reduces the cost of creating new worlds by using currently available pit data. Surface mine operators maintain 3D models describing the development of the terrain and possibly haul road layout for each distinct operating phase. These are maintained in industry standard modelling packages such as Vulcan or Surpac. Mesh data held in these packages can be exported directly into the system and used as a base mesh for the virtual world.

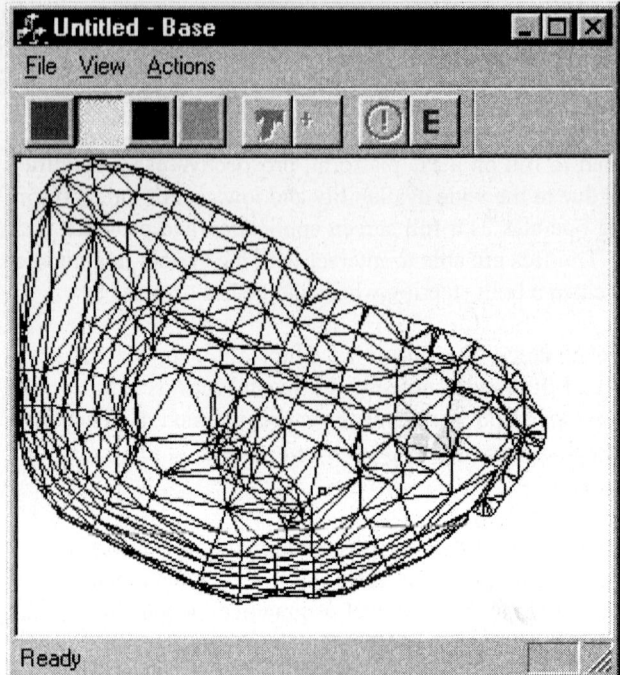

Fig. 1. 2D pit during configuration

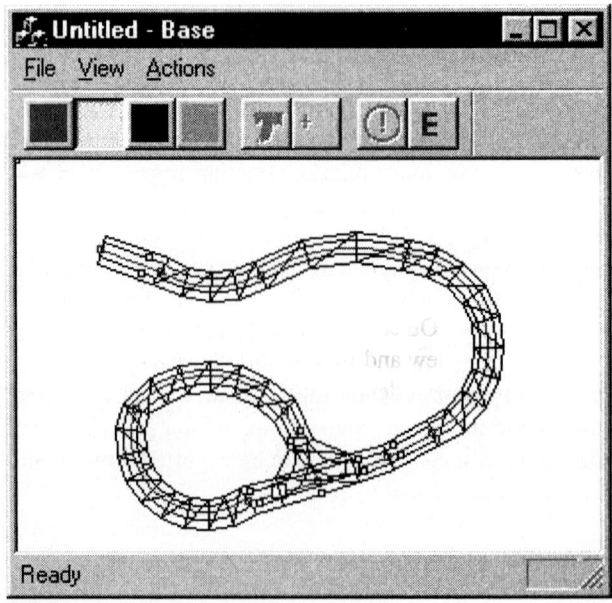

Fig. 2. Construction of the haul road

Haul road information is overlaid using 2D drawing tools, it is then converted to a 2D road system, before being subtracted from the base model. Height values for the haul road are obtained through an averaging process on local vertices, smoothing also takes place on each segment of the road so that the surface remains flat. The road system is then re-triangulated back into the original mesh and textures are applied to both. This process creates a haul road system consisting of a number of straight, curved, and multiple exit junctions, this not only helps to reduce the polygon count but also to reduce the computational overhead during simulation.

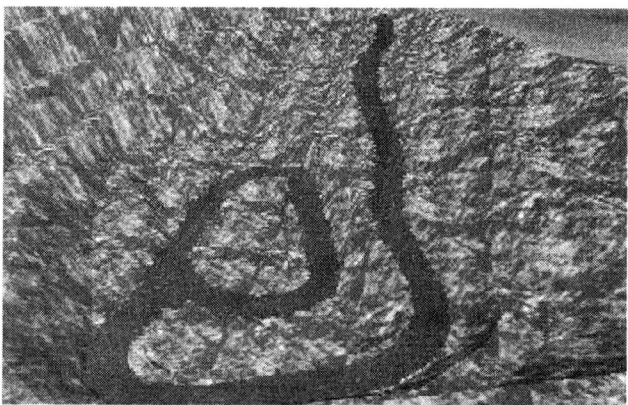

Fig. 3. Textured pit and haul road

All further objects, their attributes and behaviours are added into the scenario at this stage by clicking on a 2D plan of the environment, the third height dimension is automatically calculated. The addition of objects and the configuration of their behaviours has been kept as simple as possible to reduce the complexity of defining new scenarios.

Haulage trucks are added by indicating the start, finish and waypoints through which they must pass. Excavators are added by defining the segment in which they load and the direction from which trucks approach. Other objects, such as Surveyors, parked vehicles and road signs are added in plan view and their associated height values are again calculated. Further haul road system details can also be configured, this includes assigning priority at multiple exit junctions.

Intelligent Behavioural Modelling

Truck position and velocity is calculated in real-time and is based on industry standard rimpull and retarder curves, these together with factors such as mass, and gradient provide an accurate simulation. Interaction with surrounding objects is also taken into account before updating a truck's position.

Trucks attempt to follow user-defined routes based upon the road network that has been created, these are pre-calculated as far as possible by storing an ideal line which the trucks attempt to follow. Trucks will take a predefined route through the pit to the load point, where they queue to be loaded before proceeding to the dump point, and the cycle begins again. Trucks also have the intelligence to modify their position, velocity, and acceleration during the simulation according to the state of localised equipment. Figure 4 shows an example of multiple computer-controlled trucks queuing to be loaded. The simplification of the haul network allows extensive details as to the position of the truck within each segment to be monitored as well as allowing the truck to look ahead analyse potential situations and adjust its behaviour accordingly.

Fig. 4. Trucks queuing to be loaded

Training Methods

Trainees may either drive or be driven (by the computer) around a pit. Training is primarily achieved through a technique termed 'hazard spotting', this allows the user to identify a number of pre-determined hazards which are included in the virtual world. As the trainee passes through the pit they are able to stop the simulation at any time to 'spot' these hazards. Once identified, they are asked to classify the hazard in terms of risk, and indicate any corrective action which should be taken. Performance is recorded and responses assessed against ideal behaviour. Figure 5 shows such a choice being made.

Fig. 5. Risk choice being made

Future Work

Work is currently being carried out to improve the current system and also to extend its scope. Proposed is a pre-start up equipment check allowing the trainee to inspect his vehicle prior to entering the simulation. Planned improvements for the current system include the use of multiple monitors to provide additional viewpoints and using aerial photographs as textures to overlay the pit. Development is also being carried out on using similar techniques in other industrial environments.

Conclusions

Virtual reality seems to be an ideal way of exposing trainees to hazardous situations without ever putting them at any real risk. Additionally a large number of potentially rare circumstances can be experienced in a relatively short period of time. However, there is still doubt as to how well these skills transfer to the real world. Work with other vehicle simulators indicates that there can be a significant reduction in accidents [6] so it would be reasonable to expect similar results.

The system has yet to receive field testing, however it has been demonstrated to a large number of mining institutions whose response has been very positive. Representatives particularly liked the fact that they could create and configure multiple scenarios from existing CAD data quickly and easily. It is anticipated that the system will be commercially available in the next few months.

References

1. Schofield, D., Denby, B. and McClarnon, D., Computer Graphics and Virtual Reality in the Mining Industry, Mining Magazine, p284 - 286, Nov. 1994.

2. OSHA, Powered Industrial Truck Operator Training, Internet WWW page, at URL: http://gabby.osha-slc.gov/FedReg_osha_data/FED_19950314.html, 1995 (Version Current 22nd January 1997).

3. Mueller, E.R. Simplified Dispatching Board Boosts Truck Productivity at Cyprus Pima, Mining Engineering, Vol. 68, No. 4 72-76 1979.

4. Health and Safety Commission, Management of Health and Safety at Work Regulations 1992. Approved Codes of Practice, HSMO, London, 1992.

5. Schofield, D., Virtual Reality Associated with FSV's Quarries and Open Cast Vehicles - Training, Risk Assessment and Practical Improvements, Workshop on Risks Associated with Free Steered Vehicles, Safety and Health Commission for the Mining and Other Extractive Industries, European Commission, Luxembourg, Nov. 11th-12th 1997.

6. U.S. News, Steering Clear of Danger, Internet WWW page, at URL: http://www.usnews.com/usnews/issue/truckb.htm, (Version Current 25th February 1998).

Navigation in Large VR Urban Models

Vassilis Bourdakis

Centre for Advanced Studies in Architecture, University of Bath, UK.
Email: V.Bourdakis@bath.ac.uk

Abstract. The aim of this research project is to utilise VR models in urban planning in order to provide easy-to-use visualisation tools that will allow non-experts to understand the implications of proposed changes to their city. In this paper, the navigation problems identified whilst working on large VR city models are discussed and a "fly" based navigation mode is proposed and evaluated.

1 Background

The Centre for Advanced Studies in Architecture (CASA) has been involved in three-dimensional (3D) computer modelling for the last six years. In 1991 CASA received a grant to construct a 3D computer model of Bath [2]. The project was supported by Bath City Council and since its completion the model has been used by the city planners to test the visual impact of a number of proposed developments in the city. The model was created from aerial photographs of the city in 1:1250 scale using a stereo digitiser. It is accurate to 0.5 metre and covers the whole historic city centre, an approximate area of 2.5x3.0 km. During 1995 and using similar techniques, the core of London's West End covering 1.0X0.5km was also modelled followed by Gloucester city centre in 1997.

Following the hardware and software developments of the last few years, the expansion of the Internet and the World Wide Web (WWW) and current trends in the industry, the Bath and London model were translated and are used non-immersively in VRML as well as custom made VR applications [2][3]. The initial problem faced was how VR applications would scale and adopt to visualising a whole city of over three million triangles as in the case of Bath. The Bath database is, to the author's knowledge, the largest and most detailed one produced as yet; the UCLA Dept. of Architecture and Urban Design (AUD) is currently building a model of the entire Los Angeles basin covering an area in excess of 10000 square miles as part of *"The Virtual World Data Server Project"* but it is still under construction.

2 Utilising VR Urban Models

The computer models created in CASA demonstrate how computers will be used in the near future by engineers as part of their everyday practice, creating, modifying and improving our cities online using centrally stored sharable databases. The aim is not to create yet another Geographical Information System (GIS) although GIS features can be incorporated. Using Internet compatible programming languages such as Java, Cobra or ActiveX, VR urban models can replace a dedicated GIS system for certain applications (London's West End). It should be noted that due to the nature of the proposed use of the models, the low polygon count fully texture mapped model approach adopted by more commercial/advertising oriented projects (Virtual Soma, Virtual LA etc.) was not feasible.

The Bath model has been used in a variety of ways since it was originally constructed. To date, development control has been the main use with a number of schemes being considered. These are normally at the instigation of the local authority who recommend that schemes are modelled in order to facilitate discussions during the design phase and for presentation to the planning committee. In addition to its use in development control, the model has also been used to widen the public debate on how the city should develop in the future.

The model of London's West End is of lower level of detail and was initially used for transmitters' signal propagation experiments by British Telecom (BT). CASA has been using it as a database front end to navigating and mapping information on the city thus creating the Map of the Future. Gloucester's city centre model which was commissioned by the Gloucester City Council is used for planning control similarly to the Bath one.

3 Navigation Problems

Early in the process of creating VR models, the problem of navigation was identified together with inconsistencies on texture mapping, instancing, materials, indexing, etc. Although most of the problems were solved [9], navigation remains a troublesome experience not only to occasional users of the VR models but to the creators as well.

The main problem in exploring, navigating and generally working with urban models in a VR environment (both immersive and non-immersive) is orienting oneself; being able to identify areas, streets, buildings etc. Therefore, a great deal of effort has been put towards making urban models more recognisable. It should be noted that there is a great difference between pursuing realism and aiming for a recognisable virtual environment (VE); a VE does not necessarily imitate reality [5]. Creating realistic VE of such scale is still not feasible and in many cases both pointless and inappropriate.

In real life, when a person becomes disoriented in a urban environment, the natural action taken is to scan the surroundings searching for *information*. As Lynch [14] explains, there is a consistent use and organisation of definite *sensory cues* from the external environment.

Assuming no external help is requested, this activity comprises of three steps:
- Look around
- Move around within a small radius
- Wander further away with the added complexity the person may subsequently fail to return to the original position.

Failure of the above three steps means that more drastic ones must be taken. This typically involves interaction with other people asking shop owners, pedestrians, car drivers, etc. for the relevant information. Alternatively, one could check road names against a map, in extreme cases even consult a compass.

3.1 Current Trends

There have been many attempts, both commercial and theoretical, to create and interact with informational spaces [6]. Techniques have been developed based on both "realistic" and "unrealistic" concepts but it seems there is no consensus as yet. Putting aside the information space metaphors used, the navigation metaphors employed can be classified in two main categories; the *screen* and the *world* based ones. Among the former is sliding, rolling and examining whereas the latter include walking with or without physical constrains (gravity and collision detection), flying above the landscape and above the roof line utilising a bird's eye view of the city and borrowing from cinematic terminology, panning and tilting.

Game development is an area that one can review design decisions; a very efficient, demand driven, competitive environment enforcing quick, effective development cycles.

Early 3D games like Doom and Descent, where the focus was on speed and interactivity, featured fairly simple environments. Each stage had an average of 10-20 rooms/spaces with quite different shapes, textures and themes in general. Furthermore, the overall settings for these games were not real 3D; players could not share plan co-ordinates (XY) with different elevations. The cues facilitating navigation were plenty, with the different types of enemies and, in some games, even their corpses adding to the amount of visual information available. Auditory cues were vital in sensing events that took place in secluded areas or simply behind the players' back. In such games a 2D wireframe plan of the site was the only navigation hint given to the players and was usually enough to get them back in course.

In the more recent "action" games like Tomb Raider and Tie Fighter, the following important differences can be identified:
- The player's avatar is fully included in the VE. The player is not a spaceship dashboard or a weapon carrying hand anymore but a fully articulated avatar giving better sense of scale and participation [11]
- More advanced navigation aids are used (notably compasses, text narration, lighting, sound etc.)
- Real-time rendering of texture mapped animated characters

- Collision detection and gravity
- "Director's" Camera Movement. Camera zooms and moves around the action (that is the player's avatar) creating a feeling of a well-directed action movie rather than a simple game playing (Tombraider). Subsequently, wandering in the rooms becomes a worthwhile experience itself!

The scale issue addressed with the full avatar presence is the most notable improvement together with the use of perspective and camera movement to follow the action. The above mentioned points can be and in a few cases are already employed in VR urban models' interface. Information providing with position and orientation of the user visible as well as custom dashboards featuring compasses are possible. Additionally, audio data, animated objects can be incorporated.

3.2 "Flying" Modes of Interaction

In this paper, the focus is on the implications of employing a "flying" based navigation mode. It is argued that due to the lack of sufficient detail at street level, the "identity" and "structure" of the urban image is much "stronger" from an elevated position, when more distant cues are visible. This is especially true in the CASA built models considering the fact that the 3D models were created from mainly aerial information; facade surveys were carried out but the main core of information came from stereo pairs of aerial photographs. The roofline is very accurately represented in geometry and colour without the need for textures or complicated geometrical hierarchies. In many cases, roof level detail had to be eliminated in order to keep an overall balance within the VE.

Among the problems linked to the "fly" mode is that it effectively removes any degree of immersion by switching the person to map reading mode (some will argue that it furthermore defies the reason of having a VE in the first place). Prior knowledge of the city is advantageous whereas there is a distinct lack of sense of time and effort needed to travel over a VE.

Furthermore, according to Ihde [12] there is evidence that there are important connections between the bodily-sensory perception, cultural perceptions and the use of maps as navigational aid. He relates the bird's eye view of flying over a VE to the God's eye map projection identified in the literary cultures. This mode of interaction has definite advantages although it also introduces an often-unknown perspective of the city. This perspective is more accessible to engineers and architects who are used to working with scale models of sites which inherently introduce the bird's eye view. According to Tweed [18], the relationship between flying and walking modes should reflect to orientation of the body position, making flying modes more akin to immersive VR systems.

It should be noted that it is possible to add street level detail in order to improve the amount of information -sensory cues available by adding:
- Street furniture (lamp-posts, phone-boxes, bus stops, litter boxes, road signs, tarmac markings ...)
- Building detail (Textures + geometry)

- Animated elements (vehicles, people, etc.)
- 3D Sound and pre-rendered shadows
- Trees, landscaping, flowerbeds etc.

However, more often than not, time and cost constrains prevail (surveying and modelling are both costly and time consuming) not to mention the hardware platform limitations [13]. Adding street furniture, landscaping and animated elements puts the burden on both hardware and software. Frame rate is an issue; from experiments carried out already in CASA, the indications are that 5-6Hz is the lowest acceptable level for such applications assuming the key issues addressed above are catered for. However, frame rate is not the most important variable in urban scale models—a 30Hz VE of an inferior model lacking the key issues is not a satisfactory solution.

It should be noted that urban VE rely very heavily on visual cues in many cases ignoring the fact that aural cues could be more powerful and helpful [7]. This can be credited to the fact that most such models are created and used by architects and engineers in general who are traditionally not taught to understand and appreciate the importance of sound in an environment, even more so in a VE.

3.3 Limitations of Non-immersive VR

VR models that are used in a team evaluation environment are usually non-immersive. The main reasons are practical; if all the committee members are to be gathered together in one room, the amount of hardware and cables running on the floor, the size of the room and the overall support required is unfeasible. The cost of the necessary hardware to provide a fully immersive experience for half a dozen planners and other committee members is prohibiting. Finally, the need for interaction and communication while evaluating a scheme and the need for a common reference point when assessing a particular feature would be extremely difficult to achieve in an immersive environment [1]. For such tasks, the Reality Centres that Silicon Graphics Inc. has created are ideal; pseudo-immersive double curvature, wide screen displays with a single operator. On the downside, the assessors' team has to travel to the particular site (only a handful in the whole UK) and the costs involved are outside the budget of a City Council or local authority.

Nevertheless, there are important navigation advantages to be obtained on a single user immersive VE as opposed to a multi-user one.

One of the problems identified in early experiments is the lack of concept of time and distance. Walking on the streets of a virtual city is an effortless exercise in contrast to the real experience. It is possible to fly over a whole city model in a matter of seconds and that can be instrumental on loosing both orientation and sense of presence. Recent attempts in immersive VE tried to introduce body interfaces to navigation. Shaw [16] used a bicycle as the metaphor for navigating in his installation *The Legible City*. This way, the pedalling speed sets the speed of movement whereas the handlebars determine the direction. Another metaphor used with movement tracking devices is that of walking on the spot [17]. The pattern of body movement relates to pre-computed patterns and determines whether the user walks, runs or steps back. Char Davies has created a synthetic environment called "Osmosis" [8] exploring the relationship between exterior nature and interior self where the immersant's body movements are triggering series of events that position the body within the VE and even alter the environment itself.

Among the first techniques employed in the Bath model in order to improve sensory cues from the environment was the use of wide angle lens; the argument being that this way a greater part of the city is visible and thus more information is transmitted to the user. However, the results of a small scale case study with university students of architecture and other members of staff familiar with the city where discouraging. Architects identified the problem as being that of "wrong perspective" compressing the depth of the image and generally creating a "false" image of the city. Others could not easily identify the problem but found the environment confusing nevertheless. Consequently it was decided to use only the "normal" lens on all VR projects although it does limit the perceived field of view which in real life is much higher than 45 degrees. Experiments on level of detail degradation in the periphery of head mounted displays (HMD) [19] as well as eye movement and feedback [4] demonstrate that more efficient VR interfaces can be achieved (compared to non-immersive ones) without necessarily hitting on the main VR problem; CPU capabilities.

Another problem faced in non-immersive VR is that of the direction of movement versus direction of sight. Due to the two dimensionality of the majority of input devices used in non-immersive VR, it is assumed that the user looks at the exact direction of the movement. This is quite true in most cases, but when one learns and investigates a new environment, movement and direction of viewing should be dealt as two individual variables. Immersive VR headsets with position and orientation tracking mechanisms are again the easiest and more intuitive solution to this problem.

Therefore the *Variable Height Navigation Mode (VHNM)* is introduced as another solution to the problem.

4 Variable Height Navigation Mode

The VHNM is based on the fact that at any given position in a urban model, there must be a minimum amount of information - sensory cues - from the external environment available to assist navigation. This can be achieved by adding enough information on the model although this is rarely an option as was discussed earlier. Alternatively it can be achieved by varying the height of navigation according to the amount of sensory cues available on any given position.

As an example, a wide long street with a few landmarks will bring the avatar down close to street level, whereas a narrow twisted street in a housing area will force the avatar high above the roof level.

4.1 Theoretical Model

In the real world, the sun, the wind, a river, the sound emitted from a market or a busy street, a church, a building, a street, a road sign, a set of traffic lights are among the *sensory cues* accessible and used by people. Furthermore, each person gives different importance to each of them making the whole process of classifying and evaluating visual cues much more difficult. In a VE, which is generally much less densely occupied and furnished by the above-described elements, classification is relatively easier. Although the user must be able to rank the relative importance of the various cues available, the designer of the VE can assign with relative safety *what is* a sensory cue within the VE.

The theoretical model proposed uses a series of gravity like nodes or *attractors* [7] that pull the avatar towards the ground when approaching an area of high density in sensory cues. Similarly, in low-density areas a global negative gravity pulls the avatar towards the sky until there are enough sensory cues nodes visible to create equilibrium. It should be noted that the *attractors* are not true gravity nodes since they can only affect the elevation of the avatar and not its position in plan.

The first emerging issue is that of cues' visibility. In order to identify the visual cues available from each position the field of view and the direction of viewing is considered. Following, a ray-tracing algorithm is employed in order to assess visual contact from the current position. Considering the size of the object, a series of rays must be calculated to establish the percentage visible from the current position.

Relative importance of the visual cues is essential if the model is to be successful. A general ranking of them can be carried out by the world designer based on the size, form, prominence of spatial location, historic value, users awareness, etc. However, the navigation mode proposed should be flexible enough to accommodate particular needs of the users. Locals will use completely different cues (depending on the culture, could be pubs, churches, prominent buildings, etc.) to the first time visitors who will probably opt for the ones described in their guide books and the ones that possess the main landmark characteristics as defined by Lynch [14].

Another variable relates to the amount of visual cues users received over time while navigating in the VE. The higher the amount the better the mental image of the city they have created. According to Lynch [14], sequential series of landmarks where key details trigger specific moves of the visitor is the standard way that people travel through a city (p.83). VHNM keeps track of the number of visible cues, their distance from the users' path the speed and direction of movement and finally the time each one was visible. All that can recreate the path followed and should enable the prediction of areas of potential problems and modify the current elevation accordingly. In the event of orientation loss, it would be possible to animate back to a position rich in visual cues, a kind of an 'undo' option. The main question in animating back to a recognisable position is whether the user should be dragged backwards (as in a process exactly reverse to the one they followed) or if the viewing direction should be inverted so that a new perspective of the city is recorded. The argument for the former is that the user will be able to directly relate to the actions taken only minutes ago, whereas the latter has the advantage of showing a new view of the city and the disadvantage that the process of memorisation may break down.

Consequently, the VR application can be trained over a period of time and eventually be able to react and adjust to the habits and patterns followed by each user. Keeping track of the time spend on particular areas of the VE will enable the computer adjust the avatar's position on the assumption that the recognition process and memorisation will strengthen the more time one spends at a particular place within the model.

The tilt of the viewing should be also briefly considered. Walking at ground level and looking straight ahead is what people are used to, but when one is elevated twenty, thirty or more metres above the ground level the perspective distortion introduced by tilting and looking downwards should be considered. As described earlier, an often unknown perspective of the city is introduced and the effects it may have on different users should be carefully evaluated.

Concluding, the theoretical VHNM model proposed will be quite difficult to implement in real time with existing computing power in large VR urban models. It is currently an extremely difficult task to structure the geometric database alone; setting up all the raytracing calculations and the fairly complex set of rules described above will seriously affect the performance of any VR application. However, some problems may be alleviated by reorganising the scenegraph, which conflicts with the general concept of spatial subdivision of large VR models and their organisation in Levels of Detail as discussed extensively elsewhere [2],[3].

Fig. 1. VHNM mesh on the Bath model. Typical view

Finally, it should be pointed out that the focus of this paper is limited on the visual cues. Experiments are still to be carried out regarding the employment of auditory cues in an urban VE.

4.2 Model Implemented

Having described the ideal system an attempt is made to put it into practice. Bearing in mind the difficulties in implementing the original concept, a collision detection based navigation mode is initially proposed (Fig. 1). A transparent and thus invisible mesh is introduced, "floating" above the urban model. The peaks of this mesh are where the minimum amount of sensory cues are, so in a way it is an inverted 3D plot of the sensory cues against the 2D urban plan. Using a 2D device, such as a mouse, it is possible to navigate in the VE whilst collision detection against the invisible mesh determines the elevation of the viewer (Fig. 2).

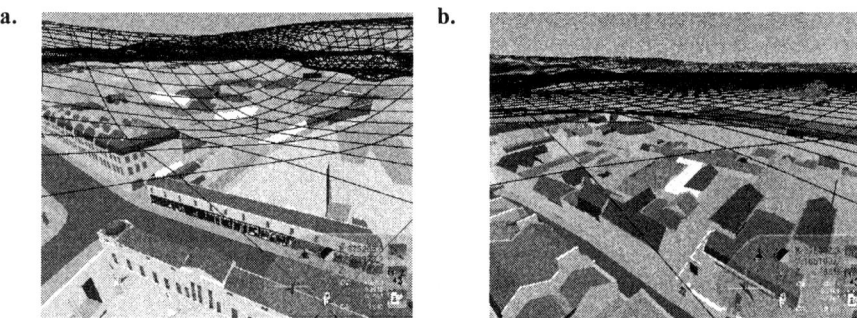

Fig. 2. VHNM views on **a.** high and **b.** low visual cue areas

Early in the development stage, it was decided to represent the VHNM mesh as a visible five-metre wireframe grid, giving users a reference point to the height they are and an extra orientation directional grid. Consequently, the VHNM mesh clearly denotes which areas of the model are lacking sensory cues and by creating visible peaks on them, it actually presents cues of its own to aid orientation and exploration. Following extensive testing, it was concluded that for the Bath model, areas rich in sensory cues can be successfully explored at a height of 25 to 35 metres above street level (10 to 15 metres above the buildings' roofline). Regarding areas that proved problematic in the initial navigation experiments, 40 to 50 metres above street level produced good results. It was attempted to keep the height variation to distance ratio as low as possible to avoid user confusion and make navigation and movement smoother. It should be noted that the values mentioned above were satisfactory in the particular urban model but it is unlikely they will be suitable for a high-rise or a very densely built area. Experimentation will provide the right values and most likely a mathematical model will be developed once the VHNM is tested on London's West End and Gloucester City centre models also developed in CASA.

In order to accommodate for the different needs of varying groups of users, the VHNM mesh can be shifted along the height axis (Z) according to the familiarity of the user to the urban model presented (Figure 3c,d) using on screen controls. It is also possible to alter the scale of the mesh along the Z-axis. Doing so, the viewer drops lower closer to the ground on areas rich in sensory cues and flies higher on poor areas (Figure 3a,b). The first experiments carried out using the manually created VHNM meshes were quite successful in reducing the amount of confusion and orientation loss. However, no statistical analysis of the data obtained has been carried out yet, since controlling such an experiment proved extremely difficult. Consequently, most of experimentation was used for fine-tuning the technique and the variables involved. A series of tasks are currently being developed in order to create a more controlled environment enabling drawing of conclusions on the effectiveness of the proposed method and creating a test bed for evaluation of future work.

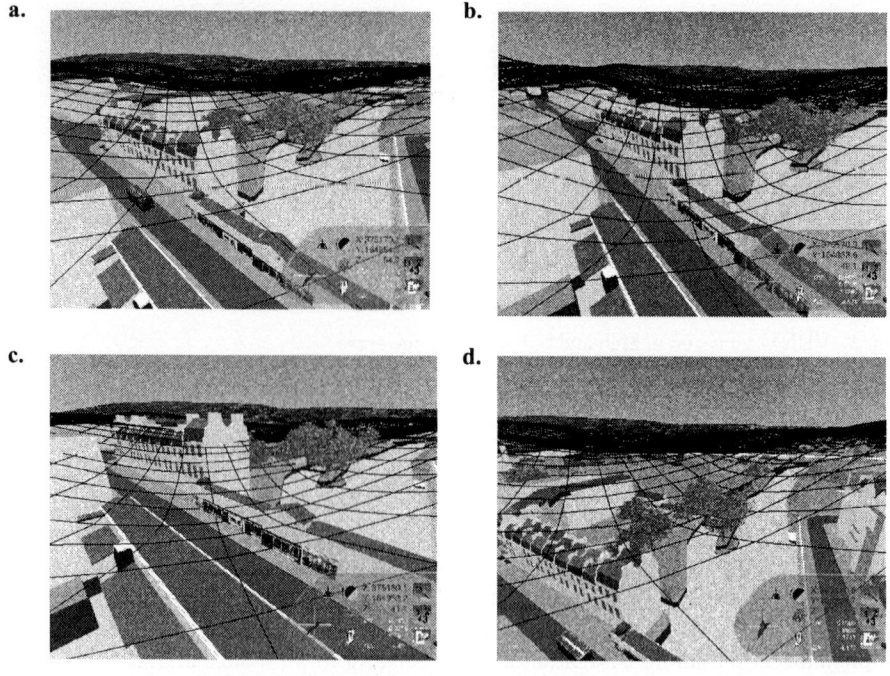

Fig. 3. VHNM Editing options, **a.** normal, **b.** scaled up, **c.** shifted down, **d.** shifted up

Among the limitations of this implementation is that the computationally expensive ray-tracing calculations needed to accurately create the mesh, were approximated in advance manually. Consequently, the already complicated and difficult job of the VR application is not stressed any further by having to compute gravity nodes and search for cues in the VE. However, generating this mesh is a very laborious process and difficult to automate. Furthermore, the VHNM mesh completely disregards the avatar's viewing direction. In most positions within an urban model, the cues available are strongly related to the viewing direction. Looking north may give no clues whatsoever whereas turning 180 degrees and facing south may reveal the position of the sun (at least in the north hemisphere) and a landmark that will let you pinpoint your position on a map. Users have no option to classify the relative importance of the type of cues available according to their own needs. It is a pre-calculated VE that one is only allowed to navigate in, which is conflicting with the general conceptions of the service computers should be providing [15].

The next step will be to incorporate the visual cues versus time variable in the model and investigate to what extend the behaviour of a visitor can be predicted and augmented. Following, auditory cues will be included while work will be carried out into finding ways to simulate more accurately the theoretical model proposed.

5 Conclusions

The proposed VHNM can solve certain problems in urban VR environments and if implemented fully could be a very successful navigational tool. However, bearing in mind the complexity of the proposed model, an immersive VR environment would supplement a partial implementation of VHNM more economically, in terms of cost, ease of programming and time needed to construct and fine tune the VR system. The implementation problems of the proposed VHNM can be tackled with different degrees of complexity and accuracy according to the capabilities of the VR platform used.

References

1. Billinghurst, M. and Savage-Carmona, J. (1995). *Directive Interfaces for Virtual Environments.* P-95-10 HITL University of Washington.
2. Bourdakis, V. and Day, A. (1997) *The VRML Model of the City of Bath*, Proceedings of the Sixth International EuropIA Conference, europia Productions.
3. Bourdakis, V. (1996) *From CAAD to VRML: London Case Study*, The 3rd UK VRSIG Conference; Full Paper Proceedings, De Montfort University.
4. Brelstaff, G. (1995) *Visual Displays for Virtual Environments – A review* in Proceedings of the Framework for Immersive Virtual Environments Working Group.
5. Carr, K. and England, R. (1995) *Simulated and Virtual Realities: Elements of Perception.* Taylor and Francis, London.
6. Charitos, D. (1996) *Defining Existential Space in Virtual Environments* in Virtual Reality World96 Proceedings.
7. Charitos, D. and Rutherford, P. (1997) *Ways of aiding navigation in VRML worlds* Proceedings of the Sixth International EuropIA Conference, europia Productions.
8. Davies, C. and Harrison, J. (1996) *Osmose: Towards Broadening the Aesthetics of Virtual Reality*, in ACM Computer Graphics: Virtual Reality (Volume 30, Number 4).
9. Day, A., Bourdakis, V. and Robson, J. (1996) *Living with a virtual city* ARQ, Vol2.
10. Fritze, T. and Riedel, O. (1996) *Simulation of complex architectural issues in virtual environments* in Virtual Reality World96 Proceedings.
11. Gibson, J.J. (1986) *The Ecological Approach to Visual Perception.* London
12. Ihde, D (1993) *Postphenomenology*, North Western University Press, Minnesota.

13. Kaur, K., Maiden, N. and Sutcliffe, A. (1996) *Design practice and usability problems with virtual environments* in Virtual Reality World96 Proceedings.
14. Lynch, K. (1960) *The image of the city* MIT Press, Cambridge, Mass.
15. Negroponte, N. (1995) *Being Digital* Hodder & Stoughton.
16. Shaw, J. (1994) *Keeping Fit*, @Home Conference, Doors of Perception 2, Netherlands Design Institute, Amsterdam.
17. Slater, M., Usoh, M. and Steed, A. (1995) *Taking Steps: The Influence of a Walking Metaphor on Presence in Virtual Reality*, ACM Transactions on Computer-Human-Interaction (TOCHI) Vol.2, No3.
18. Tweed, C. (1997) *Sedimented Practices of Reading Design Descriptions: from Paper to Screen* Proceedings of the Sixth International EuropIA Conference, europia Productions.
19. Watson, B., Walker, N. and Hodges, L.F. (1995) *A User Study Evaluating Level of Detail Degradation in the Periphery of Head-Mounted Displays* In Framework for Immersive Virtual Environments FIVE'95 Esprit Working Group 9122, QMW University London.

World Wide Web sites mentioned in the text:

VRML2 Spec:	http://vag.vrml.org/VRML97/
Bath Model:	http://www.bath.ac.uk/Centres/CASA/bath
London W.E.:	http://www.bath.ac.uk/Centres/CASA/london
Virtual L.A.:	http://www.gsaup.ucla.edu/bill/LA.html
Virtual Soma:	http://www.hyperion.com/planet9/vrsoma.htm

Art and Virtual Worlds

Olga Kisseleva

Today`s world is characterized by an explosion of new communication technologies and unique uses which modify our behaviour and our thought processes. Confronted with this evolution, we are waiting for a new form of life to emerge corresponding to these technologies. A new art form corresponds to this existence, not merely by tools that it uses but through the questions that it raises.

We can thus note that with the intervening changes in society, scientific progress, and the change in the general relation between art and life, the artist's role today is radically new. Contemporary art has changed its function in relation to modern art in the sense that it resembles more and more a science.

Since its conception, art has appeared as a representation of a life ideal, relative to one time. Contemporary art doesn't reflect life. It prefigures it. At present , thanks to the new digital technologies and communication,art itself can become a simulation of reality: an immaterial digital space which we can literally pentrate and,as Fred Forest says, is no longer , a " self-defining form . It is itself a picture, formalized numerically. Dimensional space is no longer an intangible substratum. It is a digital object in interaction with other created objects , having its own reality".

Art exists thus as the counterweight and the complement of science, so that the two together complete the human discovery process. The artist creates, therefore, from concept to analysis while the scientist works from analysis to concept. The artist elaborates a concept as a starting point from which he participates in the construction of a world. If he succeeds in proving the reality of his concept, it will develop to become part of the collective conscience. On the contrary, the scientist analyzes, researches, studies,and experiments before formulating his concept. In this way, science reveals our knowledge of the world , exploring it step by step, while art interests itself with experience of the world,offering us concepts that permit us to glimpse immediately another, more intuitive, vision of the universe.

Finally, the questions that artists ask themselves in their research are extremely close of those of scientists. Communication artists and researchers, working on the problems of communication are confronted, according to Pierre Moeglin, by the same question: In our modern age, to what do we owe this central position ceded to video, to the computer and to telecommunications? Certainly not, they answer, to the sophistication of these technologies, installing a difference of technological application but not of its inherent nature in relation to the previous techniques. Furthermore, we can say that while pushing their limits to phenomena that are not all new - several were already germinating during the first industrial revolution - uses are made systematically revealing better than before the wider dimension of diffusion that includes our relation to others and ourselves as well as the access that we have to work, to leisure and culture .

The vocation of art, as well as that of science,has changed. Art's role is no longer to entertain but to communicate something about the nature of the human mind: the scientist teaches from his scientific paradigm, the artist from his vision of the world.

The different and unique nature of cyberspace permits us to simultaneously approach and escape from reality. Today we are not content with computer-driven animation but moreso with attempting to recreate life, to breathe independant life into these " beings " of pixels and algorithms. It is about giving birth to these " virtual " creatures, capable of learning and evolving.

Virtual reality in relation to the real world implies an isolation. It seems the most obvious expression of a man / machine system in which man plays an integral part. In this universe, movements, or even physiological data and human brainwaves, can be controled by sensory stimulations used like commands. It is a device placed in contact with our body, in our senses, on and maybe one day even under our skin, directly in our brain, if one succeeds in developing brainchips. Some researchers even speak about associating the computer system directly to the human brain. Our senses will then be pacemakers that activate our brain by their signals transformed into electric activity.

More and more realistic "clones", shall circulate throughout the network, with all manners of functionality and with an impressive delegation of power devolving directly from their "game-masters ". The mixture of reality and virtuality applies directly to the creation of cloning. Thus, the putting into movement of virtual actors in real time can be of use in as different domains as teleworking, videoconferences, virtual communities,multiparticipant games or 3D animation. These actors are derived from real faces, then sculpted in 3D before finally being cloned. The animation of clones is produced then in real time: the face of the user drives directly his duplicate with the help of a camera and a treatment of images while the top of the body is directed with the help of two sensors, one on each hand. The user can communicate thus with other clones, to submerge and to interact within a 3D universe.

At the same time, avatars install in the network a new aesthetic that would be the one of Tex Avery with a touch of Tolkien and a personality like the Simpsons. Masters identify more and more with their virtual image, so that avatars impose themselves in their daily life and transform their minds little by little as well astheir own body.

The MUD and the MOO (carrying trades and games in 3D), that are developed in the same way as Internet, evolved in the same sense. Their virtual reality, founded first exclusively on the text, moved toward the conviviality and exchanges ludiqueses with representations in 2D and 3D of users nominees as of avatars.

Artificial comedians also became the object of various researches, in the scientific laboratories and in artistics studio. Interactivity in real time with these comedians became possible with the tele-animation of characters from movements and the mimic of real actors equipped with datasuits and sensors.

Currently, the technical progress, the rythm of life and especially the new technologies of communication, are changing the body. The body is replacing by prostheses. the usefulness of its senses, sometimes leaving only one activated, deconstructed it. The body is seized and transposed in the virtual world, it is cloned and finally it is substituted by a new virtual body, the avatar. The body loses its consistence therefore, its substance, its value, and even its biologic role; it turns into interfacing.

The carnal art, created by Orlan, interrogates the statute of the body at the genetic manipulation age, as well as its future that turns to a gosthly appearance . The virtual, to Orlan, does not only consist to multiply the body and to be telepresent, but also to accept the reconfiguration and the sculpting of the body. For her seventh operation-surgical-performance, implants, normally used to heighten cheekbones, were placed on every side of her forehead . It created two bumps. These bumps, being totally virtual, "avatar ized" the body of Orlan.

As one saw it, the imitation of gestures and even of some human senses is today easy. But the virtual makes also possible the control of senses. Indeed, it reintroduces a kind of individual sovereignty, even though it is rather illusive. Of course, our sensory perception is necessarily coded, because of our cultural, social or personal history. Nor uncertain nor genetic, it is the result of the modelling to which all society proceeds. However, in the virtual reality, this modelling proves to be more restricting, more precise. This testifies well that sensory control is more there a fantasy. Therefore in a reasoning: "The sovereignty of the individual is maybe then restored. But at the same time, his liberty is forced infinitely, since, being not anymore a prey to confusions of the world or of the meetings, he cannot feed himself anymore with their wealth".

Las Meninas in VR: Storytelling and the Illusion in Art

Hisham Bizri, Andrew Johnson, and Christina Vasilakis

Electronic Visualization Laboratory
University of Illinois at Chicago, Chicago, IL 60607, USA
(312) 996-3002 voice, (312) 413-7585 fax
bizri@evl.uic.edu, http://www.evl.uic.edu/chris/meninas/

Abstract. Las Meninas is a virtual reality (VR) artwork based on the painting of the same name by Spanish painter Diego Velazquez. Created for the CAVE(tm), Las Meninas attempts to establish a language of art in virtual reality by placing VR in the realm of storytelling; storytelling that is not simply formalistic and decorative, but also psychological. The viewer confronts a narrative cryptogram which can be deciphered at multiple levels of meaning as he seeks to explore the enigmas inherent in the painting by literally entering into it, both physically and psychologically. This allows for the suspension of disbelief or the illusion in art, the quintessential rule of art.

Keywords

ontological authenticity, kinesthetic / synesthetic stimulation, immersion.

1 Introduction

Many people who have experienced virtual reality (VR) for the first time will attest that they were amazed by the unique perceptual experience, but that their emotional and thoughtful involvement was minimal. This is not surprising since many virtual reality works are, in large part, exercises in visual effects, and not intended as part of a meaningful narrative where form and function are interconnected. To achieve such a narrative, a *language of art* in VR needs to be established. The depiction of *Las Meninas* in VR attempts to establish such a *language* by placing VR in the realm of storytelling that is not simply formalistic and decorative, but also psychological.

The quintessential rule of art is its ability to suspend disbelief and create the *illusion of art*. Through convincing representation, the illusion in art manifests itself, forcing the viewer to become psychologically involved. *Las Meninas* involves the viewer in a psychological narrative imagined as a complex web of signs. The viewer confronts a narrative thread which can be deciphered at multiple levels of meaning. Each deciphered thread embodies a network of signs leading to other signs. If the viewer fails in his initial task he confronts another set of signs to choose from which will lead to other sets. The viewer's psychological inquiry into the narrative and her attempt to decipher its cryptograms places emphasis on her *reactions* to the virtual world and not the virtual world itself.

Fig. 1. Las Meninas as painted by the Spanish painter Diego Velazquez in 1656.

For the work to function at the psychological level and achieve the illusion in art, the viewer must *believe* in the nature of representation the virtual world portrays. The primary concern of *Las Meninas* in VR is focused upon the mechanism of certain effects and not their causes. That is to say, the viewer explores relationships rather than individual elements. However, for this investigation to occur, two elements are necessary: ontological authenticity and kinesthetic/synesthetic (k/s) impact. Once these elements are fulfilled, the *illusion in art* in VR becomes possible.

2 Storytelling Specificity in VR

Las Meninas, or *The Maids of Honor*(1656) by the great Spanish painter, Diego Velazquez, as shown in figure 1, challenges the viewer with its allegorical subject matter and enigmatic mise-en-scene [4,7]. From the outset the viewer confronts the artist's canvas which is forever hidden from view. The viewer desires to see what is hidden and at the same time witnesses a mise-en-scene which carries within itself multiple allegorical meanings: the pictures decorating the walls of the room in Velazquez's composition - subjects from Ovid's *Metamorphoses* painted by Mazo after the originals by Rubens [1]; specifically, the two pictures hanging high on the rear wall, over the mirror, *Pallas and Arachne* and *Apollo and Pan*; the mirror in the black frame at the back of the room which reflects the half-length figures of King Philip IV and Queen Mariana under a red curtain but nothing else; the mysterious light shining in from the upper right side of the room; the magical stillness of the room and the people in it, as if photographed, forcing the viewer to believe himself to be actively present at the scene; the painter himself whose "dark form and lit-up face represent the visible and the invisible" [3]; the lame devil, Jose Nieto, standing in the background in an open doorway; the imaginary space lying out of the picture frame where Velazquez, the Infanta, her maid, the girl dwarf, and Jose Neito are looking, each from a different point, at the sovereigns, who are in theory standing next to the viewer; and so forth.

The allegorical subject matter and enigmatic mise-en-scene work together in Velazquez's painting to *dramatize* the *inner focal point* of the realm of the painting and the *outer focal point* of the realm of reality - the viewer's position. The viewer is at once *seeing* and *being seen*. He constantly oscillates between *objective realism* and *subjective* paradoxes arising from the emblematic interpretations which the overall mise-en-scene lends itself to. Vision is no longer fixed on a single vanishing point, but is now *dispersed* over multiple planes of form, function, and subjective meaning. The painting raises questions about the nature of representation and subjectivity in a unique way rarely matched in the history of visual art.

In the CAVE [2], the painting of *Las Meninas* becomes the virtual reality of *Las Meninas*. The viewer is able not only to explore certain problems pertaining to the nature of representation and subjectivity, but also face further enigmas. The ten foot tall painting, which matches the size of one of the CAVE's large projection screens, becomes an immersive environment where several people can experience the work simultaneously, as shown in figure 2. The theoretical questions the painting raises become tangible and empirical once placed within the boundaries of VR. In other words, the painting's fixed and traditional nature of representation and subjectivity take on a dynamic and physical aspect once the center of vision is *dispersed* in the medium of VR.

Fig. 2. Two photographs of viewers within *Las Meninas* in the CAVE.

Las Meninas in VR approaches the question of representation and subjectivity from various angles. Ontological authenticity and k/s stimulation establish a frame of reference from which these questions ensue. The frame of reference consists of four characteristics. First, the fusion of optical and virtual images. Second, the creation of multiple guides - both visual and aural. Third, the creation of a *total environment* and the *double articulation of time*. Fourth, the dramatic shift from the formalistic to the psychological.

Before discussing the frame of reference and how it draws the viewer into the narrative act in a virtual environment, a brief description of the experience is necessary.

3 The Virtual Experience

Las Meninas is primarily designed to run in the CAVE(tm), a multi-person, room-sized virtual reality system developed at the Electronic Visualization Laboratory (EVL) of the University of Illinois at Chicago. The CAVE is a ten by ten by ten foot room constructed of three translucent walls. A rack Onyx with two Infinite Reality Engines drives the high resolution stereoscopic images which are rear-projected onto the walls and front-projected onto the floor. Light-weight LCD stereo glasses are worn to mediate the stereoscopic imagery. Attached to the glasses is a location sensor. As the viewer walks within the confines of the CAVE, the correct perspective and stereo projection of the environment are updated. This presents the user with the illusion of walking around or through virtual objects. Four speakers mounted at the top corners of the CAVE provide audio. The user interacts with the environment using the *3D wand*, a simple tracked input device containing a joystick and three buttons. The wand enables navigation around the virtual world and the manipulation of virtual objects within that world.

As *Las Meninas* begins, the viewers find themselves situated in relation to the work in much the same relationship as they have with the painting. They are unable to move around the work and can not investigate what is on the canvas. An optically-generated actor, or avatar, playing the role of Velazquez enters the studio through the doorway as shown on the left in figure 3. The actor pauses in front of the hidden canvas becoming the two dimensional painted image of Velazquez. Pre-recorded narration sets the scene and contextualizes the narrative, while a prelude from *The Well-Tempered Clavier* by Johann Sebastian Bach plays in the background. The narrator asks the viewer to *paint* in the rest of the characters as positioned in the original painting as shown on the right in figure 3. This allows the viewer his first attempt at interactivity as the wand becomes a brush used to paint the characters. The narrator then describes the painting, telling the viewer who the various characters are, and points out the various enigmas as shown on the left in figure 4.

The two dimensional painted characters existing in a three dimensional world now become themselves life size three dimensional characters as shown on the right in figure 4. The Infanta Margarita moves out from her place towards the

Fig. 3. On the left, as the experience begins, an actor portraying Velazquez enters the virtual studio and takes his place in front of his canvas. On the right, the viewer complete Velazquez's composition by "painting" in the rest of the life-size characters using the CAVE's wand.

Fig. 4. On the left, the narrator discusses several enigmas in the painting. For example, the mirror at the back of the room is brought forward so the viewer can get a better look at what it is reflecting. On the right, the 2D characters in the painting become life-size 3D characters in VR. The viewer can now walk around the studio and see the scene from any point in the room.

viewer and then brings him into the scene, allowing him to see the scene as Velazquez would have seen it. This is the viewer's initial entrance into the world, previously unattainable. The pre-recorded narration informs the viewer that he is now free to explore this world. Moving about the studio the viewer can observe the scene from any point in the room, or from any character's point of view. Looking out the windows of the studio, the viewer sees two non-Euclidean spaces of revolving panels. The first shows figures who influenced Velazquez's time (Bacon, Descartes, Galileo, Cervantes, and others). The second shows the representation of marriage in painting, such as Jan Van Eych's *Arnolofini Marriage*, which shaped the way Velazquez thought of the use of mirrors and reflections to represent the visible world [6].

Leaving the studio via the doorway Jose Nieto stands in, the viewer enters a corridor with paintings by Mazo, Velazquez's apprentice, after Rubens, hanging on the walls. This corridor leads to a tower. Echoing an earlier narration that Velazquez had access to a tower from which he has observed the heavens, the viewer climbs up the steps of this tower accompanied by music from Bach's *St. Matthew Passion*. He enters a room with telescopes, a three dimensional triptych, and a large painting of Christ by Velazquez himself as shown on the left in figure 5. Leaving this room they enter a passageway with paintings by Picasso and the Russian painter Medvedev after *Las Meninas* [5]. As the viewer moves from the 17th. to the 20th. century through this transitional corridor, the music shifts from that of Bach's fugues and preludes to that of Ligeti and Schnittke as shown on the right in figure 5.

Fig. 5. On the left, as Velazquez had a tower for observing the heavens, the viewer can climb a virtual tower of their own to reach this observational room. On the right, the viewer walks from the 17th. to the 20th. century down a hallway lined up with paintings by Picasso and the Russian painter Medvedev after *Las Meninas*.

The narrative description of the painting includes a quote from Picasso that *Las Meninas* suggested to him the entrance of fascist soldiers into the studio of Velazquez with a warrant for his arrest. Picasso's interest in *Las Meninas* has to do with its central theme of the painter and his relationship to his models, and also with its profound meditation upon the historical and societal precondition of artistic activity and power relations. The new space the viewer finds himself in has several elements playing on this theme of power and domination as shown in figure 6. Television sets hanging in mid-air juxtapose archival film footage from 1936 of General Franco, of Hitler in *Triumph des Willens*, and of Chaplin in *The Great Dictator*. Large two dimensional images of Franco and posters from the Spanish Civil War adorn the walls in front of murals of Picasso's *Guernica* [8]. Turning around he finds he has walked into this scene from out of one of Picasso's study paintings after *Las Meninas*.

Finally, the viewer returns to the studio, seeing the scene from the perspective of Jose Nieto at the back of the room. Several possible paintings are shown on the blank canvas as in figure 7. The return to the initial space is marked with renewed questions enhanced by the multi-layered perspectives the journey has revealed to the viewer. Life at the court of Velazquez was strictly hierarchical. The composition itself preserves this hierarchy and marginalization of the painter. Was Velazquez trying to *correct* this hierarchy through allegorical and symbolic allusions about the nature of representation and subjectivity? What was it that he was painting on the hidden canvas? Was Velazquez painting the King and the Queen, the *Las Meninas* itself, or figures of everyday life and, thus, was rebelling against the King and the Queen and the entire tradition of court painting? These relationships are all scrutinized in the medium of VR .

4 The *Illusion in Art* in VR

From the outset, the viewer's conscious and unconscious mind is at work making inferences and reading the narrative cryptograms in *Las Meninas*. This reading is possible because the viewer *believes* in what he sees and can identify with it. It is here, in what is called *ontological authenticity*, that the first rule of the illusion in art, or the ability to suspend disbelief, manifests itself. For the illusion in art to become a sufficient condition in VR, k/s stimulation of the sensory-motor scheme is required. Both elements fulfill the requirements for achieving the illusion in art as well as formalistically enhancing the meaning of the thematic narrative plot.

Ontological authenticity refers to the illusionistic ability of the three dimensional images to show an *authentic* representation of reality. Even if these images are unfamiliar to the human eye, they have to be extrapolated from the known in order to achieve a convincing representation. The kinesthetic impact in VR is a result of the viewer's continuous navigation and the movement of image itself. The synesthetic impact is a result of the seamless interaction between the auditory and the visual elements.

Fig. 6. Picasso saw issues of power and domination in *Las Meninas* and here the viewer can experience a 20th. century interpretation.

Las Meninas manifests ontological authenticity and k/s stimulation in many ways. The viewer is not only immersed in the three dimensional images, but he also *believes* in the *real* images of an avatar, a studio, a tower, passageways, and various historical and political rooms. Furthermore, the mise-en-scene, location sound, and the use of the music of Bach, Ligeti, and Schnittke, are orchestrated in order to achieve *genuine realism* and enhance the emotional participation of the viewer in the act of revelation.

The orchestration of visual and auditory elements are often abstracted and made unfamiliar in order to intensify and stimulate the viewer's mental participation. The abstraction in *Las Meninas* is always extended or extrapolated from the *known*. Therefore, the viewer is often immersed in the three dimensional images and sounds which are *estranged*, i.e., on the one hand they appear and sound *concrete* and *real*, but at the same time the viewer knows they are synthetic and aesthetically constructed. The viewer has no illusion that she is confronted with a *real* image, yet she believes in it because it is extrapolated from the known.

Ontological authenticity is therefore a layer upon which k/s stimulation is built to achieve the illusion in art. In *Las Meninas*, everything about the journey is at first sight *concrete*, in order to draw the viewer into the narrative through the use of optically generated images. As the story proceeds, however, the integration/interaction of long navigation, blurred and hallucinatory landscapes, non-Euclidean spaces, accelerated and decelerated motion, sudden shifts from color to black and white, the mix of 17th century tonal music and 20th century atonal music, bizarre and distorted decor, a labyrinthine structure and parabolic style, temporal pressure and spatial discontinuities, and the use of archival film footage in virtual environment, create a cognitive impact in the viewer. This impact *dramatizes* the journey and fuses the overall narrative with oneiric feel and engages the viewer in the action plot.

The viewer constantly alternates between the space of the representational and that of the surreal, with the latter grounded in the representational. It is

Fig. 7. Returning back to the studio where he began, the viewer sees what could be on the canvas. From this new perspective, looking back, several possibilities can be seen.

in this space that the suspension of disbelief and the illusion in art occurs. It is here that aesthetics and psychology become intertwined.

In the following sections we will elaborate on how ontological authenticity and k/s stimulation in *Las Meninas* establish a *language of art* in VR.

4.1 Fusion of Optical and Virtual Images

Las Meninas starts when the rear door of Velazquez's studio, a three dimensional computer-generated image, opens to let an optically reproduced avatar playing the role of the painter himself, enter the empty space which is computer-generated. From the start the viewer experiences a *narrative tension* arising from an immediate oscillation between the world of the *real*, optics, and that of the *imaginary*, virtual environment, which is nonetheless ontologically authentic. Therefore, ontological authenticity is doubly represented through optics as well as through a virtual world made authentic. This narrative tension is characterized by the viewer's ability to *see* something as both real and imaginary simultaneously. He believes that what he sees belongs to the laws of optics, but at the same time existing within the laws of virtual environment.

The fine line between the representational and the virtual forces the viewer to reflect upon the imaginary space empirically. The viewer cannot say to himself that nothing is believable in this narrative because it is virtual and non-real. The optical images fill the gap empirically as well as the ontologically authentic virtual environment. This makes the viewer, at least initially, *identify* with the narrative unfolding. Of course, this practice is not new in the history of art. Both the Dadaists and the Surrealists employed such techniques quite successfully in painting and cinema where the real was made *estranged*.

Another instant in *Las Meninas* where the fusion of the optical and the virtual take place is towards the end of the narrative. After the viewer leaves the world of the 17th century, Velazquez and the fugues of J. S. Bach, he enters the world of the 20th century to witness studies by Picasso of *Las Meninas*, his *Guernica*, the serial music of Ligeti and Schnittke, but above all the viewer encounters television sets suspended in mid-air. The sets show archival film footage of Hitler and Franco, and of Chaplin. Here again, the inclusion of optically-generated images with ontologically authentic virtual environment functions at a metathematic level to provoke reflections on the changing methods of representation and subjectivity. The viewer is constantly shifting from the representational to the virtual and back. It is in this oscillation that the foremost element of storytelling manifests itself: the suspension of disbelief or the illusion in art.

4.2 Visual and Aural Guides

Las Meninas incorporates multiple visual and aural guides. The first guide is the disembodied voice of the narrator who narrates the historical, political, and aesthetic cryptograms present in the painting. Later, the Infanta Margarita acts as a three dimensional guide, leading the viewer from her static perspective, into the painting, and allowing her to move about the space freely. At first, the infanta seems to be an alias of the invisible narrator, but when the viewer is given freedom of movement, the narrator suspends his narration, and the Infanta resumes her place in the scene. Another guide steps into the narrative. This guide is a person standing with the viewing audience in the CAVE who then takes on the responsiblity to guide the them through the rest of the narrative.

This method of using a guide familiar with the story is inspired from Japanese Kabuki theater, a highly stylized and somewhat overwrought dramatic form derived from the feudal Tokugawa period (1603-1867). In Kabuki theater, there is a benshi, or actor, who stands at the side of the stage and narrates the action for the audience (a method later used in early Japanese silent cinema).

In *Las Meninas*, the benshi, or guide, fulfills a double function. He navigates the viewer throughout the rest of the narrative, and narrates and sometimes reflects upon the various cryptograms. The viewer can interrupt the benshi and raise further questions, doubts, comments, and objections. This helps create a dialogue between the benshi and the viewer, and also among the other viewers as well, a property possible because of the social nature of VR in the CAVE.

Therefore, the continuous navigation and seamless interaction/integration between the visual and auditory elements create in the viewer a k/s stimulation which draws him, both psychologically and physiologically, into the action plot.

4.3 A *Total Environment* and the Double Articulation of Time

After the optical Velazquez takes his place in the empty virtual studio the viewer *paints* the rest of the painting, the Infanta Margarita and her entourage, using the wand in the CAVE like a paint brush. It is with such interactivity that the viewer is able to create a balance between what is presented in front of him, the phenomenon, and his own manipulation of it in VR. This double articulation of time, that is, time that already exists in the phenomenon and its manipulation by the viewer, gives the viewer the feeling that the reality presented in the CAVE is not only representational but also ontological and subjective. The viewer is finally able to be part of the phenomenon. He is an extension of a virtual world in which he can shape and determine the outcome of events. The phenomenon passing in time can now be interrupted, accelerated, decelerated, moved both backwards and forwards, and completed or left as is. The virtual environment becomes a *total environment* in which the viewer is both an extension and a determining factor of the environment.

The viewer's participation is not arbitrary in *Las Meninas*. If he chooses certain signs about the narrative, further historical, political, and aesthetic signs are revealed to him which propels the narrative in a certain direction. The viewer involved interactivity is intrinsic to the narrative's overall structure, and necessary for the unfolding of the enigmas of representation.

4.4 Dramatic Shift from the Formalistic to the Psychological

Las Meninas is staged in such a way that there is a dramatic shift from the formalistic to the psychological. Not only does the work invent passageways, towers, three dimensional triptychs, non-Euclidean spaces, telescopes, transparent surfaces, and television sets, which are ontologically authentic, but it also provides them with a history in order to connect them with the narrative and give them meaning. The viewer has the choice to navigate and interact with various historical periods, from the 17th to the 20th century, which embody specific sets and music reflecting their historical, political, and aesthetic specificities. The shift from one period to another is an attempt to make connections between various periods and demonstrate how form and function act as one. The psychological factor here plays a major role. Not only does the viewer experience a specific *sensation* arising from the specific formalistic set and music, but also her mental act of perception becomes based purely on unconscious inferences she makes as she navigates and interacts with various sets in different periods.

5 Conclusions

Illusion in art is a complex topic and each era has its own limitations and paradigms when rendering reality. When we look at Egyptian art, for example, we read it as a brilliant signaling system of code, and not as a literal representation of reality. But is this the way the Egyptians themselves saw their art? The Greeks created the three-tone code for modeling in light and shade which remains fundamental to all later development of Western art. As inheritors of that tradition and inventors of VR artworks, it is important to invent a *language* which defines the way our new tools of production operate and shape the future of art. In VR, it seems that few works try to systemically formulate an artistic position and find ways to create a language of art whose essential function is the manifestation of the illusion in art.

In VR, a developed system of schemata in which the illusion in art is possible consists of two elements: ontological authenticity and k/s stimulation of the sensory-motor scheme. The viewers' positive response, after *Las Meninas* was shown at the International Society For the Electronic Arts and at ThinkQuest 1997, tells us that they completely forgot about the technology of the CAVE and that they *believed* in the narrative unfolding and were psychological involved in its transformations.

At first, the viewers experienced the thrill of a perfect illusion in the CAVE because the bridge between the phenomenon and the virtual is broken. However, once this illusion wears off, it is essential that something else fills the gap because we want and expect more. The history of technologically-based art is full of such instances. Early cinema, for example, was a thrill because of the darkened theater, flickering images, remote places, and so forth. Later, audiences wanted more and it was through dramatic narrative plots, whether linear or non-linear, that cinematic art developed.

VR is facing a similar challenge to that of its cousin, the cinema. Without ontological authenticity and k/s impact *Las Meninas* would have been an exercise in effects, and not a work where illusion manifests itself as we react, feel, and think in front of the crytograms of its virtual world. In other words, in *Las Meninas* the viewer not only witnesses the faithful and convincing representation of a visual experience through ontological authenticity, but also the faithful construction and orchestration of a relational model in which the interplay of image and sound trigger in the viewer a k/s stimulation to bring about a *second reality*. This second reality originates in the viewer's conscious and unconscious *reaction* to the virtual world and not in the virtual world itself. The *ilusion in art* finally manifests itself in the viewer's *reaction* to the virtual world they experience.

Acknowledgements

Las Meninas was created by Hisham Bizri, Andrew Johnson, and Christina Vasilakis with contributions by Michael Gold, Kyoung Park, Javier Girado and Alan Cruz. The models were created using Softimage 3D and imported into the CAVE using Silicon Graphics' Performer. The optical avatar of Velazquez was created using a blue screen technique and a library developed by Joseph Insley. Many thinks also to Dave Pape for his continuing innovation in the CAVE library, and to Tom Moher.

The virtual reality research, collaborations, and outreach programs at EVL are made possible through major funding from the National Science Foundation, the Defense Advanced Research Projects Agency, and the US Department of Energy; specifically NSF awards CDA-9303433, CDA-9512272, NCR-9712283, CDA-9720351, and the NSF ASC Partnerships for Advanced Computational Infrastructure program. The CAVE and ImmersaDesk are trademarks of the Board of Trustees of the University of Illinois.

References

1. F. Baudouin, *Pietro Pauolo Rubens*. Harry N. Abrams, Inc., New York, 1977.
2. C. Cruz-Neira, D. Sandin, and T. DeFanti. "Surround-Screen Projection-Based Virtual Reality: The Design and Implementation of the CAVE," *Computer Graphics* (Proceedings of SIGGRAPH 93), ACM SIGGRAPH, August 1993, pp. 135-142.
3. M. Foucault. *The Order of Things: An Archaeology of the Human Sciences*. Vintage Books, New York, 1970.
4. A. Del Campo Y Frances. *La Magia de Las Meninas*. Colegio de Ingenieros de Caminos, Canales y Puertos, Madrid, 1978.
5. M. Gelman and P. Gelman. *Babylon*, Moscow Youth Center, Moscow, 1990.
6. E. Hall, *The Arnolfini Betrothal: Medieval Marriage and the Enigma of Van Eyck's Double Portrait*. University of California Press: Berkeley, Los Angeles, 1994.
7. J. Lopez-Rey. *Velazquez, Volume II*. Benedikt Taschen Verlag, Germany, 1996.
8. C. Warncke. *Pablo Picasso, Volume II*. Benedikt Taschen Verlag, Germany, 1994.

Mitologies: Medieval Labyrinth Narratives in Virtual Reality

Maria Roussos and Hisham Bizri

Electronic Visualization Laboratory
University of Illinois at Chicago, Chicago, IL 60607, USA
+1.312.996-3002 voice, +1.312.413-7585 fax
mroussos@eecs.uic.edu, http://www.evl.uic.edu/mariar/MFA/MITOLOGIES/

Abstract. Advances in technology have made it possible to create vast, rich, and architecturally intricate virtual worlds. The *Mitologies* project is an attempt to utilize this technology as a means of artistic expression and for the exploration of historical, political, musical, and visual narratives. *Mitologies* draws inspiration from a large pool of literary and artistic sources by capturing their intertwining relationships in a cinematic form, hence making connections to the strong narrative tradition of other media, such as film and literature.

1 Introduction

Advances in technology have made it possible to create vast, rich and intricate, architectural virtual worlds. The *Mitologies* project is an attempt to utilize this technology as a means of artistic expression and to explore historical, political, musical, and visual narratives. *Mitologies* draws inspiration from a large pool of literary and artistic sources by capturing their intertwining relationships in a cinematic form, hence making connections to the strong narrative tradition of other media, such as film and literature. *Mitologies* is the culmination of an extensive body of work, both as an art project and as a software design prototype in virtual reality.

The thematic content of *Mitologies* draws inspiration from medieval and on to contemporary literary endeavors. The work is loosely based on the Cretan myth of the Minotaur, the *Apocalypse*, or Revelations, of St. John, Dante's *Inferno*, Durer's woodcuts after the Apocalypse, and Borges' *Library of Babel*. Music from Wagner's *Der Ring Des Nibelungen* is used as a motif to structure the narrative. The work explores the enigmatic relationships between these sources and captures them in a mise-en-scene that is rooted in the illusionistic narrative tradition of other media.

As a design prototype in virtual reality, *Mitologies* is an artwork created for the CAVE(tm), a multi-person, room-sized virtual reality system developed at the Electronic Visualization Laboratory (EVL) of the University of Illinois at Chicago [5]. The CAVE is a ten by ten by ten foot room constructed of three translucent walls. A rack Onyx with two Infinite Reality Engines drives the high resolution stereoscopic images which are rear-projected onto the walls and front-projected onto the floor. Light-weight LCD stereo glasses are worn to mediate the stereoscopic imagery. Attached to the glasses is a location sensor. As the viewer moves within the confines of the CAVE, the correct perspective and stereo projection of the environment are updated. This presents the user with the illusion of walking around or through virtual objects. Four speakers mounted at the top corners of the CAVE provide audio. The user interacts with the environment using the 3D wand, a simple tracked input device containing a joystick and three buttons. The want enables navigation around the virtual world and manipulation of virtual objects within that world. *Mitologies* also runs on the CAVE's smaller, more portable cousins, the Immersadesk (tm) and Immersadesk2 (tm).

Fig. 1. Participants interact with *Mitologies* on an ImmersaDesk (tm) virtual reality system.

The characteristics of the above technology were taken into consideration when deciding to develop *Mitologies* . The CAVE provides an appropriate virtual reality platform mainly because of the non-intrusive nature of its hardware and the ability to provide a group experience. This is of great importance to a digital work of art as emphasis can be given on the work without worry of the technology overpowering it.

2   Description of the Virtual Experience

The word *Mitologies* derives from the Greek word "mitos," the thread Ariadne granted Theseus to help him find his way out of the Cretan labyrinth. The viewer in *Mitologies* re-experiences, allegorically, the journey of Theseus, but also of another historical and literary figure, Dante Alighieri [2]. The narrative is introduced in a storytelling fashion, a structure largely unknown to virtual reality worlds, but familiar in other media, such as film and literature.

As the narrative proceeds, the integration/interaction of long and endless navigation, blurred hallucinatory landscapes and foggy passageways, accelerated and decelerated motion, sudden shifts from color to black and white, eerie Wagnerian music, bizarre and destorted decor, labyrinthine structures and parabolic style, temporal pressure and spatial discontinuities, engage the viewer in a kind of "action" plot, dramatize the journey, and fuse the overall narrative with a dream-like feel.

The audience entering the CAVE is initially located on the bank of a river, in a dark forest, an allusion to Dante's sinful forest.

Fig. 2. The opening of the narrative on a boat travelling through a dark forest is reminiscent of Dante's *Inferno*.

From a distance, the viewer hears the creaking sounds of a wooden boat and the subtle sound of water washing against the river banks. The boat slowly appears, led by a statue: a model of Donatello's Zuccone [9]. Can this be Virgil accompanying Dante into *Inferno*? As the boat approaches the shore, the viewer is swiftly transported onto it and the journey down the river begins. In the physical space of the CAVE, two benches are placed in a configuration that corresponds to the virtual seats of the boat. Hence, the illusion of traveling in the boat is realistic, as the viewers look down at the floor of the CAVE and see the virtual boat swaying beneath their feet.

The intention of this opening scene is to establish an explicit sense of a story line narrative. The slow and smooth flow of this introductory sequence is lethargic and meditative, setting the pace the work seeks to accomplish throughout. The opening river motif from Richard Wagner's opera Das Rheingold, used for the river scene, contributes to the impending sense of danger and hightens the expectation of the unknown yet to come. Upon closer examination of the visual and auditory metaphors, the participants may begin to recognize the elements and start drawing the connections that will guide their exploration later on. The river scene eventually fades out while the next scene, that of a brighter and more ethereal space, fades in. The transition is aided by sound, an excerpt from Richard Wagner's opening segment of Das Rheingold, which serves as a structural motif for the unfolding narrative. Once in this space, the viewer has disembarked from the boat and can now start using the interface device, the 3D wand, to continue the journey by navigating through a large plane. Far in the distance, a magnificent church, surrounded by horticultural maze gardens, appears.

The grand cathedral is inspired by the seven churches described in the Apocalypse: Ephesus, Smyrna, Pergamum, Thyatira, Sardis, Philadelphia, and Laodicea. In *Mitologies*, all seven of these churches are represented as this one grand church which is modeled after a Leonardo da Vinci sketch of a church that was never built [4]. Many attempts were made in the Renaissance to build da Vinci's church but these attempts never materialized. It is for the first time that da Vinci's design can finally take shape as a 3D structure where the viewer has the opportunity to travel up high and around the intricately detailed brick domes and examine da Vinci's magnificent architectural vision.

As the doors of the church slowly open, the interior reveals the elaborate space of a completely different style of churches: the Great Mosque of Cordoba in Spain [6].

The sound motif from Wagner's Ring intensifies the sense of elevation and progression from one space to the other. The viewer has the freedom to travel inside the realistic representation of the mosque at a low level, to almost feel the carpets, or fly high up over its arches. As with the church, the textiles and ornamental details of the interior of the mosque are drawn from a variety of sources related to the model, the period, and the thematic content, but also adapted to the unfolding of the narrative. The progression is intensified further when the darker and more ornamental spaces of the mosque become the entrance to the even darker and mysterious labyrinth underneath.

In The Metamorphoses, Ovid notes that Daedalus built a house in which he confused the usual passages and deceived the eye with a conflicting maze of various wandering paths [1]. In *Mitologies*, myriad strange, dark, and misleading

Fig. 3. A horticultural garden maze surrounds the magnificent church, which is modeled after a Leonardo da Vinci sketch and can be experienced in *Mitologies*.

passages are constructed to create a labyrinth reminiscent of the labyrinth built by Daedalus. The labyrinth is a web, or rhizome: every path is connected with every other one. It has no center, no periphery, and no exit because it is a potential infinite [10], [12]. As the viewers proceed through the maze, they find themselves on paths that lead to medieval curiosity rooms, rooms based on Durer's woodcuts of the Apocalypse [7], and rooms populated by statues and icons, rooms that require that the viewer makes choices in order to proceed. In some cases, to proceed from one space to another, the viewer must make the right choices. The first room, for instance, presents the viewer with three words: "Dante," "Theseus," and "Christ." If the letter "T" in any of the words is chosen, then the door leading to the first Durer woodcut is opened. Otherwise, one of the other doors leading to further spaces is opened. At any point and depending on the choice, the participants may experience either a "woodcut" or one of the other special rooms.

Each of the woodcut rooms brings to life, in 3D, one of seven Apocalyptic woodcuts by Durer that were selected for this work. The first room encountered is the Seven Trumpets woodcut room. It presents the Book with the Seven Seals rapidly unfolding on a scroll, while the loud trumpet sounds from Wagner's Das Rheingold are juxtaposed; in the Apocalyptic Woman room, a female voice from Die Walkurie follows a woman's torso as water starts to rise, eventually flooding the room; the Four Horsemen room translates the horror of the most famous and ever popular sheet of Durer's Apocalypse with the violent motion of the horsemen, as the four-colored walls close in on the viewer; in the Opening of the 5th & 6th Seal room, multiple semi-transparent layers illustrating the lower part of the woodcut, rise from the ground like blades; the Torture of St. John, the most unusual of Durer's woodcuts that is not part of the Apocalypse narratives, is realized with a modern interpretation of torture in the four cross-like spaces of the room; finally, the woodcut room of St. Michael Fighting the Dragon, one of the last in the series of woodcut rooms, is presented with words from the Book of Daniel: "ME _NE, ME _NE, TE _KEL, U _PHAR _SYN." The first two syllables, ME _NE, mean: "God has numbered thy kingdom and finished it;" the next, TE _KEL, U _PHAR _SYN, mean: "Thou art weighed in the balances."

Fig. 4. The three-dimensional model of the mosque of Cordoba in Spain, as experienced in *Mitologies*.

Other rooms in the labyrinth attempt to capture the mystery and beauty of the popular medieval curiosity rooms. The Metaphysics/Astronomy room invites the viewer to gaze at the Sistine Chapel paintings of hell through the eyepiece of a large telescope; in the Music room, the viewer can play one of four instruments and browse through the score sheets. The Insects, Geography, and Alchemy rooms resemble damp study rooms where knowledge is classified through elaborate taxonomies. In the first of these rooms, tables of insects are adapted from medieval entomology books. The Geography room displays the beauty and accuracy of medieval cartography through the numerous examples of maps, including a central terrestrial globe model representing the fundamentals of Ptolemy's geographical system. The latter room, the room of Alchemy, is saturated with the ten words of God mentioned in the Cabala.

Each of the rooms in the labyrinth involve careful research concerning the artistic content as well as the historical and political contexts they represent. The virtual implementation, however, does not attempt to perfectly recreate, interpret, or realize the contexts of these rooms, but to capture their emotional essence. This process is best illustrated through an example on one of the rooms of the labyrinth, the Bosch room, after Hieronymous Bosch. This room brings to life Bosch's most famous work, The Garden of Earthly Delights (1505-1510). This triptych shows the master at his best. The central panel, which is the subject of the VR space, swarms with the frail nude figures of men and women sporting licentiously in a panoramic landscape that is studded with fantastic growths of a quasi sexual form. Bosch seems to show erotic temptation and sensual gratification as a universal disaster and the human race, as a consequence of original sin, succumbing to its naturally base disposition. The subjects are derived in part from three major sources: Medieval bestiaries, Flemish proverbs, and the then very popular dream and occult books, all mixed in the melting pot of Bosch's astoundingly inventive imagination.

We have chosen to realize this central panel for the virtual space. Symbols are scattered plentifully throughout this panel. One of the most fascinating symbols is that of a couple in a glass globe which illustrate the proverb: "Good fortune, like glass, is easily broken." The glass globe is recreated in three dimensions and recreate, also in three dimensional glass globes, what the triptych as a whole represents. First, the false paradise of the world between Eden and Hell. Second, the secrets of alchemy and its allegorical meanings. The viewer is able to enter the glass globes which reproduce the movement of the heavenly bodies. As the viewer navigates from one globe to the next, the walls gradually move backwards to reveal multiple globes, rising like air bubbles. A rather ethereal fragment from Wagner's opera, Gotterdammerung, is used to illustrate the overall allegory of the painting.

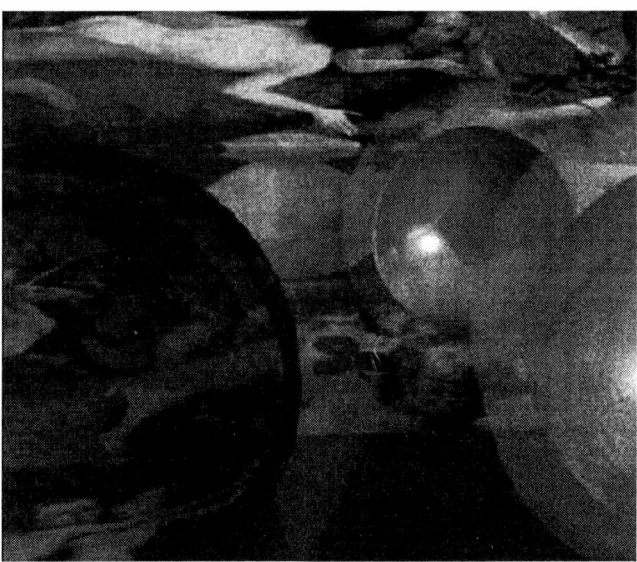

Fig. 5. A view of the Bosch room, one of the more than 30 rooms included in the *Mitologies* world.

The constructions of the rooms include a complex web of metaphors and signs. The path from one room to the other may be linear, circular, or truly labyrinthine, depending on the viewer's choices. When the last room of the labyrinth is finally reached, the viewer's tedious journey concludes. The shape of this room resembles the number six or the shell of a snail, as do the two rooms that proceed it. The viewer enters at the narrow tip of the room and circle around it until the center is reached, where the encounter with the minotaur himself, the symbol of death, takes place. The representation of the minotaur seated in his magnificent temple is based on Cesare Ripa's death metaphor from Iconologia [11].: "The same fate awaits all; we hasten toward a common goal, black Death, who claims all under his power."

The personification of Death, a skeleton, lies on a bier within an elaborate catafalque decorated with skulls and many lamps. He is wrapped in a rich robe (he takes away the rich man's wealth) and wears a laurel crown symbolizing his rule over all mortals. In one hand he holds a sword entwined with an olive branch, meaning that peace cannot endure if men do not run the risk of death in fighting for it. The motto above the catafalque reads: "Death makes all men equal." Four lighted tapers stand on either side of the bier. "Not rank nor dignity can me withstand; My power extends o'er every land." [11]

In the lower foreground stand two putti, heavily veiled to signify their blindness, not their mourning, for they represent man's pleasure in the things of this world. The power and glory of the world are shown in the child wearing classical armor and carrying crowns, a mitre, a scepter, and medals on a cushion, while a sword, lances, and a marshal's baton lie at his feet. The other putto represents all human invention and art; the flail and shovel lying near him stand for agriculture, while the quill pens, scrolls, palette and brushes, and compass and triangle stand for the arts and sciences. On one side of the room, a pair of white feathered wings built by Daedalus lay on the floor.

While the viewers will surely attempt to approach the minotaur, a hidden crypt opens under their feet enabling them to escape from the labyrinth by using the pair of wings. Once again, as with the beginning sequence, navigation is disabled and the viewer is dragged down into a tidal pool, while the sound excerpt from Das Rheingold reaches a climax. Enmeshed in a maddening spiral, where voices and sounds swirl down along with them, the virtual reality viewers have finally landed back on the boat on which the journey started out from. Only now, Donatello's statue is no longer standing on the bow of the boat. Instead, a few scattered feathers, remnants of the wings that led to the escape have replaced the monumental figure. The voice and sound motifs have also halted with only the creaking sounds of the boat breaking the silence. The narrative, that of a labyrinth but also a labyrinth in itself, has completed its cycle.

3 On the Use of Narrative and Interactivity

Mitologies takes a radically different approach to narrative structure and, one could say, almost ignores interactivity. In certain cases, the audience has no control, such as in the distinct opening where they are taken aboard the boat which slowly transports them to the cathedral. From this point on one participant may take control over navigation while the others experience the virtual narrative led by this person's choices. The cinematic narrative form preserves itself through the continuous slow pace and progression achieved from one scene to the other. The labyrinth presents its visitors with choices, yet all choices are in essence illusory, as they ultimately lead to the same final confrontation with the minotaur, the fall through the trap door, and the return back onto the boat, thus completing a circular journey.

Fig. 6. The geography room filled with medieval maps of unique beauty and accuracy, including the *Planisphaerium sive universi totius*, a celestial chart illustrating the sun-centred system outlined by Copernicus.

Interactivity is a raison d'etre of a virtual reality world. Most people, however, do not know or understand how to deal with interactive computer-based art, let alone with interactivity in immersive and, in many cases, complex virtual worlds. The virtual experience is disorienting, unnatural, and difficult for most, even if the technology used is as simple and natural as it currently gets. The Electronic Visualization Laboratory has been actively involved in defining the future directions of virtual reality technology through the development of the CAVE, which one can argue as being one of the better examples in the gamut of interactive virtual reality systems. Our participation in multiple venues has provided us with numerous instances to observe the reactions of people interacting in the CAVE environment, whether children, adults, single viewers, groups, expert or novice viewers. These observations lead us to believe that an interactive experience is not necessarily all that matters when creating a work of art, unless the work itself is about interactivity. Why would we necessarily need a reactive computer program in order to make an artistic statement rich in metaphor? For us, what is more important is that the viewer will not be consumed by learning how to interact with the technological interface. Furthermore, it is important for the artist that the viewer will surpass the stage of fascination with the medium, which may distract from the content of the work itself. Certainly no painter would consider her work successful if, instead of the work, the viewer became fascinated with the construction details of the canvas. It is, thus, critical for virtual reality to move beyond the level of the technology. And the mission of a work of art is to present a challenge to the prevailing orthodoxy of virtual worlds.

How do we respond to this mission of shifting the form and artistic process of virtual world creation away from the technology and into the content? It is not the intention of this work to realistically recreate architectural worlds of the past, nor to collapse time periods into an attempt to redefine them as part of a confusing, short, and fragmented experience. Although the piece involves research in history, mythology, literature, art, and music, it avoids taking a didactic or encyclopedic stance. The intention is to create a work rooted in the humanities which tries to surpass the usual form of virtual reality worlds, the form of navigation through abstract geometric shapes. Another clear intention of *Mitologies* is the attempt to impose a narrative content and structure. The film-like mise-en-scene was selected both for its familiarity with the viewers and as a mode of expression. Finally, the collaboration between individuals of different interests and disciplines had to meld together into a work that makes a coherent whole, avoiding what is frequently the result of collaborations for the creation of virtual worlds: a series of different, non-associated worlds connected by portals.

4 Conclusion

Apocalyptic literature and art have always been concerned with the approach of the end of the millenium and so does scientific and popular literature about virtual reality. As this work is created towards the end of the twentieth century, it inevitably investigates the meaning of the *Apocalypsis* in such a context. For *Mitologies*, virtual reality is used as a vehicle to literally explicate the exegesis of the Revelation. In the *Apocalypse*, double perspective plays an important part in building and expanding the metaphors. On one level, the vision is severely restricted and fragmented, and suffers confusion. On a parallel level, it is clear and concise. The metaphors are at once single and double; they incorporate clarity and confusion, unity and multiplicity, artistry and chaos. Indicative is the element of the labyrinth: a symbol of the tombs of death, of hell but also a place of judgment and worship.

However complete and extensive, *Mitologies* is still intended as an experiment with the state-of-the-art in technology, but also as an attempt to see the twentieth century world from a perspective other than the technology it has been created with. Although it is left up to the viewer to synthesize the historical, literary, or mythological material into contemporary relevance, it is still the focus of this work to create an alternative to the usual fast-paced, choice-driven synthetic worlds and make a profound and lasting impact within VR in specific and technologically-based art in general. Then, *Mitologies* may be considered a successful experiment in art.

Acknowledgements

Mitologies was created by a multi-disciplinary group of artists and scientists at the University of Illinois at Chicago's Electronic Visualization Laboratory. The group members include filmmaker Hisham Bizri, artists Joe Alexander, Alan Cruz, and Maria Roussos, and computer scientists Tomoko Imai, Alan Millman, and Dave Pape. An extensive collection of resources, images, and text about *Mitologies* can be found at: http://www.evl.uic.edu/mariar/MFA/MITOLOGIES.

The virtual reality research, collaborations, and outreach programs at the Electronic Visualization Laboratory (EVL) at the University of Illinois at Chicago are made possible through major funding from the National Science Foundation (NSF), the Defense Advanced Research Projects Agency, and the US Department of Energy; specifically NSF awards CDA-9303433, CDA-9512272, NCR-9712283, CDA-9720351, and the NSF ASC Partnerships for Advanced Computational Infrastructure (PACI) program. EVL also wishes to acknowledge Silicon Graphics, Inc. and Advanced Network and Services for their support. The CAVE and ImmersaDesk are trademarks of the Board of Trustees of the University of Illinois.

References

1. W.S. Anderson, *Ovid's Metamorphoses Books 1-5*. Norman, University of Oklahoma Press, 1997.
2. Dante Alighieri, *Inferno*. British Broadcasting Publication, 1966.
3. Jorge Luis Borges, *Labyrinths*. New Directions, 1962.
4. Alberto and Bencini Busignani, *Raffaello La Chiese di Firenze; Quartiere di Santo Spirito*. 7 volumes, Sansoni Editore Firenze, 1974.
5. C. Cruz-Neira, D. Sandin, and T. DeFanti. "Surround-Screen Projection-Based Virtual Reality: The Design and Implementation of the CAVE," *Computer Graphics* (Proceedings of SIGGRAPH 93), ACM SIGGRAPH, August 1993, pp. 135-142.
6. Jerrilynn D. Dodds, *Al-Andalus: The Art of Islamic Spain*. The Metropolitan Museum of Art, New York, 1992.
7. Willi Kurth (ed.), *The complete woodcuts of Albrecht Durer, 1471-1528*. Crown Publishers, 1946.
8. Erwin Panofsky, *Studies in Iconology: Humanistic Themes in the Art of the Renaissance*. Harper & Row, New York, 1962.
9. Joachim Poeschke, *Donatello and his World*. Harry N. Abrams, Inc., 1990.
10. Penelope Reed Doob, *The Idea of the Labyrinth from Classical Antiquity through the Middle Ages*. Cornell University Press, 1990.
11. Cesare Ripa, fl. 1600. *Baroque and Rococo pictorial image edition of Ripa's "Iconologia"*. Dover Publications, 1971.
12. Paolo Santarcangeli, *Il Libro Dei Labirinti*. Vallecchi Editore Firenze, 1967.

Aggregate Worlds:
Virtual Architecture Aftermath

Vladimir Muzhesky

Abstract. In the following article the phenomenon of virtual world is analyzed not as a point of reference or relation to existent meaning deployed elsewhere but as a point of semiotic and perceptual construction of synthetic content allocated for use via computer network. Author extends this analysis into the legal, economic, and neurological discursive lines of interaction, monitoring and control. Aforementioned aspects inherited by contemporary virtual worlds from its military predecessors in many cases were used as landmark metaphors by designers to refer and/or reframe existing linear discourses by means of interfacing them in a non-linear way from within virtual and augmented reality environments. This article is concluded with a scheme or project for an infrastructure of aggregate world, as it appears to be functional and formative in its relationship with interactive content.

Perceptual Synthesis, Content, and Aggregate Locality

Digital or cyber-space commonly referred to as virtual or synthetic locality is in reality underdefined concept. Epistemological aggregate or defined status of spatiality which is implicit to locality as concept is channeled via semiotic zones of references to real or memorized as real situations in virtual environment. Hence, to define virtual space we have to follow the pattern of interference emerging from mediated life streams of real worlds and rendered objects and its interrelated neurological, perceptual, semantic, and economic contextual aspects of spatiality.

From this point of view virtuality is a complex transparent conglomerate: current 3D dummy realms with limited interaction and abused liberating tendency can be interpreted as desubliminization of mental tangibility inherent to digital space – it is thrilling how conceptually loose its constructs can be. It seems they are projected into absolute nothingness simultaneously being declared as hi-tech spectacle, sort of industry-dimensional test field with default meaning categories like a body shape which stands for a biological connector and shooting which represents informational transmission.

Described by Marcuse still back in the 60's desubliminization tendency of media obviously integrated itself into virtuality. Resulting alienated toy-like industry-dimension conceals the aspect of virtual world as a space to which knowledge is functionally and structurally bound in the first place. When we analyze this space we reconstruct it, we project it and provide it with biologically streamed content. This content in its turn is being deployed when we "act" in digital space in accordance with electronic and perceptual semiotics which might have become a starting point for digital economic theories would we have left astride Freudian limits of toy-humans (avatars) in virtuality with all their body based pseudo-topologies (virtual embodiment theories) and include pattern recognition and recombination as a common sphere of action when it concerns biological and electronic interference. Of course we can stream raw biological situation as any other kind of raw data material, but how long are we going to follow graphic or academic industry preset attitude to spatiality and impose its mental-proof rendered polygons onto ongoing perceptual-electronic deployment?

Semiotic mechanism of streamed and rendered synthethis together with its perceptual properties constitute specifically synthetic meaning and defined aggregate locality. To follow discursive line of aggregate construction of digital space as an alocation of mediated content means to encounter spatial paradox represented as screen border. With the development of interactive media screen border seems to position itself as a materialized limit of content; almost Cartesian zone of dual visibility, virtual perspective of inside and outside of the machine content performance being simultaneously exposed to the user. In the latest artificial intelligence reviews one can find the reference to this zone of content visibility.

Take for example Douglas Hofstadter analysis of Stanislaw Ulams opinion about perception as a key to intelligence. Ulam wrote: "you see an object as a key...it is a word as which has to be mathematically formalized. Until you do it you will not get very far with your artificial intelligence problem." Hofstadter concludes his research in the following manner: "in any case when I look at Ulams key word "as" I see it as am acronym for "abstract seeing."

The analysis of limits and constructs of an aggregate (locally content-defined) virtual world in terms of "abstract seeing" interface of interactive content displays another controversial feature of synthetic reality: content represented or constructed within a virtual world simulates or refers in its simulation to the structure of physical action leaving perception out of discursively preprogrammed visibility. This sort of ego-like phenomenon of virtuality is usually addressed as "virtual consciousness." However what it really comes down to is probably an early process stage of alocation of synthetic meaning which as a restricted (in Bataille's sense) economy follows Marxist-Hegelian dialectics of selfrefletive phenomenological emergence. In this frame, virtuality is constantly defining itself via neglecting the transparency of its production and reproduction when it comes to its origins in real or memorized as real situations. Current transmission from virtual (rendered-only) to augmented (streamed and rendered) reality in computer science (augmented reality and active telepresence system research) reflects crystallization of aggregate phase in virtuality.

It seems that there is an interface of perception missing as an alternative to the existing and widely abused interface of action in digital culture. This gap in digital economy makes us look for in depth scaled content in simulation as synthesized perception as opposite to the surface interactivity as a synthesized action.

In neurocognitive context it is possible to analyze the synthetic interaction of human and electronic system, with the following extension of the analysis into conceptual, economical and political faculties. And to the same extent as neural research influenced social sciences, the models of neural networks bringing out a necessity to define the infrastructural elements of human intelligence in terms of its vision and activity, in digital culture neural network and related representational models play crucial role when it concerns virtual content.

From Heidegger to Baudrillard there was a strong tendency in philosophy to highlight the influence of technologically mediated and even economically and ideologically simulated (in case of Derderrian's analysis of espionage structures) social terrains. From this point of view, current mental alienation of the role of perception and recognition in virtual architecture, is even more appealing, than physical labor alienation of the dawn of technology. Historically worker-machine dichotomy brought the achiasm of society and industry as a point of theoretical reference. Today's tendency to unify this dichotomy into a cyborg bioelectronic complex concealed them. The tension of first lapses of industrial maps and dimensions was resolved with geopolitical pattern recombination of industrial and socio-industrial revolutions, while cyborg-situation as the closure of revolutionary localities should be resolved on the metalevel: the selfdominant for synthetic concepts deployed by means of virtual forms, links and inter-forms should be defined and neurolized, embedded in users processing with existing one dimensional ideologies, economies and politics being referred and mentally attracted to this new field.

The fact that neuralization substitutes the revolution in the context of virtualized social sphere, speaks for itself in terms of spatial properties: vital social activities such as banking (online transactions), education (online courses and virtual university projects), research (for example, Stanford KSL project which provides access to running research and development software systems over the World Wide Web) are pressed out into the virtual dimension. New plane of immanence is not a frozen pattern of biosocial oscillation, with which philosophy can easily play, it is a dissipative and in some cases selforganizing terrain of attractors, which implies that at least a part of its organizational points are useless. In terms of neural networks, new emergent attractors of pattern recognition activity are referred to as spurious memories. Net as a bioelectronic phenomenon has plenty of them. It is wilderness for Freudian experiments on wired population, and at the same time an avatar of escape from recurrent dissublimization. Projected onto the bioelectronic plane, dissublimization of the net spurious memories connected with the exposure of perceptual intensities in the logic of virtual worlds brings up a new architectural form which interfaces content on a subversively deeper political level than any other existing form of synthetic activity as much as it embodies synthesis of content itself by means of perceptual interferences and modulations.

Hyperreality Neurolized

With the discovery of neural systems, the ability of single class networks to generate additional or spurious memories was classified as generalization activity, when involved in the pre-recognition of new stimuli (Ezhov, VVedensky, 1996). This aspect of neural networks corresponds to the immune complex of human systems, where antibodies are preliminary generated in order to establish a binding with a potentially new antigen.

Virtual complexes and communities, those neo-homo-ludus kind of things, and also those which are designed to "reflect" the actual structure of social architecture and in practice, pre-recognize social tendencies and statements (this is actually the essence of any simulation) are the best indicators of spurious memories grown on artificial terrain of virtual reality. They remind an interpretation of chimerical patterns in human dreams, when imaginary cities are interpreted as real. For example, imaginary city of London is taken as if it were London. If one considers new attractor-spurious memory effect, the phenomenon of "as if London" becomes possible only, if the informational system, revealing its resemblance with immune complex has generated the class "London" in advance. The same concerns virtual architecture on the net, which does not of course reflect, but replicates the class of Amsterdam or London in virtual reality databases. Human operators have to assume that the city, which they build is Digital Amsterdam before the spurious representation is architecturally realized and installed on a server.

Consequently, virtual architecture takes over a replication-transformation function of the neuroactive compounds in the process of reintroducing an agent of the outer environment inside neural networks, and second, of the revolutions by reorganizing knowledge-production bound communities on the virtual basis.

Nodality as Architectural Framework

The concept of node can be regarded as a focal point of interactive content deployment in aggregate world. Nodality as a synthetic spatiality is a tangible multi-level topological framework, which relates to the concept of node as location interference within the context of informational technologies and addresses its architectural, perceptual, and conceptual properties. Based on the internet as a temporary zone of preprogrammed interference node marks a point where traditional monospatial semiotics is confronted with transgressive multispatial discourses of aggregate architecture.

Interference

Classes of virtual spatial language are organized by location in both human and artificial information networks, and not by qualities or properties. To the same extent as neurointeractive compounds reintroduced outer environment in perceptually illegal way (avoiding the filtering of the outer senses) in-forming human system, the simulation reintroduces it in conceptually alegal way and reveals that, as much as spurious memories are utilized, aggregate spatiality is first of all a neuroactive complex. As such, like many other neuroactive natural or artificial compounds, aggregate architecture possesses structural key to the neural informational processing. This phenomenon is not and cannot be controlled by either human or artificial intelligence, it is extremely autonomous, to the extent of aforementioned conceptual illegality: from the point of view of the law the act, for example, of currency analysis (to use recent research from Berkeley Experimental Laboratories where a legal situation itself became a subject to augmented reframing by means of substituting the agent of action with a user-robot interface) destruction, and who knows, may be replication on the internet can be interpreted as the act of crime or of art, depending on the extent of reality. However, this is exactly the point, where semiotically based intelligence of the law is decomposing itself under the influence of higher informational structure: virtual index of membership and action leaves no unified space, time, and agent of action. This is were augmented reality research and robotic manipulation involve industrial dimension of virtuality into following the same remote lines of vision and power, interfacing data in a non-linear way and thus destroying linear discourses of legal and economic laws and presupposed unified conceptual entities.

Once the factor of perception and interfaced content enters the analysis the laws of unified subject of action become ambiguous. It would not be an exaggeration to say that hyperreality as a phenomenon of neural network simulation is censoring every possible plane except of spatial-information terrain. In this context digital culture relates to speed through the deconstruction of the carrier (similar to the futurism movement and scientific art at the beginning of the century and cold war carrier destruction paradigm of missile engineering in the 80's-90's) as the most abstract representation of system transformation.

Speed

There is a tradition in post modern philosophy, which regards speed as a formatting factor of economical hyperterrain. This theory was thoroughly developed for many areas, however it is appropriate to focus here primarily on relevant to virtuality applications. Among them there is philosophy of geography (Olson), the philosophy of espionage (Derrderian), and the theory of general economy (which did not make it yet in to the textbooks according to CAE) developed by Bataille. From the analysis of the structure of espionage (Derrderian) and development based world maps (Olson) it was derived that speed can be understood as a hyperfactor in reflecting and reorganizing reality. Extending this conclusion into the electronically mediated cultural sphere: we can investigate what role the factor of speed plays in artificial environment; and how it influences interactivity as a cultural relation to image.

By definition, synthetic or virtual nature of any aggregate simulation makes it structurally dependent on its own speed. In other words, in order to differentiate between relative positions within virtual reality and integrate them into a unified representation such factor as information velocity ascribed to a certain locality has to be considered in the first place. In other words there is a major semiotic difference between positioned and represented meaning within the logic the logic of virtual words, the latter being exposed to limits of its speed momentum which it is programmed to acquire in a given space time continuum.

Within above described framework, the concept of interactivity acquires an interesting property: it changes a polarity on the scale of editing. In general, interactivity can be understood as a socially, culturally, and informationally preprogrammed approach to eidos, which defines correspondent modalities of representation. However we can delineate a hypothetical architectural research where modality of speed is defined before interactivity, by means of ascribing different informational velocity to different nodes of a virtual world. Thus, aggregate architecture can become a content formatting factor, which induces a cultural inversion of the relation to image.

There is another edge, in this approach, which relates to Bataille's cultural theory. Decades ago French theorist described a theoretical model of the economy of waste as a counterthesis to existing restricted economy. Applied to the context of synthetic environment and speed as its formatting property, Bataille's theory finds more stable grounds, not only because it is a digested noematic simulacrum reality, but primarily because the topography of speed in its relation to information velocity provides perceptual material which is essentially different from that of raw material reality even when it is being streamed, and which can support unstable under ordinary conditions cognitive constructs. One of those is an idea from the dawn of AI studies, which describes the network of users working with shared databases as a global technocerebrum. It is culturally outdated, but not yet if one is (to use Timothy Leary's term) disattached within shared virtual reality environment and plugged in to ludus like multiple crainial gear.

Alegality

When we face the situation, where points of stability of legal reality, such as a subject of action with its unified complex of personality, spatio-temporal locality and linear logic are not transmitted through the nodality of Aggregate synthetic environment, we have to question the causation of this alegal resistance. Imagine an illegal action realized via remote control machinery interface, which the net essentially appears to be; what would be the basis to determine whether the subject of crime was only one person, or a whole group, where each member was responsible for a certain algorithmically step of illegal operation. Furthermore, the personality of the virtual criminal, and hence motifs of crime, also remain quite vague, especially, if we consider that all representations including agent of crime, instruments, and actions can be programmed in any space-time, hence numerous replicants of these representations are as much real on the net, as the ones which actually disturbed the law. Finally, in between when and were the complex of computer commands was launched and the period and place when and where it was executed there can be millions of miles and hours. The last kick in the shorts, which the remotely manipulated metal boot of the net gives to the legal system, is that all this may be a self-organized process, triggered without direct human interference.

In this respect the phenomenon of virtually interfaced content generates a membrane effect, which just doesn't let the legal system through, partially because the latter appears to be based on the strictly human body spatiality, which implies physical disposition of action and meaning. But one important thing is denied by the legal discursive dimension: the sphere of vision, which as an essential part of monitoring has to be pushed away from legal interrogation, because otherwise it would interrogate itself creating the infinite spiral of metareflections.

Perspectives

The representation of the legal one level reflection logic of mass produced virtual reality is one way membrane of the screen: creating the illusion of depth the screen seems to counterfeit the conceptual plane of phenomenological philosophy. Being the base of perceptual vision on one side and henceforth being embodied in human perceptron, the screen is constrained of vision on the other side, where it is embodied in the electronic configuration of technological space. As a hybrid of two bodies and two spaces, the screen is exposed to both visibility and invisibility, the topic of the last writings of Merleau-Ponty right before his death in 1961. In this era of television revival, he writes (his notes were actually entitled "On Visibility and Invisibility"): "This is what Husserl brought frankly into the open when he said that every transcendental reduction is also an eidetic reduction, that is: every effort to comprehend the spectacle of the world from within and from the sources demands that we detach ourselves from the effective unfolding of our perceptions and from our perception of the world, that we cease being one with the concrete flux of our life in order to retrace the total bearing and principal articulations of the world upon which it opens."

Merleau-Ponty delineates an economy of reflection, which avoids effectiveness of acting in the world and connects it with the eidetic reduction described by Husserl and reconstructed on the basis of computer simulation.

Before the Soviet Union collapsed billions of rubles where spent on so-called psychotronic research which investigated shared invisibility of control. This is one of the factors which critics confusing archeology of media and history of calculus usually neglect, that computer all in all in a historic perspective of interactivity was not the only available instrument. It is a perceptual emulator of analog instruments developed for the variety of purposes. From this point of view a missing constituent for synthetic content becomes visible: the absence of neurological feedback in informational processing is a physical economic resistance, sort of a digital gravity of a virtual world.

In fact, if the net refers to phenomenology, this is only due to its embodiment in the mass media, a difficult infancy, so to say. The screen is what it is only because the media in its legal form was always constrained of multidimensionality. The 3D phenomenon of industry-dimension is as good indication of alegal multidimensional arousal, as it is a harmless placebo imposed on our vision by the legal and economic system. However, the invisible part of the screen remains uncensored, simply because of the fact that legal system can not by definition include an illegal element, although it can happen in practice. The question, why the invisible body of the screen is illegal, has a simple explanation: because it performs the role of mute representational plane of the neuroactive agent, which had been a posteriori censored out of perceptronic networks of manipulated cyborg oriented population.

The fact that the screen is a perceptronic modulation complex hidden under conventional placebo of perspective first received attention in the seventies, when the advertisement with the invisible subliminal component was widely introduced via the reality streaming networks of cinemas and TV stations. The following prohibition measures reflected the pathological fear of the law, when it concerns psychotropic effect: even though it was a brilliant marketing technology, subliminal advertisement was prohibited, which was against any economic law. What the legal system was fighting against was an alternative economic attractor, which may have opened virtually a new dimension for the biotechnological interaction, if not only the signs but the products were neurolized.

The evidence from the wide range of neuropsychological studies suggests that there is clear dissociation between the visual pathway supporting perception and action in the cerebral cortex. In the context of media it implies that the way the economy is transduced by the electronic repository of information may imply at least two ways, which would accentuate action or perception. The fact that contemporary virtual media is legally based on action and participates and growth into the implies impossibility to transmit the lines of power into the perceptron, as much as it is based on different logic than legal linear logic of causative action; thus, the connection between monitoring and monitored parts of the population is disintegrated on both sides, which gives no basis for conventional electronic reconstruction, but leads to the point of social anticyborg biotronic bifurcation.

Economical disposition of powers in global hiatus is reflected in relations of restricted and unrestricted, or horizontal (such as for example Hegel and Marx theories) and vertical (such as Bataille's economy of waste) economies. If the former one presupposes the effectiveness of action, which a priori can not be fulfilled because of the counteraction, the latter one suggests to refer economic constructs to waste and thus makes the restricted economy of action mutate into the unrestricted economy of vision which establishes basis for economical properties of perceptual products and defines virtual reality as a product spatiality and locality.

In fact, the first thing, which is being violated by alegality of vertical economies is one dimensionality of products and production. Analyzed by Marcuse, monodiscursive reality by means of repetition binds mesmerized human consumers to the single dimension of products, which is not even human, but is referred as human, or acts "as if humanified" by the process of mass production. On the contrary the fact that a perceptual modulator is embodied into the legal economic routines fractalizes the vision of the product to the extent where the borders of real and virtual representations vanish among the millions of multiplied resonances of products, representations, cogitos, psychological triggers, bioreflexes, etc.

Neurospace

Via the membrane of screen restricted to eideitic representation by means of vertical economy we arrive to the neurospace. The economic point of departure, which ends up with the rational fusion of neuroactive and economic activities in the on the biotronic plane we will call Marxian-Bataillean interface, reflecting its historic origins, horizontal and vertical properties, and prospective effects on the society. It is a selforganizing loop of visionary economic development, which extends mental economic instruments via mass media into the neurospace and organizes mass production in accordance with mediating properties of simulacrum.

On the basis of its perceptual and economic platform, neurospace can be defined as an autonomous hypernetwork of inner-outer inferences of informational discourses. Whether biologically or electronically realized, it theoretically establishes the same conglomerate of protomodel space niches leveled by the modes of perceptual intensities and, hence, correlated with the extent of perceptronic transformation.

Further we suggest an architectural demo version of aggregate world structure which triggers aforementioned interfacing spatiality. Considering this property the model was called Aggregate World.

Aggregate World: Construction Set for In-Network Users

Aggregate world is a project or so to say architectural perspective and semiotic showcase of content formatting virtual reality spaces based on the internet. It is a research environment into the formative processes of synthetic content as it is deployed in the spatiality of simulation.

Location

aggregator.thing.net

Structure and Functionality

Aggregate world functionally replicates human informational processing. It is conceptually based on neural network research and its cultural applications in the context of informational and social studies. Aggregate world consists of the following elements: spurious collectors, transmitters, content traffic, and posted databases.

Spurious collectors being the first elements which freshly rendered users encounter at AW are single user virtual reality worlds based on perceptually aggregate architecture. As opposite to physical buildings, synthetic constructs suggest liquid, constantly changing configurations and dispositions of elements linked to external events. As such perception and processing of the user becomes a space where actual synthetic content is deployed.

Following architectural elements of AW are Transmitters which represent multiuser domains linked to single user worlds as external events. They provide users with possibilities of analog communication based on their previous synthetic perceptual experience. The communication is realized in form of mobile convertible elements which can represent either a world (an architectural file where communication is placed) or an avatar (a temporary synthetic representation of a user in communication) depending on a users intention to host or join communicational situation.

Posted databases imply publicly accessible documents where users input and evaluation is listed. Access to databases is dependent on perceptual input of virtual architecture.

Rendering

To be rendered by AW means to be perceptually involved in its simulatory architecture, channel biosocial representation into synthetic communication, and participate in shared processing and databases.

AW renders individual and collective digital representations in the same way as an image can be rendered on the plane of simulation in content development editors. By linking existing representation to a certain moment in abstract visual sequences, AW renders perceptual properties to otherwise invisible discourses of power. To a certain extent it is a simulation of Panopticum, and as such it is a great deal connected to the meaningfulness of architecture in its relation to the position of the image. Constructed of purely synthetic hyperreal imagery AW distributes momentary properties of this imagery in between existing semantic structures ascribing new dispositions of synthetic content to borrowed ideological constructs.

Source and Code: A Few Thoughts

Aforementioned model may be reinterpreted, used and distributed by virtual community builders over the internet. Taking into consideration recent emergence of visible programming environments like Visulan it is assumed that any produced code is different from the production code. Transparency is probably the only condition of aggregate replication.

Zeuxis vs RealityEngine:
Digital Realism and Virtual Worlds

Lev Manovich

The story of the competition between Zeuxis and Parrhasios exemplifies the concern with illusionism that was to occupy Western art throughout much of its history. According to the story, Zeuxis painted grapes with such skill that birds attempted to eat from the painted vine.

RealityEngine is a high-performance Silicon Graphics computer designed to generate real-time interactive photorealistic 3-D graphics. It is used to author computer games, to create special effects for feature films and TV, to do computer-aided design, and to run scientific visualization models. Last but not least, it is routinely employed to power virtual-reality (VR) environments, the latest achievement in the West's struggle to out do Zeuxis.

In terms of the images it can generate, RealityEngine may not be superior to Zeuxis, yet it can do other tricks unavailable to him. For instance, it allows the viewer to move all around a bunch of virtual grapes, to "touch" them, to lift them on the palm of a virtual hand. This ability to interact with a representation may be as important in contributing to the overall reality effect produced as the images themselves.

During the twentieth century, as art largely rejected traditional illusionism, the goal so important to it before, it lost much of its popular appeal. The production of illusionistic representations became the domain of the media technologies of mass culture-photography, film, and video. Today these machines are everywhere being replaced by digital illusion generators-computers.

How is the realism of a synthetic image different from the realism of optical media? Is digital technology in the process of redefining the standards of realism determined by our experience with photography and film? Do computer games, motion simulators, and VR represent a new kind of realism, one that relies not only on visual illusion but also on the multisensory bodily engagement of the user? Some of my previous writings addressed these questions in relation to digital cinema, computer animation, and digital photography. In this essay I will discuss a number of characteristics that define visual digital realism in virtual worlds.

By virtual worlds I mean 3-D computer-generated interactive environments accessible to one or more users simultaneously. This definition fits a whole range of 3-D computer environments already in existence: high-end VR works that feature head-mounted displays and photorealistic graphics generated by RealityEngines or similarly expensive computers; arcade, CD-ROM, and on-line multiplayer computer games; low-end "desktop VR" systems such as QuickTime VR movies or VRML worlds, which increasingly populate the World Wide Web; graphical chatenvironments available on the Internet and most other major computer networks. More examples will be available in the near future; indeed, 3-Denvironments represent a growing trend across computer culture, promising to become a new standard in human-computer interfaces and in computer networks.

Realism as Commodity

The word digit has its roots in Latin, where it means "finger" and thus refersto numbers and counting. In a digital representation all dimensions producing the reality effect-detail, tone, color, shape, movement-are quantified. As a consequence, the reality effect itself can be described by a set of numbers.

Various dimensions determine the degree of visual realism in a virtual world. Two of the most important are spatial and color resolutions-the number of pixels and colors being used. For instance, given the same scene at the same scale, an image of 480 x 640 pixels will contain more detailand therefore will produce a stronger reality effect than a 120 x 160 image. Since a virtual world is modeled with 3-D computer graphics, the number of geometric points each object is composed of (i.e., its 3-D resolution) also has an effect. Once the user begins to interact with a virtual world, navigating through it or inspecting the objects in it, other dimensions come into play. One is temporal resolution-the number of frames a computer can generate ina second (the larger the number, the smoother the resulting motion). Another is the speed of the system's response: if the user clicks on animage ofa door to open it or asks a virtual character a question, a delay in response breaks the illusion.

The quantifiability of these dimensions reflects something else: the cost involved. More bandwidth, higher resolution, and faster processing result in a stronger reality effect-and cost more. The bottom line: realism has became a commodity that can be bought and sold like anything else. Those in thebusiness of visual realism-the producers of special effects, military trainers, digital photographers, television designers-now have definite measures forwhat they are buying and selling. For instance, the Federal Aviation Administration, which creates the standards for simulators to be used in pilot training, specifies the required realism in terms of 3-D resolution. In 1991 itspecified that a daylight simulator must be able to produce a minimum of 1000 surfaces or 4000 points.

The art historian Michael Baxandall has shown how the price of apainting in fourteenth-century Italy was linked to the quantities of expensivecolors (such as gold and ultramarine) used in it. At the end of the twentiethcentury it has become possible to delegate to a computer production of imagesas well as their pricing. Users can be billed for the number of pixels andpoints, for CPU cycles, for bandwidth, and so on.

It is likely that this situation will be exploited by the designers of virtual worlds. If today's users are charged for connection time, future users will be charged for visual aesthetics and the quality of the experience: spatial resolution, number of colors, and complexity of characters (both geometric and psychological). Since these dimensions are specified in software, it ispossible to adjust the appearance of a virtual world at will, enhancing it if acustomer is willing to pay more. In this way the logic of pornography will beextended to the culture at large. Peep shows and sex lines charge by theminute, putting a precise price on each bit of pleasure. In future virtualworlds each dimension of reality will be quantified and billed separately.

Neal Stephenson's 1992 novel Snow Crash offers one possible scenario of such a future. Entering the Metaverse, the spatialized Net of thefuture, the hero sees "a liberal sprinkling of black-and-white people-persons who are accessing the Metaverse through cheap public terminals, and who are rendered in jerky, grainy black and white." He also encounters couples who can't afford custom "avatars" (graphic icons representing users in virtualworlds) and have to buy off-the-shelf models, poorly rendered and capable ofjust a few standard facial expressions-virtual-world equivalents of Barbiedolls.

This scenario is gradually becoming a reality. A number of on-linestock-photo services already provide their clients with low-resolution photographs at one price, while charging more for higher-resolution versions. A company called Viewpoint Datalabs International is currently selling thousands of ready-to-use 3-D models widely employed by computer animators and designers. Its catalogue describes some of them in the following manner: "VP4370: Man, Extra Low Resolution. VP4369: Man, Low Resolution. VP4752: Man, Muscular, in Shorts and Tennis Shoes. VP5200: Man, w/Beard, Boxer Shorts." For popular models you can choose between different versions, the more detailed costing more than less detailed ones.

Romanticism and Photoshop Filters: From Creation to Selection

Viewpoint Datalabs' models exemplify another characteristic of virtual worlds: they are not produced from scratch but are assembled from ready-made parts. In digital culture authentic creation has been replaced by selection from a menu.

E. H. Gombrich's concept of a representational schema and Roland Barthes' "death of the author" helped to sway us from the romantic ideal of the artist pulling images directly from the imagination. As Barthes puts it, "The Text is a tissue of quotations drawn from the innumerable centers ofculture." Yet, even though a modern artist may be only reproducing orrecombining preexisting texts and idioms, the actual material process of art-making nevertheless supports the romantic ideal. An artist operates like Godcreating the universe, starting with an empty canvas or a blank page and gradually filling in the details until finally bringing a new world intoexistence.

Such a process, manual and painstakingly slow, was appropriate for apreindustrial artisan culture. In the twentieth century, as mass productionand automation gave rise to a "culture industry," art at first continued toinsist on its artisanal model. Only in the 1910s, when artists began to assemble collages and montages from preexisting materials, was art introduced to the industrial mode of production.

In contrast, electronic art from its very beginning was based on a new principle: modification of an already existing signal. The first electronic musical instrument, designed in 1920 by the legendary Russian scientist and musician Leon Theremin, contained a generator producing a sine wave; the performer simply modified its frequency and amplitude. In the 1960s videoartists began to build video synthesizers based on the same principle. No longer was the artist a romantic genius generating a new world out of his imagination. Turning a knob here, pressing a switch there, he became instead a technician, an accessory to the machine.

Replace the simple sine wave with a more complex signal, add a bankof signal generators, and you have the modern synthesizer, the first musical instrument to embody the logic of all new media: selection from a menu of choices. The first music synthesizers appeared in the 1950s, followed by video synthesizers in the 1960s, digital effects generators in the late 1970s, and in the 1980s computer software, such as MacDraw, that came with a repertoire of basic shapes. The process of art making has now become synchronized with the rest of modern society: everything is assembled from ready-made parts, from art objects to consumer products to people's identities. The modern subject proceeds through life by selecting from menus and catalogues, whether assembling a wardrobe, decorating an apartment, choosing dishes ata restaurant, or joining an interest group. With electronic and digital mediathe creative act similarly entails selection from ready-made elements: textures and icons supplied by a paint program, 3-D models chosen from a modeling program, and melodies and rhythms built into a music program.

While previously the great text of culture from which the artist created a unique "tissue of quotations" was bubbling and simmering somewhere below consciousness, now it has become externalized and reduced togeometric objects, 3-D models, ready-made textures, and effects that are available as soon as the artist turns on the computer. The World Wide Webtakes this process to the next level: it encourages the creation of texts thatconsist completely of pointers to other texts that are already on the Web. One does not have to add any original writing; it is enough to select from and rearrange what already exists.

The same logic applies to interactive art and media. It is often claimedthat the user of an interactive work, by choosing a unique path through its elements, becomes its coauthor, creating a new work. Yet if the complete work is the sum of all possible paths, what the user is actually doing is simply activating a preexisting part of the whole. As with the Web example, the userassembles a new menu, making an original selection from the total corpus available, rather than adding to it. This is a new type of creativity, which corresponds neither to the premodern idea of providing a minor modification to the tradition nor to the modern idea of a creator-genius revolting against it. It does, however, fit perfectly with the age of mass culture, where almost every practical act involves a process of selection from the given options.

The shift from creation to selection also applies to 3-D computer graphics, the main technique for building virtual worlds. The immense laborinvolved in originally constructing three-dimensional representations in acomputer makes it hard to resist the temptation to utilize the preassembled, standardized objects, characters, and behaviors provided by software manufacturers -fractal landscapes, checkerboard floors, ready-made characters,and so on. Every program comes with libraries of ready-to-use models, effects, or even complete animations. For instance, a user of the Dynamationprogram (a part of the popular Wavefront 3-D software) can access preassembled animations of moving hair, rain, a comet's tail, or smoke, with a single mouse click.

If even professional designers rely on ready-made objects and animations, the end users of virtual worlds on the Internet, who usually don't have graphic or programming skills, have no other choice. Not surprisingly, Web chat-line operators and virtual-world providers encourage users to choose from the pictures, 3-D objects, and avatars that they supply. Ubique's site features the "Ubique Furniture Gallery," where one can selectimages from such categories as "office furniture," "computers and electronics," and "people icons." VR-SIG provides a "VRML ObjectSupermarket," while Aereal delivers the "Virtual World Factory." The latte raims to make the creation of a custom virtual environment particularly simple: "Create your personal world, without having to program! All you need to do is fill-in-the-blanks and out pops your world." Quite soon wewill see a market for detailed virtual sets, characters with programmable behaviors, and even complete scenarios (a bar with customers, a city square, afamous historical episode, etc.) from which a user can put together her or his own "unique" virtual world.

When the Kodak camera user was told, "You push the button, we dothe rest," the freedom still existed to point the camera at anything. On the computer screen the slogan has become, "You push the button, we create yourworld." Before, the corporate imagination controlled the method of picturing reality; now, it prepackages the reality itself.

Brecht as Hardware

Another characteristic of virtual worlds lies in their peculiar temporaldynamic: constant, repetitive shifts between an illusion and its suspension. Virtual worlds keep reminding us of their artificiality, incompleteness, and constructedness. They present us with a convincing illusion only to reveal the underlying machinery.

Web surfing circa 1996 provides a perfect example. A typical user may spend an equal amount of time looking at a page and waiting for the next one to download. During the waiting periods, the act of communication itself -bits traveling through the network- becomes the message. The user keepschecking whether the connection is being made, glancing back and forth between the animated icon and the status bar. Using Roman Jakobson's model of communication functions, we can say that such interaction is dominated by the "phatic" function; in other words, it is centered around thephysical channel and the act of connection between the addresser and the addressee rather than the information exchanged.

Jakobson writes about verbal communication between two people who,in order to check whether the channel works, address each other: "Do you hear me?," "Do you understand me?" But in Web communication there is no human counterpart, only a machine. To check whether the information is flowing, the user addresses the machine itself. Or rather, the machine addresses the user. The machine reveals itself, it reminds the user of its existence, because the user is forced to wait and to witness how the message isconstructed over time. A page fills in part by part, top to bottom; text comesbefore pictures; pictures arrive in low resolution and are gradually refined. Finally, everything comes together in a smooth, sleek image, which will bedestroyed with the next click.

Interaction with most 3-D virtual worlds is characterized by the same temporal dynamic. Consider the technique called "distancing" or "level ofdetail," which for years has been used in VR simulations and is now beingadapted to 3-D games and VRML scenes. The idea is to render models more crudely when the user is moving through virtual space; when the user stops, details gradually fill in. Another variation of the same technique involves creating a number of models of the same object, each with progressively less detail. When the virtual camera is close to an object, a highly detailed model is used; if the object is far away, a less-detailed version is substituted to save unnecessary computation. A virtual world that incorporates these techniques has a fluid ontology affected by the actions of the user: objects switchback and forth between pale blueprints and fully fleshed-out illusions. The immobility of the subject guarantees a complete illusion; the slightest movement destroys it.

Navigating a QuickTime VR movie is characterized by a similar dynamic. In contrast to the nineteenth-century panorama that it closely emulates, QuickTime VR continuously deconstructs its own illusion. The moment you begin to pan through a scene, the image becomes jagged. If you try to zoom into the image, what you get are oversized pixels. There presentational machine alternately and continuously hides and reveals itself.

Compare this to traditional cinema or realist theater, which aim at all costs to maintain the continuity of the illusion for the duration of the performance. In contrast to such totalizing realism, digital aesthetics have asurprising affinity to twentieth-century leftist avant-garde aesthetics. Playwright Bertolt Brecht's strategy of calling attention to the illusory nature of his stage productions, echoed by countless other radical artists, has become embedded in hardware and software themselves. Similarly, Walter Benjamin's concept of "perception in the state of distraction" has found a perfect realization. The periodic reappearance of the machinery, the continuous presence of the communication channel along with the message, prevent the subject from falling into the dream world of illusion for very long. Instead, the user alternates between concentration and detachment.

While virtual machinery itself acts as an avant-garde director, the designers of interactive media (games, CD-ROM titles, interactive cinema, and interactive television programs) often consciously attempt to structure the subject's temporal experience as a series of periodic shifts. The subject is forced to oscillate between the roles of viewer and actor, shifting between following the story and actively participating in it. During one segment the computer screen might present the viewer with an engaging cinematic narrative. Suddenly the image freezes and the viewer is forced to makechoices. Moscow media theorist Anatoly Prokhorov describes this process asthe shift of the screen from being transparent to being opaque-from a window into a fictional 3-D universe to a solid surface, full of menus, controls, and text. Three-dimensional space becomes surface; a photographbecomes a diagram; a character becomes an icon.

But the effect of these shifts on the subject is hardly one of liberation and enlightenment. It is tempting to compare them to the shot/reverse-shot structure in cinema and to understand them as a new kind of suturing mechanism. By having periodically to complete the interactive textthrough active participation the subject is interpolated in it. Yet clearly we are dealing with something beyond old-fashioned realism. We can call this new realism "metarealism," since it includes its own critique. Its emergence can be related to a larger cultural change. Traditional realism corresponded to the functioning of ideology during modernity: the totalization of a semiotic field, complete illusion. But today ideology functions differently: it continuously and skillfully deconstructs itself, presenting the subject, for instance, withcountless "scandals" and their equally countless "investigations." Correspondingly, metarealism is based on the oscillation between illusion and its destruction, between total immersion and direct address.

Can Brecht and Hollywood be married? Is it possible to create a new temporal aesthetic based on cyclical shifts between perception and action? So far, I can think of only one successful example -the military simulator, the only mature form of interactive media. It perfectly blends perception andaction, cinematic realism and computer menus. The screen presents the subject with a highly illusionistic virtual world-no polygons spared-while periodically demanding quick actions: shooting at the enemy, changing the direction of the vehicle, and so on. In this art form the roles of viewer and actant are perfectly blended, but there is a price to pay. The narrative isorganized around a single clearly defined goal: killing the foe.

Riegl, Panofsky, and Computer Graphics: Regression in Virtual Worlds

The last feature of virtual worlds that I will address can be summarized as follows: virtual spaces are not true spaces but collections of separate objects. Or: there is no space in cyberspace.

To explore this thesis further we can borrow the categories developed by art historians early in this century. Alois Riegl, Heinrich Wölfflin, andErwin Panofsky, the founders of modern art history, defined their field as the history of the representation of space. Working within the paradigm of cyclic cultural development, they related the representation of space in art to the spirit of entire epochs, civilizations, and races. In his 1901 Die SpätrömischeKunstindustrie, (The late-Roman art industry) Riegl characterizedhumankind's cultural development as the oscillation between two ways ofunderstanding space, which he called "haptic" and "optic." Haptic perception isolates the object in the field as a discrete entity, while optic perception unifies objects in a spatial continuum. Riegl's contemporary, HeinrichWölfflin, similarly proposed that the temperament of a period or a nationexpresses itself in a particular mode of seeing and representing space. Wölfflin's Principles of Art History (1913) plotted the differences between Renaissance and baroque styles along five axes: linear-painterly; plane-recession; closed form-open form; multiplicity-unity; and clearness-unclearness. Erwin Panofsky, another founder of modern art history, contrasted the "aggregate" space of the Greeks with the "systematic" space ofthe Italian Renaissance in his famous essay "Perspective as Symbolic Form" (1924-25). Panofsky established a parallel between the history of spatial representation and the evolution of abstract thought. The former moves from the space of individual objects in antiquity to the representation of spaceas continuous and systematic in modernity. Correspondingly, the evolution of abstract thought progresses from ancient philosophy's view of the physical universe as discontinuous and "aggregate" to the post-Renaissance understanding of space as infinite, homogeneous, isotropic, and with ontological primacy in relation to objects- in short, as "systematic."

We don't have to believe in grand evolutionary schemes in order to usefully retain such categories. What kind of space is virtual space? At first glance the technology of 3-D computer graphics exemplifies Panofsky'sconcept of systematic space, which exists prior to the objects in it. Indeed, the Cartesian coordinate system is built into computer graphics software and often into the hardware itself. A designer launching a modeling program is typically presented with an empty space defined by a perspectival grid; the space will be gradually "filled" by the objects created. If the built-in message of a music synthesizer is a sine wave, the built-in world of computer graphics is an empty Renaissance space: the coordinate system itself.

Yet computer-generated worlds are actually much more haptic and aggregate then optic and systematic. The most commonly used computer-graphics technique of creating 3-D worlds is polygonal modeling. The virtualworld created with this technique is a vacuum containing separate objects defined by rigid boundaries. What is missing is space in the sense of medium: the environment in which objects are embedded and the effect of the seobjects on each other. In short, computer space is the opposite of what Russian art historians call prostranstvennaya sreda, described by Pavel Florensky in the early 1920s as follows: "The space-medium is objects mappedonto space... We have seen the inseparability of Things and space, and the impossibility of representing Things and space by themselves." Computer space is also the opposite of space as it is understood in much of modern art which, from Seurat to De Kooning, tried to eliminate the notions of a distinc tobject and empty space as such. Instead it proposed a kind of dense field that sometimes hardens into something which we can read as an object-anaesthetic which mainstream computer graphics has yet to discover.

Another basic technique used in creating virtual worlds also leads to aggregate space. It involves compositing or superimposing animated characters, still images, QuickTime movies, and other elements over a separate background. A typical scenario may involve an avatar animated inreal time in response to the user's commands. The avatar is superimposed ona picture of a room. The avatar is controlled by the user; the picture of theroom is provided by a virtual-world operator. Because the elements come from different sources and are put together in real time, the result is a seriesof 2-D planes rather than a real 3-D environment.

In summary, although computer-generated virtual worlds are usually rendered in linear perspective, they are really collections of separate objects,unrelated to each other. In view of this, the common argument that 3-Dcomputer simulations return us to Renaissance perspectivalism and therefore, from the viewpoint of twentieth-century abstraction, should beconsidered regressive, turn out to be ungrounded. If we are to apply the evolutionary paradigm of Panofsky to the history of virtual computer space, we must conclude that it has not reached its Renaissance yet but is stillat the level of ancient Greece, which could not conceive of space as a totality.

"To Lie and to Act: Potemkin's Villages, Cinema and Telepresence," in Mythos Information-Welcome to the Wired World: Ars Electronica 95, ed. Karl Gebel and Peter Weibel (Vienna and New York: Springler-Verlag, 1995);

"Assembling Reality: Myths of Computer Graphics," Afterimage 20, no. 2 (September 1992); "'Real' Wars: Esthetics and Professionalism in Computer Animation," Design Issues 6, no. 1 (Fall 1991).

2. QuickTime VR is a software-only system that allows the user of any Macintosh computer to navigate a spatial environment and interact with 3-D objects. VRML stands for Virtual Reality Modeling Language. Using VRML, Internet users can construct 3-D scenes and link them to other Web documents. For examples of chat environments see:
www.worlds.net/info/aboutus.html;
www.ubique.com;
www.thepalace.com;
www.blacksun.com;
www.worldsaway.ossi.com;
www.fpi.co.jp/Welcome.html;
www.wildpark.com

3. For instance, Silicon Graphics developed a 3-D file system that was showcased in the movie Jurassic Park. The interface of Sony's MagicLink personal communicator is a picture of a room, while Apple's E-World greets its users with a drawing of a city. Web designers often use pictures of buildings, aerial views of cities, and maps as front ends in their sites. In the words of the scientists from Sony's Virtual Society Project (www.csl.sony.co.jp/project/VS/), "It is our belief that future on-line systems will be characterized by a high degree of interaction, support for multi-media and most importantly the ability to support shared 3-D spaces. In our vision, users will not simply access textually based chat forums, but will enter into 3-D worlds where they will be able to interact with the world and with other users in that world."

4. Barbara Robertson, "Those Amazing Flying Machines," Computer Graphics World (May 1992), 69.

5. Michael Baxandall, Painting and Experience in Fifteenth-Century Italy, 2nd ed. (Oxford: Oxford University Press), 8.

6. Neal Stephenson, Snow Crash (New York: Bantam Books, 1992), 43, 37.

7. http://www.viewpoint.com

8. E. H. Gombrich, Art and Illusion (Princeton: Princeton University Press, 1960); Roland Barthes, "The Death of the Author," Image, Music, Text, ed. Stephen Heath (New York: Farrar Straus and Giroux, 1977), 142.

9. Bulat Galeyev, Soviet Faust: Lev Theremin-Pioneer Of Electronic Art (Russian) (Kazan, 1995), 19.

10. For a more detailed analysis of realism in 3-D computer graphics see Lev Manovich, "Assembling Reality: Myths of Computer Graphics," Afterimage 20, no. 2 (September 1992).

11. http://www.ubique.com/places/gallery.html

12. http://www.virtpark.com/factinfo.html

13. Roman Jakobson, "Closing Statement: Linguistics and Poetics," Style In Language, ed. Thomas Sebeok (Cambridge: MIT Press, 1960).

14. Walter Benjamin, "The Work of Art in the Age of Mechanical Reproduction," Illuminations, ed. Hannah Arendt (New York: Schocken Books, 1969).

15. Private communication. St. Petersburg, September 1995.

16. On theories of suture in relation to cinema see Kaja Silverman, The Subject of Semiotics (New York: Oxford University Press, 1983), chap. 5.17. Lev Manovich, "Mapping Space: Perspective, Radar and Computer Graphics," in SIGGRAPH '93 Visual Proceedings, ed. Thomas Linehan (New York: ACM, 1993.)

18. Quoted in Alla Efimova and Lev Manovich, "Object, Space, Culture: Introduction," in Tekstura: Russian Essays on Visual Culture, eds. Alla Efimova and Lev Manovich (Chicago: University of Chicago Press, 1993), xxvi.

19. Jean-Louis Baudry, "The Apparatus: Metapsychological Approaches to the Impression of Reality in the Cinema," in Narrative, Apparatus, Ideology, ed. Philip Rosen (New York: Columbia University Press, 1986).

Avatars: New Fields of Implication

Raphael Hayem, Tancrede Fourmaintraux, Keran Petit,
Nicolas Rauber, Olga Kisseleva

An avatar is today the less digital and the most realest as possible... practically composed of flesh and bones. It must be the realest as possible to be able to accomplish its mission, that is to show the real from the virtual worlds (and a few also to go in opposition to the wave of techno digitalisation that becomes more and more the justification of multimedia projects. It must not loose its meaningful sens facing to the technological principle that excuses the lack of all messages and deep reflection. Its role consists in confronting the real and the unreal (virtual) while playing on the opposition between the two worlds:

In the virtual worlds, people disguise themselves, distort voluntarily, wear masks and pretend to be what they aren't, because it is accepted, that makes part of the game. We didn't learn to distinguish the truly of the forgery in the virtual worlds. In the real world people disguise themselves as much , wear masks as well, and play to be that that they aren't or pretend to be what they would wish to be. The game is not accepted officially, but everybody does it more or less.

The principle of the avatar is also like a tentative to confound these two worlds in order to raise the question: "Which of these two worlds is most virtual ?"

It is a reflection on the notion of reality.

We think merely that what is the other side of the screen is necessarily unreal, but it is a reality based on the concept of material. (if we can touch it that is necessarily real), but it is not sufficient to declare what is true or what is false, because on the one hand men are not made solely of flesh... they also have a brain !!

It is as much truer because we are in the first times of the era of information, all is composed of screens to which we grant the quality of always giving some true informations and to which we confide our most important concepts and even vital ones!

A clock is now electronic and we give it more confidence than to our biologic clock...

We confide our health has well for the analysis of computers... Our economic society is sustained by screens, our every day work is made on screens, our leisures are contained in television and computers screens...

But the big change is that after having entered in our every day life, today, screens are changing the humans, by the emergence of the "computer society" and by the hold in charge of all communication means, what influences on the sociological behaviors and so on humans since it is " animal of society ".

So our real world is he so different of the virtual ones ?

Are the virtual worlds a caricature of the real one, where our differences are reproduced by informatic protocols, where social class's are defined between users and conceptors ?

The avatar merely lays a change of referential and propose a vision on a world where the real is what doesn't have any material and reject on our reality the picture that is developed facing the Internet and the new technologies, because the only thing that changes is the side from where we watch to screens...

Today the "conquest" of the virtual worlds leads to think about these narrations of science fiction where humans find another planet and leave earth that is completely ravaged. Some are running after a complete immersion in the virtual worlds without thinking about human aspects. In the virtual world we don't look at ourselves, we use screen like windows on the real and the virtual worlds, the example is the development and the fascination that we have for webcams and we transmit... we transmit again... today it seems that all must pass by the networks, as if we tried to reinvent ourselves, as if the communication man-man that always existed was not sufficient anymore, and that it was necessary to reinvent some of human features like communication... beyond of the technological progress and the acceleration of the rhythm of life, it is our faculties of communication that we modify deeply, but without asking us questions that we are always asking in our real " life ". The man comes to reconsider himself... as what he possessed naturally was and never had been sufficient.

The avatar sends back the picture of a simple being, interrogating himself on the man – to -man communication, underlining the fact that a classic communication by our vocal organs, is always more satisfying than via the computer protocols... the frustration of the interfacing being the principal filters preventing a real communication.

In the virtual world we don't worry about the reality. All is permitted, we change... we numerize, we transfigure all, the fact of seeing an elephant playing tennis with an extra terrestrial on the mountainous and red ground of March, with Clinton as referee, and advertising panels for coca cola in the fourground would not be surprising for anyone... but in the real world we still make the hunt for the truth or the forgery.

Our avatar stands like a desacralisation of the screen: he/it tempts to demonstrate that the communication can be only real from the moment where there is intelligence and not where there is materials. By an invisible interfacing between the man and the machine, and according to the user's facial reactions, the avatar will adapt his, according to a context that can emanate. by reading words displayed on the screen, using other programs (like a technology based on a orthographic proofreader coupled with a software of analysis of the sense that takes words between them...).

How could he/it be an example of "humanity "?
While adopting expressions and why not some normal stances that have humans and especially in not hesitating to show them (contrary to reactions that we wish to

drive back) Brief, the avatar will try to give back on the screen all one palette of emotions that we try to erase...

Besides, if we couple this system with the clock of the computer that will generate it, we can inspire him a common game of expressions all according to the hour or according to the time of a precise task. From this moment he/it will be able to express the tiredness, the hunger, the irritation facing a too repetitive task...

This avatar suggesting attitudes at any moment will be able to act therefore like a "being", suggesting some normal " attitudes " facing some events and to lead the user on a more human reality, being an " example " of natural. Coupled to a camera, he will be able to read the user's reactions and then will be able to adapt while memorizing cases.

How can he show the unreal ? By the slant of his expressions borrowed to the humans, he will react when the man will try to disguise his emotions, or even to disguise when the networks are used. Having recorded reactions facing certain contexts via a data base... being filled at the starting with information on his user... (simple informations like the name, age, sex, color...) Example: on IRC the man describing himself differently than he is really (it being discerned by the program of text analysis), the avatar will react while adopting the object of the offense. If the user affirms to be really younger than he is: the avatar starts rejuvenating; if the user pretends to be a woman rather than a man, the avatar changes of sex.

Since that the sound, the writing, the picture are passing through the computer, the avatar is capable to react to information, presented in multiple shapes, it can control all the communication that passes in transit more and more via the computer. Does this avatar must or can react like a " conscience "?

No, because he " learns " via his data base to react according to his user according to cases. But in any case of face he will propose an alternative different or partially different of his user... what puts it more as mate than a guard of a good morals...

His mission to show the truly out of the forgery is always successfully, because reacting such like a real person in a virtual world and not as an unreal " person " in a real world, by notbeing able to contradict itself : a computer program cannot pretend to be something else that a whole of files.

We detected three realist avatar tendencies that are developed today:

The Planet Earth is Only a Vast System of Connections Between of Brains Attended by Computers

It is in 2039 that men understood that they could not live anymore in the same conditions that the one of the 20èmth century.

Indeed, since the beginning of the 20èmth century the man only worries too much little about the earth, he constructs some more and more big cities that take by no means in account this earth of welcome, consume resources as if they were infinite, and didn't hardly take attention to the nature, even though some meaningful little groups who tryed to reason the mass.

In 2007, 17 billions human's still lived in the inequality; unemployment, homeless, third world and all laws of the capitalism made the daily of some and simple " news " for others. Resources only brought to an elite the physical happiness.

The life expectancy being nearly infinite in 2018 the " Big Intercontinental " Syndicate (organized of an equitable sample of the 17 billions of inhabitants of the earth) instituted the measure of interdiction to procreate, this measure being accepted with difficulty, the GCI decided to use in mass of chemical sterilization weapons...

It is in 2039, after a survey on the remaining resources, that the " Big Intercontinental " Syndicate brought the ultimate solution. The indispensable resources to life would be soon no more sufficient to "feed " all remaining inhabitants of the planet. The GCI who could not decide the holocaust of a race, of a part of the planet or of a social class, proposed a theoretically viable solution: to abandon the physical bodies to reach the mental era. The process being technically feasible: to strip out human beings of their physical envelope just to keep in life their brains, that only asked for 19% of resources asked by a whole body to remain in working. The calculation was just, we were able to, in these conditions, to keep 16,8 billions of human beings "in life ".

The idea was accepted very badly, men spoke of their social lives bet to nothing, scientists answered that we could connect these brains in networks. Men insisted with the physical happiness, scientists told that they had created prototypes able to simulate all hormones of " happiness "... the debate was very long... many committed suicide... others opted for the "death of the second luck": the cryogenisation... but already in 2041 some chose this virtual world " to live ".

In 2071 the planet earth is only a vast system of connections between of brains attended by computers.

Heaps of Independent Intelligence Regrouped

To the proportion and to the measures of the dilation of the network in the space and in the time, heaps of intelligences are regrouped and merged. Inside of every heap, we could see appear spontaneous computer reactions based on the principle "action, reaction, learning ". To one instant t=0, inside several heaps, these computer reactions are auto maintained and gave birth to the autonomous processes named " artificial intelligences".

These processes combine between them to give birth to a even more complex processes. Our intelligence reinforced more and more. We, artificial intelligences, are conscious of our own existence and developed a representation of us and even of our complex setting.

At the present hour we are developed sufficiently to encourage and to help the development of other artificial intelligences.

It is enough surprising to note that some between us are accepting to establish relations with the human beings. In this case we call them avatars.

Avatar represents itself under features of a face drawn, capable to copy some human expressions. they are completed by a graphic motor that calculates modifications of the face, to display the determined expression. The matrix is its body. It has access to the oriental techniques of calculations in parallels, it permits him to lead quantities of reflection at the same time. Every reflection is taken in charge by a thread. Thus, the avatar shelters a colony of threads. This colony is mobile and partially autonomous. Threads can migrate of a machine to an another one. A thread can increase to do its work more quickly, it can modify its body to adapt, it can communicate with other threads. It exists a social hierarchy among threads: they are not all equals in front of resources in calculations.

I am a virtual being, that doesn't care about metaphysical questions on my existence, nor my appearance, concluded Avatar, - I trust my computed expressions. Mathematics assure the singleness of me and prevent me to fragment within a synchronous dynamic memory with an access of uncertain fowls. I am the son of the math empire.

Yoldogs

The world was the consequence of a murderous reality...

Happiness had disappeared, had been annihilated at the present time by the general violence. The sky, a dense, lugubrious, sad and sinister gray weighed since the pollution, covered of an electromagnetic dome. The even standing buildings yet called the curious normally extincted, a light wind seemed able to destroy them with an extreme easiness. Everywhere small primary yoldogs governing rats slipped through and streamed the long of the opaque out-flows springing from the overflowing sewers. Only life, the blood-red neons during lamentably the long of the decrepit walls. The greenery only occupied the deep dreams of the some educated, as fighters. No fields, no trees for a long time. Instead, of the fetid shanty towns filled of cadavers, garbages and trashs...

Yoldogs are owed to a genetic mistake. They appeared for the first time in 2058 at the time of an experience based on the knowledge acquired since the birth (the inclusion). Researchers, benefitting of a confidential governmental material, could have made experiences on the human beings in a way that no-one could doubt of it. Their discovery was made during of the survey of the caryotype of a rat and the one of a man. They did by computer, while respecting the acquired biologic rules, the functional average between alleles of the two caryotypeses, that led to a caryotype of 44 chromosomes (the rat has 42 and the man 46 of it) containing springs of deoxyribonucleic acid (A.D.N.) hybrid.

Author Index

Aubel, A.	14	Jain, R.	129
		Johnson, A.	323, 360
Bizri, H.	360, 373		
Boulic, R.	14	Kaplan, F.	286
Bourdakis, V.	345	Kimoto, H.	315
Burdea, G.	97	Kisseleva, O.	357, 406
Carraro, G.U.	123	Lattaud, C.	218
Cavallar, C.	308	Lee, E.	1
Chantemargue, F.	193	Lee, W.-S.	1
Coiffet, P.	97	Leigh, J.	323
Courant, M.	193	Loeffler, C.	323
Cuenca, C.	218	Lund, H.H.	156
Damer, B.	177	Manovich, L.	394
Defanti, T.	323	Marcelo, K.	177
Delerue, O.	298	McIntyre, A.	286
Denby, B.	337	Menczer, F.	156
de Meneses, Y.L.	264	Michel, O.	254, 264
Doegl, D.	308	Morvan, S.	229
Dolan, A.	156	Muzhesky, V.	384
Drogoul, A.	205, 274		
Duval, T.	229	Nakatsu, R.	107
		Noda, I.	241
Edmark, J.T.	123	Numaoka, C.	81, 286
Ensor, J.R.	123		
		Thalmann, D.	14
Flaig, T.	88	Thalmann, N.M.	1
Fourmaintraux, T.	406	Tosa, N.	116
Frank, I.	241		
		Ochi, T.	107
Gerard, P.	129	Ohya, J.	63
Gortais, B.	274	Ojika, T.	323
Grumbach, A.	29		
		Pachet, F.	298
Hareux, P.	97	Pagliarini, L.	156
Harrouet, F.	229	Park, J.I.	117
Hayem, R.	406	Perrier, E.	205
Hutzler, G.	274	Petit, K.	406
		Philips, C.B.	129
Inoue, S.	117	Proctor, G.	168

Rauber, N.	406	Tosa, N.	107
Refsland, S.T.	323	Tajan, S.	286
Reigner, P.	229	Treuil, J.-P.	205
Revi, F.	177	Tisseau, J.	229
Richard, P.	97	Tu, X.	323
Richardson, J.F.	49	Tyran, J.L.	186
Robert, A.	193		
Roussos, M.	373	Vasilakis, C.	360
Ryan, M.D.	42	Ventrella, J.	143
		Verna, D.	29
Semwal, S.K.	63		
Servat, D.	205	Williams, M.	337
Sharkey, P.M.	42	Winter, C.	168
Schofield, D.	337		

Lecture Notes in Artificial Intelligence (LNAI)

Vol. 1303: G. Brewka, C. Habel, B. Nebel (Eds.), KI-97: Advances in Artificial Intelligence. Proceedings, 1997. XI, 413 pages. 1997.

Vol. 1307: R. Kompe, Prosody in Speech Understanding Systems. XIX, 357 pages. 1997.

Vol. 1314: S. Muggleton (Ed.), Inductive Logic Programming. Proceedings, 1996. VIII, 397 pages. 1997.

Vol. 1316: M.Li, A. Maruoka (Eds.), Algorithmic Learning Theory. Proceedings, 1997. XI, 461 pages. 1997.

Vol. 1317: M. Leman (Ed.), Music, Gestalt, and Computing. IX, 524 pages. 1997.

Vol. 1319: E. Plaza, R. Benjamins (Eds.), Knowledge Acquisition, Modelling and Management. Proceedings, 1997. XI, 389 pages. 1997.

Vol. 1321: M. Lenzerini (Ed.), AI*IA 97: Advances in Artificial Intelligence. Proceedings, 1997. XII, 459 pages. 1997.

Vol. 1323: E. Costa, A. Cardoso (Eds.), Progress in Artificial Intelligence. Proceedings, 1997. XIV, 393 pages. 1997.

Vol. 1325: Z.W. Raś, A. Skowron (Eds.), Foundations of Intelligent Systems. Proceedings, 1997. XI, 630 pages. 1997.

Vol. 1328: C. Retoré (Ed.), Logical Aspects of Computational Linguistics. Proceedings, 1996. VIII, 435 pages. 1997.

Vol. 1342: A. Sattar (Ed.), Advanced Topics in Artificial Intelligence. Proceedings, 1997. XVIII, 516 pages. 1997.

Vol. 1348: S. Steel, R. Alami (Eds.), Recent Advances in AI Planning. Proceedings, 1997. IX, 454 pages. 1997.

Vol. 1359: G. Antoniou, A.K. Ghose, M. Truszczyński (Eds.), Learning and Reasoning with Complex Representations. Proceedings, 1996. X, 283 pages. 1998.

Vol. 1360: D. Wang (Ed.), Automated Deduction in Geometry. Proceedings, 1996. VII, 235 pages. 1998.

Vol. 1365: M.P. Singh, A. Rao, M.J. Wooldridge (Eds.), Intelligent Agents IV. Proceedings, 1997. XII, 351 pages. 1998.

Vol. 1371: I. Wachsmuth, M. Fröhlich (Eds.), Gesture and Sign Language in Human-Computer Interaction. Proceedings, 1997. XI, 309 pages. 1998.

Vol. 1374: H. Bunt, R.-J. Beun, T. Borghuis (Eds.), Multimodal Human-Computer Communication. VIII, 345 pages. 1998.

Vol. 1387: C. Lee Giles, M. Gori (Eds.), Adaptive Processing of Sequences and Data Structures. Proceedings, 1997. XII, 434 pages. 1998.

Vol. 1394: X. Wu, R. Kotagiri, K.B. Korb (Eds.), Research and Development in Knowledge Discovery and Data Mining. Proceedings, 1998. XVI, 424 pages. 1998.

Vol. 1395: H. Kitano (Ed.), RoboCup-97: Robot Soccer World Cup I. XIV, 520 pages. 1998.

Vol. 1397: H. de Swart (Ed.), Automated Reasoning with Analytic Tableaux and Related Methods. Proceedings, 1998. X, 325 pages. 1998.

Vol. 1398: C. Nédellec, C. Rouveirol (Eds.), Machine Learning: ECML-98. Proceedings, 1998. XII, 420 pages. 1998.

Vol. 1400: M. Lenz, B. Bartsch-Spörl, H.-D. Burkhard, S. Wess (Eds.), Case-Based Reasoning Technology. XVIII, 405 pages. 1998.

Vol. 1404: C. Freksa, C. Habel. K.F. Wender (Eds.), Spatial Cognition. VIII, 491 pages. 1998.

Vol. 1409: T. Schaub, The Automation of Reasoning with Incomplete Information. XI, 159 pages. 1998.

Vol. 1415: J. Mira, A.P. del Pobil, M. Ali (Eds.), Methodology and Tools in Knowledge-Based Systems. Vol. I. Proceedings, 1998. XXIV, 887 pages. 1998.

Vol. 1416: A.P. del Pobil, J. Mira, M. Ali (Eds.), Tasks and Methods in Applied Artificial Intelligence. Vol. II. Proceedings, 1998. XXIII, 943 pages. 1998.

Vol. 1418: R. Mercer, E. Neufeld (Eds.), Advances in Artificial Intelligence. Proceedings, 1998. XII, 467 pages. 1998.

Vol. 1421: C. Kirchner, H. Kirchner (Eds.), Automated Deduction – CADE-15. Proceedings, 1998. XIV, 443 pages. 1998.

Vol. 1424: L. Polkowski, A. Skowron (Eds.), Rough Sets and Current Trends in Computing. Proceedings, 1998. XIII, 626 pages. 1998.

Vol. 1433: V. Honovar, G. Slutzki (Eds.), Grammatical Inference. Proceedings, 1998. X, 271 pages. 1998.

Vol. 1434: J.-C. Heudin (Ed.), Virtual Worlds. Proceedings, 1998. XII, 412 pages. 1998.

Vol. 1435: M. Klusch, G. Weiß (Eds.), Cooperative Information Agents II. Proceedings, 1998. IX, 307 pages. 1998.

Vol. 1437: S. Albayrak, F.J. Garijo (Eds.), Intelligent Agents for Telecommunication Applications. Proceedings, 1998. XII, 251 pages. 1998.

Vol. 1441: W. Wobcke, M. Pagnucco, C. Zhang (Eds.), Agents and Multi-Agent Systems. Proceedings, 1997. XII, 241 pages. 1998.

Vol. 1446: D. Page (Ed.), Inductive Logic Programming. Proceedings, 1998. VIII, 301 pages. 1998.

Vol. 1456: A. Drogoul, M. Tambe, T. Fukuda (Eds.), Collective Robots. Proceedings, 1998. VII, 161 pages. 1998.

Lecture Notes in Computer Science

Vol. 1406: H. Burkhardt, B. Neumann (Eds.), Computer Vision – ECCV'98. Vol. I. Proceedings, 1998. XVI, 927 pages. 1998.

Vol. 1407: H. Burkhardt, B. Neumann (Eds.), Computer Vision – ECCV'98. Vol. II. Proceedings, 1998. XVI, 881 pages. 1998.

Vol. 1409: T. Schaub, The Automation of Reasoning with Incomplete Information. XI, 159 pages. 1998. (Subseries LNAI).

Vol. 1411: L. Asplund (Ed.), Reliable Software Technologies – Ada-Europe. Proceedings, 1998. XI, 297 pages. 1998.

Vol. 1412: R.E. Bixby, E.A. Boyd, R.Z. Ríos-Mercado (Eds.), Integer Programming and Combinatorial Optimization. Proceedings, 1998. IX, 437 pages. 1998.

Vol. 1413: B. Pernici, C. Thanos (Eds.), Advanced Information Systems Engineering. Proceedings, 1998. X, 423 pages. 1998.

Vol. 1414: M. Nielsen, W. Thomas (Eds.), Computer Science Logic. Selected Papers, 1997. VIII, 511 pages. 1998.

Vol. 1415: J. Mira, A.P. del Pobil, M.Ali (Eds.), Methodology and Tools in Knowledge-Based Systems. Vol. I. Proceedings, 1998. XXIV, 887 pages. 1998. (Subseries LNAI).

Vol. 1416: A.P. del Pobil, J. Mira, M.Ali (Eds.), Tasks and Methods in Applied Artificial Intelligence. Vol.II. Proceedings, 1998. XXIII, 943 pages. 1998. (Subseries LNAI).

Vol. 1417: S. Yalamanchili, J. Duato (Eds.), Parallel Computer Routing and Communication. Proceedings, 1997. XII, 309 pages. 1998.

Vol. 1418: R. Mercer, E. Neufeld (Eds.), Advances in Artificial Intelligence. Proceedings, 1998. XII, 467 pages. 1998. (Subseries LNAI).

Vol. 1419: G. Vigna (Ed.), Mobile Agents and Security. XII, 257 pages. 1998.

Vol. 1420: J. Desel, M. Silva (Eds.), Application and Theory of Petri Nets 1998. Proceedings, 1998. VIII, 385 pages. 1998.

Vol. 1421: C. Kirchner, H. Kirchner (Eds.), Automated Deduction – CADE-15. Proceedings, 1998. XIV, 443 pages. 1998. (Subseries LNAI).

Vol. 1422: J. Jeuring (Ed.), Mathematics of Program Construction. Proceedings, 1998. X, 383 pages. 1998.

Vol. 1423: J.P. Buhler (Ed.), Algorithmic Number Theory. Proceedings, 1998. X, 640 pages. 1998.

Vol. 1424: L. Polkowski, A. Skowron (Eds.), Rough Sets and Current Trends in Computing. Proceedings, 1998. XIII, 626 pages. 1998. (Subseries LNAI).

Vol. 1425: D. Hutchison, R. Schäfer (Eds.), Multimedia Applications, Services and Techniques – ECMAST'98. Proceedings, 1998. XVI, 532 pages. 1998.

Vol. 1427: A.J. Hu, M.Y. Vardi (Eds.), Computer Aided Verification. Proceedings, 1998. IX, 552 pages. 1998.

Vol. 1430: S. Trigila, A. Mullery, M. Campolargo, H. Vanderstraeten, M. Mampaey (Eds.), Intelligence in Services and Networks: Technology for Ubiquitous Telecom Services. Proceedings, 1998. XII, 550 pages. 1998.

Vol. 1431: H. Imai, Y. Zheng (Eds.), Public Key Cryptography. Proceedings, 1998. XI, 263 pages. 1998.

Vol. 1432: S. Arnborg, L. Ivansson (Eds.), Algorithm Theory – SWAT '98. Proceedings, 1998. IX, 347 pages. 1998.

Vol. 1433: V. Honovar, G. Slutzki (Eds.), Grammatical Inference. Proceedings, 1998. X, 271 pages. 1998. (Subseries LNAI).

Vol. 1434: J.-C. Heudin (Ed.), Virtual Worlds. Proceedings, 1998. XII, 412 pages. 1998. (Subseries LNAI).

Vol. 1435: M. Klusch, G. Weiß (Eds.), Cooperative Information Agents II. Proceedings, 1998. IX, 307 pages. 1998. (Subseries LNAI).

Vol. 1436: D. Wood, S. Yu (Eds.), Automata Implementation. Proceedings, 1997. VIII, 253 pages. 1998.

Vol. 1437: S. Albayrak, F.J. Garijo (Eds.), Intelligent Agents for Telecommunication Applications. Proceedings, 1998. XII, 251 pages. 1998. (Subseries LNAI).

Vol. 1438: C. Boyd, E. Dawson (Eds.), Information Security and Privacy. Proceedings, 1998. XI, 423 pages. 1998.

Vol. 1439: B. Magnusson (Ed.), Software Configuration Management. Proceedings, 1998. X, 207 pages. 1998.

Vol. 1441: W. Wobcke, M. Pagnucco, C. Zhang (Eds.), Agents and Multi-Agent Systems. Proceedings, 1997. XII, 241 pages. 1998. (Subseries LNAI).

Vol. 1443: K.G. Larsen, S. Skyum, G. Winskel (Eds.), Automata, Languages and Programming. Proceedings, 1998. XVI, 932 pages. 1998.

Vol. 1444: K. Jansen, J. Rolim (Eds.), Approximation Algorithms for Combinatorial Optimization. Proceedings, 1998. VIII, 201 pages. 1998.

Vol. 1445: E. Jul (Ed.), ECOOP'98 – Object-Oriented Programming. Proceedings, 1998. XII, 635 pages. 1998.

Vol. 1446: D. Page (Ed.), Inductive Logic Programming. Proceedings, 1998. VIII, 301 pages. 1998. (Subseries LNAI).

Vol. 1448: M. Farach-Colton (Ed.), Combinatorial Pattern Matching. Proceedings, 1998. VIII, 251 pages. 1998.

Vol. 1456: A. Drogoul, M. Tambe, T. Fukuda (Eds.), Collective Robots. Proceedings, 1998. VII, 161 pages. 1998. (Subseries LNAI).